GENDERING THE AFRICAN DIASPORA

# Gendering the African Diaspora

WOMEN, CULTURE, AND HISTORICAL
CHANGE IN THE CARIBBEAN AND
NIGERIAN HINTERLAND

EDITED BY

*Judith A. Byfield, LaRay Denzer,*
*and Anthea Morrison*

Indiana University Press
*Bloomington & Indianapolis*

*This book is a publication of*

Indiana University Press
601 North Morton Street
Bloomington, IN 47404-3797 USA

www.iupress.indiana.edu

*Telephone orders*   800-842-6796
*Fax orders*   812-855-7931
*Orders by e-mail*   iuporder@indiana.edu

♾ The paper used in this publication
meets the minimum requirements of
American National Standard for
Information Sciences—Permanence
of Paper for Printed Library Materials,
ANSI Z39.48-1992.

Manufactured in the United States of
America

Library of Congress Cataloging-in-
Publication Data

Gendering the African diaspora :
women, culture, and historical
change in the Caribbean and
Nigerian hinterland / edited by
Judith A. Byfield, LaRay Denzer,
and Anthea Morrison.
    p. cm. — (Blacks in the diaspora)
   Includes bibliographical references
and index.
   ISBN 978-0-253-35416-7 (cloth : alk.
paper) — ISBN 978-0-253-22153-7 (pbk.
: alk. paper) 1. Women, Black—Caribbean Area. 2. Women, Black—Nigeria.
3. Blacks—Race identity. 4. African
diaspora. I. Byfield, Judith A. (Judith
Ann-Marie) II. Denzer, LaRay. III.
Morrison, Anthea.
   HQ1501.G464 2009
   303.48'27290669082—dc22

2009024782

1  2  3  4  5  15  14  13  12  11  10

*We dedicate this volume to two scholars who were present at the first workshop but have since passed on. Errol Hill was professor of drama and theatre arts at Dartmouth for thirty years. But before he arrived at Dartmouth, he had spent three years at the University of Ibadan in Nigeria. Samuel Asien, professor of literature at the University of Ibadan, had studied Caribbean literature with Hill in Ibadan. Their meeting over dinner at the restaurant A Taste of Africa in White River Junction, Vermont, captured many of the themes and issues that framed our deliberations.*

# CONTENTS

# PREFACE

This volume germinated from an idea first planted and nurtured by Veronica Gregg of Hunter College–CUNY. Being from Jamaica, residing in the United States, we have often discussed our experiences as migrants and as black women in the academy and the numerous ways those factors have shaped our intellectual interests, scholarship, and pedagogy. We were self-conscious of the overlapping diasporas from which we emerged. We were part of the African diaspora forged during the transatlantic slave trade and more recently part of the Jamaican diaspora forged in the tumultuous years following the island's independence in 1962. Often our conversations were comparative, as Veronica spoke of and from her position as a specialist in Caribbean literature, and I from my training in African history and my focus on colonial Nigeria. Our respective fields were linked in numerous ways. The majority of the black population in the Caribbean came from West Africa; furthermore, both regions were linked by the histories of colonialism, nationalism, migration, and structural adjustment programs. It was Veronica who first suggested that we take the elements of those conversations and build an intellectual project around it. She also suggested that we bring Verene Shepherd, a historian of the Caribbean and Caribbean women, into the conversation. This collaboration has been rich and enriching.

The first manifestation of that collaboration was a workshop at Dartmouth College in May 2001, under the auspices of Dartmouth's African and African American Studies Program and the York University/UNESCO Nigerian Hinterland Project to which Verene belonged.

The workshop, "Women's Voices, Women's Stories from the Caribbean and the Nigerian Hinterland," brought together thirteen scholars and graduate students from Nigeria, Benin, Canada, Jamaica, Barbados, and the United States to explore and historicize the linkages between the Caribbean and the Nigerian hinterland and to put women and gender at the center of our analysis. The papers presented at the workshop demonstrated the existence of a new and imaginative body of research that explored the linkages between West Africa and the Caribbean. More fundamentally, they revealed how gender analysis, rigorously and consistently applied, challenges and refines the theoretical conceptualization of the African diaspora. Equally important, the workshop provided an opportunity for scholars of both regions to have sustained intellectual and social interactions and to consider future collaborations.

The success of this workshop led us to plan a larger conference, "Gendering the Diaspora: Women, Culture, and Historical Change in the Caribbean and the Nigerian Hinterland." Under the banner of Dartmouth's African and African American Studies Program, the York University/ UNESCO Nigerian Hinterland Project, and the Text and Testimony Collective (an initiative of Hilary Beckles, Paul Lovejoy, Verene Shepherd, and David Trotman), we sent out an international call for papers and received more proposals than we could accept. In the end, we accepted twenty-five proposals. Scholars from Benin, Canada, Barbados, England, France, Jamaica, Nigeria, Trinidad, and the United States converged on Hanover, N.H., in November 2002, what one scholar from the Caribbean called the "depths of winter." It was cold, and the days were getting shorter, but the conversations were intoxicating. The conference was open to the public, and in conjunction with it, we organized a daylong workshop for New Hampshire and Vermont K–12 teachers; a screening of the film *Life and Debt,* with its director, Stephanie Black, in attendance; and two art exhibits, one by Jamaican-born artist and Vermont resident Judith Salmon, the other by Nigerian textile artist Nike Davies-Okundaye.

The original plan called for Veronica, Verene, and me to edit the volume that resulted from this conference. Unfortunately, Veronica and Verene had to withdraw, but Anthea Morrison and LaRay Denzer, who had participated in both the workshop and the conference, stepped in. Their participation maintains the interdisciplinary and comparative dimensions that have defined this project from its inception.

This series of projects could not have happened without the support of many people. Gertrude Fraser, then of the Ford Foundation, helped us bring several participants to Hanover. At Dartmouth College, we thank the Provost's Office, the Dean of the Faculty, the Dickey Center for International Understanding, the Rockefeller Center for Public Policy, and the Bildner Fund for their generous financial support. The directors of these offices during 2001 and 2002, Barry Scherr, Michael Mastanduno, Linda Fowler, and Ozzie Harris, kept their checkbooks open instead of running away each time I showed up at their door. We also thank the Departments of African and African American Studies, Latino/Latin American and Caribbean Studies, Women's and Gender Studies, and History as well as the Film Society and the Hood Museum. Verene, Veronica, and I relied heavily on the administrative assistance of Gail Vernazza. Gail, saying "Thank you" cannot fully convey the depth of our gratitude for your dedication throughout this long process. I must thank colleagues who chaired sessions, hosted participants, and contributed to the rich discussions and debates, especially Alex Bontemps, J. Martin Favor, Irene Kacandas, Deborah King, Agnes Lugo-Ortiz, Dayo Mitchell, Marysa Navarro, and Keith Walker. Together we thank all those who participated in the workshop and the conference and the members of the York/UNESCO Nigeria Hinterland Project, especially Paul Lovejoy and the Text and Testimony Collective.

Residences at the National Humanities Center in Research Triangle Park (N.C.) and Cornell University's Society for Humanities provided the time, space, and collegial support to finally bring the volume together. The contributions have been enriched by the suggestions and advice of the anonymous reader. Finally, we thank Bob Sloan at Indiana University Press for advocating for this volume.

# A NOTE ON THE STRUCTURE OF THE VOLUME

The articles in this volume are organized into three sections: Africa in the Caribbean imagination; race, gender, and agency in the shadow of slavery; and building diaspora in the web of empire. The articles in this collection address some of the themes discussed in the introduction and take us into new terrain. Denzer, MacDonald-Smythe, and Morrison examine the experiences of women who traveled to other parts of the African diaspora and to Africa. Their stories compel us to see the gendered dimensions of their journeys. MacDonald-Smythe, Sturtz, Samaroo, Adi, Denzer, and Mayers illustrate the complex ways in which women negotiated socioeconomic and political spaces in the face of racial and patriarchal constraints. Shepherd and Sturtz also add new dimensions to our discussion of race. Shepherd's study of Indian women illustrates the complex ways in which they were positioned and racialized in the Caribbean where the dominant racial framework revolved around African and European. Similarly, Sturtz's discussion of an "as-if-white" Afro-Caribbean woman highlights the fluidity of racial identities. Mayers, Chuku, and Ojo offer compelling comparative examples of the ways in which colonial policies were gendered. Smith and Morrison show how Africa was remembered and imagined by men and women of the Caribbean. Shepherd and Smith in their discussion of gender ideology call specific attention to masculinity. Finally, Okome projects the exciting new possibilities that the internet offers for diasporic connections and repositioning in gender relations.

This collection is not comprehensive; nonetheless, the conversations within and between articles raise new considerations. For example, how are women's diasporic networks different from those of men's? How did marriage and/or motherhood shape women's ability to network and the kinds of diasporic networks they created? What kind of diasporic links did the small cadre of black women professionals in teaching, communications, and nursing create during the first half of the twentieth century? Finally, how did travel transform conceptions of Africa when concrete experience collided with a diasporic culture born of creolized practices and mythical expectations? As we ponder these questions and others, we will make significant progress in gendering the African diaspora.

# INTRODUCTION

Tiffany Patterson and Robin K. G. Kelley note in their seminal article, "Unfinished Migrations: Reflections on the African Diaspora and the Making of the Modern World," that population dispersal does not by itself constitute a diaspora.[1] Drawing on the insights of historians and cultural theorists, they eloquently identify parameters that shape and define diasporas.[2] Diasporas are the product of articulated linkages that connect the disparate parts. Furthermore, the linkages that tie diasporas together are not inevitable; they are "always historically constituted." Thus "diaspora is both a process and a condition. As a process it is constantly being remade through movement, migration, and travel, as well as imagined through thought, cultural production, and political struggle."[3] As a condition, the African diaspora exists within a global context shaped by hierarchies of class, race, and gender. These hierarchies that manifest in different formulations and compositions within imperial and national boundaries inflect the ways in which diasporic linkages are made and remade.

A metanarrative constructed around diaspora, while revelatory of global conditions and networks of power and domination, can also obscure and hide important distinctions and more localized processes. For example, in much of the literature on the African diaspora, "the experiences of those located in the United States . . . have come to stand for those not in the U.S. or used as the standard of comparison."[4] A U.S.-based standard elides black identities forged from different national, regional, and imperial experiences. In its wake, it obscures "the diversity of black takes on diaspora."[5] The multiplicity of ways in which men and women built and theorized the African diaspora emerged from the geopolitical context in which they lived. The brutalizing dynamics and processes that sculpted Spanish, Portuguese, Dutch, British, French, and Danish colonies in North and South America and the Caribbean created the conditions for what Stephens calls a "multinational blackness" with multiple racial cultures and political forms.[6] Thus even though black populations experienced discrimination and marginalization, the nature of those processes varied between empires, within empires, and within specific countries. Brazil's elevation of African culture created a racial culture that diverged significantly from that within the United States. In addition, as Kim Butler points out, Brazil's racial culture was not uniform; it reflected demographic and regional variation. Black communities in Brazil's São Paulo and Salvador used different political strategies to combat racism and discrimination because the nature of the marginalization they experienced differed significantly.[7]

Architects of diasporan thought had to nurture linkages across multiple historical landscapes. These linkages were fraught with contradictions and internal tensions. Some of these tensions resulted from the asymmetrical and uneven development of different regions even within the same empire. Within the British empire, for example, freed men and women of the Baptist Church pressed the Jamaican Baptist Association to assist Africa. Their demand for missionary work in Africa grew out of their antislavery ethos, for they believed that dissemination of the gospel in areas from which people were captured and enslaved would end slavery.[8] Although this mission was ultimately unsuccessful, Jamaica and the Caribbean in general continued to be an important source for missionaries to the continent in the nineteenth and early twentieth centuries. Their inspiration for missionary service emerged from an identification with the continent and a shared sense of victimization through the slave trade. At the same time, West Indian missionaries also understood themselves as members of a worldwide Christian community, and as Smith argues in this volume, their Christian identity played a significant role in their relationship with Africa.

African descent did not encompass the full range of West Indian identity formation. Africanness sometimes existed in tension with national identities that crystallized over time. Settings such as the First

World War illuminate the complex tensions between racial and national identities among Africans and diasporan Africans. Black soldiers who fought in World War I experienced multiple levels of discrimination and marginalization. While most British colonial soldiers were not allowed to serve on the frontline, thousands of French colonial soldiers saw active service in the frontlines of African and European campaigns. Nevertheless, British colonial soldiers suffered casualties from their exposure to disease and hardship as carriers. They received poorer food and accommodations and less pay. There were further distinctions that had significant bearing on wages and material conditions. Contingents identified as laborers, for example, were considered men of low intellect or poor physique and therefore unsuitable for the frontlines. The British West India Regiment (BWIR) constantly reminded military brass that they were an all-volunteer contingent and therefore did not have the same social standing as "laborers." Similarly, they tried to avoid the designation of "native" regiment, a term often applied to African contingents, for it also denoted inferior status.

Tensions around class and national identities also manifested between different black contingents as they negotiated the military's array of discriminatory practices.[9] Despite the class tensions among West Indian soldiers and the tensions between West Indian and African soldiers, the war politicized many and exposed them to pan-African influences and radical black American thought. Smith reports that Claude McKay distributed radical literature among West Indians in the Winchester repatriation camp.[10] The war offered opportunities that both created and disrupted efforts at diasporic linkages. The war also put into high relief competing notions of masculinity. The dedication with which the BWIR protected their status as volunteers derived in part from the type of masculinity associated with volunteer soldiers. Unlike conscripts, mercenaries, or pressed soldiers, volunteers were considered the highest caliber of military men because they served "in pursuit of an ideal or just cause."[11] Wars also created opportunities for women to write new gendered scripts as well. As Antonia MacDonald-Smythe shows in this volume, Mary Seacole's activities during the Crimean war formed a centerpiece in the construction of her racial and gender identities in her autobiography.

Just as diaspora can obscure ideas of class and nation, it often obscures gender as well. Earlier generations of writing on the African diaspora obfuscated women's engagement in the heavy work of traveling, building networks, and imagining the diaspora.[12] In his critical study of black internationalism in Paris, Brent Edwards masterfully illustrates that although Leopold Senghor is credited with being the father of Négritude, the pioneers of the new black consciousness that Négritude represented can actually be traced back to Caribbean female students in Paris during the interwar period, particularly Paulette Nardal.[13] In a similar vein, studies of black radical thought and its contributions to diaspora formation often overlooked the contributions of black women. Claudia Jones, for example, was a contemporary of C. L. R. James. She was a member of the Communist Party who was deported from the United States in the 1950s and only recently has begun to receive the scholarly attention she merits. Carole Boyce Davies's study of Jones, *Left of Karl Marx,* and Edwards's work are only two of several recent studies that illustrate the significant ways in which an analysis of women and gender promises to transform African diaspora studies.[14]

We are a decade beyond the period Terborg-Penn identified as the infancy of African diaspora studies about women.[15] Nonetheless, Gunning, Hunter, and Mitchell insist that "the use of gender as a category of analysis remains something of a challenge for African Diaspora studies."[16] Their critique extends beyond integrating women into the conceptual analysis of the African diaspora. They challenge us to examine the construction of the gendered identities female and male as well as their intersection with sexuality. Furthermore, their intervention reminds us that race was not the sole component of diasporic discourses. Garvey's United Negro Improvement Association, for example, in both practice and theory expected women to play a helpmate role in the organization. Even though some women, like Amy Jacques Garvey, exercised important leadership roles, they faced opposition or resistance from men within the organization.[17] Exploring masculinity and sexuality also brings us into unexpected terrain or networks through which men and women engaged diaspora. Diasporic linkages not only originated from Africa or Pan-Africanism but sometimes emerged from other types of international organizations as well. In a close textual reading of correspondence between the Gold Coast–born teacher, D. K. Abadu-Bentsi, and Harry Williamson, a black postal worker in New York, Martin Summers illustrates how their membership in Freemason lodges provided the link through which they explored shared understandings of middle-class masculinity. Their correspondence also revealed much about their experiences with racism in their respective countries. For these gentlemen, Freemasonry provided the entry into their mutual critique of racism, colonialism, and masculinity.[18] International organizations also provided important spaces for women from Africa and the Caribbean to theorize gender roles and expectations, imperialism, and decolonization. Women like Fumilayo Ransome-Kuti from Nigeria, Constance Cummings-Johns of Sierra Leone, and Daphne Campbell from Jamaica all belonged to the Soviet-oriented Women's International Democratic Federation, while others participated in the liberal feminist International Alliance of Women in the west.[19]

This volume builds on the insights of these works and extends the discussion in distinctive ways. It considers networks of people and ideas moving between two discrete regions of the African diaspora: the Caribbean and the Nigerian hinterland. The contributions examine Africa in the Caribbean imaginary, the ways in which gender ideologies informed Caribbean men and women's theoretical or real-life engagement with the continent as well as the interactions and experiences of Caribbean travelers in Africa and Europe. The contributors make extensive use of biographical and autobiographical data, which add texture to our understanding of how these historical actors wrestled with the discourses of race, gender, class, empire, and nation. The papers are linked as well through empire. Many of the authors discuss different parts of the British Empire, allowing comparative examination of colonial policies and practices.

## Why the Caribbean and the Nigerian Hinterland?

The breadth and temporal depth of the African diaspora forces any exploration of the topic to occur within limits. The studies in this volume focus on the linkages and shared experiences of women in the Caribbean and the Nigerian hinterland, the region that extends from Sierra Leone to the Cameroons, and from the Atlantic coast north to Lake Chad and beyond to Morocco and Tunisia. An examination of the linkages and shared experiences of black women in both regions is especially fruitful because many of the enslaved African men and women brought to the

Caribbean originated from the Nigerian hinterland.[20] This volume has emerged at a fortuitous time as well. In the last decade there has been a surge of interest in diasporas broadly and in the African diaspora specifically. Africa specialists have begun to engage the issues and questions raised by using diasporic frameworks for understanding African history within a global context.[21] The expanding interest of Africanist scholars in the diaspora, coupled with a more serious engagement with Africanist scholarship by specialists in other fields, has created an important synergy of ideas, methodologies, and theorizing. This volume benefits from this synergy.

Scholars have long recognized the historic and cultural relationships between the Caribbean and the Nigerian hinterland. Most studies, however, focused primarily on two main periods: the period between the early sixteenth and mid-nineteenth centuries shaped by the slave trade and abolition, or the period from late nineteenth century through the twentieth century marked by the intellectual and activist networks forged by Pan-Africanists and nationalists. Crahan and Knight argue that "the ramifications of the transatlantic slave trade remained the end of intellectual curiosity about Africa. The result has been an abysmally superficial understanding of the impact of Africa on the evolution of American societies."[22] Recent scholarship by authors such as Gomez and Midlo Hall has responded to the challenge by Crahan and Knight. Their works have given a much more nuanced understanding of the impact of distinctive African cultures on the regional variations of African American society in the United States.[23] We are also gathering much more information on the cultures of origin of the enslaved population in the Caribbean.[24] Long an interest of scholars such as Warner-Lewis, important new studies have been published on the impact and transformation of Yoruba culture and religion in Cuba, Haiti, and Trinidad.[25]

The recently edited volumes by Heywood, Brown, and others focus attention on other African cultures that contributed significantly to the shaping of Caribbean cultures. Heywood's *Central African and Cultural Transformation in the American Diaspora* addresses a lacuna in studies of Africa's Atlantic diaspora. She quite correctly notes "the history and culture of central Africans in the Atlantic diaspora lag far behind that of West Africa."[26] Other significant holes still exist. Until recently, few scholars have examined the impact of Igbo culture, even though Igbos constituted the dominant group on a number of islands and formed a significant part of slave society in the southern United States.[27] Presentations in the "Atlantic Crossings" workshop show that current research on women and slavery in Igbo society offers significant possibilities for comparative analyses of slavery as well as the opportunity to refine our understanding of how gender and African ethnicities shaped the construction of creole culture and society in the Caribbean.[28]

The cultural relationship between Africa and its diaspora was not unidirectional. People, ideas, material objects, and plants moved back and forth across the Atlantic and in the process created dynamic creole communities on the continent as well. In *Rethinking the African Diaspora: The Making of a Black Atlantic World in the Bight of Benin and Brazil*, Mann and Bay highlight the ways in which continued communication between Africa and diasporic communities transformed Africa. Numerous examples document the ways in which returning members of the African diaspora transformed the sociopolitical and cultural landscape of the Nigerian hinterland. Repatriated Yorubas from Cuba who settled in Lagos and other towns along the Nigerian coast introduced transformed African rhythms such as the rumba into West Africa's musical landscape.[29] Similarly, repatriated Yorubas from Brazil introduced distinctive architectural elements into coastal cities. Brazilian "returnees engaged in dialogue with West Africans" and played a crucial role in the "Lagosian cultural renaissance of the 1890s."[30] The circum-Atlantic dialogue of these returnees, especially the merchants and priests, fashioned the diasporic homeland as well as national and subnational identities in Brazil, Nigeria, Cuba, and Benin.[31] Mann and Bay also highlight the importance of "bring[ing] time into an analysis of the formation of the diaspora."[32] Careful attention to periodization and developments within Africa enriches our understanding of the cultural and experiential resources Africans brought and continue to bring to the Americas and ways in which those resources shape diasporic cultures.[33]

Apart from studies on Pan-African connections, especially the importance of Marcus Garvey's ideas in the evolution of nationalist ideology, few scholars have examined the direct linkages between the Caribbean and the Nigerian hinterland after the end of the transatlantic trade in enslaved Africans. Schuler and Warner-Lewis are among a handful of scholars who have written on post-abolition African migration to the

Caribbean, specifically that of African indentured servants who were brought to the region after abolition.[34] Blyden's work shows the important contribution of West Indians in West African colonial society and administration, but further scholarship remains to be done on the role of West Indians as missionaries, railway workers, or members of the British colonial military.[35] Furthermore, few scholars paid attention to the number of Caribbean women in the twentieth century who migrated to West Africa to work or to marry. As Denzer shows in this volume, Caribbean women migrated to Nigeria in pursuit of jobs in the decades before independence. Many who made this journey were influenced by pan-Africanist ideology; nonetheless, in some instances, these women created distinctive cultural enclaves. In Nigeria, for example, Caribbean wives of Nigerian men have tried to re-create aspects of Caribbean culture. In Lagos, the West Indian association successfully established a West Indian carnival complete with a carnival king and queen. Added to the success of carnival is the tremendous popularity of reggae and Rastafarianism.[36] While Caribbean people and culture moved between the region and West Africa, Nigerians, and other West Africans also moved between both regions. West African students have studied in the Caribbean, practitioners of Yoruba religion have visited Cuba and Brazil, and more recently professionals, especially Nigerian nurses, have migrated to islands such as Jamaica for jobs.[37]

Europe has been a critical place for launching journeys to either West Africa or the Caribbean. It is in the metropoles that people from different parts of colonial empires met. Recent biographical studies of West Indian and West African women reveal the critical significance as well as the complexity of diasporic interconnections that originated in overseas student experience or participation in international organizational work.[38] Recent African migration to the United States has made cities like New York and Washington, D.C., important meeting points for large numbers of West Indians and West Africans. In these locations, West Indians and West Africans adopt new kinds of cultural and political practices that contribute to new ways of thinking about blackness and citizenship in their home and host countries.[39]

Travel is a cornerstone of many of the contributions to this volume. They engage the increasing attention that cultural theorists bring to the place of women, and black women specifically, in the discourses of travel

and migration. As Boyce Davies argues, travel involves boundary crossing on many levels. Boundary crossing is not only physical but it also
inspires shifts in identity, the creation of new identities, or the familiarity and reconnections of old identities. Travel, as MacDonald-Smythe
shows, enabled Mary Seacole to reconstruct her persona from one defined by work to one defined by care giving, the highest expression of
imperial womanhood. Morrison's examination of the boundary crossing
of Maryse Condé and Paule Marshall and the characters that populate
their novels illustrate how both novelists employ boundary crossing as a
critical platform. These authors use travel as an entrée into overlapping
meditations on race, gender, class, empire, and diaspora. Their characters reveal competing ways of realizing home and community. For
Conde, Marshall, and many other black female authors, home and the
nation are not necessarily celebratory spaces. In many instances, home,
community, and nation are places of exile.[40]

Whether places of refuge or exile, the Caribbean and the Nigerian
hinterland share much in their histories of colonialism and postcolonial-
ism. As a result, the movement of ideas and peoples between the Nigerian
hinterland and the Caribbean lend to comparative analysis of historical
processes and institutions. However, as Thomas Holt argues, a diaspora
framework does not work well in formal comparisons that require "at
least one time or place constant in order to effect a comparison and contrast of differences." Instead, diaspora supports comparative analyses that
draw on unifying themes. Building on the studies of W. E. B. Du Bois,
C. L. R. James, and Eric Williams, Holt demonstrates how these scholars
used a diaspora perspective to link the black diaspora to an evolving
global system. Their works emphasized "at once the special unities of the
black experience across the diaspora and its intimate interconnections
with broader social processes on a global stage."[41] The African diaspora
was crucial to the world order created by slavery, the slave trade, and
emancipation. As a result, the African diaspora is also linked to other
diasporas, for former slave owners turned to China and India to meet the
labor demands in post-abolition societies around the globe.[42]

The African diaspora remains important in our analysis of evolving global trends such as the virtual recolonization of Caribbean and
African economies through structural adjustment programs (SAP), the
increasing transnational movement of capital and labor, and the new

information technologies. Yet few scholars have attempted to put gender at the center of the analysis of these shared aspects of recent global history. Although the case studies were not exclusive to the Caribbean and Africa, Steady's collection *The Black Woman Cross-Culturally* was one of the earliest efforts to examine black women's experiences comparatively. More recent efforts include Emeagwali's edited collection *Women Pay the Price: Structural Adjustment in Africa and the Caribbean.* The African and Caribbean case studies in the latter volume are important challenges to conservative and radical analyses of structural adjustment that do not consider gender. Women and men do not experience the impact of these programs in identical ways. Even in West African societies where women are actively engaged in trade in the local markets and foodstuff production, their limited access to the state, land, and formal credit often means that their economic situation becomes even more precarious in the face of government withdrawal of social spending and other provisions of SAP. There is much more to learn from comparative analyses of women's economic roles under structural adjustment programs since women in the Caribbean have and continue to play similarly important roles in local markets and foodstuff production. Despite the similar economic roles women play in the Nigerian hinterland and the Caribbean, significant cultural differences exist. Thus culture and context profoundly shape women's experience of global forces.[43] SAP has contributed significantly to migration from Africa and the Caribbean, particularly to North America. The interactions of these populations with each other and with African Americans provide rich material for comparative studies of migration as well as new thinking about the fluidity of racial, ethnic, and national identities.[44]

Economic activities also become a lens through which we can view the multiple ways in which women became enmeshed in a variety of global forces and phenomena. Although few women from the colonies had experience of the military theaters during World War II, women were part of the war effort as colonial states demanded increased agricultural production and limited recruitment of cooks and nurses. Gloria Chuku in this volume shows that this is potentially a rich area for comparative work, since the war required empirewide strategic planning and logistics. Other topics such as education lend themselves easily to comparative work. As Mayers demonstrates, the architects of education policy in Barbados borrowed heavily from the British system. Nonetheless, they noted developments in education in other parts of the empire. After the Caribbean labor crises of the 1930s, when various commissions surveyed conditions across the empire, significant discussions unfolded in London about the state of women's education. Thus the postwar period was a critical moment for the development of educational facilities across the empire.[45] Collectively these contributions demonstrate that comparative analyses of women's experiences refine our understanding of global developments in both the macro and micro arenas.

## Notes

1. Patterson and Kelley, "Unfinished Migrations," 13–15.
2. In particular, they cite the important insights of Stuart Hall and his conceptualization of "articulation." See Grossberg, "On Postmodernism and Articulation"; Hall, "Cultural Identity and Diaspora"; and Hall, "The Question of Cultural Identity."
3. Patterson and Kelley, "Unfinished Migrations," 20.
4. Ibid.
5. Edwards, *The Practice of Diaspora*, 12.
6. Stephens, *Black Empire*, 13.
7. Butler, *Freedoms Given, Freedoms Won*.
8. Russell, *The Missionary Outreach of the West Indian Church*, 73.
9. Smith, *Jamaican Volunteers in the First World War*, 82–89.
10. Ibid., 137.
11. Ibid., 88.
12. For example, see Harris, *Global Dimensions of the African Diaspora*.
13. Edwards, *The Practice of Diaspora*, 125.
14. Important new studies include Griffith and Savage, eds., *Women and Religion in the African Diaspora*; Taylor, *The Veiled Garvey*; Gourdine, *The Difference Place Makes*; and Shepherd, ed., *Working Slavery, Pricing Freedom*.
15. Terborg-Penn, "Women in the African Diaspora: An Overview of an Interdisciplinary Research Conference," xvii. Some of the important early texts include Bair, "Pan-Africanism as Process"; Beckles, *Centering Women*; Bush, *Slave Women in Caribbean Society, 1650–1838*; Cromwell, *An African Victorian Feminist*; Davies, *Black Women, Writing, and Identity*; and Shepherd, Brereton, and Bailey, eds., *Engendering History*.
16. Gunning, Hunter, and Mitchell, eds., *Dialogues of Dispersal*, 2.
17. Taylor, *The Veiled Garvey*, 64–90. Also see Bair, "Pan-Africanism as Process."
18. Summers, "Diasporic Brotherhood."
19. See Johnson-Odim and Mba, *For Women and the Nation: Funmilayo Ransome-Kuti of Nigeria*; Cummings-John, *Memoirs of a Krio Leader*; and Vassell, "Women of the Masses."

20. Higman, *Slave Populations of the British Caribbean, 1807–1834*, 126.

21. Matory, "The English Professors of Brazil"; Byfield, "Rethinking the African Diaspora"; Crahan and Knight, *Africa and the Caribbean;* and Mann and Bay, eds., *Rethinking the African Diaspora.*

22. Crahan and Knight, *Africa and the Caribbean.*

23. Gomez, *Exchanging Our Country Marks;* Midlo Hall, *Africans in Colonial Louisiana.*

24. Higman, *Slave Populations of the British Caribbean.*

25. Bastide, *The African Religions of Brazil;* Brandon, *Santeria from Africa to the New World;* McCarthy-Brown, "Systematic Remembering, Systematic Forgetting"; Simpson, "Shango Cult in Trinidad"; Warner-Lewis, *Central Africa in the Caribbean;* Rodrigues, *Os Africanos no Brasil;* and Verger, *Trade Relations between the Bight of Benin and Bahia from the 17th to 19th Century.*

26. Heywood, *Central Africans and Cultural Transformations in the American Diaspora,* 8.

27. See, for example, Warner-Lewis, *Archibald Monteath;* Chambers, *Murder at Montpelier;* and Brown and Lovejoy, eds., *Repercussions of the Atlantic Slave Trade.*

28. Shepherd, Brereton, and Bailey, *Engendering History;* Lovejoy, ed., *Identity in the Shadow of Slavery;* and Brown and Osakwe, "Haunting Tales of Loss and Enslavement."

29. Watermann, *Jùjú,* 31–42.

30. Matory, "The English Professors of Brazil," 74. For earlier explorations of Brazilian-Nigerian connections, see Turner, "Some Contacts of Brazilian Ex-Slaves with Nigeria, West Africa"; and Ralston, "The Return of Brazilian Freedmen to West Africa in the 18th and 19th Centuries." For Brazilian influence in Nigerian architecture, see Vlach, "The Brazilian House in Nigeria."

31. Matory, *Black Atlantic Religion,* 7.

32. Mann and Bay, *Rethinking the African Diaspora,* 9.

33. See Okome in this volume; also L. Fields-Black, *Deep Roots;* Mercer, Page, and Evans, *Development and the African Diaspora.*

34. Schuler, "Myalism and the African Religious Tradition in Jamaica"; Schuler, "Kru Emigration to British and French Guiana, 1841–1857"; and Warner-Lewis, *Trinidad Yoruba.*

35. Blyden, *West Indians in West Africa, 1808–1880;* Blackett, "Return to the Motherland"; Bryan, *The Jamaican People, 1880–1902,* 251–55; and Russell, *Missionary Outreach.*

36. Savishinsky, "Rastafari in the Promised Land."

37. Ogbogbo, "Labour Mobility." Nurses from Nigeria as well as Ghana were recruited as part of technical assistance programs to help Jamaica address the severe shortage of nurses on the island. See "Nurses from Nigeria to Work in Jamaica," *Jamaica Gleaner* (Kingston), 12 June 2005; and "New Examination for Incoming Foreign Nurses," *Jamaica Gleaner,* 18 November 2001. The island of Dominica recently began a similar program. See "Dominican Nurses Critical of Government's Plan," *Jamaica Gleaner,* 16 August 2007.

38. Jarrett-Macauley, *The Life of Una Marson, 1905–1965;* Sherwood, *Claudia Jones;* Taylor, *The Veiled Garvey;* and Cummings-John, *Memoirs of a Krio Leader.*

39. Thomas, "Blackness across Borders."

40. Davies, *Black Women*, 1–22. Also see Stephens, *Black Empire*.

41. Holt, "Slavery and Freedom in the Atlantic World," 41.

42. See, for example, Dabydeen and Samaroo, eds., *Across the Dark Waters;* Look Lai, *The Chinese in the West Indies, 1806–1995;* and Look Lai, *Indentured Labor, Caribbean Sugar.*

43. Ajayi, "Market Women in Ibadan"; Crahan and Knight, *Africa and the Caribbean;* Harris, "The Historian and the Female Entrepreneur"; and Ojo, "Yoruba Women, Cash Crop Production, and the Colonial State, 1920–1957."

44. For examples, see Lewis "'To Turn as on a Pivot'"; Wamba, *Kinship;* Stoller, *Money Has No Smell;* and Clarke and Thomas, eds., *Globalization and Race.*

45. Education was just one of several issues discussed from an empirewide perspective. Changes in labor policies across the empire were inspired by the Caribbean labor strikes of the late 1930s. See Oberst, "Transport Workers, Strikes and the 'Imperial Response,'" 122.

# References

Ajayi, Yinka. "Market Women in Ibadan." Paper presented at the conference "Atlantic Crossings: Women's Voices, Women's Stories from the Caribbean and the Nigerian Hinterland," Dartmouth College, 18–20 May 2001.

Bair, Barbara. "Pan-Africanism as Process: Adelaide Casely Hayford, Garveyism, and the Cultural Roots of Nationalism." In *Imagining Home: Class, Culture, and Nationalism in the African Diaspora*, ed. Sidney Lemelle and Robin D. G. Kelley, 121–44. New York: Verso, 1994.

Bastide, Roger. *The African Religions of Brazil: Toward a Sociology of the Interpenetration of Civilizations.* Trans. Helen Sebba. Baltimore: Johns Hopkins University Press, 1978.

Beckles, Hilary. *Centering Women: Gender Discourses in Caribbean Slave Society.* Princeton, N.J.: Marcus Wiener, 1999.

Blackett, R. J. M. "Return to the Motherland: Robert Campbell, a Jamaican in Early Colonial Lagos." *Journal of the Historical Society of Nigeria* 8 (1975): 133–44.

Blyden, Nemata Amelia. *West Indians in West Africa, 1808–1880.* Rochester, N.Y.: University of Rochester Press, 2000.

Brandon, George. *Santeria from Africa to the New World: The Dead Sell Memories.* Bloomington: Indiana University Press, 1993.

Brown, Carolyn, and Paul Lovejoy, eds. *Repercussions of the Atlantic Slave Trade: The Interior of the Bight of Biafra and the African Diaspora.* Trenton, N.J.: Africa World Press, 2005.

Brown, Carolyn, and Nneka Osakwe. "Haunting Tales of Loss and Enslavement: Finding Women's Voices in the Oral History of the Slave Trade from the Bight of Biafra." Paper presented at the conference "Atlantic Crossings: Women's Voices, Women's Stories from the Caribbean and the Nigerian Hinterland."

Bush, Barbara. *Slave Women in Caribbean Society, 1650–1838.* Bloomington: Indiana University Press, 1990.

Butler, Kim D. *Freedoms Given, Freedoms Won: Afro-Brazilians in Post-Abolition São Paulo and Salvador.* New Brunswick, N.J.: Rutgers University Press, 1998.

Byfield, Judith. "Rethinking the African Diaspora." *African Studies Review* 43 (2000): 1–9.

Bryan, Patrick. *The Jamaican People, 1880–1902: Race, Class, and Social Control.* London: Macmillan Caribbean, 1991.

Chambers, Douglas B. *Murder at Montpelier: Igbo Africans in Virginia.* Jackson: University Press of Mississippi, 2005.

Clarke, Kamari Maxine, and Deborah A. Thomas, eds. *Globalization and Race: Transformations in the Cultural Production of Blackness.* Durham, N.C.: Duke University Press, 2006.

Crahan, Margaret, and Franklin Knight. *Africa and the Caribbean: The Legacies of a Link.* Baltimore: Johns Hopkins University Press, 1979.

Cromwell, Adelaide. *An African Victorian Feminist: The Life and Times of Adelaide Smith Casely Hayford, 1868–1960.* Washington, D.C.: Howard University Press, 1992.

Cummings-John, Constance A. *Memoirs of a Krio Leader.* Recorded and edited by LaRay Denzer. Ibadan: Sam Bookman for Humanities Research Center, 1995.

Dabydeen, David, and Brinsley Samaroo, eds. *Across the Dark Waters: Ethnicity and Indian Identity in the Caribbean.* London: Macmillan Caribbean, 1996.

Davies, Carol Boyce. *Black Women, Writing, and Identity: Migrations of the Subject.* New York: Routledge, 1994.

Davies, Carole Boyce. *Left of Karl Marx: The Political Life of Black Communist Claudia Jones.* Durham, N.C.: Duke University Press, 2007.

Edwards, Brent. *The Practice of Diaspora: Literature, Translations, and the Rise of Black Internationalism.* Cambridge: Harvard University Press, 2003.

Emeagwali, Gloria, ed. *Women Pay the Price: Structural Adjustment in Africa and the Caribbean.* Trenton: African World Press, 1995.

Fields-Black, Edda L. *Deep Roots: Rice Farmers in West Africa and the African Diaspora.* Bloomington: Indiana University Press, 2007.

Gomez, Michael. *Exchanging Our Country Marks: The Transformation of African Identities in the Colonial and Antebellum South.* Chapel Hill: University of North Carolina Press, 1998.

Gourdine, Angeletta. *The Difference Place Makes: Gender, Sexuality, and Diaspora Identity.* Columbus: Ohio State University Press, 2002.

Griffith, R. Marie, and Barbara Dianne Savage, eds. *Women and Religion in the African Diaspora: Knowledge, Power, and Performance.* Baltimore: Johns Hopkins University Press, 2006.

Grossberg, Lawrence. "On Postmodernism and Articulation: An Interview with Stuart Hall." In *Stuart Hall: Critical Dialogues in Cultural Studies,* ed. David Morely and Kuan-Hsing Chen, 131–50. London: Routledge, 1995.

Gunning, Sandra, Tera Hunter, and Michele Mitchell, eds. *Dialogues of Dispersal: Gender, Sexuality, and African Diasporas.* Oxford: Blackwell, 2004.

Hall, Stuart. "Cultural Identity and Diaspora." In *Colonial Discourse and Postcolonial Theory: A Reader,* ed. Patrick Williams and Laura Chrisman. London: Harvester, Whaeatsheaf, 1993.

Hall, Stuart. "The Question of Cultural Identity." In *Modernity: An Introduction to Modern Societies,* ed. Stuart Hall, Don Hubert, Kenneth Thompson, and David Held, 596–634. Oxford: Blackwell, 1996.

Harris, Dawn. "The Historian and the Female Entrepreneur: Reconstructing the History of the Female Traders during the Era of the Slave Trade and the Period of 'Legitimate' Commerce." Paper presented at the conference "Atlantic Crossings: Women's Voices, Women's Stories from the Caribbean and the Nigerian Hinterland," Dartmouth College, 18–20 May 2001.

Harris, Joseph. *Global Dimensions of the African Diaspora*. Washington, D.C.: Howard University Press, 1982.

Heywood, Linda. *Central Africans and Cultural Transformations in the American Diaspora*. New York: Cambridge University Press, 2002.

Higman, B. W. *Slave Populations of the British Caribbean, 1807–1834*. Kingston: University of the West Indies Press, 1995.

Holt, Thomas. "Slavery and Freedom in the Atlantic World: Reflection on the Diasporan Framework." In *Crossing Boundaries: Comparative History of Black People in Diaspora*, ed. Darlene Clark Hine and Jacqueline McLeod. Bloomington: Indiana University Press, 1999.

Jarrett-Macauley, Delia. *The Life of Una Marson, 1905–1965*. Manchester: Manchester University Press, 1998.

Johnson-Odim, Cheryl, and Nina Mba. *For Women and the Nation: Funmilayo Ransome-Kuti of Nigeria*. Urbana: University of Illinois Press, 1997.

Lewis, Earl. "'To Turn as on a Pivot': Writing African Americans into a History of Overlapping Diasporas." *American Historical Review* 100 (June): 765–87.

Look Lai, Walton. 1998. *The Chinese in the West Indies, 1806–1995: A Documentary History*. Mona, Kingston: University of the West Indies Press, 1998.

———. *Indentured Labor, Caribbean Sugar: Chinese and Indian Migrants to the British West Indies, 1838–1918*. Baltimore: Johns Hopkins University Press, 1993.

Lovejoy, Paul E., ed. *Identity in the Shadow of Slavery*. London: Continuum, 2000.

Mann, Kristin, and Edna G. Bay, eds. *Rethinking the African Diaspora: The Making of a Black Atlantic World in the Bight of Benin and Brazil*. Portland, Ore.: Frank Cass, 2001.

Matory, J. Lorand. *Black Atlantic Religion: Tradition, Transnationalism, and Matriarchy in the Afro-Brazilian Candomblé*. Princeton, N.J.: Princeton University Press, 2005.

Matory, J. Lorand. "The English Professors of Brazil: On the Diasporic Roots of the Yoruba Nation." *Comparative Studies in Society and History* 41 (1999): 72–103.

McCarthy-Brown, Karen. "Systematic Remembering, Systematic Forgetting: Ogou in Haiti." In *Africa's Ogun: Old World and New*, ed. Sandra Barnes, 65–89. Bloomington: Indiana University Press, 1989.

Mercer, Claire, Ben Page, and Martin Evans. *Development and the African Diaspora: Place and the Politics of Home*. London: Zed Press, 2008.

Midlo-Hall, Gwendolyn. *Africans in Colonial Louisiana: The Development of Afro-Creole Culture in the Eighteenth Century*. Baton Rouge: Louisiana State University Press, 1992.

Oberst, Timothy. "Transport Workers, Strikes, and the 'Imperial Response': Africa and the Post World War II Conjuncture." *African Studies Review* 31 (1988): 117–33.

Ogbogbo, Christopher. "Labour Mobility: A Recurring Decimal in Nigeria-Caribbean Relations." Paper presented at the conference "Atlantic Crossings: Women's

Voices, Women's Stories from the Caribbean and the Nigerian Hinterland," Dartmouth College, 18–20 May 2001.

Ojo, Olatunji. "Yoruba Women, Cash Crop Production, and the Colonial State, 1920–1957." Paper presented at the conference "Atlantic Crossings: Women's Voices, Women's Stories from the Caribbean and the Nigerian Hinterland," Dartmouth College, 18–20 May 2001.

Patterson, Tiffany Ruby, and Robin D. G. Kelley. "Unfinished Migrations: Reflections on the African Diaspora and the Making of the Modern World." *African Studies Review* 43 (2000).

Ralston, Richard D. "The Return of Brazilian Freedmen to West Africa in the 18th and 19th Centuries." *Canadian Journal of African Studies* 3 (1969): 577–593.

Rodrigues, Raymundo Nina. *Os Africanos no Brasil.* São Paulo: Companhia Editora Nacional, 1932.

Russell, Horace. *The Missionary Outreach of the West Indian Church: Jamaican Baptist Missions to West Africa in the Nineteenth Century.* Peter Lang, 2000.

Savishinsky, Neil. "Rastafari in the Promised Land: The Spread of a Jamaican Socioreligious Movement among the Youth of West Africa." *African Studies Review* 37 (1994): 19–50.

Schuler, Monica. "Kru Emigration to British and French Guiana, 1841–1857." In *Africans in Bondage: Studies in Slavery and the Slave Trade,* edited by Paul E. Lovejoy, 155–201. Madison: University of Wisconsin Press, 1986.

Schuler, Monica. "Myalism and the African Religious Tradition in Jamaica." In *Caribbean Slave Society and Economy,* edited by Hilary Beckles and Verene Shepherd, 295–303. New York: The New Press, 1991 [1979].

Shepherd, Verene, ed. *Working Slavery, Pricing Freedom: Perspectives from the Caribbean, Africa, and the African Diaspora.* New York: Palgrave, 2002.

Shepherd, Verene, Bridget Brereton, and Barbara Bailey, eds. *Engendering History: Caribbean Women in Historical Perspective.* New York: St. Martin's Press, 1995.

Sherwood, Marika. *Claudia Jones: A Life in Exile.* London: Lawrence and Wishart, 2000.

Simpson, George. "The Shango Cult in Trinidad." *African Notes* (Ibadan) 3 (1965): 11–21. See also the version in *Religious Cults of the Caribbean: Trinidad, Jamaica, and Haiti.* San Juan: Institute of Caribbean Studies, University of Puerto Rico, 1970.

Smith, Richard. *Jamaican Volunteers in the First World War: Race, Masculinity, and the Development of National Consciousness.* New York: Manchester University Press, 2004.

Steady, Filomina Chioma. *The Black Woman Cross-Culturally.* Cambridge, Mass.: Schenkman, 1981.

Stephens, Michelle Ann. *Black Empire: The Masculine Global Imaginary of the Caribbean Intellectuals in the United States, 1914–1962.* Durham, N.C.: Duke University Press, 2005).

Stoller, Paul. *Money Has No Smell: The Africanization of New York City.* Chicago: University of Chicago Press, 2002.

Summers, Martin. "Diasporic Brotherhood: Freemasonary and the Transnational Production of Black Middle-Class Masculinity." In *Dialogues of Dispersal:*

*Gender Sexuality and African Diasporas,* ed. Sandra Gunning, Tera Hunter, and Michelle Mitchell, 154–178. London: Blackwell, 2004.

Taylor, Ula Yvette. *The Veiled Garvey: The Life and Times of Amy Jacques Garvey.* Chapel Hill: University of North Carolina Press, 2002.

Terborg-Penn, Rosalyn. "Women in the African Diaspora: An Overview of an Interdisciplinary Research Conference." In *Women in Africa and the African Diaspora: A Reader,* ed. Rosalyn Terborg-Penn and Andrea Benton. Washington, D.C.: Howard University Press, 1996.

Thomas, Deborah A. "Blackness across Borders: Jamaican Diasporas and New Politics of Citizenship." *Identities: Global Studies in Culture and Power* 14 (2007): 111–33.

Turner, Lorenzo D. "Some Contacts of Brazilian Ex-Slaves with Nigeria, West Africa." *Journal of Negro History* 27 (1942): 55–67.

Verger, Pierre. *Trade Relations between the Bight of Benin and Bahia from the 17th to 19th Century.* Trans. Evelyn Crawford. Ibadan: Ibadan University Press, 1976.

Vlach, John Michael. "The Brazilian House in Nigeria: The Emergence of a 20th-century Vernacular House Type." *Journal of American Folklore* 97 (1984): 3–23.

Vassell, Linnette. "Women of the Masses: Daphne Campbell and 'Left' Politics in Jamaica in the 1950s." In *Engendering History: Caribbean Women in Historical Perspective,* ed. Verene A. Shepherd, Bridget Bereton, and Barbara Bailey, 318–33. New York: St. Martin's Press, 1995.

Wamba, Philippe. *Kinship: A Family's Journey in Africa and America.* New York: Plume Books, 2000.

Warner-Lewis, Maureen. *Archibald Monteath: Igbo, Jamaican, Moravian.* Mona, Kingston: University of West Indies Press, 2007.

Warner-Lewis, Maureen. *Central Africa in the Caribbean: Transcending Time, Transforming Cultures.* Mona, Kingston: University of West Indies Press, 2004.

Warner-Lewis, Maureen. *Trinidad Yoruba: From Mother Tongue to Memory.* Barbados: University Press of the West Indies, 1997.

Watermann, Christopher. *Jùjú: A Social History and Ethnography of an African Popular Music.* Chicago: University of Chicago Press, 1990.

PART ONE

# Africa in the Caribbean Imagination

# 1

# Of Laughter and Kola Nuts; or, What Does *Africa* Have to Do with the African Diaspora?

## FAITH LOIS SMITH

"What do you mean by *Africa?*" a political scientist asked a literary critic at a panel devoted to films and novels at the conference where an earlier version of this essay was presented. The question made explicit undercurrents that had been merely implied up to that point. While the question could have been interpreted as an "African" interrogation of romantic and essentialist texts and the "diasporic" critics who read them—the questioner was African, the panelists were not—the immediate chorus of "exactly" by both African and non-African historians and social scientists in the room suggested a disciplinary divide.

To my perhaps overly sensitive mind, those of us gathered in freezing Hanover were playing out an episode in the continuing ideological drama of African Diaspora Studies, wherein literary and cultural critics, and the artists and texts that we write about, are deemed to be insufficiently theoretical in our discussion of the African continent as a "home" for people in the Americas and elsewhere. What part of Africa, which time period, the precise nature of alleged continuities and traditions, are downplayed or nonexistent in such discussions, as fictional characters and social actors lay claim to "Africa" in the absence of the ability to claim a specific part of the continent.[1] The presentations of our colleagues in history and the social sciences, on the political, social, and historical transformations that have occurred in West Africa from the period of the transatlantic slave trade to the present day, were striking and thus made clear how static notions of Africa might benefit from more complex and rigorous perspectives. ("Hell, even *Af-*

*rica* isn't Africa!" as one literary critic put it.) Even more striking was the extent to which their presentations—on the social upheaval that can be obscured by statistics, or the ways in which cowrie shells and other objects might tell us about the increasing commodification of bodies in the slave trade—far from invalidating so-called "uncritical" claims on (or rejections of) Africa, seemed to make such claims even more salient. Their perspectives on the sociopolitical upheaval in late nineteenth-century Africa provided me with the opportunity to revisit my conclusions about Caribbean notions of modernity in Africa for that historical period.

When I related the following anecdote about kola nuts, I concluded that the laughter of the members of a late nineteenth-century Trinidadian audience indicated that they thought that they were superior to West Africans. This conclusion holds little interest for me now, not least because of the laughter of my Dartmouth audience at the same story! A conclusion of Trinidadian superiority becomes little more than an attempt to confirm my own good judgment in the twenty-first century, and it also downplays and so confines West African perspectives to the very stasis that irked some of our colleagues. To really come to grip with such perspectives is to acknowledge the equally anxious and imaginative mythmaking in which people on the African side of the Atlantic have been engaged—mythmaking that the quest for scientific "rigor" can sometimes discount. My presentation at the Dartmouth conference juxtaposed a missionary's story about women walking behind their husbands in West Africa with the image of, on the one hand, men and women sitting side by side listening to his lecture in San Fernando and, on the other, unruly women in public spaces such as the streets of Port of Spain. It was important, I suggested, to consider what black nationalist and Pan-Africanist men said about both the women who were in their midst *and* those who were far away. The same nationalist who might applaud middle-class women for attending lectures, because this signaled an intellectual parity between men and women that confirmed his sense of the Caribbean as modern and progressive, might very well lambaste single, working-class women in the Caribbean public sphere because their autonomy threatened his sense of normative gender relations. Walking *without* men was thus deemed to be as troubling as walking *behind* them.

The enormously fruitful, sometimes uncomfortable, and even painful exchanges of the conference have prompted a reassessment of many issues for me, including the extent to which both sides of the Atlantic were transformed in the late nineteenth century. In paying more attention to the West African dimension of a story about kola nuts I now want to consider gender, and specifically the role of women, in a more thoroughgoing discussion of issues of betrayal and upheaval, tradition and modernity, and valid and invalid diasporic claims, as two sides of the Atlantic took stock of their respective futures in the late nineteenth century.

On 1 August 1887 the Reverend P. H. Douglin, a black Barbadian-born minister of the Church of England, gave a public lecture at St. Paul's School Room in San Fernando, the southwestern city that could safely be called the center of Trinidad's black and colored middle class.[2] The lecture marked the anniversary of Emancipation Day in the British Caribbean, and the topic was the Rio Pongo Mission in West Africa, where Douglin had served until illness prompted his departure. The Mission, 120 miles north of Sierra Leone, was established in 1855 by the Church of England in the West Indies, headquartered in Barbados. By the 1880s the Mission was supervised, as well as staffed, mainly by "men of African descent," since most Europeans who had been sent to staff it had succumbed to illness, Douglin told his listeners. Thus the Caribbean-based church was sending to Africa missionaries "mainly derived from Africa, and where not derived from Africa, deeply indebted to Africa by wrongs inflicted and by benefits obtained." Pointing out the importance of Rio Pongo to Europeans because of its palm oil, and telling his audience not to confuse it with either the "River Congo" or the "Rio Pongas," Douglin reviewed the history of religious missions in the area, noting that the Church of England challenged the dominance of the Roman Catholic Church in the region and that all Christian denominations in the area competed with Islam. He told his audience the sordid history of the slave trade in the region, noting that "white men of all nations" were "rogued and tricked" by the "Mulattoes and Sosohs [Susu]" who competed with them for prominence in the slave trade. These groups exploited the "weak points" of the "natives," giving them "gaudy things" and alcohol, instigating civil wars and supplying both sides with arms.

A team of nine clergy, catechists, and schoolteachers labored among "Sosohs, Fallahs [Fula or Fulani], Mandigos [Mandingo], Bagahs [Baga] and Tomahs [Toma]," at five mission stations. "Away from civilisation and improvement, far from the light and knowledge of God, which is the center and source of all improvement and civilisation," they were "sunk in great ignorance and superstition," declared Douglin, lamenting that the African continent, once "in the vanguard of civilization," was "now so behind-hand in everything." He told his audience that "forests of ignorance, superstition, vice and ungodliness, with countless evil habits and wicked customs which lurk in them like wild beasts and venomous serpents" had to be "cleared" and "good habits and customs planted and matured and reared up in their place." While the Baga "compare[d] favorably with civilized people everywhere," *black* Baga were "dark-headed, ignorant heathens." Outside contact had "tarnished" the Susu, but time had taught Douglin to appreciate their essential honesty and to see that their religious beliefs were compatible with Christianity. They had migrated from the interior to avoid the influence of Islam. He assured his listeners that he and his team were succeeding under difficult circumstances, getting converts to promise not to sell slaves, and translating portions of the Bible and the Book of Common Prayer into the Susu language. The Susu, he told them, were fond of alcohol and believed in witchcraft, but they loved their children and were prepared to go to war if their mothers were insulted.

Douglin's account of Susu gender relations underlined his account of missionary success in the face of great odds. Susu men sat on the ground to eat the rice that was the staple of their diet, while Susu women, who did not eat with their husbands, fanned the meal so that it did not burn the hands of "their lords and masters." Women walked behind their husbands. The mission team had succeeded in teaching the Susu people "the dignity of women," raising her "from the dust," lightening "her burdens, developing her mind, and [teaching] her her true position." Polygamy was discouraged, and husbands were instructed to "love their wives and not to regard them simply as natural conveniences." Douglin explained the importance of the kola nut for the Susu: regarded as the "tree of knowledge," it was prized for its ability to satisfy hunger during periods of fasting or on long journeys, and for its efficacy in proving guilt or innocence. His account of another of its properties elicited laughter from his Trinidadian audience: it was the forbidden fruit that Eve swallowed, and that explained why women could not keep secrets. Adam, on the other hand, ate it gingerly and it lodged in his throat, and thus the Adam's apples of men indicated that they were more reflective and discreet than their impulsive female counterparts.

Notwithstanding his statement that the very word *Sosoh* meant "immigrants," and that the Susu language was the medium of trade and commerce for all visitors to the region, Douglin did not hesitate to speak with authority about innate differences among the six "nations" that lived near the Rio Pongo. A *Grammar* published in 1802 noted that teaching the Susu to read and write in their own language would enable them to communicate "religious ideas" more clearly, check "the progress of Mohamedanism," and accelerate the spreading of the gospel, since "their country is a mart for commerce on that part of the coast, and as they are visited by many thousands of people from all the countries around them."[3] Missionaries such as Douglin, then, finding themselves in a region marked by these "many thousands" and their "commerce," sought to tame what they considered to be a messy linguistic, ethnic, and spiritual situation.

Douglin spoke with the certainty of a man who knew that he and his cause represented a superior divinity and civilization, to an audience that assumed the same. If their laughter signified their amusement at customs that seemed backward to them, confirming their own modernity as believers in the equality of the sexes and as Christians, I am more interested today in how willing I was to grant to my Hanover audience a healthy sense of irony and fun, and the capacity to critique Douglin's missionary zeal, and see in a story about kola nuts and Adam's apples more than Susu "backwardness," than in my conviction of the "failure" of Douglin and his audience to do so, if indeed that is what it was. For is this really all that I can say about a narrative that is so suggestive? Douglin's account tells us something about the competition between Christians and Muslims for the souls of potential converts and about the assessments of the relative merits of white and black missionaries. We get some sense, from his account, of what we might term Pan-Africanist interpretations of slavery and the slave trade in the late nineteenth century: the outright villains, the gullible actors, the victims. Douglin measures Africa against itself—against its own past—when he laments that

Africans had once been "pioneers of mankind in the various untrodden fields of art, literature and science, alphabet, writing, history, chronology, architecture, navigation, agriculture, and textile industry." At a period when Victorian travelers discussed Afro-Caribbean people in terms of "reversion" to African "savagery," Douglin shows the Susu and the Baga to have "reverted" from prior models of African civilization.

On the anniversary of the emancipation from slavery in the British Caribbean, a Trinidadian audience had come out to hear about Africa in the context of their identity as Christians. Douglin identified Rio Pongo as "one of the sunny fountains of which you so often sing," referring to the popular missionary hymn "From Greenland's Icy Mountains," written by Reginald Heber in 1817. The intense interest in Africans and Africa on the part of missionaries such as Douglin, and the churches that sponsored them, is evident here, but so is Africa's significance for a broader base of Caribbean people—mainly, though not solely, a black and brown middle class in this instance—represented by those who turned out to hear his lecture in San Fernando. Distinctions that we might want to draw today between Caribbean Christians with an inauthentic ancestral investment in uplift and civilization, and those with a "genuine" interest in Africa's political autonomy, are complicated here if we accept that these interests converge and seem to feed on each other in the story above. Far from being indifferent to Africa or ashamed of their ancestral connection to it, Douglin's audience is anxious to bring the continent in line with its notions of "progress" *because of* rather than *in spite of* its Christian faith and to regard this as key to the continent's eventual freedom. We may attribute this to a diasporic imperative specifically but to a more global interest in Christian missions as well. The complete stanza of the hymn to which Douglin refers is, after all:

> From Greenland's icy mountains,
> From India's coral strand,
> Where Afric's sunny fountains
> Roll down their golden sand.
> From many an ancient river
> From many a palmy plain
> They call us to deliver
> Their land from error's chain.

Here, Africa is one of several locations for the spread of the gospel, and Douglin's listeners are thus part of an international web tying them, for instance, to congregations in England who were deeply invested in "civilizing missions."[4] Their missionary interest is not easily distinguishable from what may be termed their ancestral interest, and both are in turn inseparable from an imperial dimension, given black Trinidadians' colonial status as "Her Majesty's Ethiopic subjects."[5] In the twentieth century, Marcus Garvey's United Negro Improvement Association meetings would begin with the singing of "From Greenland's Icy Mountains," underscoring the strong connections between diasporic Pan-African sensibilities and missionary-imperial ones.[6]

A few months before Douglin's lecture, the well-known black Trinidadian John Jacob Thomas had lamented the absence of women, except for the white governor's wife, in the lecture halls of Grenada, where Thomas had gone to live. Trinidad had taught him to take for granted the presence of women at numerous lectures in the late nineteenth century. We might say that he had an expectation about black and brown women sitting beside their men rather than walking behind them, as Douglin told his audience was the case for the Susu. As Robert Love, the Jamaican Pan-Africanist, would put it almost a decade later:

> The race rises as its women rise. They are the true standard of its elevation. We are trying to produce cultured men without asking ourselves where they are to find cultured wives. We forget that cultured families constitute a cultured race and that a cultured race is an equal race. The elevation of women to equality with [their] white counterparts is the *Condition Sine Qua Non* of the elevation of the Negro race.[7]

The maneuvers by which various constituencies are held up as models of either modernity or the lack of it are almost dizzying, from speaker to speaker or even within the space of a sentence. For Love, "the race's" women need to be like *white* women (one presumes upper middle class and above) so that black men can take their place as patriarchs in the manner of white gentlemen, who are the absent referents here. Thus the respectable, heterosexual, middle-class black couple can function as both a model for, and a bulwark against, Susu and Bagah couples on the other side of the Atlantic, but also, closer to home, black immigrant women like "Bim-Bim" from Curaçao and her "equally vile daughters, who, every night, to the peculiar music of their Quelbays went through the most lascivious antics, indicative of the sensuous vocation to which they abandoned themselves,"[8] as well as male and female immigrants from the Indian subcontinent, to whom (ungentlemanly) Victorian travel writers compared Afro-Caribbean people unfavorably, much to the consternation of the black and brown middle class. The influx of immigrants increases anxieties in the Trinidad context, as do the "thousands of people from all the countries around them" that preoccupy the missionaries in the Rio Pongo region. We will return to immigrants and their perceived threats to a community's integrity in a moment.

Love, Thomas, and other members of the black middle class also compared themselves to black men and women outside of the region, as when Thomas praised prominent African Americans in the United States public sphere in *Froudacity*. His and others' spirited defense of Africans and the African continent is made with the full assumption that as "extra-Africans" they have *crossed over* in more than just a physical and geographical sense. When he notes in *Froudacity* that the "heathen of Africa, the man-hunting Arab, the Egyptian [and] the Turk" are "glorified" by the Christian endeavors of Charles Gordon, David Livingstone, and others, he speaks as one of "Her Majesty's Ethiopic subjects,"[9] a diasporic intellectual whose parents' crossing and enslavement on Caribbean plantations has thrust him into a particular modernity. Christian Pan-Africanist nationalists countered the charges by European naysayers that Africa was inherently incapable of "civilization" by stressing the devastating impact of the slave trade and the role that could be played in its rehabilitation by "the extra-African millions—ten millions in the Western Hemisphere—dispersed so widely over the surface of the globe, apt apprentices in every conceivable department of civilized culture."[10]

In the late nineteenth and early twentieth centuries, Indian nationalists made similar arguments, though by a different positioning of the Caribbean relative to an "old world." They lamented that Indians sent to the Caribbean and elsewhere as indentured laborers to fill perceived postslavery labor shortages were degraded as long as they remained outside of the Indian subcontinent. As Tejaswini Niranjana has argued, such nationalists, in representing the plight of Indians in the diaspora (extra-Indians?) as "victimized, pathetic, lost, and helpless," refused to

acknowledge that these migrants could "become modern" in the Caribbean, since to do so would be to admit that there could be a space for
Indians to become modern outside of India and beyond the jurisdiction of middle-class, upper-caste nationalists.[11] In speaking on behalf of
"the intra-African Negro . . . clearly powerless to struggle successfully
against personal enslavement, annexation, or [to] volunteer forcible 'protection' of his territory," did extra-African nationalists in the Caribbean
similarly think of themselves as presiding over the continent's future—
indeed that they *were* its future, as family members who, as modern
and black, represented the best of the West? And in so doing, did they
discount the long-term engagement of continental Africans with the
trade, with the horror of the traffic in bodies, and thus with the continuing consequences of modernity?

I will try to read the kola nuts in Douglin's account, then, not as a
premodern sign of Susu backwardness or quaintness (if indeed that is
what the laughter of the San Fernando audience signified), or as a late
nineteenth-century Caribbean congregation's failure to be politically
correct, but as part of an ongoing discussion about who spoke for a
community and who could represent it, as an engagement by those on
the African side of the Atlantic with what Rosalind Shaw has termed a
"vampiric modernity" caused by the "imperative to produce slaves."[12]
Recent discussions of the discourses of mid- to late nineteenth-century
participants in the transatlantic slave trade and their descendants suggest the extent of the social and moral upheaval that Douglin and his
missionary colleagues attempted to make sense of, and provide useful
perspectives on the extent to which both sides of the Atlantic attempted
to square off losses and gains. The trade—its geographical parameters, its
no-longer-African, not-yet-Caribbean names and gods and betrayals—
reveals itself as a zone that demands specific theorization.

In *Central Africa in the Caribbean: Transcending Time, Transforming
Cultures,* Maureen Warner-Lewis notes that in making a case for linkages between Africa and the Caribbean, the scholar must contend with
resistance to the idea of African provenances on the part of Caribbean
people: "The stigma of slavery and black pigmentation, the effectiveness
of colonial brainwashing, the psychological insecurities of economically
and technologically dependent peoples, and the complacency born of
majority demographic status, have made the issue of Africa more sub-

tly tortured for its peoples."[13] But the scholar must also contend with academics who assume that enslaved Africans were so traumatized by slavery that only shoddy scholarship and romantic notions of diaspora would lead the scholar to go further back in time than the history of the Caribbean plantation in trying to account for the history and culture of the majority of the region's people.

In her own efforts to address these popular and academic assumptions, Warner-Lewis examines the oral narratives that she gathered from elderly Trinidadians and Guyanese in the late 1960s, as well as the narratives collected by other researchers, to trace the presence of Central African cultural forms in the Caribbean. Besides giving us a sense of the enduring stamp of Kongo, Mbundu, and Ovimbundu ethnic groups on the region, the Caribbean interviewees shed light on the period of slavery from the perspective of Africans. Mavis Morrison of Guyana tells of her father's sale as a teenager by his uncle as they were out hunting.[14] Her father recalled that some of his captors were "clear clear" (meaning light-skinned), and some "black"; "dey chain 'e," and the uncle "Packet . . . de money. 'E tun 'e back. A sell 'e sell 'e." In the small boat in which he was placed he was chained to a post because of his incessant weeping, and then he arrived at "a big big boat" where others were chained. Family betrayal, monetary or other compensation, and the involvement of black and mulatto/a traders all tell us something of the dynamics of the trade. Furthermore, the distinction between "clear clear" and "black" in the description of the agents, a demarcation in skin color, and a corresponding social status central to and usually held to be distinguishing features of Caribbean societies, suggests that these were salient *before* the crossing of the Atlantic, a reminder of the long period of European contact prior to the mid- to late nineteenth century when these informants' parents were captured.

While Warner-Lewis attributes popular resistance to Africa to feelings of shame, Rhonda Cobham proposes that silence or negativity regarding Africa on the part of Caribbean people should be attributed to a sense of African betrayal during the period of slavery and the slave trade.[15] Turning to scholarly discussions in Africa of the figure of the Mami Wata (also Mammywata, Mammy Wata, or Mama Wata) in order to gloss its representation in Caribbean fiction, she is dissatisfied that the scholarship does not give sufficient weight to the slave trade and to the changes that occurred in Africa because of it. Cobham proposes that this figure in West Africa and the Americas (variously the Mami Wata, River Mumma, Osun) ought to be examined with careful attention paid to how the changes in its characteristics from the deities whom it most closely resembled reflected the social transformations taking place during the trade.[16] Indeed, in Cobham's discussion, the figure emerges as a symbol of the transformations of that historical moment.

Since Mami Wata has been particularly associated with rivers, Pidgin English, and the figure of the mulatto/a, Cobham links her to features of the trade with Europeans, including the increasing number of biracial children of European traders and West African women. For Cobham, then, Mami Wata was an obvious symbol of mediation, related to but very different from her traditional counterparts, including Idemili and Osun, and particularly suited to the period of the transatlantic slave trade, "when social interactions between Europeans and Africans on the West African coast were relatively fluid and when both Africans and Europeans saw in the trade lucrative possibilities for mutual enrichment." Cobham suggests that Mami Wata's self-involvement and childlessness can be read as "a community's way of acknowledging and negotiating the paradox whereby African coastal and riverine traders were able to amass considerable personal wealth by sacrificing their society's 'children' in exchange for the opportunity to accumulate capital on a scale not formerly common in African societies."[17]

Where African literature represents the encounter between Africa and Europe as a "face-off" between two powerful belief and knowledge systems that are equally rife with internal contradictions, Cobham notes that Caribbean literature positions the African-Caribbean "folk" against "modernity" in a much more complex encounter in which the Caribbean, lacking "established institutions through which to articulate the significance of commonly held beliefs and widely dispersed practices," is destined to lose out to both European *and* African systems.[18] Mami Wata offers the possibility of wealth to those on the African side of the Atlantic in exchange for the loss of their children, but there are no such gains for the Caribbean descendants of those children. This is why, for Cobham, the repudiation of African traditions by Caribbean people cannot simply be attributed to "an unsophisticated disavowal of their heritage," since Africa, like Mami Wata, failed to protect its children, and thus a wholesale embrace of the continent is also a discounting of, perhaps also a collusion in, one's own betrayal. For Cobham, this response to Africa in terms of maternal betrayal helps us to understand a text such as *The Autobiography of My Mother* by Jamaica Kincaid, a writer often accused of offering "incorrect" and hostile interpretations of Caribbean people's conceptions of blackness and the African continent in her work. As I suggested earlier, a wholesale dismissal of diasporic responses to the African continent as essentialist and uncritical, whether they are negative or celebratory, risks missing a full appreciation of the range and complexity of such responses.

In *Memories of the Slave Trade: Ritual and the Historical Imagination in Sierra Leone,* Rosalind Shaw finds in present-day practices of divination, as well as in discussions of witches and spirits, ongoing memorializations of the trade that counter perceptions that Sierra Leoneans today neither discuss nor accept any responsibility for the slave trade. The Temne-speaking region including northern Sierra Leone, on which Shaw focuses in her discussion of ritual and memory, may or may not include the region "120 miles north of Sierra Leone" where Douglin's Mission was located. I am less interested in proving that this is so than in using Shaw's insights to draw out the rich implications of Douglin's account. As Shaw shows, kola (a Malinké term) was an important trade item for Temne speakers, who traded with the Mande in exchange for iron, cotton, and gold before the arrival of Europeans in the fifteenth century. By the time the latter arrived, the region was already a "translocal sphere of commercial relations" linked to the trans-Saharan trade touching three continents. As Portuguese merchants, and then the English who replaced them as the dominant slave traders by the eighteenth century, sought slaves and other sources of trade, rivers became "extensions of the Atlantic ocean." Shaw argues that the terror of those Africans who stayed behind, "[living] for centuries with both the anticipation and the consequence of the warfare, raiding, and other means of enslavement that the transatlantic trade engendered and multiplied," is as much the story of the slave trade as the actual movement of bodies across the ocean.[19]

Shaw maintains that the consequences of the trade were gendered, since men were sent into the transatlantic trade and women were retained in the domestic trade. The following account suggests that female slaves who became wives in neighboring communities "exacerbated" prevailing notions of alien wives "as witches, as diviners' clients, or as drawing the dangers of bush-spirit incursion."[20] In the late nineteenth century, a woman from the Kpa Mende who married into the Yoni Temne was killed for publicly communicating her dream about enemies attacking her husband's town. She had violated taboos regarding the discussion of dreams with anyone other than the chief, to whom she should have reported her dream. Not only had she undermined his ultimate "control over knowledge," but she had also threatened to set in motion the transfer of harmful forces to her husband's people, since in the dream world humans "[mingled] freely with spirits, witches, and ancestors in the dream-town," and women's dreams, in particular, risked attracting hostile forces to their households and villages. Reporting the dream to the chief enabled its "dangerous potential" to be contained, and this is why the woman's failure to do so required such drastic punishment. In any event, the woman's dream *did* bring about the danger that the elders feared, since her son left the region and eventually joined forces with his mother's Kpa Mende people, the enemies of the Yoni Temne, to sack Ronietta, the town in which she had been killed and in which he had been raised.

Shaw points out that these events took place during a period when these two communities and others of Temneland in southern Sierra Leone fought each other furiously over the issue of access to trading centers and rivers. Many of these conflicts were marked by the use of marriage between warring communities to create or maintain alliances. Thus a new wife who came from a community with whom her husband's people had just been in conflict presented an obvious source of suspicion; we have just seen how the Yoni Temne of Ronietta found out to their peril how the attempt to cure the threat represented by one wife's dream resulted in their eventual destruction years later and so confirmed the danger of "alien" wives.

Here, then, is an anxiety about trade, ethnic rivalry, outsiders, and the containment of the speech of alien women that can help us to understand a story about kola nuts and women's indiscreet speech in Douglin's Susu community. A story about Adam and Eve, itself a biblical reference to originary, gendered infraction, encodes a community's concerns about controlling speech in times of war—perhaps alien women's violations of male elders' instructions in particular—at a historical period of unparalleled internecine fighting and economic opportunity, afforded by the trade in palm oil and human bodies. Wives speaking out of turn; the potential danger of women's dreams and their public disclosure outside of the proper channels; neighboring communities placated or enraged by captive women—Eve's indiscreet consumption of the kola nut potentially compromised a community's ability to control knowledge and ensure its safety.

Who presided over the consumption and distribution of the kola nut, the symbol of the community's lucrative trade, and the means by which it "spoke" to the world in economic as well as moral terms? Recall Douglin's description of the kola nut as the "tree of knowledge," the means by which hunger could be assuaged, the discloser of truth. As the key to the Susu community's ability to take care of *all* of its needs—physical, economic, ethical, and otherwise—the kola nut had to be squared off against what Douglin and other Christians offered in return. Having made a vow to discontinue the trade in slaves, would the untested promise of Christian conversion be sufficient for the Susu people? How would Christianity allow them to "speak" in the future?

If we can allow these connections between Shaw's Temneland and Douglin's Rio Pongo region, then we might see how in the late nineteenth century, narratives about women—as docile or vulgar, as the intellectual companions of middle-class nationalists, as wives who betrayed their communities, or as mothers who literally sold their children down the river—were a powerful site for the expression of culture, civilization, tradition, and modernity for Trinidadians and Susu alike. Douglin and the middle-class members of his audience used the anecdote to take stock of what Africa "needed," how it was deficient, and thus why their civilizing procedures were necessary, as they struggled to assert who could be in charge of what counted as "civilized" in the face of the influx of thousands of immigrants such as Bim Bim into Trinidad. Presiding over a trade in humans and palm oil at once potentially prosperous, violent, and horrifying, the Susu weighed Christian, Islamic, and other ideological systems. Facing uncertain times in different contexts, both communities drew on deeply gendered ways of assigning authority as well as blame, and they fashioned the various "Africas" that would allow them to navigate difficult futures.

# Notes

My thanks to the participants of the 2002 "Gendering the African Diaspora" conference and to the organizers, Judith Byfield, Veronica Gregg, and Verene Shepherd.
1. While I am interpreting the query about precision with which my chapter begins as a *disciplinary* one, between those of us in the arts, roughly speaking, and those in the social sciences, I am well aware that it is possible to find these fault lines in any number of permutations. Intellectuals associated with Négritude have been eloquently critiqued by literary and cultural critics, most recently the Martinican Créolists. See Bernabé, Chamoiseau, and Confiant, *Eloge de la Créolité: In Praise of Creoleness.* Stephan Palmié's reservations about the lack of theoretical rigor in the assessment of "African" cultural formations in the Caribbean are directed at his fellow social scientists. See *Wizards and Scientists: Explorations in Afro-Cuban Modernity and Tradition.* Sylvia Wynter's most memorable critiques of the English Department's Eurocentrism are addressed to her fellow literary critics in "The Novel and History, Plot and Plantation." David Scott's critique of Kamau Brathwaite's meditations on the cultural and geographical proximity of the Caribbean to West Africa is, to my mind, less a function of Scott's disciplinary location in anthropology, and Brathwaite's in poetry/literary criticism/history, than of *generational* differences between pre- and post-post-national(ist) intellectuals. See Brathwaite, "The African Presence in Caribbean Literature," and Scott, "An Obscure Miracle of Connection."
2. See *San Fernando Gazette,* 6 August 1887. On Douglin, see Brereton, *Race Relations in Colonial Trinidad, 1870–1900,* 93; Smith, *Creole Recitations,* 136–39; and Cudjoe, *Beyond Boundaries,* 366–69. On the Mission, see Barrow, *Fifty Years in Western Africa.*
3. Kemp, *Grammar and Vocabulary of the Susoo Language.*
4. See Hall, *Civilising Subjects,* and Thorne, *Congregational Missions and the Making of an Imperial Culture in Nineteenth-Century England.* See also Hall's "'From Greenland's Icy Mountains . . . to Afric's Golden Sand.'"
5. Thomas uses this term in *Froudacity: West Indian Fables,* 56.
6. Hill, *The Marcus Garvey and Universal Negro Improvement Association Papers,* 1:278.
7. Bryan, *The Jamaican People, 1880–1902,* 233. Bryan cites the *Jamaica Advocate,* 6 April 1895.
8. Editorial, *Trinidad Review,* 9 August 1883.
9. Thomas, *Froudacity,* 174, 56.
10. Ibid., 179.
11. Niranjana, "Left to the Imagination: Indian Nationalists and Female Sexuality in Trinidad," 119–20.
12. Shaw, *Memories of the Slave Trade,* 17.
13. Warner-Lewis, *Central Africa in the Caribbean,* xxiii.
14. Ibid., 31–32. Morrison's interview with Adeola James is from James, *Guyanese Oral Traditions.*
15. Cobham, "'Mwen Na Rien, Msieu.'"
16. At the Dartmouth conference, Akin Ogundiran's paper, "Osun, Yemoja, and Olukun: Gender, Commerce, and the Making of Atlantic Goddesses," showed how

changes in the representation of these and other deities in the Yoruba pantheon reflected "memories, actions, intentions, experiences, and possibilities that have their provenance in the context of Atlantic encounters" and anxieties about the social relations such as the "struggles between the [male-dominated] state and the [female-dominated] market." His discussion of taboos about women and palm nut divination, of witchcraft, bloodsucking, palm-oil sucking, and the process by which "human bodies and souls became convertible to cowries and commodities" during the slave trade is relevant to Shaw's discussion of Sierra Leone Temne-speakers.

17. Cobham, "'Mwen Na Rien, Msieu,'" 873.
18. Ibid., 874–75.
19. Shaw, *Memories of the Slave Trade*, 28, 32.
20. Ibid., 33.

# References

Barrow, Alfred Henry. *Fifty Years in Western Africa, Being a Record of the Work of the West Indian Church on the Banks of the Rio Pongo*. London: Society for Promoting Christian Knowledge, 1900.

Bernabé, Jean, Patrick Chamoiseau, and Rafael Confiant. *Éloge de la Créolité: In Praise of Creoleness*. Paris: Gallimard, 1993.

Brathwaite, Kamau. "The African Presence in Caribbean Literature." In *Roots*, 190–258. Havana: Casa de las Americas, 1986; Ann Arbor: University of Michigan Press, 1993.

Brereton, Bridget. *Race Relations in Colonial Trinidad, 1870–1900*. London: Cambridge University Press, 1979.

Bryan, Patrick. *The Jamaican People, 1880–1902*. London: Macmillan Caribbean, 1991.

Cobham, Rhonda. "'Mwen Na Rien, Msieu': Jamaica Kincaid and the Problem of Creole Gnosis." *Callaloo* 25 (2002): 868–84.

Cudjoe, Selwyn R. *Beyond Boundaries: The Intellectual Tradition of Trinidad and Tobago in the Nineteenth Century*. Wellesley: Calaloux, 2003.

Hall, Catherine. "'From Greenland's Icy Mountains . . . to Afric's Golden Sand': Ethnicity, Race, and Nation in Mid-Nineteenth-Century England." *Gender and History* 5, no. 2 (1993): 212–30.

———. *Civilising Subjects: Metropole and Colony in the English Imagination, 1830–1867*. Chicago: University of Chicago Press, 2002.

Hill, Robert A., ed. *The Marcus Garvey and Universal Negro Improvement Association Papers*. Vol. 1: *1826–August 1919*. Berkeley: University of California Press, 1983.

James, Adeola, ed. *Guyanese Oral Traditions: Interviews Conducted on the East Coast Demerara, West Coast Berbice, West Bank Demerara, and the Essequibo Coast*. Turkeyen: University of Guyana, mimeograph, 1989.

Kemp, John. *Grammar and Vocabulary of the Susoo Language: To Which Are Added the Names of Some of the Susoo Towns near the Banks of the Rio Pongas, a Small Catalogue of Arabic Books, and a List of the Names of Some of the Learned Men of the Mandinga and Foulah Countries, with Whom an Useful Correspondence*

*Could Be Opened Up in the Arabic Language*. Edinburgh: J. Ritchie, Blackfriars, Wynn, 1802.

Kincaid, Jamaica. *The Autobiography of My Mother*. New York: Farrar, Straus and Giroux, 1996.

Niranjana, Tejaswini. "Left to the Imagination: Indian Nationalisms and Female Sexuality in Trinidad." In *A Question of Silence? The Sexual Economies of Modern India*, ed. Mary E. John and Janaki Nair, 111–38. London and New York: Zed, 2000.

Ogundiran, Akin. "Osun, Yemoja, and Olukun: Gender, Commerce, and the Making of Atlantic Goddesses." Paper presented at Dartmouth conference "Gendering the Diaspora: Women, Culture and Historical Change in the Caribbean and the Nigerian Hinterland," Dartmouth College, 22–24 November 2002.

Palmié, Stephan. *Wizards and Scientists: Explorations in Afro-Cuban Modernity and Tradition*. Durham, N.C.: Duke University Press, 2002.

Scott, David. "An Obscure Miracle of Connection." *Small Axe* 1 (March 1997): 17–36.

Shaw, Rosalind. *Memories of the Slave Trade: Ritual and the Historical Imagination in Sierra Leone*. Chicago: University of Chicago Press, 2002.

Smith, Faith. *Creole Recitations: John Jacob Thomas and Colonial Formation in the Late Nineteenth-Century Caribbean*. Charlottesville: University of Virginia Press, 2002.

Thomas, John Jacob. *Froudacity: West Indian Fables*. London: T. Fisher Unwin, 1889; reprint, London: New Beacon Press, 1969.

Thorne, Susan. *Congregational Missions and the Making of an Imperial Culture in Nineteenth-Century England*. Palo Alto, Calif.: Stanford University Press, 1999.

Warner-Lewis, Maureen. *Central Africa in the Caribbean: Transcending Time, Transforming Cultures*. Barbados: University of the West Indies Press, 2003.

Wynter, Sylvia. "The Novel and History, Plot and Plantation." *Savacou* 5 (June 1971): 95–102.

# 2

# From Africa to "The Islands":
# New World Voyages in the Fiction
# of Maryse Condé and Paule Marshall

ANTHEA MORRISON

I come to find my vital self left back here
so that I land in Xamayca with quest fever
and all the while Africa you had my remedy
. . .
Continent of my foremothers, to reach back I have
crossed over seas, oceans, seven-sourced rivers.
Under my heartbeat is where you pitched and lodged
persistent memory, rhythm box with no off-switch.

LORNA GOODISON, "NATAL SONG"

In the evocatively titled collection *Travelling Mercies* (2001), Jamaican poet Lorna Goodison speaks in the voice of a female voyager whose journey "back" to southern Africa is suggestive of the travails, inscribed in Caribbean literature, of various traveling heroines, also afflicted/fired with "quest fever." Clearly a dominant trope in diasporic literature of the second half of the twentieth century, journeying is a powerful and poignant motif in the fiction of Maryse Condé and Paule Marshall, whose female protagonists defy the constraints—constraints informed by gender and/or race—that reined in the audacious impulses of their forebears.

The work of the two writers, one manifestly Guadeloupean, the other arguably both African American and Caribbean, reflects, on the one hand, a sharp sense of place, of island place and, on the other, a recognition of the difficulty for many West Indians of definitive homecoming.[1] For peoples fashioned by exile—both the initial *déracinement* and the subsequent voyages northward—the notion of home has not been without its charge of ambiguity. From the very beginning of French Caribbean literature, Aimé Césaire's *Cahier d'un retour au pays natal* [*Notebook of a Return to the Native Land*] foregrounded such ambiguity in the elliptical reference to return to a *pays natal,* which one assumes to be Martinique, but that might also be the African continent, site of memory and obsession. Complex affinities are similarly inherent in the title of Goodison's "Natal Song," in which this writer exploits in the South African context, as she has done in so many texts inspired by her native Jamaican landscape, the felicitous suggestiveness of place-names that highlight and also satisfy a need for belonging. For Goodison, like Césaire before her, never travels so far that the island loses its privileged place in a vision that, though resolutely generous, is also shaped—and sometimes circumscribed—by the familiar shores of a land small enough for intimate knowledge. By the end of *Cahier d'un retour au pays natal,* the poet of Negritude seems to have transcended, if not relinquished, his sense that the island can stifle as well as nurture.

But for generations younger than Césaire's—and for those less rooted than Goodison—the emergence of important diasporic communities, coupled with individual experiences of exile, has broadened and/or problematized the notion of home and, with it, the assumption of fidelity to a single "rock," to the island rock. That sometimes fertile tension between the land of the New World, if not ancestral, belonging, and the temporary home of convenience is vividly captured in a dialogue/duel between the young American-born daughter of "Bajan Yankees"—a term used with slightly pejorative intent by those who have remained on the land—and her grandmother, in the story that Paule Marshall dedicates to her own Barbadian grandmother, "Da-Duh." The latter presents, with the solemnity of ritual, and the proud certainty of those whose navel string[2] lies close to home, the sumptuous trees rising out of the Caribbean soil: "This here is a breadfruit . . . that one yonder is a papaw. Here's a guava. This is a mango. I know you don't have anything like these in New York."[3] But the older generation, however beloved, however revered, does not have the last word: the granddaughter's rejoinder, a few pages later, reveals a dual belonging, a new form of *métissage* in migrant communities where the island is a memory, inevitably diluted, and yet potent. In the face of the majestic *tropical* royal palm, the city-bred child, initially intimidated by the lush landscape that the grandmother claims with confidence, is happy to boast: "We've got buildings hundreds of times this tall in New York."[4]

That New York functions here as paradigm of difference is, of course, hardly surprising, for the city dazzles like few others (perhaps less so in the post–September 11 era, but Marshall's narrative was written at a time of relative innocence). Claude, the young Guadeloupean protagonist of Maryse Condé's short story "Three Women in Manhattan," is similarly vulnerable to New York's seductiveness, even as she is conscious of the pull of a *mythical* Africa celebrated by her friend and mentor, the much older Haitian Vera:

> There still was Africa, about which Vera would often speak. It was so far away! Who knew what went on there? Nonetheless, the evening classes at City College were almost free. She was learning English. Bit by bit, the sounds of New York—which had frightened and deafened her—were becoming intelligible. She was able to decipher the puzzles of neon signs and posters.[5]

The figure of the woman traveling alone, venturing unprotected into uncharted territory, is a recurrent one in Condé's *oeuvre,* evocative of audacity and independence of spirit, and emblematic of the will to transcend the limitations of patriarchy. New York is all the more alien to this particular young traveler because she is French-speaking. The city's strangeness derives, however, at least in part from the fact that it is the antithesis of the distant island, but an island that Claude does not idealize, for she was happy to escape the claustrophobia of a restrictive neocolonial society. (The political status of the francophone territories of the Caribbean, which became Overseas Departments of France in 1946, means that the ties to the former "metropole" remain virtually intact.) In an analysis of Julia Kristeva's work, Anna Smith makes a comment that is pertinent to Condé's portrayal of a young woman savoring the perceived freedom of urban space: "She [Kristeva] offers the figure of the female voyager as the exemplary role to assume in the face of New York's frenetic movement. The time of New York is one of rupture, of perpetual comings and goings that the female voyager can turn into a play that avoids all notions of fixity."[6]

Islands can indeed confine. They may even appear, by comparison to the big city, to epitomize "fixity." Nevertheless, both Condé and Marshall seem aware of their capacity for nurturing and for restoring ancestral linkages to the lost continent. Condé grew up on one of these tiny portions, or weighty fragments, of earth that make up the archipelago, islands that Général de Gaulle is said to have dismissed in the comment "Between Europe and America I see only specks of dust." His words appear in an epigraph to Edouard Glissant's *Caribbean Discourse*[7] and have been much cited in the French Caribbean, a Caribbean whose very existence they implicitly refute. Marshall, on the other hand, is the Brooklyn-born daughter of migrant Barbadians. Ironically, it is the fiction of the Guadeloupean writer that seems less sure of ancestral belonging, more tentative in the steps taken toward homecoming. While Marshall asserts that she is "an unabashed ancestor worshipper," Condé puts in the mouth of one of her most enigmatic characters, Spéro, the male protagonist of *The Last of the African Kings* [*Les derniers rois mages*], the provocative suggestion that the past should be "killed." In the latter novel, the male descendants of King Béhanzin of Dahomey,[8] an African monarch exiled in Martinique at the beginning of the twentieth century, are brought up to revere their royal lineage, to recognize and valorize their difference from the run-of-the-mill descendants of enslaved Africans by paying homage to the ancestral past, to a sometimes elusive forebear whom memory dresses in radiant cloth. So although a substantial section of the narrative is set in the African American community of the United States, into which Spéro has married, Martinique and Guadeloupe occupy a place of honor in a cartography of identity that ultimately provides a linkage with ancestral Benin.

Yet when Anita, the first female initiate into this familial, patrilineal cult, proposes her own physical journey "back" to Africa, Spéro seems to renounce (perhaps because he senses that myth will always be more comforting than reality) the very ancestor worship that has provided for him—and perhaps even more so for his African American wife, Debbie—a *raison d'être*, a sense of purpose:

> Can't we ever live our lives in the present? And if need be, bear the ugliness of its wounds? The past must be condemned to death . . . wasn't this the misfortune of too many blacks they knew who were so busy build-

ing imaginary family trees they had lost out on conquering their own
America?[9]

This conflict between father and daughter recalls the dispute between
Avey, the protagonist of Paule Marshall's *Praisesong for the Widow,* and
her third child, Marion: a comparison of these similarly tense relationships is suggestive, since in each case the younger generation advocates
a radical departure from conventional routes. The well-off widow of
Marshall's narrative, on the verge of a return to the African source via
the Caribbean island of Carriacou, remembers, with some irritation,
the "faint rattle of the necklace of cowrie shells and amber," implicitly
contrasted to her own classic pearls, always worn by Marion, a souvenir
of the daughter's last visit to Togo.[10] It was the outrageous, subversive
Marion who had expressed strong criticism of the very project of a cruise
devoid of cultural significance: "Why go on some meaningless cruise
with a bunch of white folks anyway, I keep asking you?"[11]

Despite the manifest differences in sensibility between the two
writers, there are other compelling echoes and signs of a similar vision, for example, if one considers the thematic correspondence between
*Praisesong* and *The Last of the African Kings.* Condé has acknowledged in
an interview both her admiration for, and her sense of difference from,
the canonical African American women novelists:

> I came to know the women writers whom everyone knows: Paule Marshall,
> Toni Morrison, Alice Walker. I loved them, yet I cannot say that I always
> identified with their writings. I always had the feeling that they wrote for
> a specifically African American public of which I was not a part.[12]

In both *The Last of the African Kings* and *Praisesong,* it is not Africa
that holds the remedy for a malady akin to Goodison's "quest fever" but
rather "the islands"—a reductive term when used from North American
distance about diverse territories as distinct from each other as guavas
and tamarinds. It is the islands that offer the possibility of reconciliation,
of making one's peace with the centuries-old but never to be forgotten rupture from another continental mass. Dorothy Hamer Denniston
rightly points out the importance of the geographical location of Grenada and Carriacou: "in *Praisesong,* she moves the locale from North
America to the Caribbean, which, symbolically, points eastward toward
Africa."[13] So in these narratives it is the islands that serve as a repository

of racial and cultural belonging, a bridge to the precolonial past. One notes, however, that Condé's attitude is sometimes subversive, colored by irony, and certainly more enigmatic than that of Marshall, who offers her character Avey a healing and liberating journey to Carriacou (symbol of the past), a far cry from the more complex and challenging Africa represented in Condé's novel by contemporary Benin.[14] Indeed, implicit in the open-ended form of *The Last of the African Kings*—we do not know the outcome of Anita's African sojourn, although there are hopeful, though tenuous, signs of reintegration—is the guarded attitude to Africa of a writer whose own itineraries seem to overlap with the fictional adventures of women who will perhaps have to come to terms with the inaccessibility of the past and to accept the challenge of *redefining* homelands lost and found.

In *The Last of the African Kings,* as in Marshall's early novel, *Browngirl, Brownstones,* the Caribbean island is essentially a fatherland; in each case a female protagonist is initiated into a cult of the homeland by a father who is proud to display his island roots, and in each of these fictions of displacement, the young woman must finally make her own journey, her own crossing, in order to appropriate and redirect the patrilineal heritage. But while for Anita, Spéro's daughter, it is distant Benin that beckons—the reader wonders if the absence of any project of return to Guadeloupe suggests an inability to come to terms with the reality of Caribbeanness—the heroine of *Browngirl, Brownstones* contemplates at the end of the narrative a return to her father's native Barbados. In the case of Marshall's *Praisesong,* the traveler will find "Africa" closer to home. Avey's unplanned crossing to Carriacou unravels both the surface of these once "British" West Indies and the poised exterior of the African American who seemed the quintessential cruise trip voyager, far removed from the forebears of whom her great-aunt talked so much, from those mythical Ibos whose memorable and yet effortless flight away from plantation servitude is well known to all readers of Marshall's fiction: "When they realized there wasn't nothing between them and home but some water and that wasn't giving 'em no trouble they got so tickled they started in to singing."[15]

In continuing an intertextual reading of the work of the two writers, both of whom have, like the little girl of "Dah-duh," complex affiliations within this "New World," another fertile comparison seemed to present itself, this time between *Praisesong* and Condé's 1997 novel, *Désirada*. Both narratives trace the decisive journey of a solitary woman, resident in the United States, to a "miniscule" Caribbean island potent in its capacity to stimulate/simulate reconnection. *Désirada* is a panoramic and sometimes dizzying representation of migrant communities from France to West Africa to the United States. Yet it is the apparently insignificant and very small island that gives the text its title, which lends some coherence to the rambling narrative, because it is the site from which Reynalda, the mother of the youngest protagonist, Marie-Noëlle, begins a series of journeys, and it is a dreamed of, unfamiliar, and yet essential destination to which Marie-Noëlle will finally return—but only provisionally—by the end of the text. In choosing La Désirade, supposedly a dependency of "mainland" Guadeloupe, as the quasi-mythical land of origin for a family of displaced women, Condé subverts the stereotype of the idyllic island, perhaps writing back to Césaire, whose 1939 *Cahier* first undermined the French colonialist fantasy of "les Antilles heureuses" [the happy Antilles]. The "home" described by Reynalda (who left Désirade in childhood for Guadeloupe, where she was supposedly raped by an unknown European, presumed to be Marie-Noëlle's father) is both sour and sweet:

> I was born in Désirade. People from Guadeloupe have negative impressions of Désirade because of the rogues and the lepers that used to be sent there and also because nothing grows there. Nothing. No sugar cane. No coffee. No cotton. No yam, no sweet potato. But for me, as a little girl, this was really "Désirada," the desired island rising up out of the water before the eyes of Columbus' sailors after so many days. I owned every nook and cranny of the island, I breathed in its smell when the sun, after heating it all day long, finally rests its head at the bottom of the water.[16]

This small island bears little resemblance to the predictably pleasing site evoked by Jamaica Kincaid in *A Small Place* or to the lush décor of so many Caribbean narratives. Yet it is in Condé's text a somewhat muted Eldorado, a peripheral but nevertheless *desirable* location, bare of the colonial taint implicit in the allusion to "King Sugar" and the rest. Though hardly Edenic, the time in Désirade was for Reynalda a period of relative innocence and independence, a time of peaceful intimacy with her mother, Nina. By the same token, the separation from this site, the time when mother and child leave for Guadeloupe, where Nina will work—and have an illicit sexual relationship—with a European jeweler, marks the beginning of discord and may be compared to the loss of the absolute security of the maternal womb that haunts Condé's fiction.[17]

By choosing to foreground, in her title and in the journeys to and from Désirade that inform the narrative structure, an island that epitomizes the condition of marginality, Condé flies in the face of the Eurocentric assumption of "small island" insignificance. At the same time, she undermines, as does Marshall, the construction of the exotic island peopled by happy natives. It is hardly coincidental that both Paule Marshall and Maryse Condé have alluded, I think with ironic intent, to a nostalgic song popularized by Harry Belafonte, "Island in the Sun." The Guadeloupean novelist chooses to entitle a chapter of the novel *Windward Heights* "O Island in the Sun," a chapter set in Marie-Galante, yet another tiny "dependency" of Guadeloupe. Marshall uses the phrase in evoking the nostalgia for the homeland of her parents' contemporaries: "Barbados—or Bimshire, as they affectionately called it. The little Caribbean island in the sun they loved but had to leave."[18]

But tiny islands can hold their own against the colonizing mainland. Of note, in this context, is the emphasis in *Praisesong* on the dimensions of Carriacou, assumed by Avey's Grenadian taxi driver to be unworthy of his interest: "Why waste my time going to visit someplace that's even smaller than here. That's so small scarcely anybody has ever heard of it."[19] Avey herself is guilty of a similar "dissing" of the tiny island in a conversation the next day with Lebert Joseph, the man who will become her guide on a journey of immersion into an identity she has forgotten; she speaks of the excursion to the island whose name she has also discarded from memory:

> "Is the same!" the man interrupted her impatiently. "Some went yesterday. The rest is going today."
> "... to someplace, some island ... I forget the name."
> "Carriacou!" he declared, and drew himself up sharply on his longer leg; he looked tall enough suddenly to reach up and touch the roof of thatch. "The name of the island is Carriacou!"[20]

The solemn, reproving, almost ritual naming of the island is, of course, proprietorial in intent. A few pages later, in a more relaxed vein,

Lebert Joseph asserts that "Carriacou is small but sweet,"[21] recalling the section from *Désirada* quoted above, which adumbrated a subaltern version of the colonizer's sense of ownership of "l'ile désirée," the desired island. The emphasis in Condé's text on the Columbian quest ("for me, as a little girl, this was really 'Désirada,' the desired island rising up out of the water before the eyes of Columbus' sailors") evokes for the francophone reader, in a less Messianic vein, of course, the concern with repossessing "his island" of Césaire's Caliban, who raged against the loss of the land that his mother, Sycorax, had left him.[22] Marie-Noëlle's island is also a matrilineal legacy, but not one as easily reconquered, and perhaps the Guadeloupean novelist is writing back to Cesaire, suggesting the complexity of a relationship to the mother-island that can no longer be taken for granted.

The young protagonist of *Désirada* is heiress to the angst borne by restless, if not entirely rootless, members of migrant communities for whom the solace of homecoming is not an option. One such character is Marie-Noëlle's mother, whose self-imposed exile from Désirade, and perhaps more significantly from Guadeloupe (the site of her alleged rape), appears permanent. Another memorable—and troubling—figure of displacement in *Désirada* is Reynalda's husband, Ludovic, the surrogate father who awaits the ten-year-old Marie-Noëlle when she goes to live with her mother in Paris, whose situation is emblematic of the condition of many late twentieth-century exiles of the new diaspora; his "homes" have been so many as to undermine the very notion of home: "Ludovic always hesitated awhile when he was asked where he was from. His father had left Haiti for Ciego de Avila in Cuba where sugar cane workers were better paid."[23] This uncertainty is painfully underscored for such exiles by the unwelcome but regular intrusion of what Caryl Phillips describes in an account of a journey to Ghana as "the problem question":

> Where are you from? . . .'
>    *The* question. The problem question for those of us who have grown up in societies which define themselves by excluding others. Usually us. A coded question. Are you one of us?[24]

And this disconcerting question also recalls Lebert Joseph's relentless interrogation of Avey about a lineage of which she is ignorant and, up to this point, uncaring;

"And what you is?" . . .

"What's your nation?" he asked her, his manner curious, interested, even friendly all of a sudden. "Arada . . . ? Is you an Arada?" He waited. "Cromanti maybe . . . ?" And he again waited. "Yarraba then . . . ? Moko . . ."

On and on he recited the list of names, pausing after each one to give her time to answer.[25]

But more fundamentally "nationless" than the Black British/Caribbean traveler that is Phillips or Avey, the occasional voyager who will finally leave Carriacou for a not unfamiliar American mainland, for her home in New York, is Condé's Marie-Noëlle. There is not even the illusion of definitive homecoming for the youngest protagonist of *Désirada* in her own journeys, whether to France, the United States, or finally back "home" to Désirade. Her condition may be read as an updated version of that chronicle of a larger displacement, told by Lebert Joseph in *Praisesong*, in a moving account of racial dispersal:

The Bongo? Have you heard of that one maybe? Is the one I like best, oui. The song to it tells what happened to a Carriacou man and his wife during the slave time. The smallest child home knows the story. They took and sold the husband—the chains on him, oui—to Trinidad and later the same day they put the wife on a schooner to Haiti to sell her separate. Their two children the people that owned them kept behind in Carriacou.[26]

And after the old man sings the Bongo, Avey and the reader are drawn into the ritual of remembrance, the ritual of mourning:

From the anguish in the man's voice, in his face, in his far-seeing gaze, it didn't seem that the story was just something he had heard, but an event he had been witness to. He might have been present, might have seen with his own eyes the husband bound in chains for Trinidad, the wife—iron on her ankles and wrists and in a collar around her neck—sold off to Haiti, and the children, Zabette and Ti Walter (he even knew the names), left orphaned behind.[27]

So, too, in a sense is Marie-Noëlle orphaned, separated early from the larger island of Guadeloupe as well as from her grandmother's land of origin. At least in the early section of the novel, set in Paris, there is no anchor for the child thrown from island intimacy into a world where migrants are not necessarily allies:

the complex was home to a large contingent of Africans, West Indians, people from Reunion. . . . The migrants from the West Indies and from Reunion got on well with each other. They spoke to each other in Creole. . . . By mutual agreement, they didn't socialize with the Africans.[28]

Yet despite the provocative allusion to the problematic of identity in the post-Négritude era (this migrant community is certainly a far cry from Senghor's and Césaire's racially based alliance in 1930s Paris), Condé, never loath to contradict herself, does not totally exclude from this saga of homelessness the African journey that inspired several of her early and most controversial texts. It is important to note, however, that in *Désirada* Africa is a *possible* destination, a road not (yet?) traveled by Marie-Noëlle; the continent beckons, but not imperiously, and the protagonist lacks the exuberant certainty voiced by the persona of Goodison's "Natal Song" ("so that I land in Xamayca with quest fever / and all the while Africa you had my remedy"). But the theme of the quest for the African origin, though apparently in minor key, is impossible to dismiss if only because of its resonance for the reader familiar with the fiction of this elusive novelist who claimed, in an interview published in 1994, that she would not write again about Africa.[29] In a memorable scene in *Désirada*, Marie-Noëlle is invited by friends of Ludovic's, a resident in Guinea but on vacation in Paris, to come for an extended stay, based on her friendship with the daughter of the visiting family. But the door is shut on an African sojourn, as her mother refuses, somewhat inexplicably given her own coldness toward the child, but perhaps because she fears that the continent will seduce the unloved daughter, that Marie-Noëlle will see it, as did Marie-Hélène in *A Season in Rihata,* as a source of solace for a motherless child.

Toward the end of *Désirada,* the adult Marie-Noëlle reflects with some irony, and yet with transparent wistfulness, on the African adventures of others in her circle:

A particular student, an African American, has decided to work on Amadou Hampate Ba. He hasn't been to Africa yet. But his father has described for him that magical world without writing, without manuscripts, without books, without libraries, and he hopes to capture the secret of the griot-poets, masters of the word. I approve of that, too. What magic does Africa hold for us, despite so many images of desolation and torture shown on screens all over the world? Soon, too, Anthea will come back from Ghana, with her head stuffed with all her imaginings. I can hear her already. . . . She will repeat for me the stories—source of so many dreams—of the ancestral Paradise. Of the Middle Passage, the terrible voyage that we all took before we were even born. Of our dispersal to the four corners of the globe and of our suffering.[30]

This ambiguous interrogation of the obsession with Africa ("Persistent memory, rhythm box with no off-switch," to borrow Goodison's compelling image from "Natal Song") recalls for me questions I posed in an earlier paper on the quest for origins in Condé's work, questions that I think are still pertinent here: "Does one have to renounce the affiliations of the past in order to assume one's present, to live it fully? . . . How does one go beyond the seduction of a mythic past, how does one relate to Africa in any other way than that of a "bastard," an "outside child," forever destined to a sense of exclusion/inferiority, that of a needy child looking in through an impenetrable window, wistfully and at the same time resentfully, at an imagined perfection?"[31] Although Marie-Noëlle is arguably a needy child, she also experiences a certain ironic detachment from these "true believers," their heads full of "imaginings" about the African past (the character Anthea is not unlike Avey's daughter in *Praisesong*, marked by a self-conscious Afrocentrism manifested in forms of dress). Yet despite a skepticism reminiscent of Spéro's desire to "kill the past" and suggestive of Condé's own fear of the mythmaking impulse, Marie-Noëlle yearns for her own sense of purpose and, above all, for a sense of place. For the time being, she will have to make do with Paris and finally with the United States, where we find her at the end of the text. But she does travel to Désirade to meet her grandmother, Nina, a foil to the frenetic mobility epitomized by Ludovic and his like, and to hear her version of the "truth," of the circumstances of the rape that led to Reynalda's estrangement from island and mother. Unlike Condé's earlier, more comforting fiction of dislocation, *I, Tituba, Black Witch of Salem* (in which a West Indian woman also found herself exiled in Boston), however, and unlike Marshall's *Praisesong*, *Désirada* does not culminate in an unequivocal reconciliation with the island and/or with self.

Like the protagonist of *Praisesong*, Marie-Noëlle must forgo the modern convenience of air travel for the small boat in which she crosses from "mainland" to small(er) island in the sun; like Avey, she is widowed (though much younger), solitary, and in need of something that would root and restore her. But ironically, although Avey has no familial ties to the island, which she discovers at journey's end, Désirada is less easy a fit than is Carriacou. No ritual of rebirth awaits the protagonist there, and the mood, as she nears the end of this voluntary crossing, is oppressive, reminiscent of the centuries-old journey of dispersal:

> At the very end of the sea, a desolate rock. . . . As the catamaran approached the coast, however, the bad memories began to retreat. On the contrary, it seemed as if the arid island was bathed in color in the sunshine, as if it were assuming a smiling countenance. The island was lifting its head out of the water to spy on the new arrival and to extend both a greeting and a reproach, as if to an ungrateful relative: "At last! I've been waiting for you for such a long time." Her eyes blinded by all the blue around her, Marie-Noëlle didn't notice anything. Her heart was becoming heavier as she saw, more and more clearly delineated against the horizon, the inhospitable land from which her people had sprung.[32]

Immersion in or even simple proximity to the sea is often symbolic in Caribbean literature of a new beginning or of a healing oneness with the landscape. A memorable example is found in Kamau Brathwaite's affirmation in "South," his poem of reunion with the "bright beaches" of Barbados that "We who are born of the sea can never seek solace in rivers." But one notes here that Marie-Noëlle is "blinded" by sea and sky, and, in fact, this potentially life-changing pilgrimage will prove strangely unsatisfactory. So the solace of real homecoming is deferred as the protagonist goes back to her life as an academic in Boston, with mixed emotions, unable to forget either the grandmother/island or the accompanying potent smell of curry, but also unable to return. As if deliberately refusing the seduction of tropical land/seascapes, the novelist, in the last two chapters of the text, exposes her protagonist to the harshness of the elements: first the snow of Paris, where she travels in search of another element of her past, her relationship with her mother, and finally the more persistent precipitation of Boston, where she seems to have "settled." Her physical position, high up in an academic ivory tower, is perhaps a disappointing sign of retreat of a once courageous traveler: "Through the windows of my office perched up on the fourth floor of the university, I can see the Charles River, a pale ribbon, between its banks which haven't yet decided to thaw. According to the calendar, spring is not far away. But nothing would suggest its approach."[33]

This final chapter is the only one in which Marie-Noëlle speaks/ writes in the first person, a coming to voice that is perhaps linked with the ability to make peace with the absence of the desired island. For Marie-Noëlle is manifestly not Tituba, the earlier Condean character, conceived on a slave ship, initially at odds with colonial Barbados where her African-born parents died tragically, who would discover in her brutal exile to Boston and then Salem a realization of belonging to "her" Barbados. No mythic heroine, Marie-Noëlle appears finally separated from the "islands," from *the* island, and from community. It is in this respect, despite the similarities adumbrated above, that she differs sharply from Paule Marshall's Avey, who is able, on return from Carriacou, to contemplate an exuberant rejoining of community, keeping the faith, the *island* faith, in the shadow of those very skyscrapers that the child protagonist of "To Da-duh, in Memoriam," had seen as a sign of metropolitan greatness. It is noteworthy that *Praisesong* is also dedicated to Marshall's beloved ancestor figure, the grandmother who rooted her in Barbados despite the many years in the dazzling North:

> Nor would she stop with the taxi driver, but would take it upon herself to speak of the excursion to others elsewhere. Her territory would be the street corners and front lawns in their small section of North White Plains. . . . She would haunt the entrance way of the skyscrapers.[34]

Characteristically, Condé's narrative is more guarded, and open-ended. Home may ultimately be, for Marie-Noëlle, an imagined, desired, but imperfect island, and possibly also a space cautiously carved out in a northern land devoid of navel strings. Perhaps what is finally important, in these narratives of journeying, is not the "planting of one's flag"[35] in a single place of origin, but rather the (re)discovery of "small islands" potent enough to serve as remedy for the continental loss.

## Notes

1. Although Maryse Condé is herself an inveterate traveler, she spends part of each year in her native Guadeloupe, where she maintains a home. Paule Marshall was born to Barbadian parents in the United States and has acknowledged and celebrated the influence of the Barbadian voices—those of her mother and her mother's friends—with which she was surrounded in childhood.

2. The term *navel string* refers to the tradition in several Caribbean cultures of burying the umbilical cord after birth in the soil under a tree. Olive Senior, in her

*Encyclopedia of Jamaican Heritage,* describes this practice as one that "was brought to Jamaica by West Africans during slavery" (349). Richard Allsopp, defining *navel string* in his *Dictionary of Caribbean English Usage,* speaks of "the folk habit of burying an infant's umbilical cord in its parents' homeground" (401).

3. Marshall, *Reena and Other Stories,* 100.

4. Ibid., 104.

5. In *Green Cane and Juicy Flotsam,* 64.

6. Smith, *Julia Kristeva,* 57.

7. *Le discours antillais* (Paris: Seuil, 1981), translated as *Caribbean Discourse: Selected Essays.*

8. *Les derniers rois mages* is a fictionalized account of an actual historical event. Behanzin, after a valiant attempt to resist French colonialism, was exiled to Martinique in 1894 and later relocated in Algeria, where he died in 1906. Nevertheless, Condé asserts playfully at the start of the narrative that "Cet ouvrage est de pure fiction" [This work is entirely fictional].

9. Condé, *Les derniers rois mages,* 82.

10. Marshall, *Praisesong for the Widow,* 167.

11. Ibid., 13.

12. Pfaff, *Conversations with Maryse Condé,* 115.

13. Denniston, *The Fiction of Paule Marshall,* 126.

14. It is worth noting here that Condé can hardly be accused of a reductive, homogenizing conflation of complex territories under the imagined simplification of "Africa," a conflation that generated some discussion and even controversy at the Dartmouth conference at which the original version of this article was presented.

15. Marshall, *Praisesong,* 39.

16. Condé, *Désirada,* 62. All translations from this novel are mine.

17. See, for example, the poignant description in *A Season in Rihata* (London: Heinemann Educational, 1988) of the impossibility for the heroine to return to Guadeloupe: "The island had symbolized one thing: her mother; a womb in which she could retreat from her suffering, eyes closed, fists clenched, soothed by the throbbing blood circulating round her. But her mother was dead" (63).

18. Marshall, "From the Poets in the Kitchen," in *Reena and Other Stories,* 7.

19. Marshall, *Praisesong,* 77.

20. Ibid., 162.

21. Ibid., 181.

22. See the translation of Césaire's *Une Tempête, A Tempest: Based on Shakespeare's The Tempest: Adaptation for a Black Theatre.*

23. Condé, *Désirada,* 38.

24. In Phillips, *The Atlantic Sound,* 98.

25. Marshall, *Praisesong,* 166–67.

26. Ibid., 176–77.

27. Ibid., 177.

28. Condé, *Désirada,* 36–37.

29. Condé, *I, Tituba, Black Witch of Salem,* 204. In this work, the author declared, "After *Segos; les murailles de terre* and *Ségou: La terre en miettes,* I had decided never to write about Africa again because the book was so terribly received by Africans and Africanists."

30. Condé, *Désirada*, 281.
31. See Morrison, "Archives of the Heart or 'Imaginary Family Trees'?"
32. Condé, *Désirada*, 175.
33. Ibid., 279.
34. Marshall, *Praisesong*, 254.
35. Condé, *Tree of Life*, 351. The image is used by Claude, the young narrator of Condé's *Tree of Life*, brought up, like Marie-Noëlle, in France, in ignorance of her island origins, who finally claims Guadeloupe in the triumphant words, "I had planted my flag on the island."

# References

Allsopp, Richard. *Dictionary of Caribbean English Usage*. Oxford: Oxford University Press, 1996.

Brathwaite, Kamau. *Arrivants: A New World Trilogy*. Oxford: Oxford University Press, 1973.

Césaire, Aimé. *Une Tempête: d'après "La Tempête" de Shakespeare: Adaptation pour un thèatre nègre*. Paris: Editions du Seuil, 1969.

———. *Cahier d'un retour au pays natal*. Paris: Présence Africaine, 1983.

———. *A Tempest: Based on Shakespeare's The Tempest: Adaptation for a Black Theatre*. Trans. Richard Miller. New York: Ubu Repertory Theater Publications, 1992.

———. *Notebook of a Return to the Native Land*. Trans. Clayton Eshleman and Annette Smith. Middletown, Conn.: Wesleyan University Press, 2001.

Condé, Maryse. *A Season in Rihata*. Trans. Richard Philcox. London: Heinemann, 1988.

———. "Three Women in Manhattan." In *Green Cane and Juicy Flotsam*, ed. Carmen C. Esteves and Lizabeth Paravisini-Gebert, 56–67. New Brunswick, N.J.: Rutgers University Press, 1991.

———. *Les derniers rois mages*. Paris: Mercure de France, 1992.

———. *Tree of Life*. Trans. Victoria Reiter. New York: Ballantine Books, 1992.

———. *I, Tituba, Black Witch of Salem*. Trans. Richard Philcox. New York: Ballantine Books, 1994.

———. *Désirada*. Paris: R. Laffont, 1997.

———. *The Last of the African Kings*. Trans. Richard Philcox. Lincoln: University of Nebraska Press, 1997.

Denniston, Dorothy Hamer. *The Fiction of Paule Marshall: Reconstruction of History, Culture, and Gender*. Knoxville: University of Tennessee Press, 1983.

Glissant, Edouard. *Le discours antillais*. Paris: Seuil, 1981.

———. *Caribbean Discourse: Selected Essays*. Trans. J. Michael Dash. Charlottesville: University Press of Virginia, 1989.

Goodison, Lorna. *Travelling Mercies*. Toronto: McClelland and Stewart, 2001.

Marshall, Paule. *Brown Girl, Brownstones*. New York: Random House, 1959.

———. *Praisesong for the Widow*. New York: Plume, 1983.

———. *Reena and Other Stories*. New York: Feminist Press, 1983.

Morrison, Anthea. "Archives of the Heart or 'Imaginary Family Trees'? The Ambiguous Quest for Origins in the Fiction of Maryse Condé." Paper presented at the conference "Atlantic Crossings: Women's Voices, Women's Stories from the Caribbean" and the conference on "Nigerian Hinterland," Dartmouth College, 18–21 May 2001.

Pfaff, Françoise. *Conversations with Maryse Condé.* Lincoln: University of Nebraska Press, 1996.

Phillips, Caryl. *The Atlantic Sound.* London: Faber and Faber, 2000.

Senior, Olive. *Encyclopedia of Jamaican Heritage.* Kingston: Twin Guinep, 2004.

Smith, Anna. *Julia Kristeva: Readings of Exile and Estrangement.* London: Macmillan, 1996.

Map supplied by the University of Texas Libraries and modified by Michael Siegel, Staff Cartographer, Geography Department, Rutgers University.

# PART TWO

# Race, Gender, and Agency
# in the Shadow of Slavery

3

# Mary Rose: "White" African Jamaican Woman? Race and Gender in Eighteenth-Century Jamaica

LINDA L. STURTZ

Historians of the Caribbean region are well aware of the social and historical constructedness of race within the context of the African diaspora in various times and geographic locations. As Franklin Knight reminds us, "Each age brought its own peculiar interpretations to bear on the way it perceived and interpreted race, ethnicity, and class, and those interpretations colour the writings of the time."[1] European notions of racial classification emerged in tandem with the colonization of the Americas and European enslavement of Africans during the early modern period. European science and social science organized humanity into races and racialized categories, with gender playing a significant role in defining individuals' race.[2] Simultaneously, relationships between European and African Jamaicans produced children who complicated those categories, leaving the taxonomists with the task of rationalizing their claims.[3] By the mid-eighteenth century, Jamaican society included a small but significant group of people descended from both African and European ancestors who sought the legal privileges of whiteness. Little documentation by these Jamaicans remains to reveal how they performed their whiteness and how they negotiated their identities.

The correspondence of Mary Rose, a woman descended from both Africans and Europeans, hints at the approach one woman took to managing her position in eighteenth-century Jamaica. This correspondence is particularly intriguing because Mary Rose wrote to Rose Fuller, her long-term partner, a white man and probably her son's father. Written between 1756 and 1760, a time when racialized classifications of people were being formulated, her letters reveal how one legally privileged wom-£an attempted to establish her own identity in a shifting social milieu.[4] In contrast to keeping a diary of her own personal reflections, she wrote these letters for a particular reader, so they hint at how she "performed" race as well as gender in mid-eighteenth-century Jamaica and across the Atlantic.

Mary Rose, who lived from about 1718 until 1783, wrote to Rose Fuller in England from her home in Spanish Town, the capital of Jamaica during most of the eighteenth century. Spanish Town, placed at the geographic and political crossroads of mid-eighteenth-century Jamaica, hosted seasonal visitors who arrived to attend the legislature and courts as well as to enjoy the social events and shopping opportunities that the town offered.[5] By providing lodgings, Mary Rose took economic advantage of this setting, and one prominent patron of her business referred to her as a "most decent landlady." Mary Rose also occupied a socially and racially liminal space. In some official records she is described as "mulatto," but she eluded simple racial classification because she successfully petitioned the Jamaica Assembly for the same legal rights "as if" she had been born to English parents, a practice shared by other eighteenth-century Jamaicans in similar circumstances. In doing so, she and others like her created a new legal and social category for themselves as persons in an Atlantic diaspora at a moment when European and American philosophers laid the groundwork for early modern and modern notions of race.

Planter law and society sought ways to manage the boundaries among racialized categories of people. One way to accomplish this was to legislate certain individuals, like Mary Rose, into a separate category of people who would share in some of the legal privileges the same "as if" they had been born of English parents.[6] By this means, elite whites granted to a few handpicked persons of color what Lucille Mathurin Mair called "surrogate white" status. Elite whites believed there was a "shortage" of white settlers to fulfill roles best trusted to whites—most notably military roles for men and reproductive functions for women.[7] The trade-off, then, was for the white elite to establish a distinct class of brown persons who would receive some of the benefits and obligations of whites in society.[8]

Across the wider Caribbean region, people resorted to social as well as legal means to define whiteness and, as Edward Cox pointed out, people with African ancestry in the islands sought to became "associationally white" when their behavior "mirrored patterns already established by whites." Wealth and education provided the means by which these individuals claimed their privileges.[9] In these letters Mary Rose presents an associational whiteness in the self-edited voice she presented to her letters' audience. "Associational whiteness" may be discursive, as it appears to have been for Mary Rose; in those letters, but intriguingly, Rose evaded placing herself explicitly within any racial category.

Mary Rose is also extraordinary because documents she wrote have been preserved in the archives when so few accounts survive that were written by women of African ancestry in the Americas during the time of slavery. Erna Brodber laments the fact that "the history of what black people felt and did in a period as vast as 1619–1865 . . . was likely to see the light of day only as figments of the imagination of powerful whites and as statistics in their log books." Even scholars of the nineteenth century have to rely on the few significant works, including *The History of Mary Prince: A West Indian Slave, Related by Herself* (1831) and *Incidents in the Life of a Slave Girl* (1861). Hearing the voices of African Caribbean women from several generations earlier, in the middle of the eighteenth century, is even more difficult, demonstrating why Mary Rose's letters are truly extraordinary.[10]

We can hear Mary Rose's private voice when, in 1758, she reported "taking in" the infant child of her niece Peg after Peg drowned while traveling between Port Royal and Kingston during a storm.[11] Her concern for her extended family is apparent in her will, in which she made bequests to her surviving son and grandson, and also to her niece, nephew, and a cousin named Jane Ann Beckford. The most sustained survival of Mary Rose's voice comes to us through her letters to Rose Fuller; thus, like Mary Prince's words, hers serve a function in addressing her particular audience. The letters were never edited or published, but she still had to edit herself to reach her reader and achieve her desired goals.

Although Mary Rose remains an exceptional eighteenth-century woman because of the number of surviving records that document her life, silence still shrouds much of our understanding of her and her understanding of her place in society. Silences, as Michel-Rolph Trouillot points out, "enter the process of historical production at four crucial moments: the moment of fact creation (the making of *sources*); the moment of fact assembly (the making of *archives*); the moment of fact retrieval (the making of *narratives*); and the moment of retrospective significance (the making of *history* in the final instance.)"[12]

Mary Rose wrote letters and legal documents, so she appears at the moment of "fact" or source creation. She squeaked into the archives due to both the nature of power relations of colonial administration and the flukes that determine whose past is preserved: she had property, so her will was recorded and preserved; she petitioned the Legislative Assembly, so her request appeared in the printed record of that body. In this respect, she resembled a small group of her contemporaries who enjoyed their position as the most prosperous, well-connected brown women who lived in mid-eighteenth-century Jamaica. What makes Mary Rose's archival survival exceptional is the preservation of a small group of her letters among the Fuller family papers.[13] This chapter ventures into Trouillot's third and fourth stages of history writing: retrieving facts and suggesting how we might determine Rose's "retrospective significance."

The letters she wrote, along with legal documents and other texts about Mary Rose, reveal the opportunities that a well-connected and skilled woman of colour could enjoy as well as the oppressive legal and cultural structures she faced in mid-eighteenth-century Jamaica.[14] This chapter does not analyze the female perspective in history; instead, it listens to the voice of a woman exceptional for many reasons and depicts the identities she claimed and the roles she adopted in mediating among cultures. I do not claim that these letters record Mary Rose's "true" voice: she corresponded with particular goals and audiences and presented herself and her ideas with those in mind. Like the later Mary Prince, who wrote an account of her life for public reading, Rose's thoughts and accounts of her own actions have been tailored for her own audience; however, unlike the Prince text, Rose's manuscript letters retain her own wording and escape the distortions and goals resulting from the editing of well-meaning advocates. Any editing remains Rose's own.[15]

Little is known about Mary Rose's early life. She was born in Jamaica's St. Catherine Parish, probably no later than 1718, to Elizabeth Johnson, who was a free woman by the time of her death.[16] Even Mary Rose's name fluctuated. In her letters from the 1750s she signed herself Mary Rose or Mary Johnston Rose.[17] A 1745 official document referred to her as Mary Johnston, but indicated she was also known as Mary Rose. Almost thirty years later, when she wrote her will, she called herself Mary Johnson Rose. She had at least one sister, Sarah Johnson; at least two children, Thomas Wynter and William Fuller; and at least two grandchildren, Mary Mede and William Rose Wynter. She lived as Rose Fuller's "housekeeper"—in Jamaica a title given to the long-term domestic and sexual partner of a white man. When Fuller returned to England without her, he provided her with a comfortable annuity and, in his will, stipulated it should continue after his death.

After Fuller left the island in 1754, Mary Rose wrote to Rose Fuller, and at least some of her letters survive. I have found no letters from Fuller to Mary Rose. Ironically, more documentation survives from their time apart than from their lives together because letters were necessary only after he left Jamaica. After his departure, she continued to supervise some of his businesses and acted as hostess to his guests and employees, continuing her role of housekeeper. She continued to express affection for him after he left. Through the gifts she received, her initiative, and her contacts, she became a wealthy woman. She died in 1783.[18]

In contrast to the sketchy information that describes Mary Johnson Rose's experiences, the life of her companion and correspondent, Rose Fuller, is thoroughly documented in manuscript and print sources. Born in 1708, Rose Fuller was a younger son of John Fuller and his wife, Jamaican heiress Elizabeth (Rose) Fuller, who gave their son the distinctive name Rose to honor her family of origin, a common enough pattern in Britain's eighteenth-century colonial families even when it resulted in an odd or, in this case, a traditionally feminine name. The Fullers owned thousands of acres in England and Jamaica, and the family made a fortune manufacturing iron and trading in guns. Rose Fuller, as second son whose elder brother stood to inherit the family fortune, trained to earn his own living, studying to become a physician in England before sailing in 1732 to Jamaica, where he served as physician to the British troops on the island. He also took an active hand in operating Mickelton (Knollis), the estate his mother had inherited, overturning the deleterious effects of three decades of absentee management, investing in new sugar mills, and increasing the income for the sugar estate and cattle pen. While in Jamaica, Rose Fuller married Ithamar Mill of St. Catherine's Parish, but she died in 1738, shortly before their first anniversary.[19] He became an active chief justice of Jamaica, battling Governor Charles Knowles. Fuller continued to live in Jamaica until 1754, when he returned to England where he exerted his considerable influence to undermine the governor with the British Board of Trade, the branch of royal government responsible for the colonies. When his older brother, who was the heir, died in early 1755 without children, Rose Fuller took over the family's English operations and political aspirations, standing for Parliament and winning a seat in 1755. Within that body, he lobbied for the interests of West Indian planters and, by extension, himself. He died 7 May 1777, without acknowledged children in England, leaving a nephew to inherit the family's estates. We even know what Rose Fuller looked like, since the Fuller family had a group portrait of themselves painted when Rose was a young man. We have no comparable picture of Mary Rose or her family.[20]

It is unclear when Mary Rose and Rose Fuller met. Because she had the same surname as Fuller's mother, it is possible she lived near or on Fuller family land.[21] It is probable that Rose Fuller was the father of William Fuller, Mary Rose's son, who predeceased her. What is certain is that she served as Rose Fuller's housekeeper during his time in Jamaica, and he publicly acknowledged her as such in his will.[22] The only verbal recognition he made of her significance to him appears in his will, when he proclaimed that she had saved his life several times. He left her a large legacy that included six slaves.

Mary Rose's phenotype is apparent neither from her letters nor from her description of herself in her own will. She refrained from adopting any label to refer to herself. By contrast, in about 1800 individuals writing wills began proudly proclaiming themselves "free persons of colour," and the practice became more common in the 1810s and 1820s.

Even if Mary Rose sought to evade racial classifications, Jamaican officials demanded that she fit into a category, and she manipulated that categorization for the benefit of herself and her descendants.

In 1745 Mary Rose sought "as if white" status before the law; in doing so, she established her public identity, constructing herself as a "white" African Jamaican woman. In this respect, she was like several hundred other wealthy, well-connected free African Jamaicans and Anglo-African Jamaicans who petitioned the Legislative Assembly for "as if white" status. Such petitioning began in February 1708 in response to growing legal restrictions being placed on free persons of color.[23] Petitioners explained the characteristics, such as religion, wealth, race, nationality, gender, and education, that they believed would allow their bills to succeed.[24] By 1745 when Mary Rose petitioned the legislature for "as if white" status on behalf of herself and her two sons, fifty-three other people had already sought similar "privileges." The overwhelming majority had their petitions approved, and the number of petitioners continued to grow in the late eighteenth century.[25]

Although legislation defined Mary Rose and her children under the classification of "as if born of white parents," officials continued to leave the family in limbo. The 1754 census of Spanish Town divided people into two large categories: the first enumerated all "white" inhabitants and the second listed all "Negroes and Mulattoes of free condition." Mary Rose, along with her son and one other individual, fit into neither category, but instead appeared in a separate section at the end of the "white" pages with a notation that they were "free Mulattoes or Descendants from them remitted to the privileges of white people by acts of the Legislature."[26] The census defined her as white, confirming her legislated "whiteness," but the officials determined she was a different kind of "white" from the other "white" householders of Spanish Town.

In 1761 the family encountered further difficulties after the legislature enacted a bill prohibiting white parents from granting their African Caribbean children more than £2,000 worth of property. Mary Rose's son, Thomas Wynter, had a personal estate worth thirty times that limit. Wynter, having been declared "as if white," could not leave his property to his two children without petitioning for two more bills, one declaring his children "as if white" and another allowing him to leave his property to his children.[27] Mary Rose and her family found that they still occupied a liminal position in society that defined people by ancestry. So how did she use her distinctive place in society? Her surviving letters suggest she served as an intermediary between island residents and Rose Fuller.

One of Mary Rose's most significant roles was serving as a link in the network of transatlantic contacts between Jamaica and Rose Fuller in London. No activist seeking to overthrow the slave society from which she benefited, she nevertheless operated to secure the freedom of a few favored individuals. After Fuller had returned to England, Mary Rose reminded him of his promise to obtain the freedom of two children, Fanny and Molly, who belonged to Ann (Rose) Isted, Fuller's aunt. Mary Rose describe Fanny and Molly as "the two children you desired me to take care of" and pressured Fuller to act on the slaves' behalf, because she was sure "a word from you would be of great service & therefore I must beg of you not to forget mentioning it" to his Aunt Ann.[28] Rose Fuller proceeded to exchange favors with Isted to obtain the deeds for the slaves, so that in the end, Mary Rose succeeded in securing the manumission of these slaves.[29]

Despite this effort to free Fanny and Molly, Mary Rose was no abolitionist. During her lifetime Mary Rose owned slaves, thus selectively sustaining the institution by her actions. In the first paragraph of her will she manumitted outright a woman named Mimba and her three children. She granted two other women to her son during his lifetime, but manumitted them on his death. Susanna, a woman Mary Rose possessed for life, was to have her freedom purchased from the Fuller family out of funds from Mary's estate. Her mitigation of the condition of these individuals, however, did not signal outright opposition to slavery as an institution. Although she favored certain enslaved women and children in her will by providing immediate or eventual manumission, she also granted four other women to her son and his heirs, perpetuating their condition for generations. She even ordered the purchase of a slave child for each of her nieces and nephews.[30] Her generosity extended far enough to secure the freedom of favored slave women, but not far enough to make an outright critique of slavery. Her own extended family could distance themselves from blackness and the stigma associated with menial labor by exploiting enslaved people to work for them.

Mary Rose maintained broad ties on the island, benefiting herself and Fuller. Her network extended from the lowest to the highest echelons of the Jamaican hierarchy. Fuller forwarded a letter to her through Governor George Haldane. After Fuller left Jamaica, he depended on her to extend the hospitality of his household to the governor. When she visited the governor, she described Haldane's reception of her as "very kindly." He also returned the favor and visited Fuller's pen near Spanish Town several times. Mary Rose told Fuller that when the governor took refuge at Fuller's pen, she would "go down and prepare every thing there proper for his Reception agreeable to your desire."[31] Another visitor to Mary Rose's lodging house understood Mary Rose's link to Fuller, and when the visitor resided in Spanish Town he took up "my old Lodgings . . . with the most Decent Landlady yr. old Friend Mary Rose."[32] Although Mary Rose remained a subordinate within this stratified society, Fuller, through his publicly acknowledged relationship to her, relied on her to stand in for him. Her role as "housekeeper" extended beyond mere sexual partner and included managing the household and, indeed, the social side of her partner's career locally.

After Rose Fuller returned to England, Jamaicans believed Fuller would rely on Mary Rose's opinions about business and individuals on the island. When Jamaica resident George Aldred sought a medical education in England, he approached Mary Rose to intercede on his behalf. He hoped to advance his knowledge about medicine by observing surgery at English hospitals, but he needed an English connection. The aspiring young man's brother served as physician on Fuller's Jamaican estates, so Aldred asked Mary Rose to write a letter of introduction to Fuller. On the young man's behalf, she wrote, "As I well know your Inclination to serve young people who are deserving of it; I take the freedom to introduce the Bearer Mr. George Aldred to your Countenance & Protection." Because Fuller was himself trained as a physician, he was well positioned to secure a place for Aldred. Mary Rose assured Fuller that George was "v[e]ry assiduous & Carefull in his Business."[33]

Another Jamaican seeking connections secured Mary Rose's assistance. When a Mr. Levien wanted to begin trading to England, he asked Mary Rose to help him, so she wrote another letter to Rose Fuller recommending Levien as a man of good character. She thought Levien could be trusted because he was "a nephew of Nathan Abrahams," and she reminded Fuller of his favorable dealings with the uncle. Not only did she hope that Fuller would bring Levien to the attention of the Fuller family but she also took "this Liberty of begging your Influence with [more?] gentlemen on this occasion."[34] White trading and professional families relied on Mary Rose to serve as the conduit for requests to their intended English patron.

In May 1756 Mary Rose received a more desperate plea from William Browne who wished to return to England before completing his term of service. Browne begged her to intercede on his behalf to Rose Fuller's local agent, Jonathan Lee. Fuller had paid William Browne's passage to Jamaica from England, where Browne had left his "indulgent" wife and "Affectionate" parents. Browne, struggling to overcome the heavy "burden of [his] mind" until he was "allmost Deprived of all reason," soon wanted to return to England, and he wrote to Mary Rose, asking her assistance in accomplishing this goal. Browne began his letter to Mary Rose in the most respectful manner, asking her pardon for his "great Freedom in Troubling" her. Later in the letter, Browne begged "on [his] knees in my flood of Tears" that Mary Rose in her "great goodness" would seek the permission he needed to break his agreement and leave the island before completing his obligations. Browne admitted he suffered from a fever, but more, he was on the edge of suicide. He wrote:

> [M]y Brain so Disordered that I shall and am Uncapable of [torn] business but still I am sencible I have an Immortle soul which is my greatest care to provide for . . . and without some relieve must now be lost here and in the world to come Dear Dear Madam my greaf is not only Unsupportable but if long in this Condition it must be Desparate.[35]

Browne believed Mary Rose and Jonathan Lee had the authority to prevent his return, and begged them not to obstruct his passage. He further assured Mary Rose that because Rose Fuller was a "Generous and good" man, he would not "the least" be displeased. A month after sending his letter to Mary Rose, Browne was on a ship headed back to England. Mary Rose forwarded the letter to Jonathan Lee, who sent it back to Rose

Fuller with a short note that Fuller would see the reasons for Browne's departure by reading the letter to Mary Rose.[36]

So what did the letters from George Aldred, Mr. Levien, and William Browne to Mary Rose reveal about the ways that white men understood her position in society? All three assumed she had the power to influence Fuller's opinions about issues extending beyond her household. All three, living in Jamaica, viewed her as acting as Fuller's immediate local representative. John Lee, also of Spanish Town, served as an official representative and wrote Fuller updates about the state of his business in the vicinity. Lee, like Mary Rose, received petitions from local residents requesting favors.[37] Lee and Mary Rose worked together and Lee passed along greetings from or news about Mary Rose in his letters to Fuller. Lee and Mary Rose, as employee and housekeeper, worked in tandem.

As an intermediary, Mary Rose generally behaved in an "associationally white" fashion. Admittedly, she encouraged Rose Fuller to secure the manumission of his aunt's two slave women; however, in all the other instances she passed along requests that white men made through her. There are several possible explanations for why this was the case. People of color may have had no reason to make requests of Fuller or believed Mary Rose had insufficient influence to advocate on their behalf. On the other hand, she may have chosen to lobby for white people, suggesting that they composed her circle of friends and acquaintances, indicating the extent to which she was associationally white.

In other ways, Mary Rose lived her life in a fashion comparable to that of other free women of color, despite her legal "as if white" status, admittedly from a particularly prosperous position. Free women of color, as Verene Shepherd has pointed out, frequently pursued three occupations: "housekeeper," lodging house keeper, and healer.[38] Mary Rose accomplished all three.

Because Mary Rose was Fuller's housekeeper before his departure, we have little information about the nature of their relationship during that time; nevertheless, in letters she wrote after he was in England, she alluded to her earlier roles and responsibilities. When Fuller's agent demanded that she remove her livestock from Fuller's grazing pen, Mary Rose fired off a letter in which she reminded Fuller that "The Service that I did you while you were here, besides the Intimacy between us left me no room to doubt that you would Remember me and Indulge me with the Libertys you usually allowed me." She worried about covering the expenses of household management "such as Taxes, Doctors Bills, &c. &c." that he had paid during his residence. Furthermore, she fretted that his lack of concern for her material well-being suggested to her a parallel lack of affection. She asked him to "continue my friend as Long as I *deserve* [author's emphasis] your Friendship. Consider Sir I am too far advanced in years to think of beginning the world a new and that I served you faithfully for several years and ought not to be Rashly discarded."[39] She had provided for his emotional sustenance during his residence, and her letters continued to express her affection for him. Early in their correspondence, she also sent him small gifts (pots of sweetmeats and bags of tamarinds) as tokens of her affection. She hoped the presents "serve to put you in mind that you are always thought of in Jamaica with the utmost Esteem." In return, he sent her goods such as carpeting and fabric.[40]

Fuller, on the other hand, refrained from describing his feelings for her. Although his letters to Mary Rose are lost, we can detect his voice through her correspondence. For example, in 1759 she noted, "I very well know your aversion to letters unless they are entirely upon Business."[41] While she continued to send him sweet nothings during their correspondence, he apparently sent nothing sweet in return. She also made it clear that she understood the tenuous claim she had on his affections, assuring him that she believed she only enjoyed his devotion for as long as he determined that she "deserved" his friendship, unlike an eighteenth-century wife who could count on marginally more secure support. The eighteenth-century Jamaican "housekeeper" certainly provided sexual favors to her man, but she also served as his domestic partner, providing emotional sustenance and caring for his other physical comforts. This aspect of gendered, often invisible, "relational work" has been generally understated in historical analyses of eighteenth-century Jamaican life. While historians rightly describe the abuse of women's sexuality in this setting, we need to acknowledge the wider exploitation of women's emotional life in other situations as well.[42]

Fuller even confirmed his expectations for Mary Rose's role and status as his housekeeper from beyond his grave. In his will Fuller granted her use of the Grange Pen house, the six slaves who lived there, and a chaise "provided . . . [she] do take upon her the supervision of my household goods and other things in the said dwelling house" and of the pen slaves.[43] A woman's work was never done.

Mary Rose began a new career as a lodging house keeper after Rose Fuller departed for England, perhaps at his suggestion, but at least with his blessing. Her prime location in Jamaica's capital city worked to her advantage because she could rent rooms to political figures. In 1756 she wrote: "Since the assembly has been held in this town I have let Lodgings in the house agreeable to what you told me. . . . I have met with very good Lodgers, Mr Morse & Mr Bayly, & hope shall do very well in it."[44] Her optimism paid off, and almost two years later, in December 1758, she reported:

> [Y]ou was so kind when you went off as to allow me to live in the House in Spanish Town that yourself lived in, from which I have made some money, by hiring out such of the rooms as I have not Use for to Gentlemen of the Assembly and other; as there is now a certainty of the Courts &c returning here the house will consequently be more serviceable & profitable to me.[45]

Knowing the capital would remain in Spanish Town after Rose Fuller's own success in defeating the protracted efforts by the merchants to transfer it to Kingston, Mary Rose could count on having a consistent customer base. The way she described her new occupation remains very genteel: she is merely renting out rooms she does not need at the present.

But Mary Rose's new business was not yet on secure foundations because Rose Fuller only held a life right to the Spanish Town house he made available to her. She would be evicted when Fuller died, though before he left the island he promised to buy out the full title to make her more secure.[46] After two years, however, he still had not bought out the titleholder. She reminded Fuller that should anything happen to him, "which God avert," she would have to pack up and leave. Perhaps despairing of his acting on her behalf, she finally decided to buy the house herself. She announced her decision in the same letter in which she congratulated him on being elected to Parliament. That letter suggests that his election was the turning point in their relationship, and she recognized that Fuller was unlikely to return to Jamaica: "When you was here you had some thoughts I believe of making this Purchase [of the remainder—providing outright ownership] yourself, but as I fear you never intend to come to the Island again, I suppose you have laid such Design aside."[47] What she did not say in the letter was that Fuller's older brother had died the year before, leaving Rose Fuller the heir with more obligations and privileges in England than he had possessed as a younger son. Perhaps as a result of these two events, she realized that she would have to take more responsibility for her own long-term welfare and that of her children. There is no indication that she wanted to emigrate in order to join him, or that Fuller asked her to, though one of her grandchildren did go to England.

Her lodging house seems to have been profitable. When she made the offer to purchase it outright, she mentioned she could pay in cash or by signing a bond, suggesting her income from renting lodgings, along with her annuity from Fuller, provided her the means of buying the house. When Fuller still had not answered her letter six months later, she wrote him again, this time in a more emotional and affectionate tone and with more vivid language, worrying about being only a tenant in the house:

> [S]hould any accident happen to you, before me, which God Almighty forbid how unhappy should I be in my old age; to loose my best and only Friend, and then again, be liable to be turned out of Doors at a Moments Warning; this is a Scene, that I dread to think of, but as the same may happen, I Beg Dear Sir, that you would make me Easy in this affair; as the thought thereof makes me quite unhappy.

She would only feel secure when she possessed outright ownership. She assured him that by letting out lodgings, "I may be enabled to support myself in my old age, and not to be dependent on I know not who; as I have heard you often mention."[48] In April 1759 a visitor reported to Fuller that Mary Rose's establishment was the "neatest of any in the Country."[49] Mary Rose enjoyed the privileges of her wealth, her business, and her connections to Fuller, but by 1759 she acknowledged his apparently growing unwillingness to help secure her future. The lodging house provided her with the means to guarantee her own well-being in case Fuller failed her.

Free brown and black women across the Caribbean region opened inns or lodging houses. They could take their capital in a house, build on their knowledge of food preparation and domestic management, and generate a cash income. Because travelers often kept diaries of their journeys, a great deal of documentation exists describing the women working in this sector. Lodging houses sometimes functioned as convalescent hospitals with the landladies serving as nurses, so we should not be surprised to find Mary Rose combining the two as well.[50]

One of the most intriguing elements of Mary Rose's story is her respected role as healer. Possibly drawing on her knowledge of traditional African healing methods, she worked on her own and with local doctors to heal the sick and injured.[51] In 1755 a boy named little Tom broke his leg when he was run over by the cattle-drawn cart he was leading down the road. Although Doctor Worth and "Mrs. Rose" took all the "care imaginable" to save him, Tom died two weeks later.[52] She took pride in her management of the affairs Fuller left to her, but most notably for "the Care of your Sick Negroes, several of whom must have perished had they not been taken due care of by me."[53] Rose Fuller, a trained physician himself, publicly acknowledged that she had saved his life several times through her "Care and attention (under God)" during the "several dangerous Illnesses" he suffered while in Jamaica.[54]

Her medical assistance to Fuller's slaves and to Fuller himself parallels the role of the "nurturing native" that literary scholar Mary Louise Pratt found in eighteenth-century fiction and travel literature describing Europe's colonies and may provide an opportunity to explore Mary Rose's position in the African diaspora. In Surinam, for example, the soldier John Stedman formed a long-term relationship, confirmed by a "pseudo-marriage," with a slave woman named Joanna. Local women like Joanna improved Europeans men's chances of survival, since they could prepare local food and provide medical care based on knowledge of indigenous medicines.[55] When Stedman returned to Europe, he begged Joanna to accompany him, but she declined, recognizing that she would not have the high status there that she enjoyed in Surinam. Mary Rose's letters do not indicate whether she ever considered going to England with Fuller or why she decided to remain in Jamaica. In at least one instance she referred to England as "home," but she, like Joanna, may have realized she would have far less respect in England than she did in Spanish Town. Her associational and legislated "whiteness," however fragile, was geographically situated in Jamaica. Although Mary

Rose never joined him in England, Rose Fuller, unlike John Stedman, did not marry again after he left Jamaica, and he acknowledged their relationship until he died.[56]

Mary Rose expressed no political consciousness based on solidarity with people of color; she articulated no protoabolitionist sentiments. Instead, by the terms of her will, she manumitted some slaves, but ordered her executors to purchase two more slaves as legacies for her relatives. In this respect, she fits Elsa Goveia's chronology of consciousness-raising among free colored people in West Indian history. Goveia found that during the eighteenth century, free colored people "were more acquiescent, and, no doubt, sought comfort in the reflection that at least they were a middle class." Only toward the end of the century, as their numbers and aggregate wealth grew, did free persons of color agitate for rights collectively.[57] Mary Rose, by contrast, acted on behalf of individuals, either family members or people who approached her to negotiate on their behalf.

Mary Rose's place in any analytical category currently proposed by scholars proves elusive. Was Mary Rose a member of an *African diaspora,* a concept under vigorous debate among scholars of African and African American studies? Was Mary Rose an *Atlantic creole,* to use Ira Berlin's phrase describing peoples on both sides of the early modern Atlantic who interacted in multilingual trading centers? Was she part of an *Atlantic world* founded on exchanges of goods, people, and ideas?

Rose certainly shares many characteristics of what Ira Berlin has called Atlantic creoles. Like them, she had knowledge and experience that "far more than color" set her apart from newly enslaved Africans. She possessed the "genius for intercultural negotiation" that "was not simply a set of skills, a tactic for survival, or an attribute that emerged as an 'Africanism' in the New World." Rather, her knowledge was "central to a way of life that transcended particular venues." Berlin writes that Atlantic creoles experienced "liminality, particularly their lack of identity with any one group," which posed numerous dangers. "While their middling position made them valuable to African and European traders, it also made them vulnerable: they could be ostracized, scapegoated, and on occasion enslaved."[58] Although her relationship with Rose Fuller lasted far longer than his brief marriage to the teenaged Ithamar Mill, she enjoyed none of the benefits and protections that a marriage with Fuller would have brought her or their descendants. Her gender precluded her from voting or holding office, as it would women of any colour, but her legally "as if white" sons were prevented from exercising those political rights, too—a limitation a white wife's sons would not have endured if they had held property. In this respect, she does resemble Berlin's Atlantic creoles.

In other ways, her experiences resemble those of economic actors with an active hand in an Atlantic world. In their world, circulation included knowledge and cultural practices as well as physical travel, and one of the key developments in mid-eighteenth-century transatlantic history was the increase in the speed and frequency of shipping coupled with the heightened access to goods, news, and the possibility of shared information even to regions once considered isolated. Taking the perspective of Mary Rose's Atlantic world, we see her experience centered on Spanish Town, Jamaica, but with links extended to England and Africa as well as across her Caribbean island. Other individuals participating in a cosmopolitan world shared parallel experiences. David Hancock has shown how London merchants during Mary Rose's lifetime were "international thinkers and actors" concerned with Britain's "expanding global empire, with a growth in territory, governance, trade, consumption and knowledge." Without firmly rooted locations, however, such international actors as Rose's contemporary, the Scots-born Jamaican planter Sir Alexander Grant, could be "nobody's child"—"neither native Creole, nor transplanted Englishman." Nor, we might add, African Jamaican.[59] Is Mary Rose, like Sir Alexander Grant, simply a "nobody's child" of an English-dominated Atlantic world? Her cosmopolitan perspective, the significance of her exchanges of consumer goods, the migration of her own descendants to England, and the importance of her relatively frequent communication by letters certainly places Mary Rose within a culture of the Atlantic world.

Can we reconcile Mary Rose's Atlantic creole outlook and Atlantic world exchanges with a place for her in an African diaspora? One of the key components to emerge from the discussions and debates over the nature of African diaspora is the notion that diaspora is a *process* as well as a *condition,* and that rather than being understood as a unidirectional movement, it must be analyzed through the innovation and dynamic of circulation.[60]

Her world certainly included the exchange of goods, information, ideas, and people across geographic space. Her ancestors included Africans and Europeans, and her granddaughter emigrated to Britain with her English clergyman husband, continuing the circulation of people and ideas that would accelerate with migrations of West Indians to Europe during the twentieth-century wars and with the post WWII *Windrush* generation of immigrants to England. Perhaps we may more accurately say that Mary Rose and her family demonstrate how "Africa was not the only diaspora to which African descendants belonged" and that she, like other "African descendants were contributors to and participants in the construction of other diasporas," allowing us to show how individuals who crossed multiple borders and subjectivities (either physically or discursively) might become part of "overlapping diasporas." Furthermore, such reconsideration allows us to escape the common scholarly assumption that "race and slavery are the only nodes around which the lives of Africans and their descendants revolved."[61] She emphasized her class connections, her economic agency, and her well-placed connections in her letters rather than calling attention to common cause with free or enslaved persons of colour. This may have merely reflected a deliberate strategy and her understanding of the limitations of Rose Fuller's patience, understanding, or sympathy with the plight of persons of colour (including his own descendants) rather than her own lack of common consciousness. Did she attempt to form community through bonds with other free persons of colour, including her own multigenerational extended family with whom she cemented relationships to assist the various members? The letters do not say, but this class is the group of educated, free people of property who would begin to form an interest group and successfully advocate for the rights of free persons of colour in the next two generations.

But the history of Mary Rose can shed further light on the notion of diaspora by demonstrating a distinctive Jamaican experience. The approach to analyzing diaspora proposed by Judith Byfield in the introduction to this volume suggests scholars move beyond the "U.S.-based standard" that "obscures important distinctions" that emerge from global networks of power and localized processes. Thus, "even though black populations experienced discrimination and marginalization, the nature of those processes varied between empires, within empires, and within specific countries." Because of these different experiences, people "used different political strategies to combat racism and discrimination because the nature of the marginalization they experienced differed significantly." In Jamaica, Mary Rose used the tools at hand including letters, social contacts with high-placed public officials, economic agency, and that most English means, written legal petitions to the Assembly, to accomplish her goals.[62]

In addition to calling for an extension of the concept of African diaspora beyond a U.S.-framed experience, scholars have pointed out the need to understand the concept in its chronological complexity. Discussion of the circular nature of diaspora focuses on nineteenth- and twentieth-century intellectual movements and cultural expressions from African descended peoples in the Americas and Europe that have influenced African culture and politics.[63] These cross-fertilizations of culture are fascinating, but one wonders how we can understand earlier connections, agency, and outlooks?

What was Mary Rose's identity in mid-eighteenth-century Jamaica? First, although she was not explicit in describing her African traditions, she drew on her heritage when she became a healer. Likewise, her work as a housekeeper to Fuller and landlady of an exclusive lodging house coincided with the occupations of other prosperous free women of color. Second, so far as legislation permitted, she defined herself legally "as if white." After her patron left for England, she took on a third role: she served as an intermediary for Jamaicans seeking to present their causes to Rose Fuller.[64] Mary Rose managed to negotiate some benefits for individuals closest to her. She cared deeply for her family and sought to advance their interests whenever possible, whether taking in her orphaned great-niece or procuring outright ownership of a grand Spanish Town house so that her descendants would be secure financially.

These observations leave us with further questions. How did she take on the identity she presents in these letters? Who was her father, and how did she spend her childhood? How was she educated, learning how to write eloquent letters but also mastering the survival skills she needed to negotiate mid-eighteenth-century life in Jamaica? How did she represent herself in other letters or in face-to-face interactions? We know she owned slaves and authorized the purchase of two more. How did she accommodate herself to her position as a slave holder? Whose decision was it for her to remain in Jamaica: hers or Rose Fuller's? What motivated that decision? In the end, the letters raise as many questions as answers. We may dream of reading a "secret diary" by Mary Rose of the sort written by eighteenth-century Virginian William Byrd, written for her eyes only and with introspective remarks. But for now, this correspondence is the best the archives have to offer.

Despite the unanswered questions they provoke, Mary Rose's letters do allow us to begin to make some comparisons among race-coded and gendered historical experiences. A century after Mary Rose wrote her letters, the more famous Mary Seacole (discussed in MacDonald-Smythe's essay in this volume) also worked as a healer and landlady to travelers. Like Rose, she descended from both African and European ancestors, yet she proudly claimed a more inclusive public identity than did Mary Rose and bristled at the racism of her contemporaries when she traversed Panama. On the other hand, Seacole may have consciously or unconsciously manipulated that figure of the "nurturing native" in establishing her own reputation as a "doctress." How do we compare these two seemingly similar women's experiences, identities, and voices? How had the meaning of race changed from the time of Mary Rose to the post-abolition period in which Seacole wrote?

Expanding our evidential base to incorporate more voices, many still buried in manuscript collections, will open a larger discussion about the changes and continuities in the performance of race in the Americas. In his analysis of a free woman of colour in sixteenth-century Mexico City, Herman Bennett demonstrates that "the subjectivities of Africans and their descendants were constantly constituted and reconstituted throughout the Atlantic world in accordance to spatial locality, evolving language, materiality of the *republica* and temporal, among other, dynamics that defy generalities associated with a nationalist framework." As Bennett has argued, not all persons in the African diaspora "classify their lives and its component parts as aspect of the same system," and instead, subjects were "defined by others and simultaneously constituted themselves." Only by historicizing individuals like Mary Rose and the "multiplicity of cultural formations" in which they lived in various times can we understand the variety of lived experiences of people who lived in the diaspora and, in an ongoing process, performed their identities and created communities.[65] Mary Rose's life and letters show how race was still under construction during the eighteenth century, and Jamaica's residents provided the raw materials that philosophers wielded when they built their new categories. The cogitating on both sides of the Atlantic led to systems of racial taxonomy operating in different ways, depending on imperial expectations, local desires, chronology, and geography among other factors.[66]

To conclude on a more concrete point, I want to turn to the material culture evidence to suggest how Mary Rose presented herself in public and used goods to mark the boundaries between herself and other Spanish Town residents. This chapter has discussed her voice, but some evidence suggests how she looked. As mentioned earlier, no portrait of Mary Rose has been found; however, because she ordered many of her goods directly from England, enclosing her shopping lists in letters, she left an idea of the image that she presented in public. Furthermore, her son described the Spanish Town house and furnishings he inherited from her, augmenting the picture of the material world she inhabited. So imagine Mary Rose preparing to venture into town in one of her carriages. Up in her "chamber" that served as a bedroom, she decided against her red shoes or her green calamanco ones and selected her blue shoes "laced with silk." She stepped to her dressing table to check her appearance in a gown made of chintz, registering the contrast between her own dress and that of her slave, attired in the cheaper, rough osnaburg the mistress had recently received from England. She stepped into the picture-lined drawing room where she dashed off a quick note to a neighbor on the writing desk before sliding the top back over the desk and leaving the note on the breakfast table, noticing that the blue china dishes had been expeditiously cleaned up from the earlier meal. To check on the weather before leaving the house, she walked into one of the piazzas, furnished with green chairs. Having decided the weather was cool but not cold, she chose not to wear her fashionable, newly imported white beaver felt hat, but instead swung an equally impressive scarlet cloak over her shoulders before proceeding out the door and beyond our twenty-first-century view.[67]

# Notes

I am grateful to Christopher Whittick for assistance with the manuscripts and to Lisa Anderson-Levy, John Campbell, Thera Edwards, Daniel Alan Livesay, Rachel O'Toole, Shakira Maxwell, Beatrice McKenzie, Debra Majeed, Melanie Newton, James C. Robertson, Verene Shepherd, and Holly Snyder for their comments on an earlier version of this chapter. Completion of this chapter was made possible by a Sanger Summer Faculty Fellowship from Beloit College.

1. Knight, "Race, Ethnicity, and Class in Caribbean History," 202. Race and whiteness are understood as social constructs throughout my essay. I have used *colour* in its West Indian sense to refer to persons who have both African and European ancestors, and retained the West Indian spelling to connote that particular concept.

2. Knight analyzes the way Edward Long used a "scientific" framework to understand race in eighteenth-century Jamaica. For a discussion of Long's history within its British context, see Wheeler, *The Complexion of Race,* 209. For the significance of gender in eighteenth-century racial taxonomies, see Schiebinger, *Nature's Body,* 117–18.

3. The absurdity of the claims failed to prevent their dissemination. For example, Edward Long claimed that "mulattoes" were sterile.

4. Two essays on later Caribbean history are useful for outlining theories and methods for analyzing women's voices and silences in Caribbean history: Brereton, "Text, Testimony, and Gender," 90, and Rowley, "Reconceptualizing Voice," 25.

5. Robertson, *Gone Is the Ancient Glory.*

6. Sturtz, "Legislating Race in Eighteenth-Century Jamaica."

7. Mair, *A Historical Study of Women in Jamaica from 1655 to 1844,* 88; Sio, "Race, Colour, and Miscegenation." On the military function of racial boundaries, see Cox, *Free Coloreds in the Slave Societies of St. Kitts and Grenada, 1763–1833.* The earliest bill (that of John Callender in 1708) requesting privileges based on an individual's service against the French passed by the House of Assembly was not assented to by the governor. *Journals of the Assembly of Jamaica* (hereafter *JAJ*), 1708, 1:439.

8. For the significance of military service in this, see the first three private privilege petitions submitted to the House of Assembly in 1708 by John Callender, Manuel Bartholomew, and John Williams. Each petitioned for a private bill "to prevent negroes and slaves" from testifying against him. Callender petitioned for this right based on his contributions to military security, claiming to have "done signal services to this island in discovering an invasion intended by the French." Although Callender's bill was passed, the governor killed it, and it never became law. Minutes, *JAJ*, 1797–1808, 1:438–39. Gad Heuman has written that the result of the private privilege bills was "not a close union of whites and browns, but rather the advancement of a small group of coloreds who were legally differentiated from the people of color as a whole." See Heuman, *Between Black and White,* 16. While Heuman rightly complicates the construction of a single "brown" interest, I have sought to distinguish between the interests of various groups of whites and argue that "white" as well as brown was less unitary than previously understood. The 1761 Act provides useful information for understanding the conflicting white interests in constructing racialized categories.

9. Cox, *Free Coloreds in the Slave Societies of St. Kitts and Grenada*, 155.

10. Brodber, "The Bagnolds District of St. Mary, Jamaica, and the Atlantic Crossings of the Late Eighteenth Century."

11. Mary Rose, Spanish Town, to Rose Fuller, London, 3 September 1758, SAS/RF/unlisted, Fuller Family Papers SAS-RF, Archive of Messrs Raper and Fovargue of Battle, solicitors, East Sussex Record Office, Lewes, England. [hereafter ESRO].

12. Trouillot, *Silencing the Past*, 26. The recovery of voices occurs in undertakings like the Text and Testimony Project at the University of the West Indies (Mona). Ziggi Alexander asks historians to consider how many more "chroniclers there are whose thoughts and words remain buried in our archives." See her preface to *The History of Mary Prince, a West Indian Slave, Related by Herself,* xiii.

13. The Fuller family of Rose Hill, England, deposited their papers with their solicitors, Raper and Fovargue, of Battle, England, in the nineteenth century. A letterbook was published in 1991 as *The Fuller Letters, 1728–1755: Guns, Slaves, and Finance.* Mary Rose's letters were not included in the published volume but are available in manuscript in the Fuller Family Papers, SAS-RF, Archive of Messrs Raper and Fovargue of Battle, solicitors, East Sussex Record Office, Lewes.

14. My use of the term *woman of colour* is anachronistic here. I have seen individuals self-identify as a person "of colour" in about 1800, but the practice picks up in the 1810s and 1820s.

15. For an analysis of the account as a published text, see Moira Ferguson's introduction to her edition of *The History of Mary Prince.*

16. Letters of Administration liber 9, f. 223, 1 November 1753, 1B/11/17/9, Jamaica Archives, Spanish Town [hereafter JA]. Mary Johnson Rose served as administrator to her mother's estate in 1753. At the time of her death, Elizabeth Johnson appeared as "late of the Parish of St. Catherine a Free negro."

17. Mary Johnston Rose, Spanish Town, to Rose Fuller, n.p., 21 March 1759 and 27 May 1759, both in SAS/RF/unlisted, ESRO.

18. I have calculated Mary Rose's birth date as follows: She had two sons, William Fuller and Thomas Wynter, by the time she petitioned the Assembly in 1745. Wynter, listed as a "millwright," must have been at least ten years old in order to be listed by his occupation. Assuming she was at least seventeen by the time her two sons were born, she could have been born no later than 1718. She may have been born decades earlier. Her surname is spelled both as Johnston and Johnson, but I have used Johnson because that is what she called herself in her will. In her will, she listed the members of her family who were still alive in 1774 and who were legatees. These included only one son, Thomas Wynter, her grandson, William Rose Wynter, her sister, Sarah Johnson, and Sarah's children, Ann Rose and John Shutz Johnson. Presumably her other son, William Fuller, died before 1774. Her will was proved 10 April 1783, so she had died by then. Will written 8 October 1774, proved 10 April 1783, located in wills (old series) liber 49: 202r, Island Records Office Twickenham Park, St. Catherine, Jamaica [hereafter IRO]. Her grandson, William, was the son of Thomas Wynter. Petitions, Mary Mede, Thomas's Town, *JAJ*, 23:681.

19. For biographical information about Rose Fuller's family, see the introduction to *The Fuller Letters*, xxv–xxvi, xxxvi. Rose Fuller's mother, Elizabeth, was coheir with her sisters, Ann (Rose) Isted and Mary (Rose) Greene. The family intermarried with the Sloane family, which included the naturalist Sir Hans Sloane. Ithamar Mill,

daughter of the Hon. Richard Mill of St. Catherine's Parish, had her marriage settlement recorded on 26 April 1737, and she died on 22 April 1738.

20. The portrait is reproduced in *The Fuller Letters,* x. In this portrait, the heir poses with a hunting gun. On Fuller's powerful influence on governance and policy, see Greene, "'Of Liberty and the Colonies': A Case Study of Constitutional Conflict in the Mid-Eighteenth-Century British American Empire."

21. Jamaica Council Minutes (1661–1758), manuscript 60, vol. 27: 127, National Library of Jamaica. Records indicate that she was born in St. Catherine's Parish, and she is consistently described as "mulatto" in public documents.

22. Wills liber (o.s.) 44, ff. 119–128, IRO. Because Rose Fuller had property in England and the colonies, his will was recorded in the Prerogative Court of Canterbury. A copy of the will (with later codicils), written 24 December 1774, was recorded in Jamaica and proved 26 November 1778.

23. See 7 and 12 February 1708, *JAJ,* 1:438–39.

24. On her petition, Mary Rose and her children were listed as "mulatto." *JAJ* (PRO 23): 681. Sometimes a petition would list the father of children or the name of a bill's "sponsor," but Rose Fuller's name did not appear on the petition of Mary Rose or her children. Although the first bills in the early eighteenth century included the petitioner's naturalization, later petitioners tended to omit discussion of nationality. Over the eighteenth century, petitions increasingly stressed wealth, education, and religion, but omitted discussion of naturalization. See Sturtz, "'Living Reputable': Legislating Whiteness in Eighteenth-Century Jamaica." When indexing the "as if white" bills, however, the English Privy Council referred to Mary Rose's bill (and comparable mid-eighteenth-century bills) as "Naturalization Acts." Entries dated 2 February 1741 to 29 March 1750, Privy Council, Plantation Book, pp. 254, 370, 397, 482, 487, and 542, PC5/9, National Archives, Kew. For the use of narratives in comparing racial categories in fiction, see Meehan, "Caribbean versus United States Racial Categories in Three Caribbean American Coming of Age Stories."

25. Individuals who obtained private privilege bills were a tiny minority of the total population. Kamau Brathwaite estimates that in 1774 about 23,000 persons of color lived on the island; of these about 4,000 were probably free. Between 1772 and 1796, only 512 free persons of color obtained private privilege bills comparable to the one Mary Rose secured for herself and her children. Even with "privileges," men still could not vote; women were excluded from the franchise by their gender, anyway. See Brathwaite's *The Development of Creole Society in Jamaica, 1770–1820,* 168, 173. For an aggregate study of petitioners in Jamaica prior to 1783, see Sturtz, "Forging a Free Coloured Identity in Colonial Jamaica." I have created a database of petitioners prior to 1783 using the *JAJ* volumes.

26. RF/17/XVIII/521/1, p. 13, ESRO. Mary Rose appeared as the proprietor and self-occupant of the land. The rent for the property was valued at £30. The census indicated she lived by herself, and her occupation was listed as "housekeeper." Her son Thomas Wynter appeared in the same section, living by himself in property valued at £20 in rent. He gave his occupation as millwright. The census was presented to the governor as evidence to oppose moving the capital of Jamaica from Spanish Town to Kingston to demonstrate the economic vitality of the town.

27. According to the inventory of Thomas Wynter's estate, he possessed personal property worth £65,820. This included 107 enumerated slaves plus uncounted slave

children; it excluded all his real estate. Returned 28 November 1789, inventories, liber 74, p. 156, JA, Spanish Town. Simultaneous bills to grant his children "as if white" status and to permit them to inherit his full estate are recorded in 1783. *JAJ*, 7:550.

28. Mary Rose, Spanish Town, to Rose Fuller, 9 May 1756, SAS/RF/unlisted, ESRO. This system of drawing on sometimes convoluted networks of intermediaries to negotiate the manumission of favorite slaves occurred in other instances. Mr. Almeyda contacted Fuller's Spanish Town agent, John Lee, to beg Fuller to sell Fanny and her son Stephen so that Almeyda might manumit them. John Lee, Spanish Town, to Rose Fuller, 30 June 1756, SAS/RF/21/48, ESRO. Duncan Thomson approached Dr. William Grant and his associates to petition Rose Fuller to contact his friends Mr. and Mrs. Arthur Gregory to free Ann and her son John from slavery on their Barbican estate where Thomson had been overseer. In exchange Thomson would provide two slaves to replace them. Walter Grant et al., "Liguana," to Rose Fuller, 1 June 1755, SAS/RF/21/8, ESRO.

29. A[nn] Isted, Northamptonshire, to Rose Fuller, 3 October 1756, SAS/RF/21/59. ESRO.

30. Wills Liber (o.s.) 49: 201v–202v, IRO.

31. Mary Rose, Spanish Town, to Rose Fuller ["copy"], 27 May 1759, SAS/RF/unlisted, ESRO.

32. Edward Clarke, Spanish Town, to Rose Fuller, 18 April 1759, RF/17, ESRO.

33. Mary Rose, Spanish Town, to Rose Fuller, London, 5 June 1759, SAS/RF/unlisted, ESRO.

34. Mary Rose, Spanish Town, to Rose Fuller, n.d., RF/17, ESRO.

35. William Browne, Albina, to Mary Rose, Spanish Town, 5 May 1756, SAS/RF 21/53, ESRO.

36. John Lee, Spanish Town, to Rose Fuller, 30 June 1756, SAS/RF 21/48; and Jonathan Lee, Spanish Town, to Rose Fuller, n.p. 24 July 1756 [Endorsed; answered 6 May 1757], SAS/RF 21/52, ESRO.

37. John Lee, Spanish Town, to Rose Fuller, 30 June 1756, SAS/RF 21/48, ESRO. For example, when a Mr. Almeyda wanted to purchase the manumission of "Fanny's child & mother" and offered to pay for their freedom, he channeled the request through John Lee.

38. Shepherd, *Women in Caribbean History*, 73–76.

39. Mary Rose, Spanish Town, to Rose Fuller, 27 May 1759, SAS/RF/unlisted, JA, ESRO.

40. Mary Rose, Spanish Town, to Rose Fuller, 9 May 1756; 20 June 1757, SAS/RF/unlisted, ESRO.

41. Mary Rose, Spanish Town, to Rose Fuller, London, 23 August 1759, SAS/RF/unlisted, ESRO. Verene Shepherd urges us to consider how individuals "ventriloquize" absent voices. In this case we hear the voice Fuller used to communicate to Mary Rose through this letter she wrote to him, reporting on his customs and explaining why she circumvented them. See Shepherd, "The Ranking Game."

42. Hochschild, *The Managed Heart*, 163. Hochschild writes that women "in general have far less independent access to money, power, authority, or status in society," leaving women to "make a resource out of feeling and offer it to men as a gift in return for the more material resources they lack.... Thus their capacity to manage feeling and to do 'relational' work is for them a more important resource" than it is for comparable

men. Although she analyzes nineteenth- and twentieth-century "marketized private life" in which poor women take on caregiving roles in rich societies, some of her findings seem applicable to earlier colonial settings as well. For the role of housekeepers and interracial sex in the creolization process, see Shepherd, "The Ranking Game," 23.

43. Liber (o.s) 44: f.127r, IRO, Twickenham Park, St. Catherine.

44. Mary Rose, Spanish Town, to Rose Fuller, 21 December 1756, SAS/RF/unlisted, ESRO.

45. Mary Rose, Spanish Town, to Rose Fuller, "Esq.," 27 September 1758, SAS/RF/ unlisted, ESRO. For the history of women keeping lodging houses in Spanish Town dating back to the 1680s and 1690s, see James Robertson, "Late Seventeenth-Century Spanish Town, Jamaica: Building an English City on Spanish Foundations," 386–87.

46. Mary Rose's first reference to obtaining Mr. Pennam's rights appeared in her letter of 21 December 1756 to Rose Fuller, SAS/RF/unlisted, ESRO.

47. Mary Rose, Spanish Town, to Rose Fuller, 27 September 1758, SAS/RF/unlisted, ESRO.

48. Mary Johnston Rose, Spanish Town, to Rose Fuller, 21 March 1759, SAS/RF/ unlisted, ESRO.

49. Edward Clarke, Spanish Town, to Rose Fuller, 25 November 1759, RF/17, JA, ESRO.

50. Kerr, "Victims or Strategists? Female Lodging-House Keepers in Jamaica," and Shepherd, Women in Caribbean History, 75.

51. Shepherd, Women in Caribbean History, 73.

52. John Lee, Spanish Town to Rose Fuller, 25 July 1755, SAS/RF 21/20, ESRO.

53. Mary Rose, Spanish Town, to Rose Fuller, 27 May 1759, SAS/RF/unlisted, ESRO.

54. Wills liber (o.s.) 44, ff. 126, IRO, Twickenham Park, St. Catherine.

55. Pratt, Imperial Eyes, 95–97; and Seacole, Wonderful Adventures of Mrs. Seacole in Many Lands.

56. Mary Rose, Spanish Town, to Rose Fuller, London, 5 June 1759, JA, Spanish Town. Mary Rose refers to England as "home" when describing George Aldred moving there for his medical studies.

57. Goveia, "An Introduction to the Federation Day Exhibition on Aspects of British West Indian History," 16.

58. Berlin, Many Thousands Gone, 22–23.

59. Hancock, Citizens of the World, 387, 1, 58.

60. See Judith Byfield's introduction to this volume. For the concept of diaspora as both a process and a condition, see Patterson and Kelley, "Unfinished Migrations," 20.

61. Byfield, "Introduction: Rethinking the African Diaspora." Byfield cites Earl Lewis's concept of "overlapping diasporas." Lewis, "'To Turn as on a Pivot': Writing African Americans into a History of Overlapping Diasporas."

62. On the hegemony of a U.S.-centered framework for understanding diaspora, see J. Byfield, introduction to this volume, and Butler, "Black History to Diasporan History: Brazilian Abolition in Afro-Atlantic Context," 132. For a more overt use of petitions to state opposition to colour prejudice in disaster relief measures in the 1780s, see Sturtz, "The 1780 Hurricane Donation: 'Insult Offered Instead of Relief,'" notes 67–70.

63. West, "'Unfinished Migrations': Commentary and Response," 63, and Patterson and Kelley, "'Unfinished Migrations': Commentary and Response," 67.

64. Sleeper-Smith, *Indian Women and French Men*. Mary Rose derived less power from her role as intermediary than Native American women of the Western Great Lakes region when dealing with their male French partners. In the Great Lakes region, mixed-race children were necessary for the success of fur trading families, and French men were fully aware of their dependence on intermediaries. For a discussion of the cultural mediator in West Indian fiction and nonfiction, see Barash, "The Character of Difference." For cultural mediators in the West African Atlantic World, see Berlin, *Many Thousands Gone*.

65. Herman L. Bennett analyzes the life of Luisa de Abrego, a freedwoman brought to trial in Mexico City in 1575 and argues that her experiences "cannot solely be seen as those of an African without doing violence to her other selves." He concludes that Africans and descendants "constantly reconstituted themselves." Bennett, "The Subject in the Plot: National Boundaries and the 'History' of the Black Atlantic," 110–11, 117–18. Rachel Sarah O'Toole shows the ways that men in seventeenth-century Peru drew on traditions, but also incorporated new cultural components (including the "pious Catholic") in revising and transforming their identities in a plantation setting. O'Toole, "From the Rivers of Guinea to the Valleys of Peru."

66. Cope, *The Limits of Racial Domination*, 84–85.

67. Inventory returned 28 November 1789. Inventories, libre 74, p.156, JA, Spanish Town. Shopping lists enclosed with two letters from Mary Rose, Spanish Town, to Rose Fuller, one dated 9 May 1756, the other written 20 June 1757, SAS/RF/unlisted, ESRO. The room-by-room inventory for the house in Spanish Town was recorded at the death of her son Thomas Wynter.

# References

Barash, Carol. "The Character of Difference: The Creole Woman as Cultural Mediator in Narratives about Jamaica." *Eighteenth-Century Studies* 23 (1989–90): 406–24.

Berlin, Ira. *Many Thousands Gone: The First Two Centuries of Slavery in North America*. Cambridge: Belknap Press of Harvard University Press, 1998.

Bennett, Herman L. "The Subject in the Plot: National Boundaries and the 'History' of the Black Atlantic." *African Studies Review* 43, no. 1 (April 2000): 101–24.

Brathwaite, [Kamau] Edward. *The Development of Creole Society in Jamaica, 1770–1820*. Oxford: Clarendon Press, 1971.

Brereton, Bridget. "Text, Testimony, and Gender: An Examination of Some Texts by Women on the English-Speaking Caribbean from the 1770s to the 1920s." In *Engendering History: Caribbean Women in Historical Perspective*, ed. Verene Shepherd, Bridget Brereton, and Barbara Bailey, 63–93. Kingston: Ian Randle, 1995.

Brodber, Erna. "The Bagnolds District of St. Mary, Jamaica, and the Atlantic Crossings of the Late Eighteenth Century." In *The Sea as History: Exploring the Atlantic*, ed. Nicole Waller and Carmen Birkle. Heidelberg: Universitätsverlag Winter, forthcoming.

Butler, Kim D. "Black History to Diasporan History: Brazilian Abolition in Afro-Atlantic Context." *African Studies Review* 43 (2000): 125–39.

Byfield, Judith. "Introduction: Rethinking the African Diaspora." *African Studies Review* 43, no. 1 (April 2000): 1–9.

Cope, R. Douglas. *The Limits of Racial Domination: Plebeian Society in Colonial Mexico City, 1660–1720.* Madison: University of Wisconsin Press, 1994.

Cox, Edward. *Free Coloreds in the Slave Societies of St. Kitts and Grenada, 1763–1833.* Knoxville: University of Tennessee Press, 1984.

Crossley, David, and Richard Saville, eds. *The Fuller Letters, 1728–1755: Guns, Slaves, and Finance.* Lewis: Sussex Record Society, 1991.

Ferguson, Moira, ed. *The History of Mary Prince, a West Indian Slave, Related by Herself.* Preface by Ziggi Alexander. London: Pandora, 1987; first published 1831.

Fuller Family Papers SAS-RF, Archive of Messrs Raper and Fovargue of Battle, solicitors, East Sussex Record Office, Lewes, England.

Goveia, Elsa. "An Introduction to the *Federation Day Exhibition* on Aspects of British West Indian History." Typescript, University of the West Indies, Mona, 1959.

Greene, Jack P. "'Of Liberty and the Colonies': A Case Study of Constitutional Conflict in the Mid-Eighteenth-Century British American Empire." In *Liberty and American Experience in the Eighteenth Century,* ed. David Womersley, 21–102. Indianapolis: Liberty Fund, 2006.

Hancock, David. *Citizens of the World: London Merchants and the Integration of the British Atlantic Community, 1735–1785* (New York: Cambridge University Press, 1997).

Heuman, Gad. *Between Black and White: Race, Politics, and the Free Coloreds in Jamaica, 1792–1865.* Westport, Conn.: Greenwood Press, 1981.

Hochschild, Arlie Russell. *The Managed Heart: Commercialization of Human Feeling.* 2nd ed. Berkeley: University of California Press, 2003.

*Journals of the Assembly of Jamaica.* St. Jago: Alexander Aikman, 1804–29.

Jamaica Council Minutes. Manuscript 60. Kingston, Jamaica: National Library of Jamaica.

Kerr, Paulette A. "Victims or Strategists? Female Lodging-House Keepers in Jamaica." In *Engendering History: Caribbean Women in Historical Perspective,* ed. Verene Shepherd, Bridget Brereton, and Barbara Bailey, 197–212. Kingston: Ian Randle, 1995.

Knight, Franklin W. "Race, Ethnicity, and Class in Caribbean History." In *General History of the Caribbean,* vol. 6, *Methodology and Historiography of the Caribbean,* ed. Barry W. Higman, 200–232. London: UNESCO/Macmillan Education, 1999.

Lewis, Earl. "'To Turn as on a Pivot': Writing African Americans into a History of Overlapping Diasporas." *American Historical Review* 100 (June 1995): 765–87.

Mair, Lucille Mathurin. *A Historical Study of Women in Jamaica from 1655 to 1844,* ed. Hilary Beckles and Verene Shepherd. Mona: University of the West Indies Press, 2006.

Meehan, Kevin. "Caribbean versus United States Racial Categories in Three Caribbean American Coming of Age Stories." *Narrative* 7 (1999): 259–71.

O'Toole, Rachel Sarah. "From the Rivers of Guinea to the Valleys of Peru: Becoming a *Bran* Diaspora within Spanish Slavery." *Social Text* 92 (2007): 19–36.

Patterson, Tiffany Ruby, and Robin D. G. Kelley, "Unfinished Migrations: Reflections on the African Diaspora and the Making of the Modern World," *African Studies Review* 43, no. 1 (April 2000): 11–45.

————. "'Unfinished Migrations': Commentary and Response." *African Studies Review* 43, no. 1 (April 2000): 67.

Petley, Christer. "'Legitimacy' and Social Boundaries: Free People of Colour and the Social Order in Jamaican Slave Society." *Social History* 30 (2005): 481–98.

Pratt, Mary Louise. *Imperial Eyes: Travel Writing and Transculturation.* London: Routledge, 1992.

Robertson, James. *Gone Is the Ancient Glory: Spanish Town, Jamaica, 1534–2000.* Kingston and Miami: Ian Randle, 2005.

————. "Late Seventeenth-Century Spanish Town, Jamaica: Building an English City on Spanish Foundations." *Early American Studies* 6 (2008): 346–90.

Rowley, Michelle. "Reconceptualizing Voice: The Role of Matrifocality in Shaping Theories and Caribbean Voices." In *Gendered Realities: Essays in Caribbean Feminist Thought,* edited by Patricia Mohammed, 22–43. Mona, Jamaica: University of the West Indies Press and Centre for Gender and Development Studies, 2002.

Schiebinger, Londa. *Nature's Body: Gender in the Making of Modern Science.* Boston: Beacon, 1993.

Seacole, Mary. *Wonderful Adventures of Mrs. Seacole in Many Lands.* London, 1857; reprint, New York: Oxford University Press, 1988.

Shepherd, Verene A. *Women in Caribbean History: The British-Colonised Territories.* Kingston: Ian Randle, 1999.

————. "The Ranking Game: Discourses of Belonging in Jamaican History." Inaugural lecture, University of the West Indies (Mona), 12 April 2002.

Sio, Arnold A. "Race, Colour, and Miscegenation: The Free Colored of Jamaica and Barbados." *Caribbean Studies* 16 (1976): 5–21.

Sleeper-Smith, Susan. *Indian Women and French Men: Rethinking Cultural Encounter in the Western Great Lakes.* Amherst: University of Massachusetts Press, 2001.

Sturtz, Linda L. "Forging a Free Coloured Identity in Colonial Jamaica." Paper presented to the Organization of American Historians, 1 April 2000.

————. "The 1780 Hurricane Donation: 'Insult Offered Instead of Relief.'" *Jamaican Historical Review* 21 (2000): 38–46.

————. "Legislating Race in Eighteenth-Century Jamaica." Paper presented at the annual meeting of the American Society for Eighteenth-Century Studies, Colorado Springs, 4 April 2002.

————. "'Living Reputable': Legislating Whiteness in Eighteenth-Century Jamaica." Manuscript.

Trouillot, Michel-Rolph. *Silencing the Past: Power and the Production of History.* Boston: Beacon, 1995.

West, Michael O. "'Unfinished Migrations': Commentary and Response." 63 *African Studies Review* 43, no. 1 (April 2000): 63.

Wheeler, Roxann. *The Complexion of Race: Categories of Difference in Eighteenth-Century British Culture.* Philadelphia: University of Pennsylvania Press, 2000.

4

# Trading Places: Market Negotiations in *Wonderful Adventures of Mrs. Seacole in Many Lands*

ANTONIA MACDONALD-SMYTHE

There is in this world no such force as the force
of a [wo]man determined to rise.

W. E. B. Du BOIS

Hard push mek mulatto woman keep saddler shop.

CARIBBEAN PROVERB

In nineteenth-century Caribbean plantation economies, the enforced labor system that defined slavery had created the circumstances in which subjectivity was defined as much by labor as by race: one was what one did or did not do for a living. Labor also dictated social position. Like race and class, it typically led to wealth and the ability to live a life that had both economic and social validity. Specifically, the occupational categories of planter, overseer, house slave, and field slave corresponded to gradations of skin color—from white, to colored, to black.[1] Speaking to the social class structure in nineteenth-century Jamaica, Linnette Vassell describes it as follows:

> Social class, racial and cultural distinctions were thus reinforced among women, with white women, expatriate or Jamaican-born, assuming and exercising positions of authority, superiority and patronage over brown and black women, and brown women standing in a similar social preeminence over black women.[2]

After Emancipation, Caribbean female subjectivity continued to occur within this labor/race matrix. Insofar as labor matters ontologically, the nineteenth-century Jamaican freeborn mulatta Mary Grant Seacole provides a ready example of the various negotiations required to establish the colonial colored self as subject. Born around 1805 to a Jamaican mixed-race innkeeper and a Scottish soldier, Mary Grant's early adult years were spent in trade and travel between England and the West Indies. She then married Mr. Seacole, a timid trader of indeterminate health. Widowed and orphaned eight years later, Mrs. Seacole independently carved out a livelihood for herself as lodge keeper, trader, and doctress.[3] These commercial activities were not unusual for her time. Mulattos and other mixed-blood women who had earned their freedom or had been born into it often had property and land to buttress their social and economic position, but if they did not, they were frequently involved in high-end trade.[4]

Seacole's participation in various labor markets, as detailed in her 1857 autobiography, *Wonderful Adventures of Mrs. Seacole in Many Lands,*[5] attests to her constant shifts between occupational categories so as to create for herself a fixed subjectivity, one that would firmly establish her worthiness as a colonial subject and, in the process, empower her socially and economically. Given a market environment defined by the twin jeopardies of race and gender, she deliberately privileged her "doctressing" services. In a space where Englishness had far greater currency than the as-yet-to-be fully constituted Caribbean subjectivity, Seacole was intent on representing herself primarily as a conscientious medical practitioner. For what such a depiction demonstrated—despite the incongruity of her social and racial location as a colored woman who needed to work for a living—were characteristics that epitomized the idea of Englishness: honor, public duty, moral integrity, and self-determination. Her other entrepreneurial enterprises did not offer the same cachet. Too closely associated with the vulgar commerce ascribed to by black women, these activities could not be readily seen as manifestations of colonial femininity. Trading on her knowledge of folk medicine, her nursing experience in Jamaica, and her expertise with tropical diseases in Panama, Seacole foregrounds her expertise as "doctress," because this profession would profit her in the advancement of a larger ideological agenda—the articulation of her bourgeois respectability, the establishment of her worthiness as a colonial female subject, and the valorization of her Englishness.

There are many challenges attendant to such a portrayal. In the nineteenth century, much of Britain's control over its colonial subjects depended on an ideology of difference, that is, on the establishment of the ways in which the colonized African differed in culture and habits from the European colonizer and was inferior by virtue of these differences. In response, the colonial Caribbean subject, male or female, sought to embody Englishness by evoking his or her similarity to the English-born, regardless of the ways in which race, culture, and geographical location continually undermined this discourse of sameness. Faced with such debilitating referents, colonial subjectivity was constantly reinventing itself to maintain sameness within contexts of difference. Self-representation for the colonial Caribbean female was further complicated by gender differences. For if Englishness was a stable category, gender together with skin color and socioeconomic location allowed for complex and largely unmappable interventions into the discursive paradigm within which the English colonial was located. Accordingly, there could not be one monolithic, essentialized representation of colonial subjectivity. Colonial femininity was always in process, always shifting and changing to accommodate the imperialist and masculinist discourses that inevitably governed it and potentially limited it. As performed by Mary Seacole, this colonial femininity is characterized by complicity and contradiction, by contrariness and collaboration, by inconsistency and complexity.

In *Maps of Englishness,* Simon Gikandi argues that in Seacole's search for an English identity, she is "casting herself . . . as capable of expressing her love for England in spite of hindrance and danger. To be in a position to serve England, to be one with the nation of her dreams, is to give that dream, the dream of being English, tangible (symbolic) value" (136–37). At its core, Seacole's autobiography has the mission to fulfill that dream of Englishness. She wishes to be read as a stellar example of Englishness and to be appropriately rewarded as a deserving English subject. To be successful in her mission, Seacole must take advantage of the market opportunities posed by a particular historical moment: the war in the Crimea and the interest it created in the British popular imagination. After her return from the Crimea, Seacole's war contribution was overshadowed by the public acclaim of Florence Nightingale's for her role in the medical care of soldiers in the Crimea. While receiving individualized appreciation for her medical assistance in the Crimea, Seacole did not gain the same degree of public acclaim. The British media recognized her as much for her lodge-keeping activities as for her "doctressing." This reflected the popular opinion at the time that Seacole's war contribution was as a *vivandiere* and lodge keeper. In 1857 she was lampooned in *Punch* as a *vivandiere*, that is, a female sutler one who accompanies the army corps selling soldiers provisions and liquor. Meanwhile, Nightingale was being lionized by Henry Longfellow as "the lady with the lamp." Thus, while Seacole's autobiography makes only passing reference to it, there was the mighty presence of Florence Nightingale against which she needed to prove her worth, both as British subject and as caregiver. Accordingly, in her autobiography Seacole makes clear to her British readers her desire to be recognized for her patriotic, doctressing services in the war effort.

Crucial to this successful portrayal of self as British subject is the articulation of a strategic vision—the guiding concept that maps what one wants to do and what one wishes to become. In *Wonderful Adventures,* the identification of this vision, the mission to realize it, and its articulation through narrative generate the adoption of various rhetorical strategies designed to achieve self-representation and self-valorization. Such strategizing was not unusual, in commerce as in rhetoric, for as many historians have shown, in nineteenth-century Caribbean society, mixed-race women used situations of potential oppression and exploitation to launch themselves into economic freedom. Speaking to this issue, Pauline Kerr, in "Victims or Strategists? Female Lodging-House Keepers in Jamaica," presents evidence that Jamaican mixed-race women capitalized on the market opportunities available in a socioeconomic community that allowed them to trade on their biracialism and gender. As managers and/or owners of lodging houses and hotels, these women had benefited from their relationships with white men (be these filial or sexual) and had consequently improved their employment options and social positions.

In exploring the relationship between labor and subjectivity, Kerr's argument provides a useful context for an analysis of the various commercial and rhetorical negotiations that Mary Seacole enters into, so as to fulfill her mission to prove that she had been "the right woman . . . [in] the right place." The rhetorical maneuvers in *Wonderful Adventures* are all geared at confirming the worthiness of her labor in the Crimean war effort. Given a market environment defined by the twin jeopardies of race and gender, Seacole used every available method of self-advertising. Reorienting the facts of her past to suit a present-day agenda, Seacole presents her readers with the details of her labor in Panama and the Crimea, deliberately headlining her contribution to the alleviation of sickness and suffering. If, as Hilary Beckles claims, "images of the mixed-race free woman disintegrate into archival fragments awaiting our reconstruction,"[6] then Seacole's vision is to reformulate her laboring self into a caregiving self, lest this portrait of an ethic of care should disintegrate into oblivion.

In order to successfully market herself as a conscientious British subject, devoted to doing her bit for the empire, Seacole's autobiography downplays the entrepreneurial acuity that allowed her to take full advantage of the trade opportunity offered by war. In locating her hotels in areas of ready demand and reluctant supply, Seacole profited from her labor in much the same way that Jamaican lodge keepers like her mother and sister had succeeded in doing in Kingston at the turn of the nineteenth century. Correspondingly, in distributing much-needed goods in economies where demand exceeded supply, Seacole was functioning in a manner similar to the lower-class nineteenth-century Jamaican market woman who, through necessity, became adept at capitalizing on market opportunities. Commerce holds a position of centrality as the discursive engine driving Seacole's wonderful adventures. Her import/export activities provide the *raison d'être* for her early travels to England and to Caribbean islands. In her autobiography, this is now reconfigured as adventure, as Seacole takes advantage of the opportunities for bartering provided through travel. Exploiting the British taste for things West Indian, she demonstrates entrepreneurial skills that are as natural to her character as is her love for adventure: "Before long I again started for London, bringing with me this time a large stock of West Indian preserves and pickles for sale" (4). She is similarly responsive to her local market: "Before I had been long in Jamaica I started upon other trips, many of them undertaken with a view to gain. Thus I spent some time in New Providence, bringing home with me a large collection of handsome shells and rare shellwork, which created quite a sensation in Kingston, and made a rapid sale" (6).

Like her Jamaican woman huckster counterpart, Seacole's survival as small trader depended on her immediate responsiveness to market demands. Paradoxically, in this autobiographical rendition there is the impending danger that she will be read as, and reduced to, the sensible black market woman who travels to sell and who plies her trade wherever it is needed. A race-sensitive reader may assume that her marketplace is international, where the black woman huckster's might have been local, because of the way in which her mixed-race status intersects labor in nineteenth-century society. As an international sutler made mobile by the economic privileges afforded to her by skin color, Seacole had the benefits of expanding her export trade to foreign markets. It was her business activity in Panama that sustained her stay there, and in the face of the British war office's rejection, it was her earlier commercial successes that helped fund Seacole's passage to the Crimea. Ironically, it was the lack of commercial success—bankruptcy after the premature end of the war—that occasioned the writing of her war memoirs as an income-generating venture, for with the premature declaration of peace in the Crimea, Seacole was left with an extensive stock of war-related supplies she was unable to sell, and she lost several hundred pounds. In order to avoid a misreading as a market-savvy entrepreneur (and the economic and racial disempowerment this portrayal could occasion), Seacole repackages her service in the Crimea as national duty and strategically relates her material poverty to the invaluable experience of serving in the war effort. This ability to see the sweet uses of adversity is Seacole's strongest bargaining piece, for it confirms to her reader her devotion to humanity rather than to self and to commercial success. Her autobiography serves ultimately to bring her economic assets into alignment with her ideological aspirations. Like her Scottish forebearers with whom Seacole is proud to claim kin, commerce and profiteering acquire the gloss of national service, and the material gain that accrues from travel to many lands becomes part of a larger British imperial discourse.

The successful marketing of *Wonderful Adventures* depends on Seacole's achievement of reader satisfaction. By virtue of the stigmas of vulgar commerce and unfeminine conduct implicit in unchaperoned travel to "many lands," these trade ventures could be read as oppositional to the espoused mid-Victorian domestic ideal; Seacole tactically offers alongside them another more compelling narrative. With great care, and with the strategic goal of affording self-ontological validation, she presents in a story of enterprise, courage, and humanitarianism, a story where patriotic duty trades places with self-advancement. Intent on garnering a sympathetic reaction from her book-buying English reader, Seacole deliberately orients the hardships to which she is exposed in her market penetration. Rather than focusing on the rejection she faces in England when she volunteers for war duty, she showcases her persistent efforts to enlist as a hospital nurse. Whatever hurts she might have felt are hidden behind the self-deprecating narrative of a woman who acknowledges that her desire to render her services interfered with the "official gravity of nice, gentlemanly young fellows" (77) and who forgives this slight because the officer has yet to mature into an awareness of her worth. The runaround that Seacole receives when she volunteers for service in the Crimea is mentioned only as an example of her tenacity, the strength of character that prevented her from being dismayed by untutored military officials who thought war was too serious a game to include female players. She does not present herself as taking these setbacks personally, and her self-funded journey to Turkey is proof of her determination and patriotism. Strategically, Seacole locates her laboring activities in the Crimea as part of a patriotic campaign that, while it ended in fiscal ruin, endowed her with the richness of friendship and rewarded her with grateful testimonials for her heroism. Thus this form of self-promotion allows for the validation of her sense of honor and public duty at a time and in a space where their value is appreciated. In the proliferation of such astute self-advertising, reader patronage and satisfaction are courted through what Cheryl Fish describes as "Seacole's . . . unique ability to negotiate successfully the cost, limits, and possibilities of the multiple communities she encounters."[7] *Wonderful Adventures* is attentive to communities of customers and readers alike, and Seacole—a hardworking businesswoman—sells a story that is rich in meticulous details of the worth of her medical labor. Presented as a series of complex rhetorical negotiations—arrangements as complex and as calculated as those employed by shopkeepers and other entrepreneurs as they seek to secure for themselves a generous clientele—her autobiography also unmasks the trade-off that such marketing maneuvers involve.

For, while she does not speak to them, there are significant personal and psychosocial costs incurred in Seacole's bid for Englishness.

Whereas the bourgeois ideology of Anglo-Victorian society had established that the place of woman was one of domesticity, subordination, and dependence, Seacole's autobiography betrays her as outside of that paradigm. While she did not choose to dwell on the limitations of her status as a mixed-race Jamaican woman, Seacole was governed by the sociopolitical precepts of nineteenth-century colonial Caribbean society. In a society that had yet to see women as subjects in their own right, instead of the contested terrain for the performance of male desire, Seacole's status as a single, black female was already problematic. Moreover, her desire for Englishness was itself unrepresentable, in the sense that Kristeva has used it, insofar as the colonial subject—regardless of gender—is racially marked as outside of the grid of status, privilege, and authority that constitute Englishness. To successfully represent her history of service, Seacole had to trade in the constituents of her Caribbeanness: her womanhood, her family history, her relations to home, and most specifically her blackness. The reality of her blackness—even though she chooses to racially represent herself in linguistically slippery ways such as "Creole," "a little brown," and "yellow"—made her private life indescribable and her goal for Englishness difficult. Therefore, her public life had to be presented as her only life. More importantly, she needed to prove that her carefully constructed subjectivity was validated by a white colonial authority. This essay will demonstrate that in *Wonderful Adventures,* strategic alignment of the interest and sympathy of a white male reader—the embodiment of Englishness—accordingly became part of Seacole's core objectives.

A dominant narrative strategy in nineteenth-century autobiography by persons of color was the establishment of one's humanity—the redemption of personal history from the assumptions of racial inferiority. However, in the instance of Mary Seacole, the compilation of information on the private life of a mixed-race woman may make up a portrait that cannot be successfully marketed, if only because blackness, according to Henry Louis Gates Jr., "is not a material object or an event but a metaphor; it does not have an 'essence' as such but is defined by a network of relations."[8] Seacole reads this metaphor as one of loss and lack: one that could engender financial insecurity, one that could align her with the socially marginal and the politically powerless blacks. The challenge therefore is to craft an identity which, while taking advantage of circulating notions of the indomitable and rebellious black, manages to simultaneously free these constructions from their racial moorings. In *The Negotiated Self,* Anne Malena describes the dynamics of identity that are integral to diasporic subjectivity: "The subject, socialized from the start, is forever engaged in a process of negotiation for acceptable political and socio-cultural definitions of . . . her identity" (8). The process of negotiation that Seacole entered would entail, in the words of the slave woman Sojourner Truth, "sell[ing] the shadow to support the substance."[9]

Among the critics who have noted Seacole's wily participation in the authentication strategies used in African American slave narratives, Sandra Pouchet Paquet has argued that Mary Seacole's autobiography is nevertheless "an enthusiastic acceptance of colonialism in the aftermath of slavery.[10] Noting her lack of concern with the hostile sociopolitical conditions endured by black Jamaicans at the turn of the nineteenth century, Pouchet Paquet goes on to argue that Seacole's autobiography reflects the successes of individualistic, colonial conformity rather than the hardships typically meted out to the black women in the diaspora. By virtue of her locating this autobiography within the context of nineteenth-century slave narratives, Pouchet Paquet judges it as inadequately representative of that genre to the extent that it is unconcerned with the idea of freedom and economic viability for all diasporic blacks. I concur with Pouchet Paquet's judgment that *Wonderful Adventures* cannot be representative. Seacole is not a slave, nor does she identify with slaves, as she was born free. In her narrative of self-actualization she does not give prominence to issues of race-related survival—these do not impact on her quest to market her differentiated self. Nor does she associate her mission to survive with that engaged in by other diasporic subjects—her subjectivity tends toward Britain for its constitution and not toward the diaspora. *Wonderful Adventures* is specifically about personal survival. As "an unprotected female," Seacole needs to make her way in the world. Ironically, like the slave, with whom she would undoubtedly eschew association, she uses whatever means are at her disposal, and her autobiography, like many slave narratives, is rife with strategic omissions.[11]

In her self-marketing agenda, Seacole relegates the particulars of her early years to the back shelf of her discourse, choosing to disclose snippets of information on her childhood, marriage, and widowhood as window dressing for a larger entrepreneurial showcase. She deliberately withholds her date of birth as a female prerogative, avoids specifics about her family set-up and its kinship arrangements, omits mentioning her mother's caste descriptor, glosses over her romantic connection with the sickly Mr. Seacole, and is provocatively vague about the racial and social backgrounds of the suitors wishing to fill her late husband's shoes. Whatever personal information we as readers are privy to is offered as specific to Seacole's presentation of her determined economic triumph over adversity and to her portrayal of herself as a "plain, truth-speaking woman" whose energy, activity, and ability to be undaunted by life's adversity are legacies of her Scottish soldier father. Truth remains elusive in the rhetorical deliberateness of Seacole's disclosures. I am suggesting that her personal history is strategically inaccessible to the reader because these facts could help the reader reconstruct Seacole's genealogy—a reconstruction that does not ably serve the self-image that she is peddling.[12] There are other useful details withheld from the reader. Seacole's family's involvement in running Blundell House—a Kingston-based lodging house that enjoyed a high occupancy—is never mentioned.[13] While we are told that she lost her house in the great fire of 1843 and that with perseverance and determination she rebuilt and restocked it, the name of the house and the fact that it served primarily as a lodging house rather than as a convalescent home remain obscured. Instead, Seacole chooses to detail the guests who lodged at her house: naval or military surgeons and high-ranking officers. These references conspicuously serve as the platform on which to showcase her gratitude for their past kindness and allow her the rhetorical space to construct her own war efforts as a reciprocal gesture.

In her essay "But Most of All mi Love Me Browning," Patricia Mohammed makes the point that in dealing with any one group in British West Indian history, it is virtually impossible to ignore the intra- and intergroup negotiations that take place in the political and social struggle of identity formation (27). Seacole's discourse, however, manages to ignore blacks. Throughout *Wonderful Adventures,* there is the deliberate separation of self from blackness. She reads blackness—as it relates to skin color or in its association with specific categories of labor—as reducing one to invisibility and to the loss of subjectivity, a fate she wishes to circumvent. Incapable of reformulating her blackness (no matter how invisible she presents it to be) into an acceptable metaphor of gain, she instead substitutes it with images of her Scottish thrift, industry, and self-reliance—characteristics from which she can gain material and symbolic profit. Her resilience, her energy, and her indomitable will to survive are showcased to her customer/reader as attributes inherited from her European ancestors That these may well be characteristics that could as aptly define the nineteenth-century Afro-Caribbean person is not an idea that holds value in Seacole's narrative quest. Hers is an individualized effort—the undisguised search for a personal identity with which to negotiate the paradoxes that constitute racial and cultural life in nineteenth-century Jamaica: "The struggles which it cost me to succeed in life were sometimes very trying; nor have they ended yet. But I have always turned a bold front to fortune; and taken, and shall continue to take . . . my hurts before" (6).

In a century where there were more than a hundred racial categories to describe mixed-raced persons, color stratification inevitably threads itself through Seacole's discourse on blackness. From the onset of her narrative, Seacole describes herself as Creole. The nineteenth-century meaning of this term varied. Sometimes it referred to persons of European descent born in the colonies; in other instances, it was a descriptor for persons of Afro-European descent. It is in this latter sense that Seacole uses the word.[14] "I am a Creole, and have good Scotch blood coursing in my veins." The use of the qualifier "good" prompts the following question: Is the non-Scottish blood—her mother's blood—that undoubtedly flows in her veins bad? Establishing "Creole" as a race, Seacole goes on to show that she is outside that group, since to be Creole is to be lazy, and she is an exemplar of "energy and activity" and unfamiliar with "what it is to be indolent." This rhetorical posturing allows the reader to construct her as a good Scot—a person of British descent born in the colonies. Seacole is also quick to remind her reader that she is not "as dark as any nigger" (6). When as a young person Seacole is jeered at by London street urchins, her representation of that event is telling:

> I shall never forget my first impressions of London. . . . Strangely enough, some of the most vivid of my recollections are the efforts of the London street-boys to poke fun at my and my companion's complexion. I am only

a little brown—a few shades duskier than the brunettes whom you admire so much; but my companion was very dark, and a fair (if I can apply the term to her) subject for their rude wit. (4)

Her reference to her complexion as a few shades darker than the much admired brunette suggests that she, like the brunette, can be admired. Her companion, by contrast, is too dark to be admired and is therefore the butt of their cruel teasing. There is a sense, too, that it is her dark companion who draws public attention to skin color, and by walking with her, Seacole, by association, becomes darkened. In a different setting, that is, in one in which her companions are lighter-hued, she becomes "the yellow doctress" (34). Thus Seacole's "yellowness" does not seem to function as a description of race, merely as a description that carries the same status as her mention of her blue bonnet and her red ribbons. Both set her off as a splash of cheerful color in the otherwise drab landscape of war. The disingenuousness of this self-representation, and her implied suggestion that she, by virtue of her "duskiness," is not a victim of racism resurface in her seeming lack of responsiveness to the racial prejudice of both the War Office and Florence Nightingale. By refusing to see her skin color as an obstacle, by constantly operating on the presumption of her worthiness as a British subject, Seacole is resisting this epistemological frame, so as to reorient those racial precepts—the cultural value system that could derail her constructions of self-value.[15] Notably, while she is careful to present the British as unmindful of race—although the thought crosses her mind and is dispelled—she is not as charitable about American racist behavior: "Doubts and suspicions arose in my heart for the first and last time, thank Heaven. Was it possible that American prejudice against color had some root here? Did these ladies shrink from me because my blood flowed beneath a somewhat duskier skin than theirs?" (79).

Also unarticulated in her autobiography are her relationships with blacks—family, friends, or helpers. In much the same way that lodge keepers had been careful to keep coloreds and blacks away from their establishment lest their presence would prejudice a white clientele, Seacole is careful to omit these groups from her narrative. When they do appear, the portrayal is often overgeneralized, caricatured, or reductive. Her impressions of the fugitive American Negroes in New Granada are conservative and carefully qualified: they are "generally superior men . . . and the people, for some reason—perhaps because they recognized in them superior talent for administration—always respected them." (51) While this representation may potentially counter the myth of the lazy Negro, Seacole does not provide sufficient textual corroboration for this opinion. Whereas the white men whom Seacole encounters during her wonderful adventures in these many lands are often viewed as her sons, black men are not similarly represented. She is not Mother Seacole to them. Instead, she is a peddler of a medical service, and her patients pay her well for her diligence. Indeed, despite Seacole's larger statement of the perniciousness of slavery, she constantly notes differences between herself and blacks. Her "nigger cooks" in Cruces are excitable and lazy, and her cooks in the Crimea are good-for-nothings who "laugh with all their teeth" (20). She further reinforces these differences in her description of her black cook's reaction to being bitten by a rat: "His eyes rolling angrily and his white teeth gleaming. . . . He made a great fuss" (115). In the landscape of war, this unmanly response to something as trivial as a mangled finger is compared unfavorably to the steadfast suffering of her white 'soldier-sons' as they lay dying on the frontline: "I attended to another . . . an officer, shot in the side, who bore his cruel suffering with a firmness that was very noble. In return for the little use I was to him, . . . he kissed my hands and smiled far more thanks than I had earned" (166).

In choosing a public space wherein to establish herself as the great mother of a nation of brave British soldiers, she separates herself from a tradition that had celebrated shared mothering. Whereas within Caribbean contexts of mothering, other women offer a supportive network of care, Seacole glosses over the presence of such networks in her young life, and in her narrative of surrogate mothering, she neither validates nor seeks to replicate them. Similarly, the discourse of West Indianness does not resonate for Seacole. While later this anxiety was to occupy a place of centrality in the West Indian intellectualization of self, Seacole resolutely locates herself beyond this conversation. Instead, she sells a more palatable story of the compliant Creole, and in her discussion of life in the colonies, she deliberately chooses to portray the Creole as fully committed to the well-being of the colonial: "Nature had been favourable in . . . instilling into the hearts of the Creoles an affection for English people and an anxiety for their welfare" (88). While this perspective may be Seacole's, it is a point of view that is consistently invalidated by the turbulent history of social unrest in nineteenth-century Jamaica. Even though her narrative makes no mention of it, however, the discerning reader may recognize that the colonial Jamaica—more specifically the British military—with which Seacole establishes kinship is very much under siege as nationalist activities seek to overthrow it. Her remarks about Jamaica suggest that Seacole is giving it a particular character. By foregrounding its loyalty to the crown and its liberal acceptance of the diverse and often nontraditional roles of women, Seacole fixes Jamaica as a site of simultaneous sameness and difference. Her definition of the Creole temperament as different from that of the English reader, while it serves to establish a contrast between Jamaica and England, is offered in the same spirit that she mentions her tendency toward adventure as a legacy of her Scottish blood. These comments never develop into statements about her racial inferiority.

In *Making Men,* Belinda Edmondson argues that "colonies were also involved in what for lack of a better term can be called a familial relationship with the 'Parent' country," and these European powers also "attempted to transfer their culture, language, and political structures to these colonies, and in this exhibited a desire to re-create themselves in their colonies" (22–23). Central to Seacole's marketing maneuvers is the facilitation of that desire. Perceiving herself challenged by life circumstances, driven by pragmatism, needing to make her way in the world as a single black female, having traded in all that could visibly identify her as West Indian, she is, ironically, proof of the Caribbean adage "When your foot short, take in front."[16] Eager to establish her labor rather than her race as an important constituent of her psychosocial status, Seacole, in her *Wonderful Adventures,* constructs paradigmatic spaces for her working body—spaces that not so much confine her but rather define her as subject. Hers is the disciplined body put to the service of capitalist production. It is also a patriotic body, voluntarily committed to military service. And it is a loyal body, deeply involved in the service of reproducing the political and social relations of colonialism. As a hardworking woman of color, hers is a body always in motion, energetically involved in service to others. There is much critical daring in this portrayal. Her working body may well be defined as a working-class body, and given her racial location, such self-determination allows for race and class to intersect with gender in ways that could undo the authority she has worked so hard to create. Simply put, the black body historically bears the weight of manual labor; accordingly, Seacole runs the risk of being dismissed by her British readers as the iconographic black servant and the physicality of her activities relegated to a discourse of plantation labor and subordination.

While Seacole draws many references to her body, these are presented as part of a discursive strategy aimed at legitimizing her claims to subjectivity. Her yellow dress and blue bonnet with red ribbons mark her body out as attractive and colorful. Her body, however, is not presented as sexual but rather as maternal—competent, capable, comforting, albeit comely. For central to the establishment of herself as the good woman is the evocation of her purity. Thus while she speaks of the comeliness of her portly form, and the fact that she draws the admiring gazes of the vivacious French and sees appreciation in the sundry sleepy-eyed Turks, Seacole recontains her body's fleshy corpulence into a narrative of comforting maternal bulk, the bosom at which dying soldiers find solace. The Turkish Pasha's interest, while recognized by the community as a discreet attempt at courtship, is dismissed by Seacole in a linguistically ambivalent statement on the Pasha's polygenic status: "the honest fellow candidly confessed he had three wives already at home, I acquit him of any desire to add to their numbers" (110). Her agenda in the Crimea is related not to the improvement of her matrimonial prospects but to the establishment of her Englishness.

Having successfully located her labor within a maternal matrix, Seacole then proceeds to reorient the Anglo-Victorian definition of the good woman, a reorientation that was already in progress as British society sought to accommodate the changing status of the nursing woman.[17] That her presence and behavior in the Crimea scarcely embodied true womanhood was a charge to which Seacole responded. *Wonderful Adventures of Mrs. Seacole in Many Lands,* while conceding to unorthodox female behavior, locates that transgression as ably serving a larger, nationalistic, and distinctly altruistic agenda. For even while she does not choose to focus on it, Seacole's skin color forecloses on her participation in a domestic narrative that could have confirmed her as nurturing and self-sacrificing, as was the wont of the Victorian angel in the house. As a mulatto woman, she is already constructed as inhabiting the space of disruptive sexuality. Her Creole blood—read elsewhere as black—disposes her to excesses in passion, a construction that Seacole herself buys into in her description of herself as the "hot-blooded Creole" (6) who is prone to fits of emotion. The ideological implications of this image of excess as core to the representation of blacks have corresponded to the depiction of blacks as icons of sexuality, as Sander Gilman so ably documented in *Difference and Pathology: Stereotypes of Sexuality, Race, and Madness*. Gilman's analysis of the ways in which Victorian ideology reduced blacks to genitalia and read them as "the object and source of sexual perversity" (116) is apropos in its suggestion of the various ways in which the black female body of Mary Seacole could be assessed in this society.

However, this construction of a disruptive sexuality is not one to which Seacole gives any credence. Whereas the specter of sexual incontinence often accompanies the image of the independent woman, Seacole manages to neutralize any such castigation on her virtuousness. As a widow who comes into contact with many men, Seacole never establishes desire to transform her single status. She does not admit to loneliness, even though she lacks female company. Instead, her energies are devoted solely to the service of others, ironically confirming the Victorian precepts of the good mother. Where a hotel/hostel may become, for the unchaperoned woman, a volatile space that could transform Seacole into the mistress of the lonely soldier, she is careful to reconfigure this familial relationship into one of asexual mothering. Further, Seacole's representation of herself as a woman of senior years, as already forty-something when she begins her medical adventuring in many lands, helps in part to counter labels of sexual misconduct. Her age, in allowing her the status of seniority, also helps to position her as beyond youthful riots of blood and beyond the passions that had characterized her response to her husband's death.

At the same time Seacole is careful to avoid the overly compensatory iconography of the "saving angel." Much of the appeal of her autobiography comes from her staging of her humanity, her womanly predisposition to joy and sorrow, and her coy confessions that as a desirable woman she has had to husband her desires: "Indeed, I do not mind confessing to my reader, in a friendly confidential way, that one

of the hardest struggles of my life in Kingston was to resist the pressing candidates for the late Mr. Seacole's shoes" (8). Thus her mode of
self-representation is necessarily wily. Hers is a carefully sexed body.
To present herself as unsexed is to disempower herself by trading in
the very humanity she is attempting to cash in. On the other hand, to
portray herself as sexed yet restrained is to marry the self-identification
of desirability implicit to the stereotyped mulatto with the temperance
inherited from her Scottish ancestors. Correspondingly, she explains
that she chose not to remarry because she is confident in her power to
make her own way in the world rather than for lack of offers. Indeed, it
is here that Seacole betrays the privilege of her class and caste location.
Poor black women in nineteenth-century society, whether free or slave,
were not blessed with "pressing candidates," and marriage was a way of
generating social and economic benefits. Her lack of identification with
this group is once more made apparent.

Conscious of the elite models of respectability circulating in nineteenth-century British society, Mary Seacole takes care in her autobiography to authorize herself through a deliberate evocation of her worthiness
as caregiver—one who fulfils the socially prescribed role of woman. In
constructing herself as Mother Seacole, her ministrations to the injured
soldiers are framed in terms of the loving care that a mother bestows
on her sick child as she describes her nursing and commercial activities
in the language of love and self-abnegation that so often constitutes the
rhetoric of mothering. Mention is made of her joy as she held wounded
soldiers to her bosom, her relating to them as the sons she never had, of
the grief she felt at their death, and the small mementos (locks of hairs,
rings, and lockets) that she kept *in memoriam*. As the bearer of good
cheer and tenderness, she evokes within the various war locations in
Turkey a moveable British home: one made welcoming by her tarts and
pies, her jellies, her broths, and her homely cakes. This insistent representation of maternalism deflects attention from the socially contradictory behavior that could preclude Seacole from being what Mary Poovey,
in her description of the roles ascribed to nineteenth-century women,
calls "the sexless, moralizing angel." Anxious lest she be devalued as
"an aggressive, carnal magdalen," a label that was readily ascribed to
the Afro-Caribbean woman, Seacole deploys authenticating strategies
that ensure that such a label cannot be applied to a woman like herself, a

woman who has, as her many testimonial letters confirm, dedicated her life to "charities and incessant labour among the army" (200). Her entrepreneurial activities—the sale of food and clothing—are presented as part of an extended maternal support, and her disregard for her personal safety on the Crimean battlefront marks Seacole as the self-sacrificing mother who is governed solely by her "children's" well-being. Safe from the label of abnormal behavior, Seacole's independence and proactivity are not read as degrading and anti-womanly but instead as the fitting characteristics of a mother of British soldiers.

Not that she ever surrenders her womanhood. Indeed, much of Seacole's autobiography is the authorizing of herself as the *right woman in the right place*. The Crimea is hardly the right place for a woman, though. Alongside testimonies of maternal behavior, Seacole offers her readers a portrait of herself as the model of respectability; she describes her faithful adherence to the garb of a genteel woman as a point of contrast to her European female counterparts, who compromised their femininity by succumbing to the convenience of cross-dressing in male attire.[18] Even while Seacole points to the incongruity of her long skirts as she clambers out of boats or makes her way up slippery mountain slopes, her refusal to surrender her womanly attire to the more appropriate masculine garb serves to reinforce how deeply entrenched is her commitment to Victorian womanhood. Moreover, it validates Seacole's presence in a place of war as a mothering mission. This rhetorical *volte face* is useful in deflecting attention from Seacole's other unladylike activities: her unchaperoned travel across Europe, her frontline involvement in commerce, her disdain for the women she encounters, and her constant association with men who are not related to her. These actions, while equally unconventional and as culturally impermissible as women wearing male garb, are recuperated within Seacole's discourse on good mothering as behavior that is essential to the physical and psychological sustenance of the English army.

Following Martha Nussbaum's argument in *Cultivating Humanity* that "the prominent assumption . . . is that the male head of household is a beneficial altruist who represents the interest of all his family members, and can be relied upon to distribute resources fairly" (189), then Seacole, widowed early and supposedly childless, becomes the family whose interest needs to be served. The able representation of her interest will generate resources that will allow Seacole not only to survive but also to gain the social visibility commonly enjoyed by the head of household. Seacole's autobiography can be read as a strategic plan that in responding to her market environment deploys various rhetorical and textual strategies designed to enable her to be a success. As such, *Wonderful Adventures* presents Seacole as a woman who is not afraid of hard work and whose labor is not restricted to commerce. The act of producing her autobiography is also an act of labor, one that demonstrates a similar awareness of the market within which it is expected to succeed commercially, one that is, appropriately, highly attentive to the demands of a British literary marketplace. Engaging the customer/reader is the key to a successful autobiography, and being a shrewd businesswoman, Seacole is well aware that credibility is crucial to the self-representation that she is peddling. To profit from her story, she must persuade her readers that she is a patriotic woman whose war effort deserves their appreciation, their love, and their patronage.

That Seacole offers her story primarily to male readers comes as no surprise. In a society bound by patriarchy, men held the political and economic power from which she wished to benefit, and Seacole, accordingly, tells her story with a masculine authority that is tempered by feminine engagement. In *Gendered Interventions*, Robyn Warhol makes a distinction between the narrative strategies employed by female and male writers. She shows how, during the Victorian period, the rhetoric of direct address was identified as "a woman's strategy to be applied at moments when a reader's emotional reciprocity should be most sensitive and to be avoided by practitioners of self-referential 'high art'" (205). According to Warhol, the aim of direct address is to provoke specific responses of sympathy, outrage, or even tears. Aware of the competition her autobiography is up against—"the more than enough . . . journals and chronicles of Crimean life" (146)—Seacole's success depends on her popularity and reputation. The style with which she writes allows for further market differentiation. In her autobiography Seacole makes use of what I wish to define as a "semi-direct address" in the manner in which she grounds her authority in rational objectivity. Having established herself as "the historian of Spring Hill," Seacole unceasingly presents evidence of herself as the exemplary British subject whose frontline war contribution in the Crimea is outstanding. She spends an entire chapter recording "the written opinions of those who had ample means of judging and ascertaining how I fulfilled the great object which I had in view in leaving England for the Crimea," so as to convince the reader of the worthiness she "held in the camp as doctress, nurse, and 'mother'" (120). At the same time, she frequently indicates her awareness of her reader and addresses him, not in the possessive intimacy of "dear reader," a convention deployed by other nineteenth-century women writers, but instead with the directness of a storyteller who understands and values the relationship between narrator and audience. As an engaging yet respectful storyteller, she constantly refers to the reader as "my reader," a phrase intended to evoke identification, sympathy, and camaraderie.

Unapologetically personal yet not making intimate disclosures, Seacole defends her selection of events and the chronology with which she offers them. Her text acquires a brusqueness that goes well with the no-nonsense activities she describes. Her involvement in the everyday process of buying and selling, of providing clothing, food, and medicine to her clients, acquires the gloss of military community service at a time when the British army's mismanagement of supplies was responsible for the malnutrition, disease, and death of their soldiers in the Crimea.[19] Undoubtedly, the practicality embedded in her accounts of her war contribution would appeal to her white male readers, who were aware that such frugality and resourcefulness were traits British women were being called on to demonstrate. Confident that her readers share her interest in detailing events in as dispassionate a tone as possible, Seacole is nonetheless keen to highlight her female reaction to the horrors of war. In a style that establishes solidarity and equality, she succeeds in achieving what Warhol defines as a "cross-gendered narrative."[20] By mixing the rhetorical modes of masculine and feminine communication in much the same way that she merges the hospital with the lodging house, and the kitchen with the dispensary, Seacole creates a space wherein her story is not seen to be solely addressing one sex. For in garnering masculine support, she is altogether aware of the female reader who would hold her closer to the Victorian ideal of proper womanhood and who would expect from her certain modes of conduct—in dress as in narration. Thus her autobiography, while it does not directly attend to the female reader, is nonetheless careful not to alienate a potential clientele.

From the outset, her autobiography seems cognizant of the insufficiencies of a suitably accommodating domestic discourse, and therefore it compensates for any potential loss of market shares by deploying a substitutive military narrative—one that ably confirms the worthiness of her war effort and carries the authoritative validation of British military officials. This narrative alignment with white men replicates her entrepreneurial strategies in Panama and the Crimea when she empowered herself in a world populated mainly by white men demanding domestic care in a context of scarcity. Seacole understands the benefits of reconfiguring the paradigmatic Victorian family in an alternative homespace that, in turn, substitutes for the one that war has denied the soldiers. This provides her narrative with a market advantage. Unceasingly she reminds the reader, albeit in blunt language and with a robust style that stands in contradistinction to the repetitive sentimentality of nineteenth-century women's memoirs, that her activities in the Crimea provided an alternative homespace. Indeed, her autobiography begins with the establishment of a natural connection to the military: her father was a soldier, and her mother ran a lodging house that was patronized by military men. The identification with the military is then cemented in a network of kinship support she creates in the Crimean war zone; there she becomes the ministering angel to whose warm hearth—the "British Hotel" in Balaclava—her soldier-sons are drawn and comforted. Where her autobiography may have been dismissed as a careerist form of self-advertising, she generates reader approval—especially those connected and loyal to the British militia—through repeated testimonies of her worthiness as mother surrogate, consistent praise of Englishness, and painstaking mapping of her support for the values that undergird colonial society.

In conclusion, in her memoir, Seacole successfully trades in her Creole identity for an English one. These market negotiations allow Mrs. Mary Seacole to establish herself as the amiable yet assertive woman whose love of adventure and dedication to imperial service make her a good British subject. While her commercial activities are not typically prized as the embodiment of respectable womanhood, Seacole redeems these sutlering activities by converting them from capitalist trade into a socialist ethic of care that is closely linked to the return to wellness.[21] In the process of rhetorical reconstruction, Seacole's activities as a *vivandiere* become reformulated into what W. H. Russell eulogistically called "the action of one who has redeemed the name of 'sutler' from the suspicions of worthlessness, mercenary baseness, and plunder" (viii). Commercial activity therefore becomes an extension of and a platform for maternal care. Productive rather than reproductive, Seacole manages the simultaneous self-portrayal as the good Victorian woman and as the new Victorian woman—a woman who is responsive to adversity, the woman that she so pithily portrayed as the right one for the job. She becomes "Mother Seacole," the stout, large-hearted woman whose presence in the wartorn Crimea stemmed from a desire to cure rather than to capitalize on the market opportunities of a captive military group. She is "doctress" Seacole, putting herself in harm's way so as to administer care to the wounded, the sick, and the dying British soldiers.

That Seacole, in foregrounding her laboring self, is able to seamlessly integrate commerce and medicine speaks to the abandoning of what Pierre Bourdieu describes in *Outline of a Theory of Practice* as "the dichotomy of the economic and the non-economic which stands in the way of seeing the science of . . . economic practices [as] directed towards the maximizing of material or symbolic profit."[22] Occurring at both the literal and metaphoric level, Seacole's trading generates different levels of reward, and her profit margin is ultimately a function of the strategies she employs in her multi-segment marketing. Ultimately, her dedicated support of an imperial power that had yet to authorize the colonial as having a legitimate claim to the rights attendant to British citizenry seems to work in her favor.[23] Her "affection for the English" and her "anxiety for their welfare" are rewarded by the public recognition of her contribution. By inserting herself in a military rather than a domestic narrative, she succeeds in achieving the active British citizenry to which her race had made her ineligible. Where gender may have disbarred her, she managed to practice health-care work without antagonizing medical men by the nontraditional nature of her labors. In inscribing her kindness and gentleness in the larger public territory of the battlefield, she also redeems the nursing woman. Where Florence Nightingale had sought to legitimize the contribution of her army of nurses through the establishment of behavior manuals, Seacole offers her life story as an alternative behavior manual—one where the worth of a woman is established through her labor and ratified by the testimonies and actions of British military men.

# Notes

The second epigraph is from Carole Boyce Davies, "Woman Is a Nation . . . ." This Caribbean proverb means that in times of hardship, even the most privileged need to work in order to survive. According to Boyce Davies, this proverb stresses the ways in which "color, gender, and privilege" work in Caribbean society.

1. Here I am using *colored* in the sense used by Gad Heuman in his article "The Social Structure of Slave Societies in the Caribbean." According to Heuman, the term *colored* referred to people of mixed race. Hence a mulatto (that is, the offspring of a Caucasian and an African) would be referred to as "colored," but so too would the offspring of a Caucasian and a mulatto. *Colored,* therefore, was an umbrella term used to classify persons whose skin color, hair, and facial features marked them as having African ancestry, while at the same time separating them from persons who were visibly of African descent.

2. Vassell, "Colonial Gender Politics in Jamaica, 1865–1945," 192.

3. While Seacole called herself a "doctress," she had no formal training. Her knowledge of folk medicine was gained from her mother; however, even if her mother's folk training had been validated as appropriate, Seacole would not have been considered a doctor, given that women were not allowed to be doctors in the mid-nineteenth century. Significantly, the term *doctress* was a Caribbean one ascribed to slaves who, by virtue of their knowledge of herbal lore, became medical practitioners. Like Seacole, these practitioners augmented their knowledge base through their interactions with white doctors.

4. High-end trade refers to trading activities that cater to and serve a wealthy clientele. Low-end trade catered for a poorer clientele and was typically conducted by black women.

5. All page references hereafter will be to the 1988 Oxford reprint of *Wonderful Adventures.*

6. Beckles, *Centering Woman,* 180.

7. Fish, "Traveling with Her Mother's Taste," 949.

8. Gates, "'Preface to Blackness': Text and Pretext," 67.

9. Sojourner Truth to Mrs. Mary K. Gale, 25 February 1864, folder 09, Sojourner Truth Records, Sojourner Truth Library, State University of New York, New Paltz. With the help of a friend, Euphemia Cockrane, Truth wrote the following to Gale: "I would have answered your letter when it first came, only I was having a new photograph taken. . . . I wanted to send you the best. I enclose all three [pictures] all in different positions. . . . Dear child, I wish Sojourner could go to you herself instead of the picture. . . . Please tell any friends who may want my pictures that they can have them by writing to me in this place. . . . I sell the three for $1 or a single one for 35 cents. . . . They will see by my card that I sell the shadow to support the substance." To my mind, Truth's peddling of her pictures is reminiscent of Seacole's peddling part of her life story, except that Seacole had the benefit of literacy whereas Truth had to depend on white abolitionists to tell her story. Both women, slave and free, required the authentication of the white establishment. Both women, anxious for adequate representation, provided excessive supporting material to their narratives.

10. Pouchet Paquet, "The Enigma of Arrival," 652.

11. Harriet Jacobs's omissions are examples of this. *Incidents in the Life of a Slave Girl* provides a detailed portraiture of the mulatto slave and the defenses she constructs to protect her virtue. Under the pseudonym of Linda Brent, Jacobs details her life as a slave girl and the "loophole of retreat" that she creates to protect herself from the advances of her master, Dr. Flint. She casts her relations with her lover, Sands, as a necessary evil—a way of protecting herself from Dr. Flint. That she continues her relationship with Sands after Flint is no longer a threat is an issue on which Jacobs does not dwell. Her narrative mission instead requires that she prove her humanity by appearing to be exceptional in her fortitude and in her virtuousness. That the violated slave woman can also be a desiring woman is a topic on which the literature written by ex-slave women is still somewhat silent—and for good reason. To focus on the slave woman's sexuality is to participate in a gendered ideology that had inscribed blackness as synonymous with sexuality.

12. In "Mary Seacole: Her Life and Times," historian Aleric Joseph presents statistical data on mixed-race marriages in Jamaica to infer that Seacole's parents were not married. According to Joseph's research, no mixed marriages were recorded in Kingston up to 1814. While in Caribbean society this illegitimacy would have hardly mattered, it would be of significance to the British middle-class reader from whom Seacole wished to gain social acceptance and economic patronage. Joseph also uses the 1881 census of Paddington Marylebourne, listing Mary Seacole as seventy-one, to support her claim that Mary Grant Seacole was born in 1810.

13. In *The West Indies and the Spanish Main* (1859), Anthony Trollope describes his visit to Jamaica and his stay at Blundell Hall. He recounts his conversation with the sister of Mary Seacole: "I took up my abode at Blundle [*sic*] Hall and found that the landlady in whose custody I placed myself was a sister of good Mrs. Seacole. 'My sister wanted to go to India,' said my landlady, 'with the army you know. But Queen Victoria would not let her; her life was too precious'" (21).

14. In this chapter, following Seacole, I will use the term *Creole* to describe a mixed-race person.

15. Of note is the fact that while this intervention may be read within the wider context of colonial politics, Seacole does not connect her acts of transgression to a wider discourse of an emerging black nationalism. Her agenda does not extend in this direction. Instead, what her narrative constantly validates is her exceptionality rather than her ordinariness. While her brother and Mr. Day both participate in her excursions in New Granada and Turkey, their contribution as men of color engaged in similar capitalist initiatives occupy no space in Seacole's recordings of her many wonderful adventures.

16. This Grenadian proverb can be best explained in the following way: those who are in some way disadvantaged must compensate for their deficiency by working harder than those who are not disadvantaged.

17. Her self-definition as a doctress/medical attendant at a time when women were excluded from medical discourse further undermined considerations of Seacole as a representation of the domestic ideal. Mary Poovey's monumental study, *Uneven Developments* (1988), discusses how nurses were often caught in the pernicious and pervasive constituents of sexuality. Women involved in health care would inevitably be attending to the intimate bodily functions of men to whom they were not related.

Such intimate and physical contact carried associations of sexuality and, correspondingly, devalued the caregiver into a woman of questionable repute.

18. In her account of the rascality and ruffianism that characterized life in Cruces, Seacole segues neatly into a description of the Irish-born dancer and actress Lola Montes, who publicly and rather ostentatiously wore male garb while on tour. Seacole's account of the flamboyance of Montes's masculine dress reminds me of Rachel Holmes's account of another nineteenth-century Irish woman who successfully passed as a man during her lifetime. In *Scanty Particulars: The Scandalous Life and Astonishing Secret of Dr. James Barry, Queen Victoria's Most Eminent Military Doctor,* Holmes details the life of James Barry, who graduated at seventeen with a degree in medicine and went on to have a distinguished medical career, serving for some time as surgeon major in the army medical corps and as deputy inspector general in the Crimean War. Barry is reputed to have performed the first successful caesarian section in Africa. While there had been some speculation during her life as to her specific sexual orientation, it was only after her death that James Barry was publicly confirmed to have been a woman. Born a decade before Seacole, Barry, in disguising her sex, was able to reform the medical profession in ways that Seacole, because of her gender and race, could not.

19. For further information on the mismanagement in the Crimean War, see Marjie Bloy's "General Comments on the Crimean War," at www.victorianweb.org/history/crimea/comment.html," and "The Crimean War," at http://athena.english.vt.edu/~jmooney/3044annotations2a-g/crimeanwar.html.

20. Warhol, *Gendered Interventions*, 207.

21. Conspicuously absent in Seacole's accounts is mention of her selling alcohol or other such stimulants, an activity typical to sutlers. While it is likely that her hotel stocked alcohol, this was not an issue she wished to highlight, because it could undermine the wholesomeness of her narrative on good mothering. Similarly she makes little mention of being involved in the menial activities that are part of housekeeping and hotel management, because the bourgeois construct of female respectability would relegate that form of labor to lower-class women.

22. Bourdieu, *Outline of a Theory of Practice*, 183.

23. By the end of her life, Seacole had gained public recognition as the much-decorated British war heroine. She was a woman of property, and a bust was done in her honor.

# References

Beckles, Hilary McD. *Centering Woman: Gender Discourses in Caribbean Slave Society.* Princeton, N.J.: Markus Wiener, 1999.

Bourdieu, Pierre. *Outline of a Theory of Practice.* Trans. Richard Nice. Cambridge: Cambridge University Press, 1977.

Boyce Davies, Carole. "Woman Is a Nation . . ." In *Out of the Kumbla: Caribbean Women and Literature,* ed. Carole Boyce Davies and Elaine Savory Fido, 165–95. Trenton: Africa World Press, 1990.

Edmondson, Belinda. *Making Men: Gender, Literary Authority, and Women's Writing in Caribbean Narrative.* Durham, N.C.: Duke University Press, 1999.

Fish, Cheryl. "Traveling with Her Mother's Taste: The Negotiation of Gender, Race, and Location in *Wonderful Adventures of Mrs. Seacole in Many Lands*." *Signs: Journal of Women in Culture and Society* 26 (2001): 949–82.

Gates, Henry Louis, Jr. "Preface to Blackness: Text and Pretext." In *Afro-American Literature: The Reconstruction of Instruction*, ed. Dexter Fisher and Robert B. Stepto, 44–71. New York: Modern Language Association of America, 1978.

Gikandi, Simon. *Maps of Englishness: Writing Identity in the Culture of Colonialism.* New York: Columbia University Press, 1996.

Gilman, Sander L. *Difference and Pathology: Stereotypes of Sexuality, Race, and Madness.* Ithaca, N.Y.: Cornell University Press, 1985.

Heuman, Gad. "The Social Structure of Slave Societies in the Caribbean." In *A General History of the Caribbean*, ed. Franklin W. Knight, 138–60. London: Macmillan, 1997.

Holmes, Rachel. *Scanty Particulars: The Scandalous Life and Astonishing Secret of Dr. James Barry, Queen Victoria's Most Eminent Military Doctor.* New York: Random House, 2002.

Jacobs, Harriet. *Incidents in the Life of a Slave Girl, Written by Herself.* Edited by L. Maria Child and Jean Fagan Yellin. Cambridge: Harvard University Press, 1987.

Joseph, Aleric. "Mary Seacole: Her Life and Times." MA thesis, University of the West Indies, Mona, 1986.

Kerr, Paulette. "Victims or Strategists? Female Lodging-House Keepers in Jamaica." In *Engendering History: Caribbean Women in Historical Perspective*, ed. Verene Shepherd, Bridget Brereton, and Barbara Bailey, 197–212. New York: St. Martin's Press, 1995.

Malena, Anne. *The Negotiated Self: The Dynamics of Identity in Francophone Caribbean Narrative.* New York: Peter Lang, 1999.

Mohammed, Patricia. "'But Most of All mi Love Me Browning': The Emergence in Eighteenth- and Nineteenth-Century Jamaica of the Mulatto Woman as the Desired." *Feminist Review* 65 (Summer 2000): 22–48.

Nussbaum, Martha C. *Cultivating Humanity: A Classical Defense of Reform in Liberal Education.* Cambridge: Harvard University Press, 1997.

"Our Own Vivandiere." *Punch,* 30 May 1857.

Poovey, Mary. *Uneven Developments: The Ideological Work of Gender in Mid-Victorian England.* Chicago: University of Chicago Press, 1988.

Pouchet Paquet, Sandra. "The Enigma of Arrival: *Wonderful Adventures of Mrs. Seacole in Many Lands*." *African American Review* 2 (1992): 651–63.

Seacole, Mary. *Wonderful Adventures of Mrs. Seacole in Many Lands.* London: James Blackwood, 1857; reprint, New York: Oxford University Press, 1988.

Trollope, Anthony. *The West Indies and the Spanish Main.* London: Chapman and Hall, 1859; reprint, London: Frank Cass, 1968.

Vassell, Linnette. "Colonial Gender Politics in Jamaica, 1865–1945." In *Before and after 1865: Education, Politics, and Regionalism in the Caribbean*, ed. Brian L. Moore and Swithin R. Wilmot, 190–201. Kingston, Jamaica: Ian Randle, 1998.

Warhol, Robyn R. *Gendered Interventions: Narrative Discourse in the Victorian Novel.* New Brunswick, N.J.: Rutgers University Press, 1989.

# 5

# Blacks in the White Imagination: Race in the Investigation of Rape on Nineteenth-Century Emigrant Ships to the Colonial Caribbean

VERENE A. SHEPHERD

For many decades economic and political history has dominated the academic discipline of history. This implies that the "public" activities and experiences of men and women (to a lesser extent) dominated the field of historical enquiry, assigning a position of lesser importance to the "private sphere." The emergence of the New Social History, Cultural Studies, and Subaltern Studies, combined with the feminist historians' call for destabilization of the public/private dichotomy and greater attention to gender analysis, opened space for the exploration of issues not normally examined by historians. Within this context, subjects like rape and women's "sexploitation" began to be legitimized as subjects worthy of scholarly investigation. Thus the rape of enslaved African women on the Middle Passage and of Indian indentured women on the "other Middle Passage" (the passage from India to the Caribbean in the postslavery period) are now familiar themes in Caribbean history. There is even a growing interest in the comparative analysis of the Indian woman's journey from India and the enslaved African woman's experience of the Middle Passage, specifically their social manipulation or "sexploitation" at the hands of empowered males.

This chapter, extracted from a larger work, sheds some light on the comparative experiences of enslaved African and indentured Indian women on their respective journeys to the Caribbean.[1] The main intention is to open a discursive space within which to situate the roles of ethnicity and racism in the perpetration and investigation of cases of nineteenth-century shipboard rape. The chapter presents a microstudy of the voyage of the emigrant ship *Allanshaw,* which sailed from India to colonial Guyana in 1885. Indentured laborers on board this voyage made several complaints of crew abuse. Official investigations of such complaints reflected the ways in which the ideologies and practices surrounding race, caste, class, power, and gender coalesced to determine the Indian female experience. Analysis of these investigations parallels my earlier study of the investigation of Maharani's complaint of rape against the African Caribbean Robert Ipson and the white European James Oliver.

### Postslavery Labor Exploitation, Sexploitation, and Race

The nineteenth-century system of labor exploitation called the "indentureship system," which replaced slavery in the colonial Caribbean, forms the historical context of this analysis. Indentureship had been used to exploit white laborers in the seventeenth and eighteenth centuries. But increasing cost, racism, antiwhite labor migration activism in Europe, and declining numbers of white migrants combined to cause this system to give way to the large-scale enslavement of Africans to feed the extensive labor demands of the sugar industry, the raison d'être of Caribbean slavery. The abolition of slavery in the British-colonized Caribbean in 1838, however, reopened the old debate about labor shortage in the sugar industry. This was solved through the import of laborers from various sources, mainly Indians and Chinese from Asia. Indians comprised the majority of the Asians imported by Caribbean landholders, with over a half million imported between 1838 and 1917. Of these laborers, 238,909 (the largest number) went to Guyana, followed by Jamaica, which received approximately 38,000. Indian immigrants—recruited initially from the non-Hindu "Hill People" in the Chota Nagpur district of South Bihar and later from around the cities of Calcutta and Madras as well as from districts within the United Provinces of Agra and Oudh (Basti, Gonda, and Fyzabad)—were primarily male, with just about a third of each shipment being females. The women recruits represented a mix of Hindus, Christians, and Muslims. The evidence indicates that the lower Hindu castes predominated, reflecting the prevailing view about the suitability of lower-class/caste women for drudge labor. Scholars have argued that this gender disparity was responsible for much of the social experiences of the Indian women, including their exploitation by the male crew on board the ships that transported them to the colonial Caribbean.[2]

From the literature available, it would seem that white men were the principal perpetrators of the sexploitation endured by subaltern women whether on their journeys on slavers or on nineteenth-century emigrant ships to the Caribbean. Yet in the case of Indian labor migration, the impression given in ships' records and immigration reports is that black men were the main culprits in the sexual exploitation of women. The claim that black men bore a large part of the blame in the sexploitation of indentured Indian women has often been disputed, not least by the alleged perpetrators themselves.

It is true that the system of indentured labor migration did not reflect only white, but also black and Indian masculinity in action. Practically all of the emigrant ships hired non-Caucasian crews; on some ships, most of the crew was black. For example, black men were the majority of sailors on the ship *Moy,* which sailed from India to Jamaica in 1891. On the *Allanshaw,* which sailed from India to Guyana in 1885, there were several African American and African Caribbean crew members, including the "yankee sailor" Robert Ipson, James Grant from Guyana, William Lee from Montserrat, and Joseph Warner from Antigua.

The presence of black men on nineteenth-century Indian emigrant ships has often gone unrecognized in the historiography of the trade in bonded laborers, but Jeffrey Bolster shows that black men (African, African American, and African Caribbean) had a long history of maritime occupations. As he recently recorded, the stereotypical view that "blacks aboard ships sailed as commodities rather than seamen" needs to be overturned. He shows that even before the abolition of slavery, individual enslaved men routinely drew on maritime work to take charge of their lives or to communicate with distant blacks and that "free and enslaved black sailors established a visible presence in every North Atlantic seaport and plantation roadstead between 1740 and 1865." This was as true for African Americans as for African Caribbean men. In the United States, a shipping boom after the War for Independence created jobs for enslaved and freed African American men. Since "seafaring in the age of sail remained a contemptible occupation for white men, characterized by a lack of personal independence and reliance on paltry wages," according to Bolster, it became an occupation of opportunity for black men.[3]

Shipboard work for black men became less significant after the abolition of slavery in the United States when white men increasingly dominated this occupation, so many African American seamen sought jobs with English shipping companies, which helps to explain the presence of "yankee sailors" (a description applied to sailors who had served in the U.S. navy) aboard Indian emigrant ships. Robert Ipson, the "yankee sailor" mentioned above who served on the *Allanshaw* in 1885, was a native of Santa Cruz (St. Croix) in the former Danish Caribbean (now the U.S. Virgin Islands), reinforcing the fact that British merchant ships hired seamen from colonies outside of the British Caribbean.

It is also clear that throughout the nineteenth-century trade in migrant laborers, black men on emigrant ships were accused of rape. These accusations appeared in the reports of emigration officials and ships' surgeons. Some surgeons-superintendent even complained that black men were more likely than white men to molest women on board emigrant ships, and they used this argument to justify their call for a reduction in the numbers, or even the total elimination, of black men on their crews. They bolstered their argument with the usual ethnic stereotype that black men had an "incorrigible addictedness to sexual intercourse," as the surgeon-superintendent of the ship *Moy* asserted in 1891. He advised that "negroes [sic], if so employed, should be in a minority on a coolly [sic] emigrant ship."[4]

How accurate was this representation? One cannot deny that gender issues arising from indentured labor migration reflect not only white but also black and Indian masculinity in action. Indeed, the age of modernity was characterized by assumptions about women's subordination and men's superordination that cut across ethnic lines. The confined space of a ship, the usual comradeship among shipmates, and shared sexual stereotypes about Indian women would have heightened men's confidence and encouraged their antisocial behavior toward emigrant women. Both black and white males shared in the exercise of hegemonic masculinity, a term that refers to the culturally dominant form of masculinity that is constructed in relation to femininity as well as various subordinated masculinities. Hegemonic masculinity emerges as the configuration of gender practice legitimizes patriarchy and guarantees a dominant position for men alongside the subordination of women.[5] Hegemonic masculinity, of course, borrows from Antonio Gramsci's use of the concept of hegemony in his analysis of class relations and has come to mean a cultural dynamic by which a group claims and sustains a leading position in social relationships.[6] But although it is now generally accepted that there are different and often conflicting images of men and masculinity, certain masculinities are clearly favored. In the context of black/white relations, however, black masculinity is subordinated to white masculinity. So race mattered, and racism as a discriminatory tool against black sailors by the white crew, no doubt, kept such sailors cautious. Shared gender ideologies and assumptions, then, did not necessarily mean that black men were the main culprits in the sexploitation of women. Indeed, despite the claim that black men had a greater tendency to molest Indian women on nineteenth-century emigrant ships, a preliminary analysis of sexual abuse of emigrant women on ships shows that a higher proportion of complaints were directed at European men, some of whom were high-ranking officers.

The reports of the Guyana agents-general of immigration are replete with complaints of "misconduct" on the part of the surgeons-superintendent, captains, and other crew, for immigrants were usually encouraged to lodge such complaints on arrival in the colony. Such complaints were made against Dr. Wilkinson on the *Bucephalus,* Dr. Galbraith on the *Devonshire,* Mr. Simmonds on the *Royal George,* and Dr. Cook on the *Assaye.* The captain of the *Thetis* was said to have indicated that he had no intention of interfering when Indian women and sailors on the ship engaged in sex. In 1860 the surgeon-superintendent of the *Canning* lost part of his gratuity because he was accused of getting three women drunk so they could not testify against him. On that same ship, two sailors had "violently assaulted" women to have sex with them, yet no one found out who the individuals were so that they could be punished.[7]

Complains of "misconduct" continued to be made through the late nineteenth century. In 1871 the crew on the *Dovercastle* to Guyana was accused of "misconduct" toward the women on board.[8] Dr. Atkins, surgeon-superintendent on the ship *Silhet* to Guyana in 1882, was said to have formed a relationship with the female emigrant Janky, despite the fact that Deemohammed, a sirdar, had staked his claim to her previously. Predictably, Atkins was absolved of the allegation of "illicit intercourse" with Janky during the voyage and was later allowed to marry her, a highly unusual occurrence for the nineteenth century. In 1884 there were complaints that the drunken captain of the *Joravur* molested women. Similar complaints were made about the crew and the steward of the *Grecian* the following year.[9]

In 1885 the ship's cook on the *Hereford* was accused of being "the cause of a great deal of anxiety and trouble to the Surgeon." The surgeon discovered that the cook and the ship's engineer had used the Indian barber as an interpreter to allow them to communicate with the women on board. The cook had allegedly "pulled up a woman's clothes" as he passed along the deck. For this offense he was logged and fined. Eleven days later another report was made that "a girl named Yeruh was going up the poop ladder when the ship's cook came behind her. . . . [She] being afraid of him, as all the women are, he having several times interfered with them, in her efforts to get out of his way, slipped and fell." The cook tried to grab her to stop her fall and cut her thumb with his knife in the attempt. The surgeon deemed this an accident and did not fine the cook, even though it was the cook's actions that led to the fall and subsequent wounding.[10]

Dr. Hardwicke was charged with misconduct on the journey of the ship *Foyle* on which he served as surgeon-superintendent in 1886. The report of the agent-general of immigration (AGI) stated that Aladin, a male emigrant on the *Foyle,* complained on arrival in Guyana that Hardwicke had taken "indecent liberties" with his wife, Asserum.[11] It seemed that Aladin had formed an alliance (a kind of "depot marriage") with Asserum in Calcutta. In fact, he claimed that she had been "given" to him by her mother. They registered their "marriage" before the magistrate as required and lived as a couple on the voyage. Predictably, after a more detailed enquiry, the AGI claimed that Aladin could not prove that any sexual intercourse had taken place and that "all that Aladin could testify to was that on one occasion he saw Dr. Hardwicke sitting in the chart room with Asserum on his lap and with his hands on her breasts." Chamela, a female emigrant on the same ship, corroborated this, though she added that "I never saw him doing anything except holding her breasts outside her clothes." Asserum herself denied that

Hardwicke had molested her. She stated that Aladin had not treated her well on the voyage and, further, that she had never really slept with him and had no wish to live with him as his wife in Guyana or to be located on the same estate. In his defense, Dr. Hardwicke claimed, and the AGI seemed to believe him, that he was only treating Asserum the way he treated all children. The fact that she was someone's wife, although only fifteen years old, did not deter him.[12] The result of the enquiry was that Hardwicke was not penalized in any way, although the AGI conceded that the manner in which he treated Asserum was "objectionable" and he should be warned not to behave this way with a girl of that age.

Such complaints about surgeons, captains, and ordinary crew on emigrant ships were not confined to colonial Guyana, but occurred in Jamaica and Trinidad as well. An early case had come to light in 1861 on a voyage to Jamaica involving Dr. Prince, surgeon-superintendent of the *Ravenscraig*. He was accused of excessive drunkenness on the voyage and also of "criminal assaults" on some Indian women "under circumstances of an extremely aggravated nature." As usual in cases of alleged offenses committed before the Atlantic crossing, the ship stopped at St. Helena where the governor ruled that Prince should be sent to Jamaica under arrest and relieved of his duties. On arrival in Jamaica, however, the police magistrates and other officials released Prince on the basis that there was not enough evidence to convict him. They paid him his salary and gratuities as per his contract. The police magistrate and his supporters felt that even if such intercourse had taken place between Prince and the women on board, "it must have been with their consent."[13] How they came to this conclusion is unclear, but it was not unusual for lower-caste women from India, as was the case with African women enslaved in the Americas, to be regarded as loose and promiscuous and therefore incapable of being raped.

Reports of voyages to Trinidad also contained complaints about illicit intercourse between crew and emigrant women. In 1885 such complaints were made concerning the *Nerbuddah*. Similar complaints also originated among emigrants to Mauritius, and one Dr. R. Brown was actually dismissed from the Mauritius service after four voyages on charges of drunkenness and pulling off the clothes of female emigrants.[14]

These cases occurred despite elaborate attempts to prevent social contact between crew and human cargo in case the Indian labor trade was charged with constituting a new form of slavery.[15] The rape of enslaved women on Middle Passage slavers had been one of the most brutal manifestations of gendered tyranny during slavery. As a result, pro-immigration forces, concerned with avoiding any charge that Indian emigration was a new system of slavery, attempted to use legislation to prevent similar treatment of emigrant women. Strict rules regulated the conduct of the sailors toward the emigrants. For example, when they were mustered on board as the *Allanshaw* started its journey, the sailors were reminded that "any member of the crew found among the emigrants talking to, or interfering with, or molesting them in any way, will be fined one month's pay each offence." Ipson appears to have been reminded about this constantly by both the captain and surgeon-superintendent. Fraternizing between the crew and Indian women was especially forbidden. The hatchways were guarded, especially the section leading down to the single women's quarters. Men were forbidden to enter this section of the ship, and this applied to both fellow emigrants and crew whose quarters were usually in the forecastle, next to the prow. Some surgeons ensured that the decks below were well lit, especially the female section, to prevent what they termed "promiscuous intercourse," but the distance between regulations and practice was evident from the ships' records. Neither sexual segregation nor spatial organization nor the maintenance of a hierarchy among sailors and officers nor the putative separation of the different races (black, white, and Indian) on the ships protected Indian women from sexual violence.

Attempts were made to implicate individual black men on several occasions, although the accusations of rape directed at black men were often false, or at best highly suspect, colored as they were by white racism and the stereotypical representation of black people as naturally addicted to sex. In his summary of the data relating to the 1892–93 voyage of the *Avon* to Guyana, the AGI reported that it had come to his attention that Steed, an African crew member, "had so often been cautioned against interfering with or molesting the immigrants that the surgeon-superintendent, on arrival at St. Helena, requested the inspector of emigrants (IOE) to have [him] removed from the ship." The IOE refused to take such drastic action on the grounds that no evidence of actual assault had been presented, so no legal charge could be brought against Steed.[16]

## The Case of Maharani

Robert Ipson was similarly accused and acquitted of the rape of Maharani, a twenty-year-old Indian woman who embarked as an indentured laborer on the ship *Allanshaw,* bound for Guyana in 1885, but who died on 27 September 1885, several days after an alleged rape. Her death took place approximately eleven weeks after the ship had left Calcutta. Several investigations were launched into the case. In the course of the investigation into Maharani's ordeal, two sailors were accused of the incident: Ipson, a twenty-two-year-old black man, and James Oliver, a twenty-year-old "youth" from Bath in England.[17] While Ipson was openly accused and grilled about his involvement, Oliver was never even questioned officially, despite the fact that before she died, Maharani had supplied enough evidence to her friends to allow both men to be identified unambiguously. She had reportedly confided in her friend Mohadaya that "two sailors had connexion with her," and that "two sailors dragged her from the closet and had connexion with her on the deck."[18] She did not know the names of the sailors, but described them as best she could. She described one sailor as "a tallish stout man tattooed on his breast and wearing red shirt." As they had stuffed her sari in her mouth, she had been unable to cry out for help. When news of her death filtered through to the rest of the ship, fingers pointed at Ipson, who denied all charges. Not much attention seems to have been paid to the other alleged perpetrator.

Why was Robert Ipson accused of raping Maharani while James Oliver, similarly implicated, was never similarly accused? Ipson's testimony indicates that the answer must be sought in the racism of the nineteenth century and the legacy of the slavery mentalities that governed interethnic relations in the colonial Caribbean. Black masculinity as constructed by whites defined the black male as sexually incorrigible, violent, and depraved.

Race was never irrelevant aboard ships, for there was no love lost between European and non-European (especially African and Caribbean) crew, as was indicated by frequent conflicts and the equally frequent requests by the surgeons-superintendent that black crew members be replaced by Europeans. As Bolster observes, "Black men understood

that among sailors, race worked in an ambiguous and sometimes contradictory fashion." So, in general, while seafaring was a way of escaping
discrimination in postslavery societies and facilitating upward social
mobility, certain roles on the ships were also assigned to blacks on racial
grounds. On the Indian emigrant ships, while black men never held the
lowliest positions, which seemed to have been reserved for subaltern
Indian men for cultural reasons (for example, Indians would never agree
to black men cooking their food), they tended to be rank-and-file seamen rather than officers. But even as seamen, they held some position of
authority over the bonded laborers on board. Still, while black men may
have felt superior to their "culturally alien" "human cargo," they were
keenly aware of the racial hierarchy vis-à-vis the European crew. Bolster
records that black men often suffered disproportionately the capricious
nature of shipboard punishments and discipline. Despite collective work
and an easy familiarity between non-European sailors and their white
shipmates, social identities still were conditioned significantly by race;
many white seamen just did not like nonwhite seamen.[19]

Ipson's claim that he had been singled out for particular attention
by the *Allanshaw*'s officers might therefore be true as well as his claim
that some Indian emigrants deliberately lied about his involvement, for
it is undeniable that interracial prejudices colored interethnic relations
on board nineteenth-century Indian emigrant ships. Nevertheless, Ipson
was freed of the charge against him after four investigations. The first
investigation was conducted on the ship, but Ipson was never questioned
at that first evidence-gathering inquiry conducted by the surgeon-superintendent, who preferred to submit the evidence in the case to the
officials at St. Helena in the hope that they would take action.

On the *Allanshaw*'s arrival at St. Helena on 9 October 1885, the colonial secretary, in his capacity as emigration agent, boarded the ship
to inspect the immigrants and to receive the reports of the captain and
surgeon-superintendent concerning the voyage from Calcutta. He in-
spected the ship, which he found in satisfactory condition, and accepted
the officers' assurances that every precaution had been used to "protect
the Coolies from the seamen." The emigrants made no complaint against
the captain and surgeon and did not mention any of the abuses they
had suffered at the hands of the crew that were recorded in the ship's log
book. The surgeon-superintendent reported the women's charge against

Ipson based on what Maharani had confided before her death as well as his own actions in the case. The colonial secretary at once communicated with Colonel Blunt, the acting governor of St. Helena, as well as with the crown prosecutor. Although all three listened carefully to the outline of the case presented by the captain and surgeon, the crown prosecutor decided that evidence from Moorti, Mohadaya, Rupia, and others was not sufficient to charge Ipson with rape leading to Maharani's death or to delay the ship for more detailed investigation. He advised that further investigation should be carried out after the ship arrived in Guyana if it was deemed necessary. This went against the views of the captain, the colonial secretary, and the surgeon-superintendent, who all wished Ipson to be placed in confinement or under some form of restraint.[20]

On 6 November 1885 the *Allanshaw* docked in Georgetown harbor in Guyana with 370 men, 178 women, 30 boys, 33 girls, and 41 infants for a total of 652 immigrants, after what the surgeon admitted was a long passage of 102 days.[21] The AGI, A. H. Alexander, was informed of the death of Maharani and the suspicions against Ipson. Again, Oliver's name was not mentioned. On the captain's recommendation, Alexander immediately ordered Ipson's arrest on suspected manslaughter and turned him over to the police, who proceeded to gather evidence and prepare the case for prosecution. Wright, a police inspector, stated that he had charged Ipson because he "unlawfully and feloniously did kill and slay one Maharani—against the Peace of our Sovereign Lady the Queen Her Crown and Dignity." Wright gathered evidence from Captain Wilson, Dr. Hardwicke, and some of the sailors and other crew members.[22]

The case against Ipson was tried in the City Police Court in Georgetown before His Worship, Henry Kirke,[23] an experienced magistrate and sheriff of Demerara, beginning on Friday, 6 November 1885, and lasting just over a week. The theory of the prosecution, led by Wright, was based on the statement said to have been made by Maharani herself about having been violently seized, gagged, and raped. He also used various testimonies, including that of an emigrant, Ramyadd, who said that Ipson had said to him, "Before we reach Demerara, I must f—— one of these girls." Ipson denied this, claiming that he had only had sex with a woman in St. Helena.[24]

Despite all of the attempts to link Ipson to the crime, the evidence was deemed inconclusive, much of it hearsay, and Kirke acquitted him, citing circumstantial evidence.[25] His view was that "the case for the prosecution was founded on the supposition that the defendant had outraged the woman and [the] evidence [presented] went rather to contradict than support that supposition." On the basis of the surgeon-superintendent's testimony, Kirke ruled that "if the deceased had been ill-treated by accused as the evidence of the witness alleged, one would expect to find corresponding injuries on the deceased," but no such injuries had been found. As none of the witnesses had presented direct evidence to convince him that rape had been perpetrated, Kirke threw out the case instead of sending it forward for trial by jury. Ipson, however, was arrested on a charge of disobeying "the lawful command of the captain of the *Allanshaw* on the 15th October" and for stealing twenty yards of canvas valued at $6.48 belonging to James Nurse, another crew member. Ipson was sentenced to four weeks in prison for the charge of disobeying the captain and three weeks in prison or a fine of $6.00 for stealing the canvas.[26] Five other "refractory seamen"—J. Smith, J. Allickson, G. Sutherland, J. Bayne, and J. Peterson—had already been accused of this offense. Allickson was acquitted, but the other four were each sentenced to one month's imprisonment. Smith, who had also assaulted the captain, was sentenced to a further ten weeks in prison. Along with Bayne, Smith got yet another month's term on a third charge of disobeying the captain on 5 September 1885. Although Ipson's case had been deferred, he was charged and later sentenced and fined.[27]

Nevertheless, the Colonial Office ordered Governor Henry Irving of Guyana to conduct an investigation. He appointed a commission of inquiry, declaring that "there still remained grounds for a suspicion that the death of this woman had been caused by one or more men having had connexion with her, and that Robert Ipson had been prominently concerned in it." The commission was chaired by the AGI, A. H. Alexander. The other members were Dr. Robert Grieve, acting medical officer to the immigration department (and later acting surgeon-general), Kirke (the police magistrate who had already dismissed the case against Ipson), and the lawyer for the ship's owners. The commissioners met for nine days and examined twenty-two witnesses, among whom were the captain and Grant (who were both called more than once), Hardwicke, Captain Wilson, Golap (the nurse), W. Urquhart (the sailmaker), Heerdayaram (the hospital doctor), James Grant (the assistant compounder), several of the forty-one crew members (sailors and officers), including Ipson, a select number of male and female fellow emigrants (including Moorti and Mohadaya), and the Georgetown medical doctor, Alexander Finlayson, with whom Grant had had conversation considered relevant to the investigation. The statements of the witnesses were taken under oath and recorded by the secretary to the commission. Those who were literate in English signed their statements to indicate their correctness, but those who were not (mostly first-time emigrants) had the statement read to them and signed with an X. At the end of the nine-day hearing on 12 December 1885, the commissioners dismissed the case. Summarizing the evidence, the chairman concluded that "a great amount of the evidence is mere hearsay, and quite inadmissible in a Court of Justice," a view opposed by Dr. Grieve, who firmly believed that Ipson was guilty of rape and that Maharani had indeed died from the effects of the rape. The decision of the majority was never overturned.[28]

And what of Maharani in all of this? Despite the elaborate inquiries, the cause of her death still seems unclear. According to the physicians that I consulted, rape itself, though an extremely violent act, is insufficient to cause death unless the rapist sets out deliberately to murder the victim. They believe that the most likely scenario was that as a result of the rape, a virulent infection such as streptococcus or gram negative bacterial infection was introduced into the vagina and from there into the cervix and uterus. The postmortem indicated "inflammation in or near the womb" or peritonitis. This could have led to a toxic shock condition, which in the absence of antibiotics at that time caused rapid death; the symptoms as given by the surgeon did indicate that Maharani's condition deteriorated rapidly. The severe fever that Maharani developed was consistent with the type of infection described. Such virulent bacteria could have been carried by an asymptomatic person in his nose, throat, or on his hands.[29]

The question of who raped Maharani remains equally problematic, with opinions divided about Ipson's involvement. Why, despite the accusation against Oliver, was the latter never even questioned or, like Ipson, made to prove his guilt or innocence? Did the obvious white prejudice and stereotype about black men's sexuality make Ipson an easier target? Was Ipson correct that he was being made a scapegoat for other people's wrongs simply because of his tendency to be intolerant of discrimination on the ship? Of greater significance, if he was indeed guilty, how was he so lucky to escape conviction within the context of a postslavery "justice" system riddled with racism? Any suggestion that a fair justice system existed in the nineteenth-century Caribbean must be taken with caution. David Trotman has noted that in the Caribbean at that time there was a tendency for judges to believe the rape accusations of women against men of color because "in the minds of many Whites, rape by an accused African or Indian man was quite believable given prevalent racist beliefs that darker peoples suffered from uncontrollable passions."[30] Brian Moore has also underscored the hypocrisy in colonial Guyana where despite the immoral behavior of some whites toward Indian women, white elites continued to pose as the moral (as well as political) guardians of Caribbean society and to ascribe looser morals to non-Europeans.[31] Was the outcome the result of gender solidarity in a Victorian, patriarchal society that cut across ethnic lines? This would surely go against all the evidence that testifies to the discriminatory practices of elites against nonelites of all genders in the postslavery Caribbean. Ipson might simply have benefited from the socioeconomic context of the time, where the feared economic effects of a discontinuation of Indian immigration filled the planter class and its supporters with dread and where racism made the acceptance of evidence by the "subaltern" Indians unlikely.

The answer could also lie in the social context of the nineteenth century when convictions in rape cases lagged behind acquittals, causing many rape incidents to go unreported because of the difficulty of securing convictions. Trotman notes that in postslavery Trinidad, the acquittal rate for rape increased between 1870 and 1899. More specifically, between 1893 and 1899, seventy-seven cases were tried of which 46 percent ended in conviction and 24 percent were thrown out.[32] That rape was treated as a capital crime in the Caribbean as in Europe was not in doubt.[33] And the definition was universal: "the imposition of intercourse by force; unlawful sexual intercourse with a female person without her consent."[34] But in the Caribbean, as in other parts of the world, the tendency was to blame women for any sexual abuse that they may have experienced unless they could prove beyond doubt that they had cried out or made some attempt to resist the attacker. This was why eyewitness accounts that a struggle had ensued between Maharani and her attacker(s) were so crucial to the commission of enquiry. Some emigrants and seamen did try to present such evidence. William Lee and James Grant both testified that they had heard some sort of struggle or "scuffle" on the night Maharani claimed to have been raped, with Lee having even seen Ipson with his hand on her shoulder. Another witness, Chitamun, stated that he had seen someone taking a woman like Maharani to the forecastle. But despite this, two of the commissioners were not convinced. The fact that Maharani did not survive to tell her own story further affected the case. Thus the official report of the commissioners ruled that there was no evidence of a scuffle or that anybody had held Maharani to enable a crew member or crew members to commit such an assault.

Perhaps if the medical evidence had been more supportive of the crime, the commissioners might have ruled differently; however, they relied heavily on the evidence of the surgeon-superintendent, ruling that "even the appearance of the woman after death repudiated the idea that she had been criminally assaulted by any man." This, of course, was contrary to Dr. Robert Grieve's professional opinion as a member of the commission of inquiry. Nevertheless, they preferred to believe that if Maharani had been taken to the forecastle of the ship, this had occurred without her "struggling or attempting to cry out," and that while there Ipson and others of the crew "had connexion with her, if not with full, at least with forced consent on her part, the latter being more probable from the previous modest retiring character of the woman," and the fact that she had gone to the toilet by herself and had not told anyone in authority about her having been assaulted. Obviously (but curiously), "forced consent" was not equated with rape.

## Notes

1. Shepherd, *Maharani's Misery*.
2. For further information on the Indian indentureship system and a profile of the immigrants, see Laurence, *A Question of Labour*; Shepherd, *Transients to Settlers*; and Shepherd, *Women in Caribbean History*.
3. Bolster, *Black Jacks*, 2, 4.
4. Report of protector of immigrants, Jamaica, 18 June 1891, enclosure in Jamaica dispatch #196, Sir Henry Arthur Blake, officer administering the government, to Baron Knutsford, 22 June 1891, National Archives, Kew [hereafter NA].
5. Parry, "Sex and Gender Constructions in the Jamaican Classroom," 77.

6. Gramsci, *Selections from the Prison Notebooks*. See also Gramsci, "Some Aspects of the Southern Question."

7. Correspondence/Letter Books, Colonial Land and Emigration Commission [hereafter CLEC], pp. 95–105, CO 386, NA.

8. Murdoch to R. H. McCade, 8 January 1873, CO 386/97, NA.

9. Correspondence/Letter Books, CLEC, pp. 95–105, CO 386, NA.

10. Ibid.

11. Report of the agent general of immigration [hereafter AGI], enclosure in British Guiana dispatch #303, Irving to Stanhope, 11 November 1886, CO 386/161, NA.

12. Asserum's age was misrepresented on the ship's list as eighteen. This should have been known to the surgeon-superintendent.

13. S. Walcott, CLEC, to A. McGregor, 26 February 1861, CO 386/135, vol. 2, NA.

14. Emigration dispatches, West Indies, CO 384/135–192: 1881–1896, NA.

15. For more on the Indian labor trade, see Tinker, *A New System of Slavery*.

16. AGI report, 10 February 1893, enclosure in British Guiana dispatch #35, Gormanston to Ripon, 21 February 1893, CO 384/186, NA.

17. Crew list of the *Allanshaw,* Maritime Museum, Newfoundland, Canada.

18. Maharaja's testimony, enclosure in CO 384/160, NA.

19. Bolster, *Black Jacks,* 69, 93.

20. Ibid., 93–101.

21. Report of G. A. Banbury, emigration officer, St. Helena, 8 October 1885, enclosures 5 and 6, J. C. Homagee, law officer of the crown, St. Helena, to acting colonial secretary, Court House, St. Helena, 9 October 1885; *Allanshaw* ship's log, October 1885, in Co 384/160, British Guiana dispatch #56, Gov. Irving to the Earl of Granville, 1 March 1886, NA.

22. "Alleged Outrage on the High Seas," *Daily Chronicle,* 7 November 1885; *Royal Gazette,* 13, 18, and 19 November 1885.

23. Henry Kirke lived in Guyana from 1872 until 1897. He was sheriff of Essequibo from 1887 to 1892. Previously he had been a government emigration agent in India at the depot in Garden Reach. He claimed to have had great familiarity with and expertise in criminal law, having acted as judge of the Supreme Court for twelve periods and three times as attorney-general. According to him, "There is not a crime in the statute book with which I have not had to deal." But he does not list rape among them. See Kirke, *Twenty-five Years in British Guiana,* 291ff.

24. "Alleged Outrage on the High Seas," *Daily Chronicle,* 7 November 1885; *Royal Gazette,* 13 November 1885, 4.

25. *Royal Gazette,* 18 November 1885, 3.

26. *Daily Chronicle,* 19 November and 6 December 1885.

27. *Royal Gazette,* 9 November 1885, 4, and 18 November 1885, 3.

28. Ibid.

29. Comments from Dr. Kamla Dixon and Dr. S. Wynter.

30. Trotman, "Women and Crime in Late Nineteenth-Century Trinidad," 254.

31. Moore, *Cultural Power, Resistance, and Pluralism,* 36–42, 102–103.

32. Trotman, "Women and Crime," 254.

33. For an extended discussion, see Vigarello, *A History of Rape*.

34. Cahill, *Rethinking Rape,* 10–11.

# References

Bolster, W. Jeffrey. *Black Jacks: African American Seamen in the Age of Sail.* Cambridge: Harvard University Press, 1997.

Cahill, Ann. *Rethinking Rape.* Ithaca: Cornell University Press, 2001.

Gramsci, Antonio. *Selections from the Prison Notebooks.* Trans. and ed. Quintin Hoare and Geoffrey Nowell Smith. London: International, 1971.

———. "Some Aspects of the Southern Question." Trans. and ed. Quintin Hoare. *Selections from Political Writing, 1921–1926.* New York: International, 1978.

Kirke, Henry. *Twenty-five Years in British Guiana.* London: Sampson Low, Marston, 1898; reprint, Westport, Conn.: Negro Universities Press, 1970.

Laurence, K. O. *A Question of Labour.* Kingston: Ian Randle, 1994.

Moore, Brian. *Cultural Power, Resistance, and Pluralism.* Kingston: University of West Indies Press, 1995.

Parry, Odette. "Sex and Gender Constructions in the Jamaican Classroom." *Social and Economic Studies* 45 (1996): 77–93.

Shepherd, Verene A. *Transients to Settlers.* Leeds: Peepal Tree Press, 1994.

———. *Maharani's Misery: Narratives of a Passage from India to the Caribbean.* Kingston: University of the West Indies Press, 2002.

———, ed. *Women in Caribbean History.* Kingston: Ian Randle, 1999.

Tinker, Hugh. *A New System of Slavery.* London: Oxford University Press for the Institute of Race Relations, 1974.

Trotman, David. "Women and Crime in Late Nineteenth-Century Trinidad." In *Caribbean Freedom,* ed. Hilary Beckles and Verene A. Shepherd, 251–59. Kingston: Ian Randle, 1993.

Vigarello, Georges. *A History of Rape.* Cambridge: Polity Press, 2001.

# 6

# Maria Jones of Africa, St. Vincent, and Trinidad

BRINSLEY SAMAROO

On a particularly cold day in January 2001, I was in the basement archive of the Angus Library at Regent's College, Oxford, reading the Caribbean records of the Baptist Missionary Society (BMS). I was following some leads regarding BMS work among the freed Africans in Trinidad. I came across a series of pamphlets published in Trinidad in 1851 by the Haversfordwest Mission Press located in Port of Spain. The gem of the collection was *Maria Jones: Her History in Africa and in the West Indies*. Upon reading the text I discovered that Maria Jones had lived most of her life in Trinidad and that she had spent many years on the Palmiste estate, a place where I had wandered extensively during my teenage years. The sugar cane villages that surrounded the Palmiste estate were so familiar that I felt I could relive Maria's experience in Palmiste. The pamphlet reminded me of the lives of Olaudah Equiano and Mary Prince, whose accounts of their experience of slavery left one so much sadder but so much wiser. Since January 2001, I have visited and revisited Palmiste, now with more seeing eyes, in an effort to give meaning to the life and times of Maria Jones. In this chapter, I will present a few vignettes of that fascinating story.

Maria's story differs from those of Olaudah Equiano and Mary Prince in that she does not tell her story herself.[1] Her account is biographical, told by the Baptist missionary John Law, who places Maria's life in the context of the work of the Baptist Church. A second source of information about Maria Jones comes from another BMS missionary, Reverend Edward Bean Underhill, who was dispatched to the Caribbean "to investigate the religious condition of the numerous Baptist churches which have been formed in the islands of the West, especially as that condition has been affected by the Act of Emancipation."[2] Eager to promote the achievements of his church in the region, he sought out and highlighted the Christian activities of former slaves. Topping the list of Africans in Trinidad was Maria Jones, whom he met in 1860 when she was "about eighty years of age."[3] Although she was "now aged and ill-able to walk," Maria visited Underhill and his wife several times during their stay in Port of Spain. When they parted for the last time, Underhill commended her Christian zeal as "she awaits death's summons to be forever with the Lord." From these two sources, the first published in 1851 and the second in 1862, we can estimate the chronology of Maria Jones's life. Born around 1780 on the west coast of Africa, "she was seized by some of those wretches who steal and sell their fellow men for slaves" while playing with her friends in the bush not far from their huts.[4] At the time of enslavement she was only seven years old, but in 1851, at the age of seventy, she clearly remembered the traumatic event. This account of the method used to capture and sell African children is corroborated by Olaudah Equiano. Because of its frequency, one of the youths would climb a tree to look out for human predators.[5]

There is no account in Maria Jones's story of the journey in coffles from the interior to the coast. We have to depend on Equiano for that harrowing tale. Nor did Maria's Baptist biographer consider it necessary to ask her about the dreadful Middle Passage from Africa to the New World, but we can get an idea of what it may have been like by reading the account of the voyage of the *Sandown* that took place in 1793–94, about the same time as Maria's Caribbean journey.[6]

If Maria was captured at the age of seven, then that year would probably have been 1787. The slaver that transported Maria to the Caribbean landed at St. Vincent, where she was sold to the captain of a small trading vessel. Her stay in St. Vincent was not long. Apparently her master found her to be too independent: "She had a very high spirit, which was not easily subdued. . . . All through her life of slavery she showed much strength and independence of mind, and would often utter sentiments and feelings which proved that she did not willingly submit to the yolk imposed on her."[7] So for a few years she remained "the unprofitable slave of her first owner." It is unlikely that Maria's first owner would have sold her only because of her high spirits, for Caribbean slave owners had devised sufficiently brutal methods of taming such recalcitrance. The whip, the branding iron, or dismal incarceration had become well-tried devices. What seems more likely was that the precarious state of the Vincentian economy during the last two decades of the eighteenth century rendered the maintenance of slaves a liability and too burdensome for their owners. The British had established an administration for the colony as early as 1672, but their tenure was often contested by the French or by the indigenous Caribs. The eighteenth century was particularly turbulent, and although the island was restored to the British by the peace of Versailles in 1783, that peace was tenuous and did not last long. With the onset of the French Revolution in 1789, the doctrines of republicanism spread from San Domingue to St. Vincent's neighbor Martinique, which enjoyed a thriving trade with the Caribs. The Caribs and their French allies again overran St. Vincent, burning the cane fields, plundering the houses, and killing the English colonists.

As late as 1795 the colony experienced violence and instability. By this time African slaves had joined the Caribs in resisting British hegemony, actively encouraged by Victor Hugues, the delegated commissary of the National Convention to the Windward Islands. From his power base in Guadeloupe, Hugues encouraged slaves and Caribs to "Attack! Exterminate all the English in St. Vincent, but give means to the French to second you." In a 1795 report, the British commanders in the region stated that "in the colony of St. Vincent . . . the specimens of republican hostility have been equally outrageous, sanguinary, and unprecedented."[8]

Compared with St. Vincent, Trinidad was a paradise. Neglected by the Spaniards, who were more interested in precious metals on the mainland, the colony was ideal for agriculture in the late eighteenth century. Its fresh soils and large expanses of cultivable land beckoned refugees from San Dominigue and would-be settlers from the older settlements northeast of Trinidad. Even before its capture by the British in 1797, a cedula had been granted to a wealthy Grenadian royalist, Roume de St. Laurent, in 1783. This permit allowed St. Laurent to bring French settlers to the then Spanish colony. By 1786 Trinidad was "still a Spanish possession, [but] had become almost entirely French in population."[9] As

British planters moved to Trinidad from the beginning of the nineteenth century, the demand for slaves shot up.

St. Vincent was a major source of slaves, and the chief supplier was Louis Bicaise, a French Creole who was born in St. Vincent in 1776 and who died in Trinidad in 1838. In 1810, Bicaise, in partnership with his brother-in-law, founded La Ressource Estate in South Naparima and went to live there with his family in 1812. Within a short time he became the sole owner.[10] Bicaise brought slaves to his estate at La Ressource and sold slaves to neighboring plantations, including Palmiste. Quite likely Maria was one of the slaves he brought to Trinidad; the evidence points strongly in that direction. Her biography states that she was sold to the Palmiste estate, where she worked alongside "other Negroes." Although the biography does not give details regarding the owner of the estate, it does provide sufficient information for us to trace the career of her boss, "the young Scotchman who was just commencing his career as a planter."[11] That young Scotchman was none other than John Lamont, who had come to Trinidad very early in the nineteenth century as "a penniless younger son."[12] During Maria's time at Palmiste, Lamont was just beginning his upward climb and had passed the first administrative rung on the estate hierarchy from the position of overseer to that of manager on the estate, which he did not yet own. In 1819 he bought his first estate of 360 acres. By the time of his death in 1850, when Maria would have been about seventy, he owned large estates in the north and the south of the island. His son, Sir Norman Lamont, inherited his property.

Maria's biography claims that the manager John Lamont did not treat her cruelly because her spirit of independence raised his fear that she could induce a similar spirit in the other slaves. He therefore "promoted" her as a house slave doing domestic chores, even allowing her to talk to him in a manner that he did not normally allow. After some years at Palmiste, Maria was transferred to another of the Lamont properties—Mount Pleasant—just north of the ancient Nepoio settlement of Arima. There she labored until she obtained emancipation in 1838 and continued to reside for another decade. Maria was about 58 years of age when she was emancipated.

What were the options available to Maria upon emancipation? For her, as well as for thousands of others, the options were rather limited. They could squat on crown lands, as many did, opening up villages to which they gave African names: Krooman Village, Sierra Leone, or Congo Hill. Others drifted away from the plantations to urban centers where they worked as porters, stevedores, sailors, or tradesmen. For the women there was the option of working in planter houses as servants. Conversion to Christianity conferred an immediate advantage, for a planter's wife preferred a Christian African to a non-Christian, and the planter himself looked more favorably on a Christian "boy" to look after his horses than a non-Christian. Maria chose to become Christian, possibly because she saw conversion as a means to upward social mobility in a society where such levers were few.

For this remarkable woman, emancipation, even at an advanced age, was no reason for retirement. In 1840 she presented herself to the Mico Charity School at Mt. Pleasant to get an education. She was one of the very early Mico students in Trinidad, and her biography sheds useful light on the early operation of this system. This charity was one of the major funders of the Negro Education Grant paid out by the imperial government for the education of apprentices and newly freed slaves. It originated in a bequest by Lady Mico, an English noblewoman who in 1690 seemed so concerned about the proper marriage of her nieces that she promised £2,000 to her nephew Samuel on condition that he should marry one of them. As an added inducement she also promised her best pearl necklace and all of her plate. In the event of Samuel's refusal to accept this dynastic alliance, the money was to be used to ransom Christians captured by the Barbary pirates. As things turned out, Samuel pursued other objectives and the Barbary pirates were subdued by European military might. By 1834 this bequest had accumulated considerable interest, and the following year it was made available "to the religious and moral instruction of the Negroes and coloured population in the colonies."[13]

The Mico Charity went about its work with considerable enthusiasm. It opened nondenominational, but clearly Protestant, schools throughout the British Caribbean. The charity also aimed to counter Roman Catholic influence in colonies where such influence was present. By 1838, when it started a normal school for the training of teachers, it was already operating day schools, Sunday schools, and evening schools. The day schools ran for three full days each week, and pupils paid a weekly attendance of two and a quarter pence. By 1839, it had established fourteen schools in Trinidad with 1,356 pupils, including 500 adults. Two years later, the number of schools had increased to twenty-one. These schools promoted the education of the ex-slave population, but they were doomed to failure because the majority of the colony's churches rejected the "secular" character of their education. The Mico system was too far ahead of its time! Although the system had broken down by 1845, Governor George Harris, with great tact and diplomacy, instituted a secular system of education in 1851 modeled on the Mico system.

According to her biographer, Maria was the oldest student at Mt. Pleasant Mico School. Although "aged and infirm, and apparently unpromising," she was a persistent scholar. Assigned to the evening class with the adults who paid no fees, she insisted on joining the day class, too, paying the weekly fee of two and a quarter pence. Her teacher, a member of the Scottish Presbyterian Church in Trinidad, saw in Maria a good prospect for Presbyterian conversion, although she was a practicing Roman Catholic.

The Scottish Presbyterian Church opened its first Trinidad branch in January 1836 in response to appeals from Scottish planters. Reverend Alexander Kennedy was the first pastor, a confirmed abolitionist, and so a poor choice from the planters' point of view. He was not too happy about the morality of his congregation. In his sermons in Trinidad and while on furlough in Scotland, he never failed to chastise the plantocracy for its treatment of slaves. He seemed like a later Antonio de Montesinos, the Dominican friar who in 1511 had similarly berated the Spanish *encomenderos*. Kennedy's biographer notes that when he returned from furlough in 1841, he "found that he had lost much of his congregation; however, because he championed the cause of the underprivileged blacks, they always filled his church to over-flowing."[14]

Kennedy served as an administrator with the Mico Charity, noting in 1839 that "I therefore hail with joy the establishment of schools on the broad basis of Christianity without reference to religious creed." In his mission work, he dared to go into areas that other missionaries avoided: Belmont (then Freetown Valley), Carenage, St. James, Dry River, Arouca, and San Fernando. Apparently it was Kennedy who dispatched Maria's Presbyterian teacher to Mt. Pleasant. Her biography describes her teacher's pastor as "Mr. K.," who paid occasional visits to Mt. Pleasant, preaching to the Africans there.

During this period of her life, Maria joined the Presbyterian Church. Kennedy not only accepted her eagerly but also performed a marriage ceremony between Maria and one Mr. Jones with whom she had lived for many years. From this time Maria made it known that she was no longer plain Maria but "Mrs. Jones and not Maria, as before time. This she said, purposely, in the hearing of several other females present," her biographer wrote, "turning to them as she spoke, as though anxious to improve the occasion by provoking them to go and do likewise."[15] For several years Maria maintained "a holy walk" with the Presbyterian Church. Although she resided some fourteen miles away from the city, she rarely ever missed the main services. At times she would spend up to a week in Port of Spain attending church services and functions, staying at the homes of church members there. Her religious enthusiasm had drawn the attention of the Baptists, who increasingly came to look upon her as a prize for baptism.

The BMS opened its Trinidad mission in 1843 when a former employee of the Mico Charity, Reverend George Cowen, sensing the demise of the charity, started a Baptist church in Port of Spain. Underhill, the aforementioned Baptist minister who visited Trinidad in 1860, reflected on the dire need that existed in the immediate postslavery era for "proper" instruction of the ex-slaves. He viewed the Roman Catholic Church, which had the largest number of adherents, as particularly harmful: "Superstitious practices, partly of Romish, partly of Pagan origin, everywhere prevailed. No progress had been made since emancipation in remedying the evils produced by slavery. As in other lands, the influence of Romanism was not merely obstructive to the spread of divine truth, its gross superstition had driven many intelligent young men into infidelity."[16]

To right these wrongs, Cowen started off by purchasing with BMS funds the Mico headquarters in Port of Spain. Soon he established a chapel and school at Dry River, a suburb. In 1846 he moved from the north of the island to the southeast, where he opened a mission among American Baptists who were part of the demobilized southern United States soldiers who had fought for Britain in the War of 1812. This mission was established just beyond Savanna Grande (near modern Princes Town), where the Cowen-Hamilton Secondary School is situated today, named after Cowen and another Baptist pioneer.

From 1845 to 1870, the Trinidad Baptist mission was joined by Reverend John Law, whose Welsh countrymen in Haverfordwest in County Pembrokeshire provided him with a press that he named the Haverfordwest Mission Press. Law's major purpose was the unrelenting chastisement of popery wherever it existed. The collection of which Maria's biography forms a part is filled with virulent anti–Roman Catholic propaganda. Luckily, he was writing in a British colony, beyond the reach of Roman Catholics. Although Maria's biography does not name Law as its author, the style of the piece closely matches his signed essays.

Cowen first met Maria at the Mico Sabbath school. She was introduced by her Presbyterian teacher as "a most remarkable woman, quite an original character, of a strong, sound understanding."[17] Law, who must have been present at this meeting, reported that "Mr. Cowen was greatly struck with her at this first interview; and continued to admire her in an increased degree, as he saw her progress in grace, under the sanctifying teaching of the spirit of God." From this time Cowen seemed determined to separate this devout Christian from the Presbyterian faith, but he hesitated to be seen poaching from another Protestant denomination. So over a period of months, he gradually wooed her, explaining the advantages of the Baptist faith, but never neglecting to tell her that she should convert only after she had thought and prayed over the matter. He even suggested that she could discuss the problem with her Presbyterian pastor.

Maria did. Finally she informed him that she wished to be baptized in the "same fashion as blessed Saviour," that is, by immersion, and she wanted him (the Presbyterian) to perform the ceremony. The Presbyterian minister lost out in the battle for this soul because he failed to appreciate the significance that many Africans attached to the ceremony. In her work on missionaries and slaves in Jamaica, Mary Turner comments on the profoundly symbolic meanings of this occasion. It recaptured, even for a brief space, many African slave aspirations: ritual, religious fervor, the missionary's personal attention, and time spent away from the plantation:

> The splendid ceremony in which Baptist candidates were admitted to membership encapsulated all the comforts the mission churches afforded the slaves. The candidates and their friends assembled in the chapel the night before the baptism. No service could be held, but it was understood that this was a time for solemn meditation. In the very early hours of

the morning the missionary joined them for prayer; then, before sunrise, the company moved to the nearest river or seashore. The candidates, all robed in white, were assembled by their class leaders while the missionary waded waist-deep into the water and the ceremony began.[18]

To the staid Presbyterian minister, all of this was of no account. His view was that he had already baptized Maria by sprinkling, so to immerse her now would be to baptize her twice, which, he said, was wrong. Such cold reasoning did not make much sense to Maria, and so she returned to Cowen. As soon as this pastor had satisfied himself that Maria had come to this decision of her own free will, he agreed to do the baptism by immersion. For Maria Jones this was a grand occasion:

> Mr. and Mrs. Cowen walked through the town with this devoted disciple, to the waterside; and there in the presence of a crowd of spectators, she was "buried with Christ by baptism" rejoicing that she had such an opportunity to testify her affection for him who endured for her reproach and sufferings of the cross.[19]

At this point the Baptist-inspired biography of Maria Jones comes to an end, with Maria exulting in her newfound faith, subsequently being received into the fellowship of the Baptist Church in Port of Spain. It was here that Underhill met her in 1860.

The story of Maria Jones raises a number of interesting issues about the transition from slavery to freedom in the Caribbean. For one thing, the prospect of freedom for the African population in the region whetted the appetites of Christian missionaries who saw a vast horde of "heathens" in desperate need of conversion to Christianity and to proper, civilized behavior. Journals published for this period warned of the dire consequences of leaving former slaves to manage on their own and stressed the need for an earlier version of the white man's burden. The Society for the Propagation of the Gospel in Foreign Parts, for example, was particularly worried about the impending moral degeneracy of freed Caribbean people:

> It is to be feared that many of the Negroes of British Guiana at least, if not of those in the large islands of Jamaica and Trinidad, are becoming morally worse, rather than otherwise, through the ill effects of the idle life encouraged by the extreme productiveness of the soil, as well as by the ruinous habit of promiscuous squatting on waste lands of many abandoned estates.[20]

Economic considerations now became intertwined with morality. Even the Scottish Presbyterian pioneer Alexander Kennedy, for all his antislavery conviction, did not have a high opinion of his wards: "with a few honourable exceptions, the black and coloured population are notoriously ignorant and unblushingly immoral."[21] The moral degeneracy referred to was the fear that the freed African, away from the control of the plantation system, would revert to the practice of transported African culture, including the worship of Sango and other Yoruba orisa, and Islam. Not only did they view such practices as un-Christian and therefore reprehensible; they also feared that they might be rallying points for resistance. The missionaries were mainly willing upholders of the plantation system and did their utmost to stamp out all forms of heathenism. Tied in with this low opinion of the black character was the missionaries' elevated view of themselves and their divinely ordained mission.

Reverend William Hamilton Gamble, who joined the Baptist mission in Trinidad in 1856 and stayed for three decades, had no doubt about his role:

> It is passing strange but the blacks are averse to their own colour; they will do their own colour what they would never think or dream of doing a white man. A white face is a host in itself—it can do what a black one cannot. Any but a white face as a minister is not appreciated. . . . I may mention that all the Churches have white men for their pastors.[22]

Fired by this missionary zeal, they came to the islands in droves, actively competing against each other for converts, even poaching their rivals' promising black Christians. Many missionaries brought their European rivalries to the Caribbean, creating schism among the population, particularly between Roman Catholics and Protestants. Established in Port of Spain in 1850, the Haversfordwest Missionary was set up with the specific purpose of denouncing popery, which in turn struck back with equal ferocity. Each side, of course, felt that they were acting in the name of the highest Christian principles! Such religious conflict was the cause of much interdenominational bitterness well into the twentieth century. So keen were these religious groups to propagate their particular theology that they joined forces to squash the commendable efforts of the Mico Charity to promote secular education in the Caribbean. After the 1850s, secular education took place through state fiat, even as the religious groups insisted on the privilege of operating their own schools parallel to the state schools and demanding state aid for their efforts. People like Maria Jones were caught, unwittingly, within this maelstrom of warring religious factions. Unable to perceive the larger forces at work, they may have simply been in search of solace for their souls following the insulting and demeaning experience of being owned as slaves.

While we are grateful for the information about Maria Jones's slave experience, there are many unanswered questions about her life and times. We have no details about her first African conversion and her second, possibly Vincentian, baptism. We learn nothing about her possible interaction with East Indians who were indentured on estates adjoining Palmiste from 1845 nor about the Nepoios who were still resident in Arima when Maria was transferred to the north of the island. There is very little about the routine of estate servitude such as we find in Mary Prince's account. Did Maria Jones have children? Sadly such considerations did not hold much interest for the Baptists, who seemed bent on stemming the onrush of heathenism and winning souls for their brand of Christianity. Despite these omissions in the text, however, we do have the opportunity to savor precious vignettes in the life of one who demonstrated such unusual independence for her gender and for her time. She clearly understood her disadvantaged position in the system, but was determined that she would create her own space within the interstices of that system. If religion was one way of rising from the degradation of the plantation, then why not make use of this device? If learning to read and write could assist her upward mobility as a free person, why not go to school—even at the age of sixty—and why not do a double shift? It is by such acts of creativity that enslaved Caribbean people were able to carve niches for themselves and hack their own spaces in an oppressive system. Maria Jones typifies those whose resilience ensured the survival of the race while others in despair committed suicide or were cowed by the brutality of their masters.

## Notes

The author wishes to thank Professor Bridget Brereton and Reverend Harold Sitahal for their valuable assistance in the preparation of this chapter.

1. For the autobiographies of Olaudah Equiano and Mary Prince, see Beckles and Shepherd, *Caribbean Slavery in the Atlantic World: A Student Reader,* section 13.

2. Underhill, *The West Indies: Their Social and Religious Condition,* v.

3. Ibid., 22.

4. *Maria Jones,* 1.

5. "The Life of Olaudah Equiano," 822.

6. Mowser, *A Slaving Voyage to Africa and Jamaica.* Olaudah Equiano's account is also very useful.

7. *Maria Jones,* 1.

8. Fraser, *History of Trinidad from 1781–1839,* 1:88–89, 91.

9. Ibid., 1:10.

10. See Uddenberg and Vaucrosson, *Lists from the* San Fernando Gazette, *Trinidad, West Indies, 1865–1896,* 331. Bicaise's tombstone still exists at La Ressource Estate, part of the Palmiste holdings.

11. *Maria Jones,* 1.

12. Lamont, *Problems of Trinidad,* 224.

13. Samarusingh, "The History of Education in Trinidad and Tobago from Earliest Times to 1900," chap. 6.

14. Rutherford, *Greyfriars of Trinidad, 1837–1937,* 12.

15. *Maria Jones,* 4.

16. Underhill, *The West Indies,* 16, 18.

17. *Maria Jones,* 4.

18. Turner, *Slaves and Missionaries.*

19. *Maria Jones,* 6.

20. Society for the Propagation of the Gospel in Foreign Parts, *Quarterly Paper,* January 1849, 2.

21. Rutherford, *Greyfriars of Trinidad,* 10.

22. W. H. Gamble to Baynes, 21 July 1888, BMS Collection, Regent Park College, Oxford.

# References

Anderson, R. Mowbray, ed. *The Saint Vincent Handbook, Directory, and Almanac.* 5th ed. Kingstown: Office of the "Vincentian," 1938.

Beckles, Hilary McD., and Verene A. Shepherd. *Caribbean Slavery in the Atlantic World: A Student Reader.* Princeton, N.J.: Markus Wiener, 1999.

Equiano, Olaudah. "The Life of Olaudah Equiano." In *Caribbean Slavery in the Atlantic World: A Student Reader,* ed. Verene A. Shepherd and Hilary McD. Beckles. Princeton, N.J.: Markus Wiener, 1999.

Fraser, Lionel Mordaunt. *History of Trinidad from 1781–1839.* 2 vols. Port of Spain: Government Printer, 1891–96; reprint, London: Frank Cass, 1971.

Lamont, Sir Norman. *Problems of Trinidad: Being a Collection of Speeches and Writings on Subjects Connected with the Colony.* Port of Spain: Yuille's Printerie, 1933.

*Maria Jones: Her History in Africa and in the West Indies.* Port of Spain: Haverfordwest Mission Press, 1851.

Mowser, B. L., ed. *A Slaving Voyage to Africa and Jamaica.* Bloomington: Indiana University Press, 2002.

Rutherford, Brian C., ed. *Greyfriars of Trinidad, 1837–1937: A Historical Sketch of the Congregation of Greyfriars Church of Scotland. Port-of-Spain, Trinidad, to Mark the 150th Anniversary.* Port of Spain: Greyfriars Church of Scotland, 1987.

Samarusingh, A. R. K. "The History of Education in Trinidad and Tobago from Earliest Times to 1900." PhD diss., London University, 1964.

Society for the Propagation of the Gospel in Foreign Parts. *Quarterly Paper,* January 1849. Angus Library, Regents College, Oxford.

Turner, Mary. *Slaves and Missionaries: The Disintegration of Jamaican Slave Society, 1787–1834.* Kingston: University of the West Indies Press, 1998.

Uddenberg, Tian, and Karen Vancrosson, comps. *Lists from the* San Fernando Gazette, *1865–1896.* Westminster, Md.: Privately published, 2002.

Underhill, Edward Bean. *The West Indies: Their Social and Religious Condition.* Westport, Conn.: Negro Universities Press, 1970; first published London: Jackson, Walford, and Hodder, 1862.

# 7

# Slavery, Marriage, and Gender Relations in Eastern Yorubaland, 1875–1920

OLATUNJI OJO

Studies on the Caribbean have shown that gender and class factors differentiated the encounters of male and female slaves with slavery, imperialism, and capitalism. For women, the plantation system not only impacted their reproductive and productive rights but also altered the preexisting gender division of labor. Ultimately the family structures brought by slaves from Africa were profoundly altered by European ideas.[1] Caribbean women, however, fought against their lowly status. Studies on Yoruba women's encounters with slavery and colonialism in West Africa demonstrate similar trends showing that women embraced elements within local and colonial institutions to uplift their position. For instance, Kristin Mann and Judith Byfield show how Lagos and Egba women in western Yorubaland seized new opportunities in the British legal system to accumulate wealth and power through trade and property acquisition. Others, including many slaves, left their unwanted husbands and sought divorce in the colonial courts or new marriages sanctified by church weddings.[2] More than their western counterparts, eastern Yoruba women had more in common with Caribbean women. The constant engagement of eastern Yoruba men in warfare, their high mortality rates in battles, and frequent enslavement depleted the region of male labor. This in turn drew women into agriculture and produced female-headed households at a level not seen in other Yoruba districts. Thus women on Caribbean plantations and eastern Yoruba farms shared similar experiences in employment and single-parent families.

This chapter explores the impact of slavery and British colonialism on women in eastern Yorubaland. It also discusses women's selective appropriation of British colonial and Christian institutions and laws that improved their circumstances. These included the abolition of slavery, forced marriages, child betrothal, warfare, debt seizure, and human sacrifice. It also included sanctuary for fugitive slaves and wives, legal divorce, access to resources such as land and education, and freedom of religion.

## Slavery in Yorubaland

In 1807 Britain passed an act abolishing the right of its subjects to participate in the Atlantic slave trade. Over the next two decades a number of European states supported the efforts of the British antislavery squadron to seize slave cargos in West African waters and liberate the slaves on board. Such freed slaves were often settled in Sierra Leone, but many ultimately were moved to the Caribbean as indentures working under conditions similar to plantation slavery. Ironically, Yorubaland did not become a major slave exporting region until after 1820, when the bulk of Yoruba slaves were transported to Brazil and Cuba. Although many Yoruba slaves were exported to the Americas, most remained in the homeland where they were employed in producing crops for the "legitimate" trade. Increased demand for slaves, coupled with economic and political competition, generated a century of warfare with major consequences for political, economic, and demographic change.[3] Not surprisingly, starting around 1840, the power of large-scale Yoruba slave owners increased at the expense of those who had few or no slaves. Slave owners emerged as the leading power brokers. The possession of wealth in the form of material goods, land, and a large contingent of clients surpassed hereditary or kinship affiliations as essential power indicators.[4]

## Female Slaves and Slave Wives

In discussing slavery in Yorubaland, more attention is being paid to the impact of slavery on the family system.[5] Warfare and slave raiding resulted in the death and export of predominantly male slaves, while captured women were retained locally and eventually incorporated into the society as slave wives. To many slaveholders, the accumulation of female slaves and children provided cheap labor. Thus the recruitment of slave wives made gender a central issue during the period under study. Female slaves utilized different strategies to improve their low status, and these avenues expanded toward the end of the nineteenth century. According to Samuel Johnson, "The fair young women are added to the harems of the great [men], and young men save themselves the expenses of a dowry by making wives of any that come into their hands." While Johnson reported his observations on Ibadan and other western districts, Charles Phillips, writing contemporaneously about eastern Yorubaland, reached the same conclusion: "As Itebu is without jurisdiction (that is outside British control) they have been increasing their respective household by slaves whom they purchased from the interior. The male ones are employed as laborers but the female slaves are added to their harems."[6] These statements demonstrate not only the development of a strong relationship between slavery and marriage but also unequal sex ratios in the population left behind and the expansion of polygyny in nineteenth-century Yorubaland.

The preference for female slaves may be located in the differential social status between slave wives and freeborn women as well as the rising demand for labor. A freeborn girl was generally betrothed at an early age, and her future spouse would confirm his interest in her with yearly presents in labor and kind. He would work periodically on his future father-in-law's farm, repair his house, and make gifts of drinks and yams. When the prospective bride reached the age of puberty, her suitor could arrange the final wedding ceremony. As a general rule, girls were not married until they were between sixteen and twenty years old.

Despite the advantages and power wielded by Yoruba men, freeborn women also enjoyed important rights. Even though some women might have grudgingly consented to their marriages, they had the protection of their families against poor treatment from their husbands. Payments of bridewealth, which might not be returned, and sanctions, including rejection of marriage proposals by abusive men and their relatives, imposed constraints on how husbands could treat their wives. Since the wife retained certain rights in her natal home, the bridewealth transaction constituted a nominal payment to symbolize the transfer of a girl from one lineage to the other.

Slave wives, on the other hand, were married without bridewealth payments or labor requirements. They were bought or captured in war or received as gifts, and most often they were married against their will. The absence of bridal obligations between consenting families subjected a slave wife to the control of her owner-husband with fewer constraints. Children of slave wives inherited their mothers' inferior status even though their fathers were freeborn, which meant that fathers had greater control over them than their children from freeborn wives.[7] In essence, the husband of a slave wife had proprietary rights over her and her children, as the children of such marriages belonged not to the couple but to the man. Thus a man commanded a larger percentage of his slave-wife's production. Even as late as 1910, a report on the Yoruba stated that it was much easier to marry a slave wife than a freeborn.[8]

The distinction between freeborn and slave wives in Yorubaland corresponds with the status of women in Hausaland, where freeborn women and female slaves were classified as "wives" and "concubines," respectively.[9] Although the Yoruba did not make this distinction, they did distinguish between wives of superior and inferior social status, which often correlated with the status of freeborn and slave wives.[10] While marriage to the owner had the potential for improving the condition of a female slave, especially if she gave birth, her slave status remained. Slave wives were permanently held and were reminded of their status when occasion called for it. More often than not, the relative freedom enjoyed by slave wives married to their owners tended to end, or at least diminish, after the death of their husbands. At that stage they could not leave the family unless they redeemed themselves and their children.[11] Therefore, the assertion that "any slave woman taken as a wife becomes *ipso facto* a free woman" is incorrect. Johnson himself attested to this in the 1880s when he described how Ibadan soldiers sold their slave wives for firearms and food.[12]

In eastern Yorubaland the practice of human sacrifice shows that marriage to the owner did not necessarily integrate a slave wife into her owner's household. During some religious ceremonies, for instance, slave wives were specifically reserved for sacrifice at the death of their husbands. Contemporary observations on the treatment of slaves in Yorubaland throw some light on the pattern of slave integration. According to Phillips, "Slaves at Ondo were more at risk, the newer they were the closer to being total strangers." This indicated that the community regarded it as unacceptable to sacrifice assimilated slaves or those "who had formed attachment in the compound," such as slave wives who had borne children for the community and had already started to become members of it. It is not known when the law against the sacrifice of "assimilated" slaves began, but Phillips suggested this was to prevent the inconvenience of killing a mother in the presence of her children.[13]

Yet some women were killed, including one said to have been buried alive with her children at Ondo in 1882.[14] Slave wives selected for sacrifice were in fact treated as "special" wives. Destined to die, they were often prevented from becoming pregnant by the application of contraceptives that would destroy their reproductive system.[15] These wives were thus denied a significant opportunity for integration into the owner's community and used primarily for the sexual gratification of their owner-husbands.[16]

## "Big (Wo)men," Polygyny, and Concubinage

The character of Yoruba marriage reflected the elitist nature of the larger society. Parents gave their daughters to successful men and women. Consequently, the older, well-to-do, and influential personalities had the capability of marrying more wives than young men who could not afford the cost of marriage. Wealthy and powerful chiefs used their resources to amass women, resulting in the expansion of polygyny and the size of elite compounds in the nineteenth century.[17]

The disparity in slaveholding and economic opportunities in the different parts of eastern Yorubaland was reflected in the number of women in the harems. For instance, the richer districts of Ondo and southern Ekiti had more slave wives and polygynous households than areas where slaveholding was less extensive. In Ondo, an unnamed Osemowe was reputed to have 1,000 wives.[18] According to Phillips, the Lisa Edun of Ondo had between 300 and 400 wives, most of whom he kept "for the pleasure of seeing them."[19] Figures for Ekiti were considerably smaller. In 1874, the Ewi of Ado had 41 wives, and his defense chief Aduloju had more than 150, mostly slaves.[20] Similarly, a slave wife, Fadolapo of Ikere, whose owner-husband died in 1904, informed a court that her husband had between 60 and 80 wives, 12 of whom were slave wives.[21]

Material acquisition and accumulation of political power can also be seen in another institution of eastern Yorubaland: the female husband. As in southeastern Nigeria and other parts of Africa, this custom allowed women to marry their own wives—both female slaves and freeborn—whom they gave to their male relations to raise children for them. Thus the "husband" could create and control her own estate. The wives, their lovers, and children worked for the husband, who appropriated the surplus. Alternatively, a woman might marry another woman for the purpose of perpetuating her own lineage. For instance, in families with no male children or where a brother had died childless, daughters in such lineages could marry wives to raise children for their fathers and/ or brothers. More importantly, political and economic changes in the nineteenth century provided opportunities for some female entrepreneurs to use this institution to marry wives and thus establish their own lineages with a view to entrenching their power.[22]

The reproductive function of a slave wife is evident in the preference given to a woman's color and age. In Yorubaland, female slaves of prime age were taken as junior wives while old women and very young girls were employed on agricultural estates. When the girls reached the age of marriage, they were sent back to the town and married as junior wives. The palace structure of Ado Ekiti in the nineteenth century clearly demonstrated Ekiti concepts of beauty, desirable age, and conduct for the Ewi's wives. His wives occupied the fifth courtyard of the palace, the Ùwà Àdèlé (Adele court), where their rooms were located close to the Ewi's chamber, so that he could be with the wife of his choice. The rooms in the Ùwà Àdèlé were arranged so that the beauty, complexion, and age of a queen determined her proximity to the monarch: young, beautiful queens occupied the rooms closest to the Ewi. The only male outsider allowed into this courtyard was the Ologun Adele, the head of the palace slaves, who was charged with the duty of selecting new wives for the monarch.[23]

Slave marriages had significant ramifications for Yoruba ethnic and gender relations and ultimately the birth of Yoruba nationalism.[24] As women crossed political and ethnic boundaries as trade goods, they married and raised children beyond their subethnic groups, adopting new cultures and identities. They contributed to the creation of a creolized society. Studies on the Caribbean have discussed how slavery turned women into labor producers and household heads, supplanting the African family structure with a neo-European model.[25] There were parallels in Yorubaland as polygyny altered the social organization of elite families and the socialization of children. Court cases provide evidence of this. For example, on 18 March 1898, Okolu of Ijesa accused Chief Otunba of Italemo ward, Ondo, of seizing his sister Osun, who had been enslaved with her daughter in 1894. The following year, Osun and her child managed to escape from Ikale, only to be captured and enslaved by the accused. Otunba forced Osun into marriage and sent her to hoe his farms. He gave her daughter Ondo marks, a major feature of Ondo identification.[26] We do not have enough information about how many children were in similar positions or became reacculturated by virtue of their parents' marriages, but we do know that many were, including several Ondo chiefs in the 1920s whose ancestors were slaves.[27] Others could trace the ancestry to a mixture of people of slave, immigrant, and freeborn descent. The family background of Chief Folayegbe M. Akintunde-Ighodalo illustrates this type of multiple ancestries:

> [Her] paternal grandfather, Makinde, had settled in Ife territory after the destruction of Old Oyo. Around 1850, he joined Derin Ologbenla's army and settled in the Odo Bada ward of Okeigbo. At roughly the same time, Akinlalu, who would become his father-in-law, had also fled from Ogbomoso to Ibadan, settling in Oje quarter. As the Yoruba wars waged relentlessly, some people from Oje migrated to Okeigbo, perhaps initially as soldiers in the conquering Ibadan armies. Eventually they stayed behind and built homes in Ita Otun.[28]

Akintunde-Ighodalo's father, Olojomo Akintunde, was born around 1885. Her mother, Sarah Ogunkemi, was the daughter of Adelekun Ajero of the Ile Balagbe household in Ita Orisa ward, whose father was Owa Aponlese of Ijesa. Sarah's mother, Adetola, was one of the elder daughters of Ologbenla through his wife Safunke, herself the daughter of the Olukoro of Ikoro Ekiti.[29] From these two lineages we see that the paternal lineage derives from a probable military family while the maternal lineage, especially the women, were probably Ekiti slaves captured in the wars of the 1840s and 1850s. These multiple ethnic backgrounds were reflected in religious and linguistic practices in the upbringing of Akintunde-Ighodalo and her parents. For example, while a Muslim uncle, Belo Aromoye, raised her father, her mother frequently mocked her husband with songs in the Ekiti dialect. Responding to a question about her ethnic background, Akintunde-Ighodalo replied rhetorically, "You are asking me if I am an Ondo or not. . . . I do not know where my Ondo starts and where my Ekiti, Oyo, or Ife stop. That is why I am the Wabodu of Ile-Ife and Iyalode of Okeigbo."[30]

## Patronage and Adultery: Clients and Concubines

Unequal access to women led to late marriages and eventually to tension between dependent men and women and their overlords. In the 1910 Yoruba Report, the compilers observed that "as a general rule males do not marry before the age of 25. But the sons of kings and chiefs and rich men marry between the ages of 18 and 25."[31] My survey of Ekiti marriages for men and/or parents born between 1880 and 1930 shows that the scarcity of women arising from warfare and slavery pushed up the cost of marriage and caused many men to marry five to ten years later than their counterparts in Ibadan, Egba, and Ijebu, where most female slaves were settled. The average age of marriage for Ekiti men born during this half-century, except for the sons of powerful chiefs and soldiers, was about 30. Dowry jumped from 2s in the 1890s to between £2 and £12.10s in 1903, forcing many young men to pawn themselves in order to raise marriage fees.[32]

In Yorubaland, once the stipulated marriage payments are made, only the husband has the exclusive right to have a sexual relationship with his wife. Adultery, therefore, is *àlè* (the taking of someone's wife). Like in Asante, *àlè yíyàn* (choosing a concubine) or *yàn (mú) l'ọrẹ* (choose or take as a lover) is viewed as theft, that is, "the taking away" of a husband's sexual right to his wife.[33] The scarcity of women therefore posed a major obstacle to young and poor men because there were no women for them to marry. This resulted in friction between married and single men, particularly between the elite and their dependents. Eastern Yoruba society appeared to have been conscious of the dangers inherent in polygyny and the scarcity of unattached women. No doubt this led to the evolution of a special form of concubinage or adultery that has been derogatorily termed by some of the Yoruba elite as "polyandry among backward and promiscuous tribes of Ondo."[34] Under this system young, unattached males arranged with elite men to have sexual relations with their wives and concubines in return for payment of a fee and/or agreement to perform labor services.[35] According to Charles Young:

If a man has a wife [she] must be known to be the concubine of the son or a brother of his. That in case the husband hears that his son or one of his relatives has any connivance with his wife, and keep her as his concubine the case will be brought forward and if it is proved to be real, the husband will then lay a fine upon the son or brother, that is, one goat, and one or two calabashes of palm wine. After this is done, the husband is to swear himself, the son or brother together with the woman to their . . . god that the woman and the man should continue to [be] together till such time as they will choose to part . . . , that he will no more trouble them or charge the man of it again. But he is only considered to be the right husband—the woman is to look upon both of them as husband and concubine and should there come any child in so doing, the child is the husband's and [the child is only] a brother or sister to the [lover].[36]

Although it cannot be ascertained when this system began, the origin must have been closely connected with a disproportionate male-female ratio, the scarcity of unattached women, and the high cost of bridal fees. The practice, which also facilitated the entrenchment of clientage relationships, might also be connected to the vagaries of the Yoruba wars. Whatever the case, concubinage and adultery increased after 1850 when commercial wealth and warfare enabled elite men and women to acquire many female slaves and male clients. Young men were essential to the military prowess of warlords as the immediate instruments of any chief's power. Their continued loyalty, however, depended on the ability of the overlord to provide, among other things, weapons and financial loans as well as wives and lovers. For this purpose, powerful chiefs through polygamy established large pools of women who were given out as rewards to successful clients as wives. The power to reward or punish soldiers with women provided a mechanism through which chiefs attracted young men and exerted control over them.

Data on Ondo show that concubinage—licensed or not—was fraught with tension. The implementation of the judicial system showed that the polygynists fought against encroachment on their "property" rights. Class considerations, especially the status of a woman and her husband, were central to punishments meted out to those found guilty of adultery and seduction. A wronged husband could receive between five shillings and ten bags of cowries (c. £2.10s) from anyone who committed adultery with his wife.[37] Indeed, adultery became a lucrative revenue source for some men with numerous wives.

In some instances, however, fines were not considered sufficient punishment. Among the Mahin no penalty was attached to killing a slave, so adulterous slave wives sometimes were sentenced to death. For instance, Okiti Taworoko murdered his slave wife Samoko for committing adultery with Okoro, another slave, in 1898.[38] Adulterous royal wives and their lovers suffered more. In Ekiti and Ondo, fines for rape and adultery with a commoner's wife were much lower, ranging from two to thirty bags of cowries and two goats payable to the council of chiefs. Owing to their sociopolitical status in society, the adultery or seduction of an oba's wife was punished with death. Consequently offenders were left with few options other than suicide or exile.[39] Even exile might not be safe, for efforts might be made to extradite the offenders, and if these failed, war could be declared against the host communities.[40]

Attempts to undermine the exploitative arrangements of polygynists met stiff resistance. For example, on 26 October 1878, there was a great uproar in Ondo after Chief Lisa Edun found out that about twenty-five of his wives and concubines had engaged in adultery with men of whom he did not approve. Therefore he ordered his supporters to attack those he suspected of the crime. They pillaged the houses of the accused, confiscated their property, and imposed heavy fines. According to Phillips, "The commotion caused by his anger [was] so great in the town that one should think a foreign army was approaching to besiege the town."[41]

While it was easy to reach judgments and impose fines in marital cases involving people from the same community, cases involving parties from other communities were more difficult to settle and even more problematic during periods of hostilities. During such times, adultery, seduction, and rape might even be viewed as legitimate political weapons. Considered as injurious to the legal husband and as an affront against his community, protracted marital disputes or unsatisfactory judicial decisions sometimes produced violent conflicts. Between March and April 1880, for instance, Mahin and Ijo combatants clashed twice over a case of adultery between the Ijo man Kemurerin and the Mahin wife of Merugbo.[42] When the spouses or lovers came from different ethnicities or polities, adultery disputes could turn into regional crises.[43] Local traditions show that some of the interethnic conflicts between Ondo, Mahin, Ijo, and Ijebu during the 1880s and 1890s stemmed from cases of wife seduction and adultery. The legal husbands considered such offenses personal and communal, and these might pitch individuals and communities against each other. Occasionally the conflicts induced road closures as punishment against the adulterers' communities or against traders fleeing due to insecurity.[44]

In her explanation of adultery in eastern Yorubaland, Francine Shields postulates that the system "had a practical consequence in that to some extent it helped to offset the number of women (and children) leaving marriages through desertion or divorce for another man outside the family." She concludes that the system was a "relatively progressive policy in comparison with practices in other areas" where women were only allowed to commit adultery with nonfamily members.[45] It is difficult, however, to see adultery in Ondo as "progressive," given the tensions it generated. Very few young men were satisfied with living in concubinage with their relation's wives, for the children resulting from such relationships did not belong to them.[46]

## "Antislavery and Antiestablishment": Attack on Slave Marriages

If antislavery underpinned Britain's initial intervention in Yoruba affairs, trade promotion reinforced the integration of both societies. Starting in the 1840s, British merchants in the Bight of Benin began to complain about troubles posed by local trade brokers, many of whom cut off European traders from the source of commodity production. Local traders, described as "trade ruffians" in imperial documents, relished their role as trade brokers even though Europeans viewed the brokers as obstacles to trade. A related issue, as noted above, was the persistence of slavery and violence that frequently cut off trade routes and sabotaged productive activities. Therefore, there were concerns, perhaps genuine, that Britain should mediate between the local combatants to prevent trade blockades. The implementation of these policies, which began in coastal towns, provided an excuse for intervention in politics and commerce on the Lagos lagoon. In 1851, a British consulate was established in Lagos, and ten years later the island became a colony. In piecemeal fashion, Lagos colony extended its frontiers into eastern Yorubaland, culminating in the establishment of a protectorate in 1897. British political officers assumed power to establish colonial institutions, including a new legal system, police powers, and new laws that abolished the slave trade and "inhumane" customs. In carrying out their duties, political officers embarked on periodic tours of their constituencies. Slave women seized upon the new opportunities provided by British rule and the concomitant reduced power of the Yoruba male elite over their clients to obtain their freedom and expand their economic choices. Current research on African women enduring colonialism has emphasized the complexity of their responses to the new dispensation.[47] Of particular importance was the ideology of liberation from slavery and gender oppression as well.

British policies against enslavement enabled slave wives to secure freedom. Although the practice of paying redemption fees was well established in Yorubaland, slaveholders hitherto were under no obligation to free their slaves. Consequently, as slavery reached its last days, high redemption fees became a ploy to hold on to female slaves. Not surprisingly, slaveholders were generally opposed to the liberation of slave women. For example, even though Yoruba women predominated in commerce, profits accruing to female trader-slaves were often not substantial enough to facilitate quick redemption. Male slaves had much better opportunities to obtain employment to pay for their freedom as well as better opportunities to escape.[48] Having fewer sources of independent income, female slaves hesitated to escape, especially if they had to abandon their children.

Despite such difficulties, some slave women quickly grasped the implications of British antislavery ideas, and some erroneously believed that the British imposition of political control meant automatic freedom for every slave. This belief pushed some women to resist violently, such as assaulting or murdering their husbands, abandoning their children, or suing their husbands in British courts.[49] For instance, Ado tradition traces the death of Ali Atewogboye, the Ewi of Ado (1836–85), to one of his slave wives. Although a very old man, the Ewi had married a young slave from Idoani because she was beautiful. The woman was not happy, and because she could not leave the palace, she contracted a sexual relationship with a young palace slave. When the secret affair was detected and her lover killed, she expressed her dissatisfaction with the punishment. The monarch became angry and began to beat her. Instead of running away, she "wound her arms around [the monarch's] waist until the man fell down."[50]

In addition to paying redemption fees, female slaves could become free by fleeing to colonial administrative centers and Christian mission stations and later to towns. Such escapes followed a common pattern. Women fled while in trade missions or working on farms.[51] In 1882, Chief Adaja of Ondo reported to Young and Phillips the flight of a female slave belonging to one of his wives. This woman had run away the previous year, but was recaptured toward the end of February 1882. Barely a week after her return, she carried her three-week-old baby as if she were going to bathe it, but she abandoned it by the riverbank and fled.[52]

Although Yoruba men wished to retain their slave wives, and the colonial authority hesitated to disrupt the socioeconomic system, the government nevertheless allowed slaves to procure their freedom by paying a redemption fee of £3.15s. Slave wives were aware of the rules regarding redemption and the ambivalence of the colonial government when it came to cases involving their freedom. They also knew that it was a major avenue to freedom. Those who received favorable judgments from the district commissioners set an example for others.[53] A case reported in 1875 pointed to this practice. After regaining her freedom from slavery in Lagos, a woman returned to Ondo with her children. Soon after her arrival, a man who claimed to be a relative of her former owner-husband wanted to inherit her according to Ondo custom, but she refused to accept his claim. The man then seized her children and distributed them to relatives of the deceased husband. The woman reported the case to Obayomi, Governor Glover's agent, who in turn instructed the Ondo council to intervene. The council ruled that the woman's children should be returned to her and she was free to return to Lagos or reside in Ondo where a powerful chief would watch over her to prevent any future harassment.[54]

Colonial policies could be confusing and contradictory. For instance, Britain distinguished between the colonies where the ban on slavery technically granted freedom to slaves on arrival. Contrarily, even though the slave trade was outlawed in the protectorates, slavery was tolerated and British laws were not enforced. Slaves seldom recognized these fine distinctions. While the government discouraged the mass flight of slaves, the slaves viewed European posts as freedom havens.[55] In eastern Yorubaland, there was an indigenous tradition allowing slave owners to reclaim fugitive slaves and to reward the captor with gifts. Colonial agents followed this law haphazardly. Confused policies merged with the latitude enjoyed by individual officials to interpret antislavery laws to suit personal egos. Some officers recognized the rights of masters over their slaves and returned fugitive slaves, but others favored the right of slaves to freedom.

Slave owners broadly understood British antislavery policies, but they could not comprehend why the Lagos government would not hand over runaway slaves. For instance, many of them queried why after having stopped slave trading, they should lose slaves acquired legally without any compensation. More confusing was Britain's demand for legitimate trade when workers recruited for this purpose, mostly slaves, fled to British territories as fugitives. Even though there were prior instances of slave flights, the opening of the Ondo road through eastern Yorubaland in 1871 and the nearness of British territory accelerated the process. Indeed, by 1872, it had become common for slaves sent to Lagos by their owners not to return. Three such cases were cited as underlying reasons for the lukewarm attitude in Ondo and Ikale toward the British and the Church Missionary Society (CMS).[56]

Governor Glover had envisaged that the opening of the Ondo road would increase the return of ex-slaves. To placate the people about the loss of slaves, he allowed Ijo and Ilaje chiefs to collect ten heads of cowries (one bag) from every freed slave traveling toward the interior or Lagos. This was meant to allow safe passage and to guard the returnees against reenslavement. Laudable as this might appear, it was fraught with problems. The arrangement sought to protect only slaves returning from Lagos who carried a manumission certificate. It did not address the concerns of those slaves who redeemed themselves outside colonial courts and had no freedom certificate. Illiterate or extortionist gatekeepers had little regard for papers of any kind. The practice of not giving up escaped slaves was not consistently followed, and this generated serious opposition in some communities. On one occasion, two slaves belonging to Ilaje boarded a colonial steamer. The owners demanded their return, but the governor, who was on board, refused to give them up. On another occasion, when the steamer was again on Ilaje coast, two slaves, a man and a woman, both bearing the marks of recent punishments, got on board. The ship captain, wishing not to offend local people, returned the slaves to their owners.[57] Unfortunately, the decision not to offend slave owners did not come until many slaves had fled to British-occupied areas. This increased agitation by local people who wondered why fugitive slaves could be returned in one instance and not in others. At one point Rev. James B. Wood of the CMS announced that this was a destructive British policy because it focused solely on the abolition of slavery and not on its consequences for slaves, slave owners, and society.[58]

British officers in the protectorate also sought clarification of official policy on slavery. The instruction came back that they should not encourage slaves to escape and that, when desirable, they should restore fleeing slaves to their owners. Governor Gilbert Carter observed that "though we do not recognize slavery, yet we intend not to interfere with the existing system of slaveholding where the slaves are kindly treated and they voluntarily remain with their owners."[59] Thus when slaves ran away, British officers sometimes repatriated them. When some slaves fled to Idoani from Alo of Ibokun-Ijesa in 1897, Captain Humphrey ordered the king of Idoani to return them. When the king refused to comply, Lieutenant Alfred Scott sent soldiers to retrieve the slaves and restore them to Alo. Scott premised his decision on his understanding that "the policy of the Lagos governor . . . was to get back all runaway slaves if possible and that they could redeem themselves for 15 bags of cowries or £3.15s."[60] This incident marked a stage in policy dissonance between the Colonial Office and the European "men on the spot." The new governor and Carter's successor, Henry E. McCallum, queried Scott on using soldiers to retrieve fugitive slaves. Not getting a good answer, he reiterated the official policy of minimal intervention in domestic slavery matters except when a slave is maltreated. By this law he banned British officers from becoming bounty hunters:

> Questions relative to domestic slaves are to be dealt with by the native authorities only that we should interfere as little as possible in such matters provided that no complaint of cruelty or inhumanity is made to us. It is when a slave however well treated does run away that the difficulties of our position come in. We will not allow the exercise of native custom, which would mean raid for recovery or reprisals on members of the tribe to whom the slave has bolted. As we have to passively tolerate domestic slavery in places outside our protectorate (slavery which is of a patriarchal character and very mild in form) so we must endeavour to keep the peace however unwilling we may be to recognize slavery in any form.[61]

As we have seen above, there were some gray areas in the abolition process. Sometimes it was unclear when flight was legitimate. Slave wives

sometimes went to court to plead poor treatment, ask for clearer definitions of what constituted redemption and freedom, or get a proper inter-
pretation of their status.[62] Disputes over seduction and adultery, some dis-
guised as fugitive cases, constituted other forms of resistance by slave wives
as well as proof that these women were not always the victims of sexual
harassment. Although available records were unduly biased toward men,
women sometimes initiated sexual contracts with men or at least appeared
favorably disposed to such initiatives. In Shields's opinion, adultery could
lead to either formal or de facto divorce.[63] This was applicable in many
polygynous families where slave wives were allowed to choose their own
lovers or lived in concubinage with the approval of their legal husbands.

The strategies of "runaway" slave wives also showed that most
women were not escaping into an unknown world. Instead, they entered into alliances that they had already forged during their original
marriages. Hence many slave wives were supported by lovers who agreed
to pay redemption fees or help them flee. Court records testify to the
effectiveness of this strategy. Although our data concerning the redemption of slaves and pawns before 1920 is incomplete, post-1920 figures
from Ondo province show that women resorted to colonial institutions
to obtain their freedom. Between 1921 and 1926, 103 female slaves and
42 male slaves obtained their freedom. As tables 7.1 and 7.2 in the appendix show, important modes of redemption were those where men
were very visible. Sixty-nine women (48 percent) were set free in native
courts presided over by male judges in cases where relatives paid the
redemption fees, while another thirty-nine women (27 percent) had new
husbands who paid their redemption fees. Only three women redeemed
themselves. Similarly, having realized that flight offered only a limited
form of resistance, conditioned by the circumstances in which women
lived, the men with whom slave wives sought refuge tended to possess
influence and power. By 1920, the divorce rate had become quite high,
accounting for about 75 percent of all civil cases during the decades that
the government established special matrimonial courts.

## Christianity and Marriage Reform

More than British officers, Christian missionaries encouraged marriage
reform. Another element of social change was the plea from Christian

missionaries for support from their home governments. For our area, the CMS was the dominant mission. It spread from Sierra Leone through the agency of mostly Yoruba ex-slaves or their descendants. Sierra Leone made a unique impact. As the haven for liberated slaves from very early in its history, it had also received populations of American ex-slaves— mostly maroons and army loyalists from Jamaica, the United States, Nova Scotia, and the Black Poor from England. Sierra Leone was a mixed pot of cultures. Therefore, Yoruba Christians were already exposed to a range of Euro-American ideas and practices, so it was not surprising that they condemned slavery, polygyny, adultery, and the institution of female husbands. The clergy also supported divorce, female education, and social welfare and provided safe havens for divorcées and runaway slave wives.

These reforms began to be implemented in the 1840s, and by 1860 divorce had become accepted among the modern Lagos elite.[64] Christianity was introduced into eastern Yorubaland in 1875. Converts were sanctioned for engaging in unchristian practices such as polygyny and adultery and for allowing the practice of female husbands. Punishments for matrimonial offenses included excommunication, suspension, and denial of other benefits, such as Christian burials, protection against local authorities, and financial assistance.[65]

The inferior status of slave wives and their children constituted a big obstacle to the Yoruba Christians, as unmarried freeborn males preferred to live in adultery rather than marry female slaves. A priest noted that "with the scarcity of wives, young [Christian] men resorted to seizing the wives of polygamists (Christians and non-Christians) who were mainly elders."[66] After 1886 this problem was exacerbated by the shortage of fresh slave supplies and the decline in the number of unattached women. In Phillips's opinion, this impeded the spiritual growth of his congregation. Consequently, he adopted what some considered unchristian options, including the importation of girls from Lagos and the engagement of Christian converts to non-Christian women, redeemed slaves, and widows.[67] Unfortunately, these were not easy options in eastern Yorubaland where, unless the redemption fee was fully settled, slaveholders could for some time reclaim their female slaves and their children, even if the father was free. Because it was easier to control a slave wife, many Ondo men preferred to marry slaves rather than redeem them or marry freeborn women. These men regarded redemption as an instrument of female empowerment, improved social status, and loss of male control.

The problem of the redemption of slave wives and their status relates to another issue: slave ownership. One of the resolutions passed at the Yoruba Church Missionary Society conference in 1857 prohibited Christian converts from keeping or selling slaves, but did allow them to buy slaves, provided they intended to free them.[68] This meant that Ondo men could not sell unwanted slave wives or retrieve them if they escaped. Thus some Christian converts preferred to buy, but not redeem, slave wives. The missionaries decried this as an extension of slavery. Phillips concluded that it would be difficult to find suitable husbands for slaves because freeborn males were afraid that their children might one day be claimed as slaves.[69] Nevertheless, the church did not relax its rules concerning slavery, restating them at its conferences in 1877, 1878, and 1880. While it no longer forced owners to liberate their slaves, it prohibited them from treating such women as slaves. It also encouraged monogamy. By 1898, the Ondo Young Men's Christian Association had been persuaded to sign a document whereby members agreed to live monogamous lives, a condition that forced members to set free excess wives.[70]

Polygyny and adultery were not peculiar to the old Yoruba elite. The commitments of Christian converts to the "civilizing" mission varied depending on location, generation, and gender. Many in fact professed Christianity and adopted aspects of European culture because these provided opportunities for freedom from enslavement and facilitated contacts with British rule and the Atlantic trade. But as soon as they prospered in trade, they failed to comply with the other proscriptions of the new culture: monogamy, chastity, and abstinence from holding slaves or pawns.[71]

Although the missionaries Phillips and Young represented the radical "modern" group, many Christians still believed in slavery, polygyny, and adultery as much as non-Christians. Phillips cited the example of an Itebu headman, a Christian of forty years, who had been baptized at Sierra Leone in 1849. When he was old and weak, this polygynist, probably Frederick Haastrup,[72] became very protective and jealous of the activities of his many wives, whom he suspected of living adulterous lives. As a result of his suspicions, he brought all Itebu young men, including the Christians, before a Mahin orisa to prove their innocence of these charges.[73]

Many women quickly embraced the opportunities implicit in Christian campaigns about marriage. They did not wait for the men to comply with the restrictions, particularly since several men preferred to leave the churches rather than abandon their wives, even sometimes members of the clergy. In January 1899, Charles Phillips received a report of a case involving the Anglican missionary Charles Hoffman Famorokun. Famorokun was accused of harboring Aleke of Irun Akoko, who had been pawned to Arogunmatidi of Ise for her husband's debt of thirty-two bags of cowries. Aleke did not want to serve her new master, hence her flight to Famorokun's house. Famorokun ignored every plea from Ise authorities to release the woman, and this degenerated into an anti-Christian protest. Due to the uproar, Famorokun sent Aleke to the district commissioner, who ruled that the woman must be freed and that Arogunmatidi must recover his money through another means. Soon after Aleke returned from the commissioner, she moved in with Famorokun.[74] Although this case seemed to suggest that Famorokun had other motives for assisting the woman, it is evident that he was influential and that the woman utilized the situation to her advantage.

Given the alliance between British colonialists and missionaries, women found it advantageous to embrace Christianity, not necessarily for salvation but for its worldly advantages. In eastern Yorubaland —renowned for polygyny, human sacrifice, concubinage, and twin murder—the church saw the liberation of female slaves as necessary for reducing "unchristian" vices. Consequently, the missionaries began to focus on the compounds of polygynists and slaveholders as good hunting grounds for new converts.

### Hausa Soldiers, Ethnicity, and Runaway Slave Wives

Because of the weakness of the antislavery crusade, those who were close to British officialdom seized on personal initiatives to facilitate the redemption of slave wives. For example, Hausa soldiers helped destroy slavery through "unauthorized actions."[75] Although we do not have enough evidence about the impact of the military on the freedom of slave wives, there is evidence to show that military barracks served as safe havens for runaway slave wives. This illustrates how slavery intersects with gender, marriage, and ethnicity. For the period 1875–1900, nearly every district in Yorubaland premised their support for British influence on the assurance that their wives and slaves would not be taken away by soldiers and traders and that runaway slaves would be restored to their owners.[76] Despite such assurances, female slaves had a different goal, patronizing not colonial officers but their institutions as refuge from oppression. Some of them married soldiers, while others entered into informal sexual alliances, hoping that such arrangements would protect them from former masters and offer them the chance to return to their old homes. Two incidents in Ondo district illustrate the links between first slavery marriage and ethnicity and women's negotiations with colonialism. In the first case, Mekunserun claimed he had bought two Hausa slaves, Adisatu and Lade, from Amodu, a Hausa slave dealer at Iwo. Shortly afterward, a Hausa soldier seized the women and took them to the barracks. Captain Ross L. Bower, the British resident, restored the women to Mekunserun, but they escaped again—Adisatu to another Hausa soldier, Private Musa Kanu, and Lade to the acting traveling commissioner of Igbobini, Major Ewart. Ewart ordered the women to return to Mekuserun, but allowed Kanu to redeem Adisatu for £5.[77] In the second case, Fatumo, a Nupe slave wife of Awoyele's late father, refused to be inherited by a relative of her owner-husband, and informed Awoyele that she had married Private Abba Kanu. Her decision to marry Kanu was supported by the traveling commissioner, who asked Kanu to redeem her for £5.[78] Women like Adisatu and Fatumo attracted other Hausa women to the barracks for the purpose of declaring their enslavement illegal.[79]

These two cases are significant because they highlight the divergent motives of British officials, African soldiers, and female slaves. The women believed in the liberation ideology of the British government, and this might explain Fatumo's reason for refusing to be shared out as property. On the other hand, there was the British ambivalence on the abolition of slavery and the poorly defined British antislavery laws. British ambivalence left major decisions to the whims of individual officers, and this might explain why Adisatu and Lade fled from Ibadan, which was Bower's jurisdiction, to Igbobini under the jurisdiction of the more favorably inclined Ewart. Hausa soldiers fully exploited their position to keep Yoruba slaveholders from reporting the loss of their slave wives. The behavior of the Hausa soldiers—Galadjima, Musa Kanu, and Abba Kanu (perhaps ex-slaves themselves)—represented a continuous pattern of Hausa slave resistance in Yorubaland. Furthermore, ethnicity was involved, since these women were Hausa. It seems plausible that their ethnicity, common slave experience, and desire to return home were the main motives for the alliances that were formed, not marriage.

The illegal activities of soldiers and other agents of British rule continued for several years. The agents capitalized on the poor communication between local authorities and the new government, and the awe in which British officers were held, to abuse the system.[80] Between 1894 and 1901, Captains Lugard, Bower, and Ambrose itemized cases of impostors who posed as government staff and extorted trade goods and money from the people of Ekiti. According to Ambrose, the impersonators only required "a delapedated [sic] pair of boots, a red fez or cap, a shirt and dark trousers," and "an old uniform, no matter of what regiment" to achieve the semblance of absolute legitimacy, since the people could hardly differentiate between genuine and fake officers.[81]

## The End of Slavery and the Legalization of Divorce

The end of slavery and the slave trade had profound effects on the status of women. Both led to a clampdown and condemnation of the custom of female child betrothal, forced marriage, and the poor treatment of women. Women saw these developments as practical demonstrations of the government's commitment to the principle of emancipation. In some respects antislavery laws and the process of implementation were based on official ignorance of the indigenous slavery system, hence regulations were inadequate. The crisis facing female slaves continued into the 1920s. Because of the nature of the inheritance system, homeborn female slaves sometimes could not precisely identify their owner and therefore could not easily arrange redemption. Although Emmanuel Oroge correctly states that the status of *eru idile* (homeborn slaves) was slightly better than other categories of slaves, the transformation of homeborn slaves from private to collective properties made their emancipation more complex.[82] This sometimes occurred when family members disagreed over how to manage the property of deceased relatives. When several family members could invoke individual property rights in homeborn slaves, they could set high dowry fees in order to drive off potential suitors or provide enough money for distribution. According to P. E. M. Richards, the district officer at Ondo, problems for homeborn female slaves included instances of their leaving one man for another within the same family with subsequent disputes regarding dowry rights.[83]

Disputes of this kind compelled the colonial government to address issues related to the remnants of slavery. In Ondo, the problem became acute for the status of homeborn female slaves who had reached the age of marriage, many of whom had lost their parents through flight, redemption, or bondage. In such cases, slaveholders and their descendants became the de facto parents for the girls. Under these circumstances, there arose the question concerning who should give the girls out in marriage and whether the girls had any right to reject the spouses chosen by their owners.[84] Harry Claude Moorhouse, the secretary for the southern provinces, responding to a request for guidelines on the status of marriageable female homeborn slaves, wrote that the government did not recognize the status of these girls as slaves nor the right of their "owners" to force them into marriage. He threatened that "it will be necessary to place the girl in the care of some institution or disinterested person until such time as she does marry," if the local authorities continued to do so. Apparently this was an empty threat. Richards, like Samuel Johnson, believed "it is a local custom that when slave girls marry a member of the family in which she is a slave she automatically becomes free." Subsequently, Moorhouse contradicted himself by suggesting that the government should not interfere with the payment of dowries on such girls to their owners who acted in loco parentis: "As long as the dowry system continues, the owner should receive what would ordinarily be paid to the parents. It is in accord with native custom."[85] Despite the inconsistency, frequent colonial intervention in people's daily lives enabled female slaves to petition against forced marriages, maltreatment, and unwanted husbands. By the 1920s, girls under the age of 20 (the pool from which wives were naturally recruited) were technically nonenslavable. By the same token, colonial authorities intensified their condemnation of slavery and the related institution of pawnship.

## Conclusion

The above analysis has shown how warfare and commercial success during the era of the slave and legitimate trade enabled successful men and women to accumulate a large pool of women as freeborn and slave wives and concubines. In particular, it demonstrates the advantages of marrying slave wives, the rarity of divorce, and easy control over such wives and their labor. In the harems, female and freeborn junior wives were also subjected to the control of senior freeborn wives, thereby reducing the access of the former to their husbands.[86] In captivity, many of the women and their children endured a variety of conditions. Slave wives risked being sold away to distant markets, maltreated, or offered as sacrifices during the funerals of their owners, being forced into sexual relations with clients for a variety of reasons, and serving as a store of capital. Until the late 1870s, wealth rested largely with the gerontocratic aristocracy, after which socioeconomic change provided greater access to wealth. In many cases changes such as Christianity, wage labor, and commerce favored young men and women who soon acquired the financial and social power to secure independence from the old elite. The drying up of aristocratic privileges led to the increased inability of chiefs and other wealthy men to support their harems, with the result that the number of runaway wives of chiefs quickly soared. As soon as divorce courts were established, matrimonial disputes proliferated. The central issues of gender, generational conflict, and insecurity were germane to rising divorce rates. Until the 1890s, insecurity reduced the extent of mobility and free will. Colonialism, however, presented new opportunities for freedom and autonomy, divorce, protection from maltreatment, and independent sources of income—all of which accounted for multiple cases of "husband-wife palaver" and the frequency of divorce summons. Finally, with new economic opportunities and the huge demand for paid labor, it became almost impossible to restrict a wife to the confines of her husband's compound. The adjustment by women to new socioeconomic conditions represented a revolution against the consequences of polygyny and social repression.

This study demonstrates the historical trajectory through which female headed households emerged in Ondo society. It shows similarities to changes that took place in Caribbean slave societies. Domesticity took different shapes according to local circumstances. Nevertheless, we can see that the global phenomena of evangelical Christianity, European imperialism, and antislavery ideas had complex socioeconomic and political impacts that led to changing or expanding opportunities for women and family life coming out of slavery.

## Appendix

Table 7.1. Distribution of Freed Slaves by Sex in Ondo Province, 1921–26

| Year | Men | Women | Total | Women % of Total |
|------|-----|-------|-------|------------------|
| 1921 | 26 | 42 | 68 | 61.8 |
| 1922 | 15 | 16 | 31 | 51.6 |
| 1923 | 1 | 10 | 11 | 90.9 |
| 1924 | — | 2 | 2 | 100 |
| 1925 | — | 31 | 31 | 100 |
| 1926 | — | 2 | 2 | 100 |
| 1921–26 | 42 | 103 | 145 | 71 |

Source: Annual reports for Ondo Province, 1921–26, CSO 26/1/03996, 26/1/09166, and 26/1/11874, vols. 1–3, NAI.

Table 7.2. Mode of Redemption for Female Slaves in Ondo Province, 1921–26

| Year | District | Native Court | Self | Intending Husband | Relative |
|------|----------|-------------|------|-------------------|----------|
| 1921 | Ekiti | — | — | 29 | 20 |
|  | Ondo | 19 | — | — | — |
| 1922 | Ekiti | — | — | 7 | 12 |
|  | Ondo | 11 | 1 | — | — |
| 1923 | Ekiti | — | 2 | 3 | 2 |
|  | Ondo | 4 | — | — | — |
| 1924 | Owo | 2 | — | — | — |
| 1925 | Owo | 31 | — | — | — |
| 1926 | Owo | 2 | — | — | — |
| Total (%) |  | 69 (48) | 3 (2) | 39 (27) | 34 (23) |

Source: Annual reports for Ondo Province, 1921–26, CSO 26/1/03996, 26/1/09166, and 26/1/11874, vols. 1–3, NAI.

# Notes

1. See Beckles and Shepherd, *Caribbean Slave Society and Economy*, 228–86.

2. Mann, "Women's Rights in the Law and Practice," and Byfield, "Women, Marriage, Divorce, and the Emerging Colonial State in Abeokuta (Nigeria), 1892–1904."

3. On the Yoruba crisis, see Johnson, *The History of the Yorubas*, 178–283; Law, *The Oyo Empire c.1600–c.1836*, 245–302; Akinjogbin, *War and Peace in Yorubaland, 1793–1893;* Akintoye, *Revolution and Power Politics in Yorubaland, 1840–1893.*

4. Less than ten of Ondo's about one hundred chieftaincies were hereditary. Many titles were awarded on merit, as were Yoruba war titles.

5. Mann, *Marrying Well,* "Women, Landed Property, and the Accumulation of Wealth in Early Colonial Lagos," and "Owners, Slaves, and the Struggle for Labour in the Commercial Transition at Lagos." See also Awe, "Iyalode Efunsetan Aniwura"; Awe and Olutoye, "Women and Warfare in Nineteenth-Century Yorubaland"; Denzer, "Yoruba Women"; Lindsay, "To Return to the Bosom of Their Fatherland"; Byfield, *The Bluest Hands;* Shields, "Palm Oil and Power"; Shields, "Those Who Remained Behind."

6. Johnson, *History,* 324; Phillips to James Buckley Wood, 9 January 1890, Phillips 1/1/3, National Archives of Nigeria, Ibadan [hereafter NAI].

7. Minutes of Abeokuta Clerical Conferences, 25 September 1877 and 2 July 1878, Church Missionary Society—Yoruba papers [hereafter CMS(Y)] 3/1/2, NAI.

8. Hopkins, "A Report on the Yoruba, 1910," 82.

9. Lovejoy, "Concubinage and the Status of Women Slaves in Early Colonial Northern Nigeria" and "Concubinage in the Sokoto Caliphate (1804–1903)."

10. Hopkins, "Report on the Yoruba," 81.

11. Abeokuta Clerical Conference, 25 September 1877, CMS(Y) 3/1/2, NAI.

12. Johnson, *History,* 325, 459, 490, 492; *Lagos Annual Report, 1899.*

13. Charles Phillips's journal, 20 November 1878, Phillips 1/3/3, NAI.

14. Ibid., 25 September 1882, Phillips 3/4, NAI; interviews with Chief Seriki Awoyele, Akinkunmi Fagbohungbe, and Madam Iyadunni Ayobami, Odosida Street, Ondo, 23–25 July 2001.

15. Oroge, "The Institution of Slavery in Yorubaland with Particular Reference to the Nineteenth Century," 141–42; Hopkins, "Report on the Yoruba."

16. Phillips's journal, 26 August and 20 November 1878, Phillips 1/3/3, NAI.

17. Roper, "What I Saw in Africa, Part II," 38.

18. Hunt to resident, 13 January 1915, Ondo Div 8/1, NAI.

19. Phillips's journal, 26 August 1878, CA2/078/21, Church Missionary Society papers; Wood to Lang, "Account of Visit to Kiriji Camp in March 1885," 19 August 1885, CMS(Y) 1/7/5, NAI. Like the Lisa of Ondo, Ekiti chiefs used every available opportunity to display their "wealth in wives," and no occasion was too dangerous for such manifestations. At the peak of the Kiriji war in 1885, and many miles away from their palaces, several middle-aged women accompanied the Ore of Otun and the Ajero of Ijero to meetings. On one occasion the Ajero had between twelve and fifteen women of various ages present at his meeting with Rev. J. Buckley Wood of the CMS mission in 1885.

20. Johnson, *History,* 391; Oguntuyi, *History of Ado,* 39.

21. Judgment by G. E. H. Humphrey in Ogunmolaji of Ikere vs. Anjorin of Ido, 1 November 1910, criminal and civil record book for the Northeastern district, Ondo Div 7/2, NAI.

22. Memo by Mrs. Temple, 15 January 1915, and memo by E. F. Lang to district officer, Kabba, 7 February 1919, Ilorin Prof 104/1919, National Archives of Nigeria, Kaduna; Temple, *Notes on the Tribes, Provinces, Emirates, and States of the Northern Provinces of Nigeria*, 7, 104–105; Oguntuyi, *History of Ado*, 17–21; Ijagbemi, *Christian Missionary Activity in Colonial Nigeria*, 39. For information about female husbands in other African societies, see Amadiume, *Male Daughters, Female Husbands;* Bohannan, "Dahomean Marriage: A Re-evaluation"; Burton, "Woman-Marriage in Africa"; Greene, "The Institution of Woman-Marriage in Africa"; Melville Herskovits, "A Note on 'Woman Marriage' in Dahomey"; Huer, "'Woman Marriage' in Some East African Societies"; Krige, "Women Marriage, with Special Reference to the Lovedu"; O'Brien, "Female Husbands in Southern Bantu Societies"; Oboler, "Is the Female Husband a Man?"

23. My appreciation to two Omode-Owa (palace officials) at Ado-Ekiti who showed me around the palace on 17 January 1993.

24. Ojo, "Warfare, Slavery, and the Transformation of Eastern Yorubaland c.1820–1900," chap. 2.

25. Craton, "Changing Patterns of Slave Families in the British West Indies"; Morrissey, "Women's Work, Family Formation, and Reproduction among Caribbean Slaves."

26. Traveling commissioner's journal, 18 and 22 March 1898, Ondo Div 8/1, NAI.

27. Memo, P. R. Foulke-Roberts, district officer, Ondo, enclosed in memo, secretary Southern Provinces to G. C. Whiteley, chief secretary, 17 March 1937, CSO 26/11799, vol. IV, NAI.

28. Denzer, *Folayegbe M. Akintunde-Ighodalo: A Public Life*, 5.

29. Ibid., 5–10.

30. Interview with Chief Folayegbe A. Akintunde-Ighodalo, Ibadan, 26 July 1999. "Wabodu" is the senior female title in Derin Ologbenla's family at Ile-Ife.

31. Hopkins, "Report on the Yoruba," 80–81.

32. Civil record book, 14 July 1903, Ekiti Div 4/4, NAI.

33. Allman, "Adultery and the State in Asante," 30.

34. Hopkins, "Report on the Yoruba," 81–82.

35. An approved adulterer could sue another adulterer. See Fadase and Kinyokun vs. Fletcher, Phillips's diary, 15 November–3 December 1901, Phillips 3/11, NAI.

36. Young's journal, 27 June 1875, CA2/098/10, CMS. Also see Phillips's journal, 23 November 1877, CA2/078/24, CMS; Phillips to R. Lang, 13 January 1890, Phillips 1/1/3, NAI; Phillips, "A Statement of the Peculiar Difficulties Which Impede the Progress of the Infant Church at Ondo," 14 February 1891, CMS(Y) 2/2/4, NAI; Ondo Intelligence Report, p. 61, CSO 26/30172, NAI. The proper word for concubine in this context is *paramour, lover,* or *adulterer.*

37. Carter to Ripon, 27 September 1894, CSO 1/1/14, NAI.

38. Traveling commissioner's diary, 17 May 1898, Ondo Div 8/1, NAI.

39. N. A. C. Weir, Intelligence Report on Ado District of Ekiti Division, 1933, para. 156–63, CSO 26/29734, NAI; Weir, Intelligence Report on Akure District of Ekiti Division, Ondo Province, 1934, para. 207, CSO 26/30014, NAI; A. F. B. Bridges,

Intelligence Report on Ondo District of Ondo Province, 1934, para. 89, CSO 26/30172, NAI; Chiefs in Oyo Prof (1) Adultery with Wives of (2) Runaway Wives of—Principle to Be Adopted as to Treatment of, 1920–1950, Oyo Prof 1/1324 vols. 1 & 2, NAI. This confirms the common saying "ẹni bá gbé kàkàkí ọba, kò sí ibi tí yóò ti fọn," which means "he who steals the royal bugle will have no place to blow it." Kàkàkí (bugle) is a euphemism for a royal wife.

40. Intelligence Report on Akure, appendix D, CSO 26/30014, NAI; J. O. Jegede, *Itan Ise-Ekiti* (Ibadan, n.d.); Atandare, *Iwe Itan Akure.*

41. Phillips's journal, 26 October 1878, Phillips 1/3/3, NAI; Phillips to James Maser, 30 October 1878, CA2/068, CMS.

42. "Report of Charles Philips' visit to Itebu, Leke, and Palma Stations, 2–26 April 1880," and entries for 6–9 April 1880, Phillips 1/3/1, NAI.

43. Ikale District Assessment Report, 1927–31, 19–21, MLG (W) 8/1, NAI.

44. Phillips to Maser, 20 September 1877, CA2/068/169, CMS; Ikale Assessment Report, paragraphs 24–33, 190–92, 275.

45. Shields, "Palm Oil and Power," 267.

46. Phillips's diary, 17 March 1887, Phillips 3/2, NAI.

47. Mann, *Marrying Well* and "Women, Landed Property"; Denzer, "Yoruba Women"; Byfield, "Women, Marriage, Divorce"; Kaplan, "Runaway Wives, Native Law and Custom in Benin, and Early Colonial Courts, Nigeria"; Allman, Geiger, and Musisi, *Women in African Colonial Histories.*

48. Johnson, *History,* 325; Ogba of Agbado vs. Basaya of Addo [*sic*] and Abere of Efon Alaaye, 16 March 1906, Ekiti Div 4/4, NAI. A soldier slave could ransom himself by bringing another slave to his owner.

49. Oguntuyi, *History of Ado,* 48–49; Ikale assessment report, paras. 25, 68, 80.

50. Oguntuyi, *History of Ado,* 49. In her dissertation, Shields has shown that in Yorubaland, while domestic violence by a man against a woman, "particularly in marital relations, was socially acceptable and sanctioned, it was not socially or officially acceptable for a woman to be violent against her husband, especially among the higher class." See Shields, "Palm Oil and Power," 255. Women who violated this rule were severely punished. See Nathaniel Ogbonaye's journal, 4 and 6 December 1879, CA2/011/117, CMS.

51. Young's journal, 2 January 1875, CA2/098, CMS. Manuwa of Itebu only agreed to receive missionaries in his town when he was told that Christianity would teach wives and slaves how to serve and obey their masters and husbands.

52. Phillips's diary, 1 March 1882, Phillips ¾, NAI; Derin, Oni-elect of Ife, to Moloney, 1887, enc 2 in Nigeria dispatch #353, CO 147/61, National Archives, Kew. In 1887 the Ile-Ife authorities demanded the return of a woman who had ran away from her husband to Okeigbo; the Okeigbo authorities refused, saying that many of their women and slaves had also run away to Ife.

53. Appendix F, *Lagos Annual Report, 1899,* 83; Annual Reports, Ondo Province, 1921–26, CSO 26/1/03996, 26/1/09166 & 26/1/11874, vol. I–III, NAI.

54. Young's journal, 20 July 1875, CA2/098, CMS.

55. See Oroge, "Institution of Slavery," 282–359; Mann, *Slavery and the Birth of an African City,* 160–236.

56. Maser, journal, 24 and 30 December 1873, CA2/068, CMS. Cases of slave flights featured prominently in archival records on Ikale district from the 1860s

through 1900. See missionary and colonial reports and interviews with Gbenga Ebisemiju, Olufemi Bankole, and Yemi Adepoju (all Ilaje), University of Ibadan, 8–20 May 1998; Chief Jerome Akinsipe, the Sara of Igbindo, 7 August 1998, and Charles Takuro, a descendant of Takuro of Ayesan, at the Ibadan Archives, 23–25 March and April 1999. For Lagos and Abeokuta, see Oroge, "The Fugitive Slave Crisis of 1859" and "The Fugitive Slave Question in Anglo-Egba Relations, 1861–1886"; Mann, *Slavery and the Birth of an African City*.

57. Rowe to Kimberley, 7 December 1881 and 5 May 1882, CSO 1/1/8, NAI. On antislavery, see Oroge, "Institution of Slavery," 360–420; Miers and Roberts, *The End of Slavery in Africa;* Miers and Klein, *Slavery and Colonial Rule in Africa;* Lovejoy and Hogendorn, *Slow Death for Slavery;* Sylvianne Diouf, *Fighting the Slave Trade.*

58. Wood to Lang, 28 October 1885, CMS(Y) 1/7/6, NAI.

59. Carter to Alaafin, 26 June 1892, dispatch #164, CSO 8/5/6, NAI.

60. Lt. Alfred O. Scott to Henry E. McCallum, 3 November 1897, CSO 1/1/20, NAI.

61. McCallum to Chamberlain, 8 December 1897, CSO 1/1/20, NAI.

62. Omofin of Ise vs. Fagun of Ise, 15 March 1910, Ondo Div. 7/2, NAI.

63. Shields, "Palm Oil and Power," 268.

64. Hinderer, *Seventeen Years in the Yoruba Country,* 82, 131–33; Ayandele, *The Missionary Impact on Modern Nigeria, 1842–1914,* 48; Adewoye, *The Judicial System in Southern Nigeria, 1854–1954;* Mann, *Marrying Well,* 114.

65. Meeting of Ondo church elders, 25 November 1889 and 24 February 1890, Phillips 1/4/4, NAI.

66. Payne to commissioner, 17 December 1913, Ondo Div 8/1, NAI.

67. Phillips to Lang, 13 January 1890, Phillips 1/1/3, NAI; Phillips, "Peculiar Difficulties"; Ondo Intelligence Report, 61, CSO 26/30172, NAI.

68. Conference on Polygamy, February 1857; Conference on Slavery, March 1880, CMS(Y) 2/2/3, NAI; Phillips's diary, 17 March 1887, Phillips 3/2, NAI.

69. Phillips, "Difficulties of Ondo Church," 14 February 1891, CMS(Y) 2/2/4, NAI.

70. Agreement on Monogamy Marriage Made by the Young Men's Christian Association of St Stephen's Church, Ondo, 17 October 1898, Phillips 3/8, NAI.

71. Phillips's diary, 15–23 May 1901, 2 April 1902, and 25 May–10 June 1903, Phillips 3/11–3/13, NAI.

72. Phillips, "Journey to and from Ilesa," February 1882, encl. 7 in Haastrup to Rowe, CO 147/48, National Archives, Kew. Captured by Ilorin soldiers in the 1820s, Haastrup was sold into slavery but later rescued and settled in Sierra Leone, where he became a Christian. After his return to Yorubaland, he traded on the lagoon and lived in Lagos and Itebu. He also traded in goods essential to the prosecution of the Kiriji war. He was one of the leaders of the Ekitiparapo society and also served periodically as secretary to his cousin, Owa Bepo of Ilesa (d. 1892), and as Governor Rowe's special agent to Ilesa in 1882. In April 1896 he was elected king of Ilesa and assumed the title Owa Ajimoko I.

73. Phillips to Wood, 9 January 1890, Phillips 1/1/3, NAI.

74. Phillips's diary, 19–20 and 25 January 1899, Phillips 3/9, NAI.

75. Oroge, "Institution of Slavery," 375–78.

76. Young's journal, 24 December 1873, 2 January and 25 May 1875, CA2/098, CMS; Phillips's journal, 30 September 1878, Phillips 1/3/1, NAI.

77. Adisatu as a second wife and Lade as a trader-slave. See commissioner's journal, 22 and 28 April 1898, Ondo Div. 8/1, NAI.

78. William Macgregor to Chamberlain, 19 June 1900, CSO 1/1/30, NAI.

79. McCallum to Chamberlain, 12 August, and Fuller to Chamberlain, 3 December 1897, CSO 1/1/20, NAI.

80. Albert Erhardt's journal, 25 September 1897, enclosed in McCallum to Chamberlain, 2 November 1897, CSO 1/1/20, NAI.

81. Ambrose, "Annual Report on Northeast District," *Lagos Annual Report 1901–1902*, 220. Captain Bower, the traveling commissioner into the Yoruba interior, arrested and jailed twenty impostors in 1893 and 1894.

82. Oroge, "Institution of Slavery," 135–38; CMS(Y) 2/2/3, NAI. The CMS slavery conference in 1880 also pointed out that members of a large family must agree on the process of emancipating a house slave.

83. Annual Report for Ondo Province, 1923, 59, CSO 26/1/11874 vol. 1, NAI.

84. P. E. M. Richards, district officer, Ondo, to resident, Ondo, 4 September 1923; H. C. Moorhouse to chief secretary, Lagos, 4 October 1923, CSO 26/2/11009, NAI.

85. Memo, H. C. Moorhouse, 29 September 1923; Moorhouse to chief secretary, 4 October 1923, CSO 26/1/11009, NAI.

86. See *Ogunwunmi of Ilesha vs. Chief Losare of Ilesha, 26 July 1905,* in "Notes on Two Cases of Slave Dealing," CSO 16/7/105/157/1905, NAI.

# References

Adewoye, Omoniyi. *The Judicial System in Southern Nigeria, 1854–1954: Law and Justice in a Dependency.* London: Longman, 1977.

Ajayi, Jacob F. Ade. *Christian Missions in Nigeria: The Making of a New Elite, 1841–1891.* London: Longman, 1965.

Akinjogbin, Adeagbo, ed. *War and Peace in Yorubaland, 1793–1893.* Ibadan: Heinemann Educational Books, 1998.

Akintoye, Stephen A. *Revolution and Power Politics in Yorubaland, 1840–1893: Ibadan Expansion and the Rise of Ekitiparapo.* London: Longman, 1971.

Akintunde-Ighodalo, Chief Folayegbe. Interview, Ibadan, 26 July 1999.

Akomolafe, Ade. Interview, Aaye Street, Ilawe Ekiti, 20 August 2001.

Akosile, Pa James. Interview, Okebedo Street, Ilawe Ekiti, 21 August 2001.

Allman, Jean. "Adultery and the State in Asante: Reflections on Gender, Class, and Power from 1800 to 1950." In *The Cloth of Many Colored Silks,* ed. John Hunwick and Nancy Lawler, 27–65. Evanston, Ill.: Northwestern University Press, 1996.

Allman, Jean Marie, Susan Geiger, and Nakanyike Musisi, eds. *Women in African Colonial Histories.* Bloomington: Indiana University Press, 2002.

Amadiume, Ifi. *Male Daughters, Female Husbands: Gender and Sex in an African Society.* Atlantic Highlands, N.J.: Zed Books, 1987.

Ambrose, W. Gerald. "Annual Report on Northeast District." *Lagos Annual Report 1901–1902.* Lagos: Government Printer, 1902.

Atandare, J. O. *Iwe Itan Akure.* Akure: Fagbamigbe Press, 1976.

Awe, Bolanle. "Iyalode Efunsetan Aniwura." In *Nigerian Women in Historical Perspective,* 57–71. Lagos: Sankore; Ibadan: Bookcraft, 1992.

Awe, Bolanle, and Omotayo Olutoye. "Women and Warfare in Nineteenth-Century Yorubaland: An Introduction." In *War and Peace in Yorubaland, 1793–1893,* edited by Idowu Akinjogbin, 121–30. Ibadan: Heinemann Educational Books, 1998.

Awoyele, Chief Seriki. Interview, Odosida Street, Ondo, 23 and 25 July 2001.

Ayandele, Emmanuel E. *The Missionary Impact on Modern Nigeria, 1842–1914: A Political and Social Analysis.* London: Longman, 1966.

Ayobami, Madam Iyadunni. Interview, Odosida Street, Ondo, 23 and 25 July 2001.

Beckles, Hilary McD., and Verene A. Shephered, eds. *Caribbean Slave Society and Economy.* New York: New Press, 1991.

Bohannan, Laura. "Dahomean Marriage: A Re-evaluation." *Africa* 19 (1949): 273–87.

Bridges, A. F. B. Intelligence Report on Ondo District of Ondo Province, 1934. CSO 26/30172, National Archives of Nigeria, Ibadan [hereafter NAI].

Burton, C. "Woman-Marriage in Africa: A Critical Study for Sex-Role Theory?" *Australian and New Zealand Journal of Sociology* 15 (1979): 65–71.

Byfield, Judith. *The Bluest Hands: A Social and Economic History of Women Dyers in Abeokuta (Nigeria), 1890–1940.* Portsmouth, N.H.: Heinemann, 2002.

———. "Women, Marriage, Divorce, and the Emerging Colonial State in Abeokuta (Nigeria), 1892–1904." *Canadian Journal of African Studies* 30 (1996): 32–51.

Colony of Lagos, Nigeria. *Lagos Annual Report, 1899.* Lagos: Government Printer, 1900.

———. *Lagos Annual Report 1901–1902.* Lagos: Government Printer, 1902.

Craton, Michael. "Changing Patterns of Slave Families in the British West Indies." *Journal of Interdisciplinary History* 10 (1979): 1–35.

Denzer, LaRay. "Yoruba Women: A Historiographical Study." *International Journal of African Historical Studies* 27 (1994): 1–39.

———. *Folayegbe M. Akintunde-Ighodalo: A Public Life.* Ibadan: Sam Bookman, 2001.

Diouf, Sylvianne, ed. *Fighting the Slave Trade: West African Strategies.* Oxford: James Currey, 2003.

Eltis, David. "Fluctuations in the Age and Sex Ratios of Slaves in the Nineteenth-Century Transatlantic Slave Traffic." *Slavery and Abolition* 7 (1986): 257–72.

Eltis, David, and Stanley L. Engerman. "Was the Slave Trade Really Dominated by Men?" *Journal of Interdisciplinary History* 22 (1992): 237–57.

———. "Fluctuations in Age and Sex Ratios in the Transatlantic Slave Trade, 1663–1864." *Economic History Review* 46 (1993): 308–23.

Eltis, David, and David Richardson. "West Africa and the Transatlantic Slave Trade: New Evidence of Long-Run Trends." *Slavery and Abolition* 18 (1997): 16–34.

Fagbohungbe, Akinkunmi. Interview, Odosida Street, Ondo, 23 and 25 July 2001.

Fawehinmi, Rasheed O. *Makers of Ode-Ondo.* Italy: Tipolitografia di Borgosesia, 1992.

Greene, Beth. "The Institution of Woman-Marriage in Africa: A Cross-cultural Analysis." *Ethnology* 37 (1998): 395–412.

Herskovits, Melville. "A Note on 'Woman Marriage' in Dahomey," *Africa* 10 (1937): 335–441.

Hinderer, Anna Martin. *Seventeen Years in the Yoruba Country.* Edited by C. A. and D. Hone, with an introduction by Richard B. Hone. 3rd ed. London: Seeley, Jackson, and Halliday, 1873.

Hopkins, Anthony G. "A Report on the Yoruba, 1910." *Journal of the Historical Society of Nigeria* 5 (1969): 67–100.

Huer, H. "'Woman Marriage' in Some East African Societies." *Anthropos* 63/64 (1969): 745–52.

Ifayinminu, Madam Comfort. Interview, Ogbon Oba Street, Ado Ekiti, 15 August 2001.

Ijagbemi, Adeleye. *Christian Missionary Activity in Colonial Nigeria: The Work of the Sudan Interior Mission among the Yoruba, 1908–1967.* Lagos: Nigeria Magazine, 1986.

Ikale District. Assessment Report, 1927–31. MLG (W) 8/1, NAI.

Jegede, J. O. *Itan Ise-Ekiti.* Ibadan: Micho Printing Works, n.d.

Johnson, Samuel. *The History of the Yorubas from the Earliest Times to the Beginning of the British Protectorate.* Lagos: C.S.S. Bookshops, 1921, 1976.

Kaplan, Flora E. S. "Runaway Wives, Native Law and Custom in Benin, and Early Colonial Courts, Nigeria." In *Queens, Queen Mothers, Priestesses, and Power: Case Studies in African Gender,* ed. Kaplan, 245–313. New York: New York Academy of Sciences, 1997.

Krige, E. J. "Women Marriage, with Special Reference to the Lovedu—Its Significance for the Definition of Marriage." *Africa* 44 (1974): 11–36.

Law, Robin. *The Oyo Empire c.1600–c.1836: A West African Imperialism in the Era of the Atlantic Slave Trade.* Oxford: Clarendon Press, 1977.

———. "'Legitimate' Trade and Gender Relations in Yorubaland and Dahomey." In *From Slave Trade to "Legitimate" Commerce: The Commercial Transition in Nineteenth-Century West Africa,* edited by Robin Law, 144–214. New York: Cambridge University Press, 1995.

Lindsay, Lisa. "To Return to the Bosom of Their Fatherland: Brazilian Immigrants in Nineteenth-Century Lagos." *Slavery and Abolition* 15 (1994): 22–50.

Lovejoy, Paul E. "Concubinage and the Status of Women Slaves in Early Colonial Northern Nigeria." *Journal of African History* 29 (1988): 245–66.

———. "Concubinage in the Sokoto Caliphate (1804–1903)." *Slavery and Abolition* 11 (1990): 159–89.

———. "Central Sudan and Atlantic Slave Trade." In *Paths Towards the Past: African Historical Essays in Honor of Jan Vansina,* edited by Robert W. Harms, Joseph C. Miller, David S. Newbury, and Michelle D. Wagner, 345–70. Atlanta: African Studies Association Press, 1994.

———. "The Yoruba Factor in the Trans-Atlantic Trade." In *The Yoruba Diaspora in the Atlantic World,* edited by Toyin Falola and Matt D. Childs, 40–55. Bloomington: Indiana University Press, 2004.

Lovejoy, Paul E., and Jan Hogendorn, *Slow Death for Slavery: The Course of Abolition in Northern Nigeria, 1897–1936.* Cambridge: Cambridge University Press, 1993.

Mann, Kristin. "Women's Rights in the Law and Practice: Marriage and Dispute Settlement in Colonial Lagos." In *African Women and the Law: Historical Perspectives,* ed. Jean Hay and Marcia Wright, 151–71. Boston: Boston University Press, 1982.

———. *Marrying Well: Marriage Status and Social Change among the Educated Elite in Colonial Lagos.* Cambridge: Cambridge University Press, 1985.

————. "Women Landed Property, and the Accumulation of Wealth in Early Colonial Lagos." *Signs* 16 (1991): 682–706.

————. "Owners, Slaves, and the Struggle for Labour in the Commercial Transition at Lagos." In *From Slave Trade to "Legitimate" Commerce: The Commercial Transition in Nineteenth-Century West Africa*, edited by Robin Law, 144–71. Cambridge: Cambridge University Press, 1995.

————. *Slavery and the Birth of an African City: Lagos, 1760–1900*. Bloomington: Indiana University Press, 2007.

Miers, Suzanne, and Martin Klein, eds. *Slavery and Colonial Rule in Africa*. London: Frank Cass, 1998.

Miers, Suzanne, and Richard Roberts, eds. *The End of Slavery in Africa*. Madison: University of Wisconsin Press, 1988.

Morrissey, Marietta. "Women's Work, Family Formation and Reproduction among Caribbean Slaves," *Review* 9 (1983): 339–67.

Obayemi, Madam Alice. Interview, Erekesan market, Ado Ekiti, 17 August 2001.

Oboler, Regina S. "Is the Female Husband a Man? Woman/Woman Marriage among the Nandi of Kenya." *Ethnology* 19 (1980): 69–88.

O'Brien, Denise. "Female Husbands in Southern Bantu Societies." In *Sexual Stratification: A Cross-Cultural View*, ed. Alice Schlegel, 109–26. New York: Columbia University Press, 1977.

Ogbonaye, Nathaniel. Journal, 1879. CA2/011/117, CMS.

Ogundana, Kayode. Interview, Ereguru Street, Ado Ekiti, 15 August 2001.

Oguntuyi, A. O. *The History of Ado Ekiti*. Part 2. Ado Ekiti: Bamigboye Press, 1978.

Ojo, Olatunji. "Warfare, Slavery, and the Transformation of Eastern Yorubaland c.1820–1900." PhD diss., York University (Toronto), 2004.

Oroge, E. Adeniyi. "The Institution of Slavery in Yorubaland with Particular Reference to the Nineteenth Century." PhD diss., University of Birmingham, 1971.

————. "The Fugitive Slave Crisis of 1859: A Factor in the Growth of Anti-British Feelings among the Yoruba." *Odu* 12 (1975): 40–54.

————. "The Fugitive Slave Question in Anglo-Egba Relations 1861–1886." *Journal of the Historical Society of Nigeria* 8 (1975): 61–80.

Perham, Margery, and Mary Bull, eds. *The Diaries of Lord Lugard*. 4 vols. Evanston, Ill.: Northwestern University Press, 1959–63.

Phillips, Charles. "Report of Charles Philips's visit to Itebu, Leke and Palma Stations 2–26 April 1880." Phillips 1/3/1, NAI.

————. "Journey to and from Ilesa, February 1882." CO 147/48, National Archives, Kew.

————. "Account of Visit to Kiriji Camp in March 1885." 19 August 1885, CMS(Y) 1/7/5, NAI.

————. "Difficulties of Ondo Church," 14 February 1891. CMS(Y) 2/2/4, NAI.

————. "A Statement of the Peculiar Difficulties Which Impede the Progress of the Infant Church at Ondo," 14 February 1891. CMS(Y) 2/2/4, NAI.

Pullen, A. Phillip. Assessment Report of Ekiti Division of Ondo Province, 1929–1930. CSO 26/51597, NAI.

Roper, Edward. "What I Saw in Africa: Sketches of Missionary Life in the Yoruba Country, Part II." *Church Missionary Gleaner* 3 (1876): 35–38.

Shields, Francine. "Palm Oil and Power: Women in an Era of Economic and Social Transition in Nineteenth-Century Yorubaland (South-western Nigeria)." PhD diss., University of Stirling, 1997.

———. "Those Who Remained Behind: Women Slaves in Nineteenth-Century Yorubaland." In *Identity in the Shadow of Slavery,* ed. Paul E. Lovejoy, 163–82. London: Continuum, 2000.

Temple, C. L., ed. *Notes on the Tribes, Provinces, Emirates, and States of the Northern Provinces of Nigeria,* Compiled from Official Reports by Olive Temple. New York: Barnes & Noble, 1967.

Vandeleur, Seymour. "Nupe and Ilorin," *Geographical Journal* 10, no. 4 (1897): 354.

Weir, N. A. C. Intelligence Report on Ado District of Ekiti Division, 1933. CSO 26/29734, NAI.

———. Intelligence Report on Akure District of Ekiti Division, Ondo Province, 1934. CSO 26/30014, NAI.

Young Men's Christian Association, St. Stephen's Church, Ondo. Agreement on Monogamy Marriage Made by the Young Men Christian Association of St Stephen's Church, Ondo, 17 October 1898. Phillips 3/8, NAI.

Young, Charles. Journal, 1873 and 1875. CMS(Y) CA2/o98, CMS.

8

# On Equal/Unequal Footing with Men: Diaspora Linkages and Issues of Gender and Education Policy in Barbados, 1875–1945

JANICE MAYERS

While provision is made, as on April 1st, 1945, for the secondary education of 1,543 boys, similar provision is only made for 878 girls; there are 651 boys in 1st Grade schools and 316 girls. It would appear that, should any further secondary school accommodation be envisaged, the question of girls' education should receive some priority of attention.

HOWARD HAYDEN, *THE PROVISION FOR SECONDARY EDUCATION IN BARBADOS*

When Howard Hayden, the first director of education in Barbados, reviewed the status of education in 1943, he suggested that colonial schools should discriminate in favor of girls, for despite the rhetoric of previous reports, the record of girls' secondary education was lacking. Barbados was not unique in this regard; gender imbalance was echoed elsewhere in the diaspora. Data for Jamaica shows that fewer girls than boys entered high school up to 1942. In 1911, 52.4 percent of the 1,544 students in public and private secondary school were boys. Of those in the public system, 64.7 percent were male.[1] Similarly, in Nigerian registered secondary schools in 1942, only 1,500 of 11,500 students were girls.[2] These similarities suggest that in attempting to document the philosophy underpinning the slow rate of change in secondary education for Barbadian girls, it is useful to establish linkages between the educational experiences of women across the diaspora.

The ideology of domesticity significantly influenced girls' education at home and in the British colonies. In England the ideological ideal was for all women to be at home engaged in domestic pursuits; however, class added important caveats. British society did not oppose labor for working-class women, but frowned on waged labor outside the home for middle-class and upper-class women. Thus while both groups were prepared for domesticity, middle-class girls received added tutelage in "ladylike" behavior.[3] Cole argues that girls' education in Barbados and other British West Indian societies "was predicated on the ideological assumption prevalent in Britain at the time that a woman's place was in the home and that her true vocation was that of wife and mother."[4]

Europe and the Americas were not the only parts of the Atlantic world where such ideologies influenced women's lives. The essays in Hansen's edited volume illustrate the adoption/adaptation of European domesticity ideology in Africa.[5] Musisi maintains that the missionaries who controlled education "were greatly influenced by the ideologies of domesticity prevalent at the turn of the century in both Uganda and Britain."[6] Denzer contends that "Victorian-Edwardian beliefs coincided with important elements in Yoruba cultural concepts about women's roles and status." Yet these concepts diverged in some respects. For example, Yoruba women were expected to participate in supporting the household, particularly in farming and selling surplus produce.[7]

Gender as a social construct provides areas of convergence. As Berger and White observe, "Commonalities in the construction of gender point to women as generally less privileged human beings than men." Further, "the fundamental construction . . . everywhere . . . has been to separate women from men—in role, status, privilege, access, and other ways."[8] Cole has probed such issues of gender as they appear in reports on primary, secondary, and teacher education for Barbados from 1875 to 1945.[9] This chapter extends the scope of the discourse on secondary education across the Caribbean and African diaspora. As a preliminary exploration of the shared experiences of women in Africa and the diaspora, it identifies beliefs about gender implicit in changing emphases and examines the extent to which women were mainstreamed in the discussion—mainly in official pronouncements.

In addressing these issues, we must be cognizant of differences between Barbados and other British-colonized territories in the West Indies and Africa as well as areas of divergence and convergence in these localities from and with metropolitan practice. Sometimes an examination of parallels and similarities reveals explanations of differences, for then we see more clearly the endogenous concerns that affect our differing responses to similar stimuli. As Goodridge asserts that, "despite the obvious social differences stemming from a historically different cultural evolution, the women of West Cameroon and their counterparts in the Caribbean shared a common existence in the six decades after 1900. This assertion is based upon the fact that both were subject to the pervasive influence of the plantation; and their lives were regulated to a greater or lesser extent by British colonial policy."[10]

The discourse on domesticity admits other connections to race, class, and gender aspects of girls' education. Bailey, for example, notes the intersection of class and gender in schooling and employment in Jamaica.[11] For Barbados, Mayers has demonstrated that "race and class were determining factors for access to education for both boys and girls, but gender was an added dimension for girls."[12] In the case of Britain, McDermid considers that between 1850 and 1950, the factors of gender, class, religion, and nationality all influenced female education.[13]

This study covers three periods: 1875–1919, 1920–39, and the early 1940s. Events in Barbados and the former British-colonized Caribbean are used to delimit the discussion, providing the backdrop against which issues in other parts of the Atlantic world are highlighted. Although these periods were chosen with Barbados in mind, they are also relevant to other areas. For example, the starting point for the first period is the year 1875, when the report of the commission chaired by Bishop John Mitchinson was published, five years after the passage of the Education Act in England, which greatly influenced the structure of education at home and in the empire. The Mitchinson report set the tone of Barbadian education for the next century.[14] The second period is seen within the context of evolving British imperial education policy in the late 1920s, with its emphasis on Africa. It encompasses the socioeconomic and political turbulence of the 1920s and 1930s, a time of ferment marked by struggles for middle-class advancement and greater democracy in Barbados. In addition, there was the Great Depression, which contributed to labor protests in the Caribbean and fueled demand for political change and educational reform. In the final period, ending in 1945, the main issues were related to international pressures from bodies such as the League of Nations that led to reforms throughout the diaspora after the Second World War.

## The Development of Girls' Education

Unlike other Caribbean islands, European settlement in Barbados began in 1627 and involved only the English. As the home of the seventeenth-century "sugar revolution," the island soon hosted a majority population of African descent, cultivating sugar as the major export crop, a pattern that was extended to other British territories in the region. As the Moyne commission observed later in the twentieth century, these territories differed from other parts of the empire in that they had "entirely lost the benefit of their original native cultures."[15] This may exaggerate the extent of dislocation, but it is true that enslaved Africans who had been transported to the region to work on the plantations would have suffered cultural dislocation and they would have necessarily restructured their West African heritage under conditions different from those on the continent. The continued presence of significant features of that heritage provides a link with the diaspora and underscores the desirability of exploring it.

Education in colonial Barbados developed along different lines than in other British colonies in the West Indies and Africa. For example, Miller and Gordon remark on the twenty- to thirty-year interval between the development of secondary education in Trinidad and Barbados and that in Jamaica.[16] Unlike territories such as Trinidad, which imported East Indian labor to compensate for the loss of African slave labor after emancipation, and unlike parts of Africa, such as Nigeria and the Cameroons, Barbados did not have to confront Islam in dealing with gender issues in education. Such considerations had a bearing on the nature of educational development.

Unlike Barbados and Jamaica where British colonization was a seventeenth-century experience, Nigeria's colonial era crystallized in the late nineteenth and early twentieth centuries when Britain consolidated its rule there. In 1906 the Colony and Protectorate of Lagos and the Protectorate of Southern Nigeria was reconstituted as the Colony and Protectorate of Southern Nigeria. In 1914 the British combined their northern and southern protectorates to form the Colony and Protector-ate of Nigeria.[17] Before the British arrived, there were two major types of education outfitting persons for participation in traditional society: the indigenous and Qur'anic.[18] To this milieu Christian missionaries intro-duced formal western education in the 1840s. The substantial progress of this system in the south contrasted sharply with its virtual nonexistence in the north where Qur'anic education remained dominant.[19] For pur-poses of comparison with the Barbadian situation, this chapter therefore focuses on southern Nigeria and on government-aided institutions.

The foundation of the Barbadian educational system was based on the earlier mentioned report of the Mitchinson commission, which rec-ommended a two-tiered system of primary and secondary education. It embraced universal primary education, dispelling fears of loss of labor for the vital sugar industry by introducing the notion of "better labour-ers for being educated." A narrow scholarship ladder encouraged the best stratum to do well in the primary schools. The formerly neglected education of the middle class, "an important section of the commu-nity," engaged the attention of the commission. It wanted to promote an educational system that would channel the middle class into "second grade" schools (this was the terminology used by Barbadian education authorities) as the lower rung of secondary education intended to end at age sixteen. Despite the protests of the commission, second grade education was clearly linked to the middle class. First grade education, on the other hand, would end at age eighteen, proceeding beyond the second grade curriculum "to impart . . . that indescribable something which we call culture." This level was intended to supply the leaders and thinkers of the society. This class-based philosophy of the Mitchin-son era allowed middle-class advancement, but virtually excluded the masses from participation in the higher educational system and limited social mobility.[20]

The education system of the British West Indies and West Africa was modeled on the British Education Act of 1870.[21] While in England the expansion of nondenominational schools followed along the lines delin-eated in the legislation, the opposite occurred in Ghana, indeed across West Africa, with education remaining largely in the hands of mission-aries. After emancipation, government in Barbados assumed a more cen-tral role in the provision of both primary and secondary schools. The

Mitchinson commission acknowledged its debt to the British Education Act, but observed that there were marked differences in practice between the metropole and the colony. Whereas in English primary schools, girls and boys were separated under the tutelage of their own sex, in Barbados a master taught primary school pupils, and infant schools were defined as "schools taught by a Female at a lower salary than a male Teacher, in which young children of both sexes are taught."

Despite the strong feelings of some clergymen about the moral "inexpediency of this mixture," the commission noted no general objection, and in light of the expense and scope of reconstruction to the system that change would entail, they hesitated to make recommendations on the issue. They were, however, perturbed that girls' education usually ended at the elementary stage where "very many girls receive all the education they ever get." Still the main body of the report stressed issues pertaining to the education of males except for a revealing concluding paragraph:

> Whether girls should receive identically, the same education as boys, whether their capacities are precisely the same, and if not, what ought to be the subjects on which their studies should be concentrated, are still unsettled questions. One thing seems clear, that if female education here is unsound and flimsy, narrow in range, and wanting in thoroughness; if moreover, the most valuable part of a young child's education, including the formation of its taste, and the development of its mental capacities depends mainly on early maternal teaching, it is idle to expect the boys in our first and second grade schools to go there well prepared and receptive of culture till this defect is remedied. So that after all, perhaps, the key to the problem of education really is to be found in the establishment, if possible, of thoroughly sound female education in the colony.

Although this paragraph purported to discuss the education of females, the discussion took place in the context of male needs: of serving males, of preparation of (especially middle- and upper-class) boys for life, and of girls' maternal role.

Even when the commission returned to female education in its conclusion and recommendations, slightly less than one of about eighteen pages was devoted to prescriptions for "sound female education in the middle and upper classes of society." Its recommendations included the establishment of one secondary school in Bridgetown to be headed by a lady principal from England and with a curriculum similar to that enjoyed by boys at the second grade level. Parents would have the option of paying for additional subjects such as music, drawing, and singing. Success with this institution was seen as a prelude to the later establishment of a school offering a higher-level curriculum.[22]

The nature of the discussion of gender issues in this and succeeding reports suggests that even though girls' secondary education was a recognized need, its provision for boys was considered the more pressing need. At this time gender ideology seemed to favor male domination and the preparation of girls for subordinate roles, reflected by the unequal footing of women and men in the teaching profession. In Barbados at the end of the nineteenth century, female teachers received three-quarters of the salary of males, the justification being that males married and had families to support. Married women were "not to be regarded as suitable persons to be teachers"; the education board considered a wife's proper place to be her home.[23]

The recommendations of the Mitchinson commission were embodied in the 1878 Education Act, and its successor, the consolidating 1890 act, which designated Harrison College (HC) and the Lodge School as first grade schools for boys. No provision was made for girls at this level until 1883 when Queen's College was established. Significantly, only the boys' schools offered a curriculum leading to university admission. By 1909 secondary school provision discriminated in favor of boys, with two of three first grade schools catering to boys and one of six second grade schools for girls. This was the situation that existed when the first local commission of the twentieth century met between 1907 and 1909 under the chairmanship of Bishop William Proctor Swaby.

The Swaby commission accepted that boys and girls should be afforded equal opportunity for elementary schooling; however, it retained class as the guiding principle for the two levels, with laborers confined to elementary schooling and middle-class students going on to secondary school for training as "thinkers" and "leaders and organisers." Recognizing that the time was long past when elementary instruction and a few accomplishments sufficed as suitable education for girls, the commission revived the idea of expanding higher female education and recommended the establishment of a second grade school for girls in Bridgetown. They also considered that a need for more girls' education existed in the windward parishes. The receipt of a "numerously signed" petition from St. John, St. Philip, and St. Joseph urging the establishment of such a school for those parishes and for parts of St. George and Christ Church seemed to be the motivating force behind this expressed need. The commission argued the value to the entire community of a sound education for the "mothers of the next generation."[24] Such arguments resonated with the evolving "eugenic ideologies of motherhood" in England, which linked healthy mothers to the health of the nation.[25]

The commission observed that the limited number of subjects available to girls meant that the expansion of higher education scholarships for girls would be "a barren gift, and will remain so until they are put on equal terms with boys." In lieu of establishing a separate scholarship, they recommended adding to the existing three, a subject that would accord with the curriculum at Queens College and thus place girls on equal footing in competition with their male counterparts.[26] As our discussion has shown, by the beginning of the twentieth century in Barbados, as in Britain, the prevailing expectations and assumptions of gender and class heavily influenced female education.[27]

In Jamaica, as in Barbados, the 1879 education ordinance had in effect "defined secondary education as middle-class education."[28] Girls were usually not allowed to take either the classics or the vocational subjects readily available to boys. A similar bias toward grammar school education was evident in southern Nigeria. In his study of the evolution of secondary education in Nigeria, Ajayi contends that since the mid-nineteenth century the accepted theory of education encouraged technical and agricultural schools for the many and literary schools for the few, but eventually literary education became established as the almost exclusive form of secondary education.[29] When secondary education was provided with state funding, King's College in Lagos, the first government secondary school, founded in 1909, catered to boys. During this period throughout the empire, middle- and upper-class boys received longer and qualitatively better educational training than working-class boys or girls. Indeed, few girls received more than three years of elementary education.

### Changing Colonial Policy during the Interwar Period

During the period between the two world wars, secondary education expanded, including education for girls. Ajayi shows that this demand in Nigeria came from Africans. He identifies the main pressure groups as the clergy, teachers, professionals, merchants, and politicians.[30] Black, colored, and white creole families in Trinidad also demanded the expansion of local educational facilities so that they could take advantage of slowly expanding employment opportunities for women. The economic crisis of this period affected every segment of Caribbean society and restricted the ability of even those families who could have afforded to send their daughters to school in Barbados or Europe.[31]

In the case of Barbados, Blackman notes the period after the First World War as "a time when blacks and browns were redefining democracy and attempting to make it more real to those who were not among the more privileged in Barbados." He argues that "blacks could only really be free if greater educational opportunities were available to them."[32] Middle-class businessmen in the urban vestry of St. Michael provided an example of the possible influence of blacks who perceived this connection. One of these, Washington Harper, strongly criticized the system for its emphasis on educating boys and not girls.[33] This vestry made the establishment of a second grade school for girls a political issue.[34] In response to demands for expanded middle-class and female education in the 1920s, two second grade schools were approved. The Christ Church Foundation girls school was recognized as second grade, and largely through the efforts of the St. Michael Vestry, the St. Michael Girls' School [SMGS] was built.

Francis "Woodie" Blackman discusses the expectations of middle-class education for girls in his biography of Dame Nita Barrow, the former governor-general and past scholar of the SMGS. Before the 1930s protest movements, educated blacks had few employment opportunities, and women fewer still, especially in the civil service.[35] The contemporary debate over the SMGS curriculum indicated some of the issues surrounding middle-class education. When the scheme for the school came before the House of Assembly, middle-class members objected to the inclusion of domestic science and needlework in the curriculum. While debate on the curriculum centered on the virtues of Latin over domestic economy, it nonetheless revealed a common desire to provide training for the future mothers and wives of middle-class men. The debate also revealed strong feelings among some members that SMGS girls should not aspire to the curriculum enjoyed by Queen's College girls, the sole first grade school for girls. Rather, as late as 1938, some reactionary members of the upper chamber of the legislative council considered subjects such as laundering to be more acceptable for the pupils of SMGS. In their view, the Queen's College type of curriculum constituted education beyond their station in life.[36] Meanwhile, a glance at the curricular offerings of secondary schools in 1937 reveals a generous offering of the classics in first grade boys' schools such as Harrison College and Latin in second grade boys' schools and Queen's College. Mathematics and science were emphasized for boys who would go on to higher studies at a university.[37]

Around the same time as the SMGS, Queen's College was founded in 1927 in Lagos (Nigeria). Here the issue of girls' secondary education and curriculum sparked a similar debate. Initially the curriculum included literary subjects, domestic science, and singing, with mathematics and foreign languages taught only if parents requested and paid for it separately. The continuing importance of the basic tenets of domesticity was highlighted in the prospectus's stated aim to produce "cultured women, practical housewives, and wise mothers."[38] Despite protest by several parents who desired a more academic or vocational curriculum, the principal in 1929 wrote that "the character of girls' education should be of a particular kind. It is almost universally agreed that it should not be a copy of that which is given to boys."[39]

Johnson observes that "neglect of women's education reflected both the sexism and class bias of British society." In this regard McDermid maintains that even after the 1918 Education Act, secondary education in England remained the preserve of the middle classes, with emphasis at both primary and secondary levels for curricula appropriate to gender.[40]

Among the developments taking place in Nigerian education in the interwar years was the appointment in 1929 of Eric R. J. Hussey as director of education on transfer from Uganda, where the government had supported the continuing emphasis on domesticity.[41] Tibenderana describes Hussey as "a strong advocate for girls' and women's education."[42] Taiwo notes that his 1930 Memorandum on Educational Policy in Nigeria accorded girls' education special attention. Although Hussey made impressive strides in education in the south, in 1929 only 39 of 181 secondary school pupils in the two government secondary schools were girls. Gender inequality was still evident.[43]

The Mayhew-Marriot commission report of 1933 showed a similar situation in the British West Indies where they identified 18 secondary schools for boys and 14 for girls.[44] Eleven of these schools were located in Barbados. The Marriott-Mayhew report recommended the introduction of two types of secondary schools: grammar and modern. The former would continue the academic tradition while the latter would cater to vocational needs. Male students would benefit from industrial and commercial courses in preparation for employment in carpentry, teaching, agricultural training to equip them to serve as estate managers, or other skilled occupations. Female students in the modern school, however, would receive training in domestic science or commercial studies for those interested in modern jobs. Thus females still did not have equal footing with men in either quantity or quality of education.

In the 1930s similar curriculum debates unfolded in British West Africa. The seemingly conservative nature of domestic science curriculum obscured the fact that it became a vehicle for promoting the expansion of female education and employment opportunities. Denzer details efforts to develop domestic science training for marriage training and mothercraft as well as to provide vocational training.[45] Goodridge shows that during the interwar years, Britain's "unimaginative proposals" for raising the perceived low status of Cameroon women included instruction in mothercraft, housewifery, and midwifery. Classes in needlework, laundry, cooking, and infant welfare were expanded. He further observes that international pressure for amelioration of women's circumstances was exerted through a League of Nations Assembly resolution in 1935 calling on the International Labor Organization to investigate the existing political civil and economic status of women. The international campaign emphasized the need for an expanded educational program so that women could assume their "'true' vocation of teachers, midwives, and district and hospital nurses."[46]

## Balance Sheet of the 1940s

The worldwide economic depression of the 1930s continued into the early 1940s resulting in reduced spending and contraction at a time of increased demand for education in southern Nigeria and the Caribbean.[47] It resulted in unemployment, economic distress, and social unrest in the

Anglophone Caribbean, prompting local and imperial investigation. Social unrest prompted the British government to appoint a commission of
inquiry under the chairmanship of Lord Moyne. By the time the Moyne
commission report (completed in 1939) was released in 1945, the more
overt and lengthy discussion of female education in its own right seemed
to have shifted to recognition of the need to improve the low status of
the region's women, which was also discussed at length in the report.
"Essential equality of educational opportunity between the sexes" was
deemed crucial to dealing with this challenge. Yet Mohammed pinpoints
the contradiction inherent in the commission's subsequent statement that
wide cultural education was necessary for happy marriages in which girls
would be companions to their husbands and the recommendation that
girls should begin vocational training earlier than boys. She contends
that the answer to the contradiction lies in the interplay between ideology
and the economic reality confronting working-class women who had to
labor outside as well as within the household.[48] Indeed, the commission
itself remarked on the lower rate of wages for women than men in light of
the reality that "the woman so often is the supporter of the home."[49]

The Moyne commission found that West Indian girls were generally
disadvantaged in secondary education because government provision
for them was lower than for boys. Moreover, girls "desirous of entering
the professions" had difficulty in obtaining instruction in subjects required for higher academic training. Like the Swaby commission some
thirty years earlier, the Moyne commission concluded that "in justice
either the [scholarship] regulations should be so modified as not to discriminate against girls, or the appropriate teaching should be made as
readily available to them as to boys."[50]

Similar to the findings of the Moyne commission in the British West
Indies, the Cameroons Provincial Development Committee was dissatisfied with the seeming backwardness of Cameroon women and shared the
view that education could remedy socioeconomic backwardness. According to the resident, "Until we do something to educate the women of this
province, we will never improve the economic situation and thus create
the wealth from which the general education of women will follow."[51]

In some parts of the West Indies (for example, Barbados), criticism
of the shortcomings of educational provision for girls must be viewed
against the background of a persistent excess of females over males in

the total population.[52] The higher level of provision for male education needs explanation. It may be partly explained by perceptions of the relative value to the society of educating the two genders, a point made by Campbell and Cole for Trinidad and Barbados, respectively.[53] Privileging boys' education over girls' occurred throughout the colonies. In the case of Cameroon, Goodridge cites the 1943 statement of the women's education officer, Gladys Plummer, who concluded that comparatively little had been done to educate west Cameroon girls because families preferred to invest in boys' education first.[54]

This attitude toward unequal provision of girls' education must be viewed as part of existing attitudes toward women in general and their participation in the society. Among the indicators of the low status of women cited in the Moyne commission report were the absence of the right to vote and limited participation in public administration.[55] By the 1940s in the British West Indies and Africa this had slowly begun to change. In Barbados, the first woman was appointed to the education board in 1932 and the franchise was extended to women in 1943. As argued elsewhere, the operation of "patriarchal hegemony" is significant in the Barbadian context. Since males had greater access to the locus of power than women did, they could exercise superior political power, facilitate political debate, and lobby effectively for specific causes.[56] Thus, whereas the SMGS was successfully completed because of persistent lobbying from black middle-class assemblymen who fought the opposition of authorities to such a school, in the case of Queen's College in Lagos it was prominent Lagosian women, supported by the wives of European officials, especially the governor's wife, who stood up to the authorities.[57] Even where circumstances dictated a positive response to female issues and concerns, the resulting official reports were delivered through a male lens.

So what, then, was the balance sheet by 1945? In official reports, girls were acknowledged to be on unequal footing with boys. The question was: Should they be placed on equal footing? This question resonated throughout the British empire, persisting to a greater or lesser degree throughout the period under review. As shown in this chapter, by the 1920s and 1930s, girls' education was accepted, but its quality and content were heatedly debated. By the 1940s, public discussion about the expansion and quality of girls' education became intertwined with its role in elevating the status of women. Some gains were evident in secondary education overall, even if not always resolving the issue of gender disparity.[58]

Howard Hayden was appointed as director of education in 1943 in Barbados, precipitating a new era in education. In 1945, he quickly produced three memoranda evaluating the system and outlining policy.[59] Hayden's remarks on the inadequacy of provision for female education cited at the beginning of this chapter were made against the backdrop of intensified demand for secondary education in Barbados. The island record of 7.7 pupils per 1,000 of the population was highest in the Anglophone Caribbean in 1942, while its jump to 9.4 per 1,000 in 1945 compared favorably with the 1938 figures in England of 11.4 per 1,000. However, the number of secondary schools remained unchanged from the eleven available in 1928. Despite conceding the need for according priority to facilities for girls, Hayden's proposal for additional funding by a grant under the Colonial Development and Welfare Act projected the continuation of discrimination in favor of boys, according them approximately eighty-three more places than girls.[60] Three years after his appointment, he was transferred to Fiji, before approval of plans such as that for a new modern secondary school for girls went into effect.

In England, despite the 1944 Education Act, which extended the right to free secondary education to all children and was meant to encourage social mobility, "there remained a class basis to domestic education for girls, which represented continuity with nineteenth-century ideas." Such education was "targeted at less able and lower classes," so was more significant in the low-status secondary modern sector than in grammar schools. Whether it concerned the working class in England or the descendants of former enslaved laborers in the Caribbean, it was neither expected nor intended that education would remove the majority of students from their parents' status. Girls remained at a disadvantage over the period under review. Many of the prescriptions for their education "reflected the continuing assumption that girls were to have an education in domesticity, that their future was motherhood."[61]

## Conclusion

Philip Foster concluded that the 1920s were extraordinary in terms of the extent of discussion of colonial, and particularly African, education: "Several definitive proposals were made concerning the proposed context and nature of colonial educational practice."[62] Other commentators opined that, in the immediate postwar period, public demand for educational expansion was as important and dynamic as the demand for nationalist autonomy. Leaders recognized that education was imperative in the development of skilled professionals and administrators to develop a national infrastructure. They urged the necessity of all hands being on deck, cooperating in the task of nation building. Educated women were viewed as essential in creating an informed citizenry and united nation. Thus decolonization in the British empire resulted in the rapid growth of more access to education for girls at every level. In spite of the substantial growth, a report on the status of women in Barbados in 1978 noted that the unequal provision of education for boys and girls still remained a challenge.[63]

## Notes

1. Miller, *Jamaican Society and High Schooling*, 69, 218.
2. Coquery-Vidrovitch, *African Women*, 152.
3. McDermid, "Women and Education," 107–108.
4. Cole, "Official Ideology and the Education of Women," 3. For a comparison with Trinidad, see Campbell, "Good Wives and Mothers."
5. Hansen, *African Encounters with Domesticity*.
6. Musisi, "Colonial and Missionary Education," 173.
7. Denzer, "Domestic Science Training in Colonial Yorubaland, Nigeria," 116–17.
8. Berger and White, *Women in Sub-Saharan Africa*, lxi.
9. Cole, "Official Ideology and the Education of Women."
10. Goodridge, "Women and Plantations in West Cameroon since 1900," 385. It should be noted that Britain governed western Cameroon as a mandated territory in conjunction with the administration of colonial Nigeria.
11. Bailey, "Sexist Patterns of Formal and Non-formal Education Programmes," 145.
12. Mayers, "Access to Secondary Education for Girls in Barbados, 1907–1943," 261.
13. McDermid, "Women and Education," 126.
14. Barbados, Education Commission. *Report of the Education Commission*, 1875 (hereafter Mitchinson report].
15. Great Britain, West India Royal Commission, *Report of the West India Royal Commission*, 1945 (hereafter Moyne report).
16. Miller, *Jamaican Society and High Schooling*, 55; Gordon, *Reports and Repercussions in West Indian Education, 1835–1933*, 31. The explanations offered in each case are indicative of the differences existing between territories.

17. Tibenderana, *Education and Cultural Change in Northern Nigeria, 1906–1966*, 25.

18. For a useful outline of these systems, see Fafunwa and Aisiku, *Education in Africa*, chap. 1.

19. Ibid., 207.

20. See Mitchinson report.

21. Foster, *Education and Social Change in Ghana*, 84.

22. The foregoing discussion and quotations derive from Mitchinson report, 17–18, 21–22, and 33.

23. Barbados, Board of Education, *Rules and Regulations for Public Elementary Schools*, 1898, rules 1c and 21.

24. Barbados, Education Commission, *Report of the Education Commission, 1907–1909*, 2, 17–18, 21 (hereafter Swaby report).

25. D'Cruze, "Women and the Family," 73–74.

26. Swaby report, 23.

27. McDermid, "Women and Education," 120.

28. Miller, *Jamaican Society and High Schooling*, 95.

29. Ajayi, "The Development of Secondary Grammar School Education in Nigeria," 517.

30. Ibid., 517, 522.

31. Employment opportunities for women increased in education and secretarial fields. Campbell, *Colony and Nation*, 90.

32. Blackman, *Dame Nita*, 17–19.

33. St. Michael Vestry Minutes, 22 February 1917, Barbados Department of Archives, St. James.

34. Ibid., 21 January and 1 April 1924.

35. Blackman, *Dame Nita*, 14, 21.

36. Barbados, *Legislative Council Debates*, 16 August 1938. For a fuller discussion of the SMGS issue, see Mayers, "Access to Secondary Education for Girls in Barbados."

37. Annual Report, Department of Education, Barbados, 1937.

38. Denzer, "Domestic Science Training," 122–23.

39. Johnson, "Class and Gender," 239–40.

40. McDermid, "Women and Education," 122.

41. Musisi, "Colonial and Missionary Education," 180–81.

42. Tibenderana, *Education and Cultural Change*, 83.

43. Taiwo, *The Nigerian Education System: Past, Present, and Future*, 75–77.

44. Great Britain, *Report of a Commission Appointed to Consider Problems of Secondary and Primary Education in Trinidad, Barbados, Leeward Islands, and Windward Islands, 1931–32* (chaired by Frederick Claude Marriott and Arthur Mayhew).

45. Denzer, "Domestic Science Training," 123ff.

46. Goodridge, "Women and Plantations in West Cameroon," 392–93.

47. See, for example, Taiwo, *The Nigerian Education System*, 84, and Denzer, "Domestic Science Training," 125–26.

48. Mohammed, "Educational Attainment of Women in Trinidad-Tobago, 1946–1980," 43–44.

49. Moyne report, 220.

50. Ibid., 131.
51. Goodridge, "Women and Plantations in West Cameroon," 391, 395.
52. See, for example, Barbados, *Report on the Census, 1921,* tables VII and IX.
53. Campbell, "Good Wives and Mothers," 1; Cole, "Official Ideology and the Education of Women," 3.
54. Goodridge, "Women and Plantations in West Cameroon," 395.
55. Moyne report, 217–20.
56. Mayers, "Access to Secondary Education for Girls in Barbados," 272.
57. Mba, *Nigerian Women Mobilized,* 62–64; Coker, *A Lady,* 55–59.
58. For example, by 1943 in Jamaica, public secondary schools had increased from thirteen to twenty-three: eight for boys, ten for girls, and five coeducational. See Miller, *Jamaican Society and High Schooling,* 117–18.
59. Hayden, *The Evaluation of Education in Barbados;* Hayden, *A Policy for Secondary Education in Barbados;* Hayden, *Provision for Secondary Education in Barbados.*
60. Hayden, *Provision for Secondary Education in Barbados,* 2–3, 7.
61. McDermid, "Women and Education," 123.
62. Foster, *Education and Social Change in Ghana,* 156.
63. Lynch, "The Education of Women in Barbados," 68.

# References

Ajayi, J. F. "The Development of Secondary Grammar School Education in Nigeria." *Journal of the Historical Society of Nigeria* 2, no. 4 (1963): 517–35.
Bailey, Barbara. "Sexist Patterns of Formal and Non-formal Education Programmes: The Case of Jamaica." In *Gender: A Caribbean Multi-disciplinary Perspective,* ed. Elsa Leo-Rhynie, Barbara Bailey, and Christine Barrow, 144–58. Kingston: Ian Randle, 1997.
Barbados. Board of Education. *Rules and Regulations for Public Elementary Schools,* 1898.
Barbados. Department of Education. Report, 1937.
Barbados. Education Commission. *Report of the Education Commission, 1875.* Chaired by Bishop John Mitchinson.
———. *Report of the Education Commission, 1907–1909.* Chaired by Bishop William Proctor Swaby.
Barbados. *Legislative Council Debates.* 1938.
Barbados. *Report on the Census.* 1921.
Berger, Iris, and E. Frances White. *Women in Sub-Saharan Africa: Restoring Women to History.* Bloomington: Indiana University Press, 1999.
Blackman, Francis "Woodie." *Dame Nita: Caribbean Woman, World Citizen.* Kingston: Ian Randle, 1995.
Campbell, Carl. "Good Wives and Mothers: A Preliminary Survey of Women and Education in Trinidad, 1834–1981." Women and Society Seminar #2, Department of History, University of the West Indies, Mona, November 1985.
———. *Colony and Nation: A Short History of Education in Trinidad and Tobago, 1834–1986.* Kingston: Ian Randle, 1992.

Coker, Folarin. *A Lady: A Biography of Lady Oyinkan Abayomi*. Ibadan, Nigeria: Evans Brothers, 1987.

Cole, Joyce. "Official Ideology and the Education of Women in the English-Speaking Caribbean, 1835–1945, with Special Reference to Barbados." In *Women and Education*, ed. Joycelin Massiah, 1–34. Cave Hill, Barbados: Institute of Social and Economic Research, University of the West Indies, 1982.

Coquery-Vidrovitch, Catherine. *African Women: A Modern History*. Boulder, Colo.: Westview Press, 1997.

D'Cruze, Shani. "Women and the Family." In *Women's History: Britain, 1850–1945*, ed. June Purvis, 51–83. New York: St. Martin's Press, 1995.

Denzer, LaRay. "Domestic Science Training in Colonial Yorubaland, Nigeria." In *African Encounters with Domesticity*, ed. Karen Tranberg Hansen, 116–39. New Brunswick, N.J.: Rutgers University Press, 1992.

Fafunwa, A. Babs, and J. U. Aisiku, eds. *Education in Africa: A Comparative Survey*. London: Allen & Unwin, 1982.

Foster, Philip. *Education and Social Change in Ghana*. London: Routledge, 1965.

Goodridge, Richard. "Women and Plantations in West Cameroon since 1900." In *Engendering History: Caribbean Women in Historical Perspective*, ed. Verene Shepherd, Bridget Brereton, and Barbara Bailey, 384–402. Kingston: Ian Randle, 1995..

Gordon, Shirley. *Reports and Repercussions in West Indian Education 1835–1933*. London: Ginn, 1968.

Great Britain. West India Royal Commission. *Report of the West India Royal Commission*. Cmd 6607. Chaired by Walter Edward Guinness, 1st Baron Moyne. London: His Majesty's Stationery Office, 1945.

Hansen, Karen Tranberg, ed. *African Encounters with Domesticity*. New Brunswick, N.J.: Rutgers University Press, 1992.

Hayden, Howard. *The Evaluation of Education in Barbados: A First Experiment*. Bridgetown: 1945.

———. *A Policy for Secondary Education in Barbados*. Barbados: Advocate Co., 1945.

———. *The Provision for Secondary Education in Barbados*. Barbados: Department of Education, 1945.

Johnson, Cheryl P. "Class and Gender: A Consideration of Yoruba Women during the Colonial Period." In *Women and Class in Africa*, ed. Claire Robertson and Iris Berger, 237–54. New York: Africana, 1986.

Lynch, Enid. "The Education of Women in Barbados." In *The Report of the National Commission on the Status of Women in Barbados*, vol. 2, ed. Norma Monica Forde, 67–80. Bridgetown: Government Printer, 1978.

Marriott, Frederick Claude, and Arthur Mayhew. *Report of a Commission Appointed to Consider Problems of Secondary and Primary Education in Trinidad, Barbados, Leeward Islands, and the Windward Islands, 1931–32*. London: His Majesty's Stationery Office, Colonial No. 79, 1933.

Mayers, Janice. "Access to Secondary Education for Girls in Barbados, 1907–1943: A Preliminary Analysis." In *Engendering History: Caribbean Women in Historical Perspective*, ed. Verene Shepherd, Bridget Brereton, and Barbara Bailey, 258–78. Kingston: Ian Randle, 1995.

Mba, Nina Emma. *Nigerian Women Mobilized: Women's Political Activity in Southern Nigeria, 1900–1965.* Berkeley: Institute of International Studies, University of California, 1982.

McDermid, Jane. "Women and Education." In *Women's History: Britain, 1850–1945: An Introduction,* ed. June Purvis, 107–30. New York: St. Martin's Press, 1995.

Miller, Errol. *Jamaican Society and High Schooling.* Mona, Kingston, Jamaica: Institute of Social and Economic Research, University of the West Indies, 1990.

Mohammed, Patricia. "Educational Attainment of Women in Trinidad-Tobago, 1946–1980." In *Women and Education,* ed. Joycelin Massiah, 35–77. Cave Hill, Barbados: Institute of Social and Economic Research, University of the West Indies, 1982.

Musisi, N. "Colonial and Missionary Education: Women and Domesticity in Uganda, 1900–1945." In *African Encounters with Domesticity,* ed. K. T. Hansen, 172–94. New Brunswick, N.J.: Rutgers University Press, 1992.

St. Michael Vestry Minutes. 1917 and 1924. Barbados Department of Archives, St. James.

Taiwo, C. O. *The Nigerian Education System: Past, Present, and Future.* Lagos: Nelson, 1980.

Tibenderana, Peter K. *Education and Cultural Change in Northern Nigeria, 1906–1966.* Kampala: Fountain, 2003.

Map supplied by the University of Texas Libraries and modified by Michael Siegel, Staff Cartographer, Geography Department, Rutgers University.

# PART THREE

# Building Diaspora in the Web of Empire

# 9

# Amy Ashwood Garvey and the Nigerian Progress Union

HAKIM ADI

Although Britain played a key role in creating the African diaspora, and Africans in Britain were at the forefront of Pan-African struggles against slavery and colonialism and for the rights of all, historical research on African and Caribbean women in Britain is still very much in its infancy. In recent years there have been important new studies focusing on the lives and work of key women of the twentieth century, such as the Jamaican writer Una Marson and the Trinidadian communist and political activist Claudia Jones.[1] Much work remains to be done, however, before we have a more general understanding of the histories and significance of women of African descent in Britain.

Certainly Amy Ashwood Garvey was one of the key figures in the twentieth-century British diaspora. Born in Port Antonio, Jamaica, in 1897, Amy Ashwood was only seventeen years old when she first met Marcus Garvey. In 1916 she played a leading role with Garvey in forming the Universal Negro Improvement Association (UNIA) in Jamaica and in reestablishing it in New York two years later. She married Garvey in 1919, but their married life was short-lived and they separated in the early 1920s. By that time Amy Ashwood had served as secretary of the UNIA and its women's division and as a member of the Black Star Line's board of directors. In 1922 she left New York for London, which remained one of her homes for the rest of her life.[2]

Her political activities in Britain began with her crucial role in the founding of the Nigerian Progress Union (NPU), the first Nigerian organization to be formed in the country. Although of limited duration, the NPU was a significant organization and the immediate predecessor of the West African Student Union (WASU), which became the main African anticolonial organization in Britain for more than thirty years. Although Amy Ashwood Garvey's papers and reflections on her links with Nigerians in Britain have not yet been made public, this article will sketch out her role in the NPU and document the main features of its brief history.

In the early twentieth century Britain was the center of many Pan-African activities, an important networking place for black activists and intellectuals from the United States and the Caribbean as well as the African continent. Interaction between Africans from the continent and those from the diaspora in Britain played an important role in the development of Pan-African consciousness and was crucial in the political development of key individuals, including Marcus Garvey, Paul Robeson, Jomo Kenyatta, and Kwame Nkrumah. Robeson proclaimed that he "discovered" Africa in London, but perhaps Amy Ashwood Garvey could make almost the same claim, for it was in London that she first confirmed that her African roots were to be found among the people of the Asante kingdom and she became actively involved with Africans from the continent.[3]

African student organizations had existed in Britain since the beginning of the twentieth century. African students were often radicalized by their sojourn in Britain as a consequence of the ubiquitous color bar and by the treatment meted out to them as colonial subjects. In the heart of the empire they came into contact with various political ideologies, individuals, and organizations. They quickly found themselves in a strong position to lobby the imperial government and represent the interests of their compatriots in Britain's African colonies. Students, professionals, and seaman from Britain's four West African colonies constituted the majority of the African population in Britain during the first half of the twentieth century.

One of the earliest organizations to include West African members was the African Association, formed by the Trinidadian Henry Sylvester Williams in 1897. The association convened the first Pan-African conference in London in 1900. Several other Pan-African organizations of this type were formed in London, Liverpool, Edinburgh, and other British cities in the early part of the century. In 1916 West African students formed their own African Students' Union in London, and in the same year a West African Christian Union was also formed in the capital. But it was not until the founding of the West African Students' Union (WASU) in 1925 that Africans formed an organization which had a clear anticolonial orientation designed to campaign in their interests in Britain.[4] The founding of the NPU therefore played an important role in the period when Nigerians were developing the political consciousness that was a central feature of the WASU.

As indicated above, this consciousness was in many cases shaped by the experiences Africans encountered when they arrived in Britain. The early experiences of Ladipo Solanke, who arrived in London from Nigeria in 1922, are fairly typical.[5] Solanke came to London when he was already a "mature student" of 38, to complete his legal studies and to enter the Bar. He was enrolled at University College, London, but whatever his expectation may have been, he soon found that he was thoroughly miserable and living in some poverty. According to his diary, he spent the summer of 1924 teaching Yoruba at University College in London "to get my daily bread." He wrote that he had to "borrow here and there" to survive, and what he calls "my trinkets" were given to his landlady "for security of debts."[6]

But poverty was only one of Solanke's problems. He also had to deal with the racism that accompanied Britain's colonial conquests and empire. In 1924 the British Empire exhibition was held at Wembley, London, which was organized to boost morale following the difficult years occasioned by the First World War. For Solanke and other students, the exhibition had quite a different effect. In his diary he wrote a full page concerning a "simply degrading Nigerian film," which one of his friends had seen at Wembley and what was to become a notorious article, "When West Africa Woos," which appeared in the *Sunday Express* of 4 May 1924. The empire exhibition seems to have been the excuse for the appearance in the press of several anti-African articles, and Solanke soon made a name for himself as the champion and defender of African interests. In March 1924 the *Evening News* carried an article entitled "Empire Making in Nigeria," in which the author had credited the colonial government with abolishing within twenty years what was referred to as "cannibalism" and "black magic." The article had also alluded to a recent speech delivered by Governor Sir Hugh Clifford to the

Nigeria Legislative Council, in which he had allegedly referred to areas of Nigeria in which "human meat was sold quite openly in the markets in quite recent times."[7]

Solanke immediately made his protest to the *Evening News,* but not content with the space they accorded his reply, he forwarded a copy to *West Africa* as well. He complained that the newspaper article had distorted Clifford's speech, that there were no records of cannibalism in Nigeria, and that such reports would "do serious harm to those of us from Nigeria who are now in London for educational purposes."[8] The vice president of the Union of Students of African Descent (USAD), A. Kasumu Soetan, also wrote to *West Africa* in support of Solanke's letter, arguing that such racism could only undermine what he saw as the good work of colonial administrators and missionaries in West Africa.[9] Unfortunately, the article in the *Evening News* was followed by a series of others ridiculing the West African section of the Empire exhibition, particularly a specially constructed mock Gold Coast village.[10] This time the USAD passed a resolution denouncing the articles, which was sent to the colonial secretary, James Henry Thomas, and demanding that the Colonial Office take measures to ensure more sensitive reporting by the press. Although the Colonial Office was reluctant to comply, the matter was eventually settled by Sir Frederick Gordon Guggisberg, the governor of the Gold Coast, who intervened to bar the press from the village, while the publicity council of the exhibition also took steps to prevent the publication of further derogatory articles.[11]

The protest by the USAD and Solanke succeeded partly because it had occurred during the Wembley exhibition, when West Africa and general colonial matters assumed greater prominence at home. It also highlighted the growing political influence of West African students, especially those from Nigeria, who made up the largest group of West Africans in Britain. Solanke had certainly made his mark, and following his letter in the *Evening News,* he received encouragement from an unexpected quarter. Amy Ashwood Garvey, recently estranged from her husband Marcus Garvey, was living in Streatham in south London and had seen the articles in the *Evening News* and *West Africa.*[12] She immediately wrote to congratulate Solanke and enthusiastically talked of racial pride and a novel she was proposing to write about Nigeria. Solanke, somewhat dejected by the racism and poverty he found in London, despairing of his friends and the enticements of white women, clearly welcomed her letter. He invited her to visit him, and they quickly became friends. It seems that Solanke had some hopes of romance, but had to settle for a more platonic relationship based on politics.[13] Largely thanks to Ashwood Garvey's enthusiasm, they began to plan the formation of the first Nigerian student organization in Britain, the NPU.

The relationship that developed between Ashwood Garvey and Solanke was clearly important and interesting, but we only catch glimpses of it from Solanke's diaries and personal notes. The evidence suggests that the relationship was a close one, even if it initially lasted only for a few months. For Solanke, Ashwood Garvey became Adeyola (his sister's name), and he did not hesitate to state that the NPU was "conceived, born, and mothered by Miss Amy Adeyola Ashwood."[14] Exactly what role she played is difficult to establish from the limited information that exists. Even before the formal founding of the NPU, Amy Ashwood Garvey had organized for the Nigerian students an outing to Windsor Castle in honor of Henry Carr, who had recently retired as resident of the Colony of Lagos. The students read their special address to Carr, presented him with a photo album of the trip and a quill pen, toasted the great achievements of the race, and stressed the need for unity and cooperation. To underscore the importance of this event, the students published a commemorative pamphlet, *The Nigerian Students and Henry Carr*.[15] It seems likely that Amy Ashwood inspired and helped organize these students, but her political views may also have had some influence on them. She certainly believed, as she later stated in an interview published in the *Gleaner* in Kingston, Jamaica, that her former husband had been wrong in his political orientation and had abused what she referred to as the "intelligentsia." For her, however, education was the prerequisite for politics. She said, "The Negro as a race is not yet ripe for political emancipation. You must educate him before he will be able to understand anything about politics."[16] She also took issue with Marcus Garvey's conception of Pan-Africanism, stating publicly that his "idea of an African Kingdom was a geographical blunder," based on his ignorance of African realities. She argued that "there are too many tribes each differing from the other in customs," and therefore "that it is quite impossible to form them into a simple people." She argued that Garvey had also been wrong to create "peers" for Africa and concluded, "The native African is a suspicious creature. He has his doubts about all outsiders and he was practically [sic] doubtful about Marcus Garvey."[17]

For Solanke and many Nigerian students, the issue was more how Nigeria could play its rightful role in the world. Ironically, they were partly influenced by the thinking of Marcus Garvey, as well as by the ideologies and politics of emergent nationalist organizations in West Africa, such as the National Congress of British West Africa (NCBWA) and Herbert Macaulay's Nigerian National Democratic Party (NNDP). Solanke wrote, "When one talks of anything relating to Nigeria, he is touching upon a question in which perhaps more than eighty per cent of the Negro race the world over are more or less concerned . . . [It was] the Negro country within the British Empire full of immense possibilities, with undeveloped resources and wealth capable of being exhausted within another century or more." It was a country such that "the possibility of a mighty Negro Empire or Republic in Nigeria is not a statement beyond the prophetic horoscope of its future."[18] The problem, as the students considered it at the time, was not that Nigeria was a British colony but that, for all its potential greatness, it had no university college to educate its inhabitants. What secondary education it had was limited and "not national enough," whereas women's education was almost totally neglected. Through the NPU they hoped "to solve the social industrial, economic, and commercial problem of Nigeria from the platform of Education of the masses of the Nigerian peoples; co-operating of course, with the Government, Missionaries and other bodies that have hitherto been bearing the brunt of the whole burden."[19]

The NPU was founded on 17 July 1924 at a meeting at the house of F. Ola Vincent (a student at the Inner Temple) in Ladbroke Grove, West London. Thirteen students gathered for the inaugural meeting, at which F. Oluwale Lucas, a law student of the Middle Temple, presided. Amy Ashwood Garvey did not attend this meeting; however, she had sent an invitation for the students to join her for tea at her residence in Streatham to discuss her education policy for Nigeria. The members decided that her role was such that she should be given the Yoruba title of "Iyalode" of the new organization "as an honour for life."[20] The meeting elected an executive committee, with Daniel Ekanem Esin (of the Middle Temple and London School of Economics) as president, F. O. Lucas (of the Middle Temple) as vice president, F. O. Vincent as treasurer, and Solanke as honorary secretary. Solanke and three others were appointed to draft the union's rules.[21] Most of the NPU members were studying law or medicine. At least three founding members were women, a significant number when compared with other organizations in Britain at this time. Two of the female members were daughters of Dr C. C. Adeniyi-Jones, one of the NPU patrons and a member of the Nigerian Legislative Council, and the other was Doris Williams, a student at Tryon College; nothing more is known about their contribution to the new organization. In addition to Adeniyi-Jones, the NPU decided to invite Henry Carr, J. H. Doherty (a wealthy merchant), and Chief Richard Henshaw of the Calabar National League to serve as honorary patrons.

The NPU drew up five "articles":

1. To promote the spirit of unity and cooperation among its members;
2. To further the interests of Nigerian students;
3. To foster the habit of self-knowledge and self-help;
4. To promote the general welfare of Nigeria;
5. To inculcate a high sense of duty as well as the spirit of loyalty and devotion toward the cause of our country and race.

Its main objectives were as follows:

1. To promote the education of the masses of the British Colony and Protectorate of Nigeria;
2. To secure a hostel in London furnished with a good library and common rooms for Nigerian students in Great Britain;
3. To establish national schools throughout the length and breadth of Nigeria equipped with trained teachers;
4. To send Nigerian students to various countries and universities to be trained as teachers, mechanics, engineers, and other necessary professions for the progress of Nigeria;
5. To promote Negro or African literatures, customs, and institutions through research.[22]

NPU objectives echoed Marcus Garvey's program for self-help and self-reliance, although these were also popular ideas among nationalists in West Africa. They combined a strong nationalism and concern for African customs and institutions with the belief in educational reform as the major mechanism for bringing about economic and political changes.

It is difficult to judge how much political influence Amy Ashwood Garvey had on the students. Clearly, they had a great deal of respect for her, demonstrated by bestowing on her the honorary title "Iyalode" (literally, mother has arrived) in appreciation of her love, interest, and services for the union as an organizer and on behalf of her future activities for the NPU.[23] These future activities included fund-raising for the NPU when she returned to the United States in the autumn of 1924.[24] Her fund-raising seems to have been closely linked to her plans to establish an education program to further the development of mass vernacular education in Nigeria. It seems that she saw herself as the driving force behind the NPU. In her 25 September 1924 interview with the *Gleaner* she explained:

> I am working on my own lines now, and I am concerned particularly with Nigeria. I have started an Association in London, known as the Nigerian Progress Union, and it is intended for the well-being of Nigerian students in England and the Continent. There is already a large membership and it is growing. We intend to build a hostel in London. We have some funds towards it already. And I am not working single handed. I have the support of some able men. Mr. Henry Carr, late Resident of Lagos is one of them . . . and the hon. Dr Adeniyi Jones, one of the three elected members of the Legislative Council of Lagos. Then the kings of several African tribes have written to me assuring me of their support. They understand what I am driving at and they want it. They want education— not politics.

Ashwood Garvey was at pains to explain how her views differed from those of her estranged husband, but she very likely helped to consolidate the Garveyite opinions already held by many of the Nigerian students. Solanke made it clear that although the students "may disagree with some of the methods of the great Negro organiser," the UNIA "has achieved much among us here in the fact that it has aroused in us in a material way our race consciousness."[25] Amy Ashwood Garvey herself acknowledged that her former husband had "awakened the race consciousness of the negro and created the desire in him to raise his status."[26] A similar consciousness can be seen among WASU members in its early years of the WASU, which also advocated self-help and self-reliance, "devotion towards the cause of country and race," and the promotion of African customs and institutions. Thus Ashwood Garvey's ideas—the role of the intelligentsia, the centrality of education to self-determination and coalition building between Africans at home and abroad—reinforced ideas they had already developed. Her support and encouragement served to clarify their ideas.

Solanke had no doubts about the debt he and the NPU owed her. When she left Britain, he wrote to her:

> I must confess you have been a real sister to me for this period of five months and I have achieved many successes through you and only through you alone. . . . Remember the Union you and I have brought into existence, it is full of many possibilities and at the same time it may stand to show whether the Negro has any organising ability. Remember the Union has now become a sacred trust in our hands.[27]

Ashwood Garvey's departure further distanced her from the day-to-day activities of the NPU, but the organization's activities continued to reflect critical dimensions of her political insights. The students, for example, maintained close links with nationalist politicians like Adeniyi-Jones and Macaulay. Certainly their activities were partly stimulated by the formation of the NCBWA in Accra in 1920, but perhaps even more important was Macaulay's NNDP. Solanke hoped for Macaulay's support, but at the same time explained to Macaulay how the students were extremely concerned "at the disunity which yet continues among our elderly men," and how they wanted "you all to find a way to unite for the purpose of giving us (your children) a helping hand for progress." Solanke stressed the absolute necessity for the unity of Nigerian politicians: "Neither the Government nor the (commercial) European Industrialist are strong enough to constitute our formidable or unconquerable foe if we really unite and co-operate."[28]

From their central position in the metropole, they built links with visiting African dignitaries, professionals, and business people. The newly formed NPU first came to the notice of the Colonial Office after they had arranged a reception for the emir of Katsina during his visit to London in September 1924. The emir was greeted with a speech from Adeniyi-Jones, who explained that the existence of the NPU was "wholly and solely for the purpose of fostering the love of learning in the mind of every true child throughout the length and breadth of United Nigeria." Adeniyi-Jones encouraged the emir to develop education in his province and to promote teaching of the English language as "most essential" for the progress of British West Africa and the creation of greater unity between northern and southern Nigeria.[29] What the emir replied is not reported, but it is clear that the NPU had some difficulty honoring the visiting dignitary and was constantly impeded by his official interpreter, who had sent the emir elsewhere on the first occasion when the NPU had arranged a reception. The NPU therefore decided to complain to the Colonial Office.[30] The Colonial Office was unimpressed by NPU complaints. Although the officials knew nothing about the organization, they were rather wary of Adeniyi-Jones's involvement and the NPU's link with politicians in Nigeria. In July 1925 the Colonial Office once again came into contact with the NPU, when the secretary of University College, London (UCL), asked whether the officials approved of the union and its aims, which appeared to be "harmless and even useful" as well as "a concealed form of political propaganda."[31]

The NPU, and Solanke in particular, had been very active at UCL, where they held a number of meetings. Solanke and some of the students were members of the Faculty of Laws Debating Society and disciples of Professor J. E. G. de Montmorency who delivered a series of talks to the NPU, including one entitled "The Significance of the Humanism of the Negro Races." The professor seems to have been a firm supporter of the NPU and a confidant of Solanke. He was photographed with NPU members and even helped to draft one of its letters to the Colonial Office, even though he also believed that Britain was civilizing the "barbaric nature" of Africa. Although a proponent of self-help, he thought that educated West Africans must aid their less fortunate brethren by learning the benefits of "western civilisation," assisted by their "elder brother(s)"—the Europeans.[32] The Colonial Office appears to have known little about the NPU, apart from the reports of its activities and Solanke's writings in *West Africa* and other journals, but the secretary of the UCL promised to make further enquiries.

A few months later, Solanke sent the Colonial Office a copy of the NPU constitution and aims. The officials felt that the objectives were ambitious, "unless it gets hold of some soft-headed American millionaires." They replied with an encouraging letter. In October 1925, Colonial Office officials met with the NPU executive for the first time.[33] At the meeting the NPU appealed for financial support. Solanke explained the activities of the NPU, which by that time had a membership of about thirty, mostly in London, but also among students in Birmingham, Bristol, and Edinburgh. He stressed the welfare concerns of the NPU and their plans for a hostel to meet the needs of African students, pointing out that so far British welfare organizations, the USAD, and the APU had not yet established a hostel. The Colonial Office representatives argued that the NPU must prove itself before it could expect help from the imperial authorities, but it shared NPU's concern about the growing number of destitute West Africans in Britain and the problem of supervising the students.[34] Meanwhile, the NPU had already secured support from the Etubom, a traditional ruler in Calabar and Chief of the Ekpenyon Nsa family. E. I. Ekpenyon, the chief's brother and a member of the NPU, had written to the colonial secretary, seeking a meeting during the chief's next business trip to London to "personally urge the Colonial Office to do what is possible to forward the interests of many Nigerian students now in London." This letter made it clear that one of these interests was the establishment of a "Hostel for Nigerian Students."[35] WASU had been established in August 1925, but the NPU meeting with representatives of the Colonial Office shows that NPU continued its activities independently. Eventually WASU would succeed in organizing a student hostel, and it did so in rivalry with the secret plans of the Colonial Office.[36]

Communication and publication were important goals of the organization as they tried to network. The NPU hoped to publish a monthly newsletter and a collection of members' memoirs of their student days, but it apparently never materialized, although WASU would establish a magazine. The NPU did publish one of Montmorency's lectures, though, and Solanke wrote on various issues for *West Africa*. The main literary efforts of the NPU appeared in the African American monthly journal, the *Spokesman*, based in New York, to which Ashwood Garvey had introduced the NPU.[37] There were few, if any, accounts of the NPU in British or Nigerian publications. According to an article entitled "The Why of the Nigerian Progress Union," the organization had recently issued a pamphlet "with a view to appealing to the Negroes of West Africa and everywhere, particularly those of Nigeria for unity and co-operation." The results had been so favorable that it planned another publication.[38] The NPU claimed to have branches at the universities of Edinburgh, Glasgow, Dundee, Cambridge, Birmingham, and Bristol, as well as in

Lagos, Abeokuta, Aba, and Calabar. It also claimed to have widespread support for a Nigerian National Education Fund that was being organized to realize its aims.

Of particular interest in the NPU reports in the *Spokesman* were those that show Solanke's attempts to enlist the support of African Americans and his acceptance of the Garveyite concept of the unity of "Africans at home and abroad." He sought to enlighten "the American Negro" about African culture and in return hoped for financial and other support for NPU education plans.[39] Solanke's "Open Letter to the Negroes of the World," addressed to both West Africans and African Americans, indicates that he and the NPU were developing a political platform based on what they considered to be the most pressing problems in the British West Africa colonies, particularly Nigeria, "the mighty home of the American and West Indian Negroes." There was not much questioning of colonial rule itself, although there was concern that, as had occurred in East and South Africa, land might be seized by "British capitalists" like Lord Leverhulme. Emphasis was placed on the primacy of education and its importance to the West African masses if they were to acquire the necessary skills to exploit their own natural resources. Solanke argued that West Africans themselves, not the colonial government and not the missionaries, should establish their own "Tuskegees," assisted by their "brethren in America," to produce trained specialists of all types. Ironically, as Solanke acknowledged, this was the very policy favored by the British government. The year before the establishment of the NPU, the Colonial Office had sent one of its own specialists, Hanns Vischer, to Booker T. Washington's Tuskegee Institute, to study how "Negro Education" was organized, with a view to applying its principles in the African colonies.[40]

Solanke's articles concerning the NPU in the *Spokesman* demonstrate that the NPU were confident enough to present their views to an audience in the United States as well as in West Africa and Britain. He argued that it was up to Nigerians themselves to raise the money necessary for mass education, for only then could they call for the assistance of their brethren in the United States. Here we see little of Amy Ashwood Garvey's views about the alleged "suspicious" nature of Africans nor doubts about Garvey's motives. One of Solanke's appeals concludes with the Garveyite view: "The time has now come when the Negro at home and the Negro abroad should find the way out to understand each other better with a view to co-operating for the final emancipation of the whole of the Negro race educationally, industrially, politically, and commercially."[41]

Although Ashwood Garvey played a key role in establishing the NPU, Solanke was clearly its most active and articulate member. He seems to have been keen to involve himself in all the major political questions of the day and often contributed letters to the editor and articles to *West Africa* on colonial issues, such as "indirect rule," land alienation, and other matters.[42] In April 1925 he called on the NCBWA to support the NPU plans for mass education in Nigeria, self-reliance, economic development, education, and eventual national independence. Although this represented a very early demand for "national independence," Solanke insisted that education, not politics, was the key to advancement, echoing the views of Ashwood Garvey on the subject. Clearly, not all students agreed with his views, and some members left the NPU for the new organization, WASU.[43] Solanke and other NPU members also belonged to USAD, but had grown weary of its lack of concern for West African issues and its emphasis on social events. Solanke, who was a member of the USAD executive, had even proposed that the USAD join the NCBWA and that all the existing Pan-African organizations, including the APU, "be incorporated into one or establish one union called the United Africa Society or the Central Committee of Students of African Descent."[44] This dissatisfaction, however, did not lead to the founding of a new Pan-African body, but instead resulted in the Nigerian students establishing first their own organization and then WASU in August 1925.

Although the NPU was in existence for just over a year, its significance lies in the fact that it marked the first time that Nigerian students felt confident enough to strike out and form their own organization, concentrating on those issues that particularly concerned them. It took up the whole question of colonial rule and the need for unity between nationalists in Nigeria and Britain. It desired to find ways to promote and present African customs and institutions to a wider audience, and it began to explore how Africans, basing programs on the principle of self-reliance, could solve their own problems, including establishing a hostel for Africans in London. In these and many other ways it paved the way for the formation of WASU, an organization that lasted more than thirty years and played a major role in British, Pan-African, and West African politics. No doubt NPU was a vehicle for the aspirations and personality of Ladipo Solanke, a most energetic nationalist, who devoted his life to organizing for the benefit of students in Britain and the independence of Nigeria and British West Africa.

Yet much of the inspiration for the formation of the NPU, and some of the ideas underpinning its aspirations, were contributed by a Jamaican woman, Amy Ashwood Garvey, who left Britain soon after the NPU had been created. She continued her interest in West African affairs as well as women's education and emancipation, and she maintained links with the NPU and with Solanke and other West Africans in Britain and on the continent. After some years in the United States, she returned to Britain and played a significant role in Pan-African politics and entertainment. In the mid-1930s, she opened a night club in London, the Florence Mills Social Parlour, which became the haunt of many political figures, including George Padmore and C. L. R. James. In 1935, she was one of the founding members and treasurer of the International Friends of Abyssinia, and then she became a vice president, with Jomo Kenyatta, of the International African Service Bureau, led by I. T. A. Wallace-Johnson, Padmore, and James. Politically active in Jamaica and the United States during the Second World War, she returned to Britain in 1945 and played a prominent role in the historic Manchester Pan-African Congress.

Her concern with the emancipation of African women became more evident during the 1940s. In 1944, she announced plans to publish an international women's magazine to "bring together the women, especially those of the darker races, so that they may work for the betterment of all." She added, "There must be a revolution among women. They must realise their importance in the post-war world. . . . Women of the world must unite."[45] But no such magazine was ever published. At the Manchester Pan-African Congress, she was the first speaker to raise the question of the "black woman" who, she claimed, had "been shunted into the social background to be a child-bearer."[46] One of only two women speakers at the congress, she has been credited with ensuring that the final conference resolutions included five clauses particularly relating to women. Following the congress, Ashwood Garvey renewed her acquaintance with Solanke, staying with him in London, before leaving on a journey to Liberia and several French and British colonies in West Africa where she aimed to "work for the education of native women." In a newspaper interview at the time she warned: "A nation without great women is a nation frolicking with peril. . . . Let us go forward and lift the degradations which rest on the Negro woman—God's most glorious gift to all civilizations."[47]

During this first visit to West Africa, she traveled extensively in Liberia, Sierra Leone, the Gold Coast, and Nigeria from 1946 through 1949. Although her movements were monitored by the U.S. government,[48] she was able to contact and speak to individual women and women's organizations throughout the region, such as the Women's Party in Nigeria, and to conduct research on the position of women in West Africa. Her lectures and talks frequently focused on the issue of women's emancipation and education, and in Abeokuta, Nigeria, she urged that the title of "Iyalode," which had been conferred on her by the NPU, should be resuscitated.[49] But perhaps even more important for her personal development, during her trip to the Gold Coast in 1946–47 she established that her own African roots could be found in Asante. In this she was helped by lawyers J. B. Danquah and Cobina Kessie, both of whom she had met in London.[50] She also began to research the position of women in West African societies, something which her biographer suggests may have been inspired by her links with Solanke and the NPU in the 1920s.[51]

Ashwood Garvey continued to travel extensively in the Caribbean and West Africa. She returned to Britain in 1957 to open a business, the Afro-Woman Service Bureau; a hostel and advice center, the Afro-Women's Center; and a political organization, the Association for the Advancement of Colored People, whose secretary was Claudia Jones. She continued her political activities in Britain, the Caribbean, the United States, and Africa until her death in May 1969. Yet despite her lifelong political activism and central role in many of the key British-based African organizations of the twentieth century, there is still much that remains unknown about Ashwood Garvey's life and politics. She is a woman who needs to be appreciated in her own right as a political activist and not merely as "Wife No. 1" of a famous man. Amy Ashwood did her own thinking, had her independent analysis of the world around her, and at appropriate times openly expressed her disagreement with the views of her former husband. Clearly a lifelong Pan-Africanist, she participated in many of the most important political events of the century from the founding of the UNIA to the historic 1945 Pan-African Congress to the independence of Ghana in 1957. But it is not easy to characterize her political views. She demonstrated a concern with all the major problems confronting Africa and the diaspora and aligned herself with those who presented a Marxist-Leninist analysis of these problems. What is most apparent about the life and work of Ashwood Garvey, although we have little evidence of this in relation to the NPU, is her determination to contribute to the emancipation of women. Here, too, her approach was internationalist as well as Pan-Africanist, but as she pointed out at the Manchester Pan-African Congress: "Very much has been said about the Negro, but for some reason very little has been said about the black woman." Through her activities in the United States, Britain, the Caribbean, and Africa, Amy Ashwood Garvey attempted to highlight the plight of black women and to encourage women to affirm themselves. In this regard she was very much a pioneer among the major Pan-African figures of the twentieth century.

## Notes

1. Jarrett-Macauley, *The Life of Una Marson, 1905–1965*; Sherwood, *Claudia Jones*.
2. This account is largely based on Marika Sherwood's brief biography of Amy Ashwood Garvey in *Pan-African History: Political Figures from Africa and the Diaspora since 1787*. For more biographical information, see Martin, *Amy Ashwood Garvey*, and Yard, *Biography of Amy Ashwood Garvey*. See also Martin's shorter studies, "Amy Ashwood Garvey, Wife No. 1" and "Discovering African Roots."
3. See Martin, *Amy Ashwood Garvey*, 87, 217.
4. For a political history of West Africans in Britain, see Adi, *West Africans in Britain*.
5. Ladipo Solanke (c.1884–1958) was born in Abeokuta in southern Nigeria. He had been educated at St Andrew's Teacher Training Institution, Oyo, Nigeria, and Fourah Bay College, Freetown, Sierra Leone, before arriving in Britain.
6. See "Mr. Solanke to Broadcast," *West Africa*, 21 June 1924, 618, and "My Hardship in London" in his diary 1920, p. 92, Solanke Papers [hereafter SOL] 35, Gandhi Memorial Research Collections [hereafter GMRC], University of Lagos [hereafter Unilag]. Solanke taught Yoruba at London University's School of Oriental Studies (now School of Oriental and African Studies) and was the first Nigerian to broadcast in Yoruba.
7. "Empire Making in Nigeria," *Evening News*, 5 March 1924, 3.
8. Ladipo Solanke, "An Outrage," letter to editor, *West Africa*, 22 March 1924, 247. To put matters into perspective, Solanke referred to reports made in 1884 about cannibalism among shipwrecked British sailors and an Essex man who had sold his wife.

9. A. Kasumu Soetan, "Africans and Britons," letter to editor, *West Africa*, 10 May 1924, 445; Adi, *West Africans in Britain*, 23–24. The USAD had grown out of the West African and West Indian Christian Union, founded in 1917 under the auspices of the Student Christian Federation of Great Britain and Ireland. After attracting a number of non-Christian student members, the union changed its name to the Union of Students of African Descent. Its membership rose from 25 in 1921 to around 120 by 1924. Its first president was Percy Acham Chen. In its early years the union seems to have been dominated by West Indian rather than West African students; however, in 1923 C. F. Hayfron-Benjamin from the Gold Coast was elected president, and many more West African students became members.

10. These articles are located in CO 554/64/23120, National Archives [hereafter NA], Kew.

11. USAD to the Colonial Secretary, 14 May 1924, CO 554/64/23120, NA, Kew; "Manners Makyth—Empire," *West Africa*, 10 May 1924, 433; and USAD, "When West Africa Protests," letter to editor, *West Africa*, 17 May 1924, 484. It is quite likely that Solanke was the original mover of the resolution, since his diary reveals that he had already proposed a motion "that this Union begin a campaign to suppress the every day ridicule against the Blacks in this country." He regularly scoured the pages of *West Africa* and other publications for examples of offensive reporting. See his diary, SOL 59, GMRC, Unilag.

12. According to an interview published in the Kingston *Gleaner* on 25 September 1924, Ashwood Garvey went to Europe "to study conditions, social problems, human nature . . . as part of an educational and social and educational programme which I am working on in behalf of Nigeria."

13. Entry for 26 March 1924, private and personal memos, 1924, SOL 42, GMRC, Unilag.

14. Ladipo Solanke, "The Why of the Nigerian Progress Union," *Spokesman* (New York), April–May 1925, 25.

15. Entry for 3 September 1924, NPU minute book, SOL 78, GMRC, Unilag. Over 2,000 copies of *The Nigerian Students and Henry Carr* were published. Most copies were sent to Nigeria and Sierra Leone. Other guests at the outing included Akin Adesigbin (a law student), W. Harding of Lagos, and B. Tamakloe (a Gold Coast barrister). In one speech Solanke returned to the subject of the original disparaging newspaper articles, including one by Wilson Harris in the *Daily News*. He also took the opportunity to wish Adeyola (Amy Ashwood Garvey) success when she returned to the United States. The NPU organized a farewell gathering for Henry Carr in August 1924, shortly before his return to Nigeria. He promised to promote the interests of the NPU in Africa and called on the students "as leaders of your race" to unite for common aims. For an account of this meeting, see the *Spokesman*, June 1925, 28–29.

16. Interview, *Gleaner*, 25 September 1924, 7.

17. Quoted in Martin, *Amy Ashwood Garvey*, 88

18. Solanke, "The Why of the Nigerian Progress Union," 25.

19. Ibid., 26.

20. Ibid. Solanke explained: "The term 'Iyalode' is a Nigerian word from Yoruba language [*sic*] which has no equivalent either in English or any other foreign language for it is one of the highest circuit or State titles conferred upon women in Yoruba

land and embraces such wide civil social and political jurisdiction that it appears to be a question whether the so-called Western Civilisation has any institution among women as high as this office."

21. Minutes, 17 July and 12 August 1924, NPU minute book, SOL 78, GMRC, Unilag. The other members of the commission were Ekundayo Williams, Daniel Ekanem Esin, and Jibril Martins. The other founder members were G. Rufino, Ajayi Johnson, Ernest Goyea, J. J. Martins, F. Oluwale Lucas, U. Pedro, U. Siffre, and Omosanya Adefolu. We know that Esin, Lucas, Vincent, and Solanke were law students at London colleges, and it is likely that many of the others were, too. It must be noted that at least one student, J. O. Coker, wrote to the NPU claiming that its formation was totally unnecessary.

22. These goals were published in the *Spokesman,* April–May 1925, 26. The union also adopted the motto *Sol omnibus lucet* (The sun shines for all).

23. Minute, 12 August 1924, NPU minute book, SOL 78, GMRC, Unilag.

24. Henry Carr also wrote to W. E. B. Du Bois in the United States to ask him to help NPU fund-raising efforts.

25. Solanke, "Open Letter to the Negroes of the World," *Spokesman,* June 1925, 12–15. In 1928 Marcus Garvey allowed the WASU to use his house in London as its headquarters while he was away in Jamaica. Evidently, he also provided WASU with some financial support.

26. Quoted in Martin, *Amy Ashwood Garvey,* 88

27. Solanke to Adeyola Ashwood, 7 September 1924, private and personal memos, SOL 42, GMRC, Unilag. In this letter Solanke continues to express his love for "Adeyola," and despite his own difficulties, he refers to the financial help he has provided for her.

28. L. Solanke to H. Macaulay, 16 March 1925, file 18, box 7, Herbert Macaulay papers, Manuscript Collection, Kenneth Dike Memorial Library, University of Ibadan.

29. "Speech by Dr C. C. Adeniyi-Jones, a Patron of Nigerian Progress Union, at a Reception given by the Nigerian Progress Union in Honour of the Emir of Katsina, Great Central Hall, 25 September 1924," SOL 56/4, GMRC, Unilag.

30. CO 583/131/48464, NA, Kew.

31. Secretary, UCL to Colonial Office, 16 July 1925, CO 538/138/32506, NA, Kew.

32. See Montmorency to Solanke, 21 September 1925, SOL 56/4, GMRC, Unilag. See also "Education in West Africa," *West Africa,* 28 June 1924, 646, and "The Nigerian Progress Union," *West Africa,* 28 February 1925, 167. For Montmorency's speech, see "The Significance of the Humanism of the Negro Races," *West Africa,* 7 March 1925, 178, 181. Among other things, he stressed that the union could play an important role by introducing to West Africa "the rule of law" and "the best of English civilisation." See also his address to the NPU, "Education in West Africa," *West Africa,* 8 August 1925, 985.

33. CO 538/138/44339, NA, Kew.

34. Interview with Etubom and Chief of Ekpenyon family, his brother, and Solanke, 2 October 1925, CO 538/138/44339, NA, Kew.

35. E. I. Ekpenyon to Colonial Secretary, 1 October 1925, CO 538/138/44575, NA, Kew.

36. For more details of the hostel issue and the rivalry between WASU and the Colonial Office, see Adi, *West Africans in Britain,* 57–67.

37. The *Spokesman* was published monthly in New York and edited by Thomas Anderson and W. H. Ferris. From March through June 1925, it featured a series of articles by Solanke and the NPU. See Solanke, "Nigeria: Its Institutions and Customs," March 1925, 24–26; "The Why of the Nigerian Progress Union," April–May 1925, 25–26 and 30–31; "Open Letter to the Negroes of the World," June 1925, 12–15; and "The Nigerian Progress Union—The Farewell Address of Henry Carr," April–May 1925, 28–29. Solanke apparently served as the *Spokesman*'s "foreign correspondent."

38 So far, no details of these publications have been found.

39. Solanke, "The Why of the Nigerian Progress Union" and "Open Letter to the Negroes of the World." Among other things, Solanke reminded his readers of the agreements concluded in 1859 between "Commissioners on behalf of the African race in the USA and some important Kings and Chiefs of Nigeria." According to these agreements, African American settlers would come to Nigeria and educate the brethren in agricultural, industrial, and other skills.

40. CO 554/161/8864, NA, Kew.

41. Solanke, "The Why of the Nigerian Progress Union," 26.

42. Solanke, "The Land Rights of African Races," letter to editor, *West Africa*, 16 August 1924, 834–35; Solanke, letter to editor on Lugard's theory of indirect rule, *West Africa*, 31 January 1925, 48–49; and Solanke, "Sir Hugh Clifford and the Autonomy of the Egba Nation," letter to editor, *West Africa*, 7 March 1925, 198–200.

43. Solanke, "West African Land and Self-Development," letter to editor, *West Africa*, 4 April 1925, 311; "People and Government," letter to editor, *West Africa*, 25 April 1925, 407; reply from L. A. Amponsah, "People and Government," *West Africa*, 9 May 1925, 477; and Solanke, "The Palm Oil Industry and Self-Help," letter to editor, *West Africa*, 30 May 1925, 582–83.

44. Diary, 1920, 59–60, SOL 35, GMRC, Unilag.

45. Adi and Sherwood, *The 1945 Manchester Pan-African Congress Revisited*, 72.

46. Ibid., 98.

47. "Garvey's Widow Sails for Africa," *Chicago Defender*, 5 September 1945, 8.

48. Martin, "Discovering African Roots," 122.

49. Denzer, "Intersections: Nigerian Episodes in the Careers of Three West Indian Women."

50. Martin, "Discovering African Roots," 124.

51. Martin, *Amy Ashwood Garvey*, 224. See also Solanke's "Nigeria: Its Institutions and Customs," *Spokesman*, March 1925, 24–26.

# References

Adi, Hakim. *West Africans in Britain, 1900–1960: Nationalism, Pan-Africanism, and Communism*. London: Lawrence and Wishart, 1998.

Adi, Hakim, and Marika Sherwood. *The 1945 Manchester Pan-African Congress Revisited*. 3rd ed. London: New Beacon Books, 1995.

Denzer, LaRay. "Intersections: Nigerian Episodes in the Careers of Three West Indian Women." Paper presented at the Conference on Gendering the Diaspora: Women, Culture, and Historical Change in the Caribbean and the Nigerian Hinterland, Dartmouth College, 21–24 November 2002.

Jarrett-Macauley, Delia. *The Life of Una Marson, 1905–1965*. Manchester: Manchester University Press, 1998.

Martin, Tony. "Amy Ashwood Garvey, Wife No. 1." *Jamaica Journal* 20 (1987): 32–36.

———. "Discovering African Roots: Amy Ashwood Garvey's Pan-Africanist Journey." *Comparative Studies of South Asia, Africa, and the Middle East* 18 (1997): 118–26.

———. *Amy Ashwood Garvey: Pan-Africanist, Feminist, and Mrs. Marcus Garvey No. 1; or, A Tale of Two Amies*. Dover: Majority Press, 2007.

"Mr. Henry Carr on Education and Progress." *West Africa*, 30 August 1924, 902.

Nigerian Progress Union. *The Nigerian Students and Henry Carr*. London: Caledonian Press, 1924.

Sherwood, Marika. "Amy Ashwood Garvey." In *Pan-African History: Political Figures from Africa and the Diaspora since 1787*, by Hakim Adi and Marika Sherwood, 69–75. New York: Routledge, 2003.

———. *Claudia Jones: A Life in Exile*. London: Lawrence and Wishart, 1999.

"Students' Union Meeting To-night." *West Africa*, 21 June 1924, 617.

Yard, Lionel M. *Biography of Amy Ashwood Garvey, 1897–1969: Co-founder of the Universal Negro Improvement Association*. New York: Association for the Study of Afro-American Life and History, 1989.

# 10

# "Crack Kernels, Crack Hitler": Export Production Drive and Igbo Women during the Second World War

## GLORIA CHUKU

The Second World War was one of the most distressing and militarized periods in the history of Africa, an unprecedented era in European exploitation of their colonial possessions. More than any other time in imperial history, Britain depended on her colonies for the supply of human and material resources to prosecute the war. The loss of the Asian colonies to the Axis powers in 1942 temporarily removed key suppliers of tropical produce like rubber, palm produce, and other crops, creating severe shortages of strategic materials and food supplies for the use of the armed forces and civilian population. Consequently, Britain designed new strategic planning and logistics to stimulate increased production of staple exports in her unoccupied colonies. West African colonies assumed a new importance as a major source of raw materials for Britain and her allies to make up for losses in Asia. Thus Nigeria assumed new importance in imperial wartime planning.

This chapter examines the measures adopted by the colonial government in the Igbo area of eastern Nigeria during the war. Wartime scarcity led to wide-ranging changes in the economy, especially in the development of alternative local resources and efforts to increase production in the region. This study concerns how Igbo women, the primary producers and local traders in southeastern Nigerian colonial economy, responded to new economic policies and practices. So far, little scholarly work has been done on the economic contributions of Igbo or other Nigerian women during the war. Instead, scholars have studied the role played by the ex-servicemen, the politics of the war, cassava starch production, salt scarcity, financial contributions of Nigerians to the war, and the wartime export production drive.[1] This case study may offer clues as to how the war may have transformed gender relations in other parts of the African diaspora.

Place is also important to this study. In pursuit of new commercial and employment opportunities within the British empire, major southeastern Nigerian cities such as Port Harcourt, Onitsha, Aba, and Enugu witnessed an increased influx of Syrians, Lebanese, Indians, Togolese, Gold Coasters, Gambians, and Sierra Leoneans (locally known as the Saros).[2] The war increased the tension between these communities and the indigenous elite as well as editorial criticisms of government policies in local newspapers.[3] Africa was not just the source of a diaspora. African commercial centers were part of a larger imperial matrix and sites of diasporic communities.

## The Colonial Economy and the
## Win-the-War Effort in the Igbo Region

The colonial Igbo economy was characterized by an international division of trade in which the Igbo produced palm oil and kernels for export in exchange for European products. While new economic opportunities were unleashed by colonialism, and while some Igbo women exploited such opportunities to enhance their economic power, others lost out due to the colonial gender bias against women and the unequal exchange relations of the trade. Not only did colonial policies increase the workload of women, but they also relegated women to subsistence food production and small-scale petty trading.[4]

Between 1939 and 1945, the Igbo region witnessed increased militarization and massive exploitation. A dramatic change arose from the scarcity of shipping supplies and imported goods, coupled with the increased demand for local raw materials for export. The colonial government adopted far-reaching and sometimes stringent measures to stimulate export production of palm oil, palm kernel oil, and cassava starch throughout Nigeria. A vigorous propaganda campaign was designed to promote loyalty to the British and the Allied forces and to generate financial contributions to aid the war effort.

In 1939 the administration established the Nigeria War Relief Fund (NWRF). All units of the colonial government (Lagos colony, districts, provinces, and regions) were required to contribute to the fund. Contributions also came from corporate organizations and the masses. All sorts of entertainment programs—dances, funfairs, football matches, sports events, raffle draws, and special NWRF weeks—were organized by private groups and local communities to raise funds. For example, the Port Harcourt Win-the-War Fund committee headed by Reverend Lionel R. Potts-Johnson (a Saro) and the Women's Emergency Committee (local and foreign women with substantial Saro representation) raised £600 in July 1940.[5]

In the eastern provinces, compulsory levies were imposed on government workers, villages, cultural organizations, and other groups in addition to their voluntary contributions. Between 30 September and 7 October 1942 in the eastern provinces, Port Harcourt raised £1,257. Between 28 October and 4 November 1944, Aba division contributed £1,020.5s.3d. The total raised in the eastern provinces amounted to £17,839.15s.11d.[6] When NWRF accounts were closed on 28 January 1946, Nigeria had contributed £210,999.0s.9d to the war effort.[7] These figures may look small today, but they entailed serious sacrifice on the part of the contributors. According to historian O. N. Njoku, the NWRF "was one of the most unsung strategies by which Britain squeezed out widows' mites from Nigerian citizens in aid of the imperial power's war efforts. What is more, it is not generally appreciated how heavy a burden the NWRF inflicted on its Nigerian contributors."[8] Igbo women shared this burden.

A second measure promulgated in 1939 established the British Ministry of Food (MOF) as the sole purchaser of primary export crops throughout the West African colonies. In 1942, the West African Produce Control Board (WAPCB) was set up to execute MOF decisions. The board fixed prices paid for produce, which were meager, severely compounding the hardship experienced by farmers. A third measure designated the allocation of essential imports to producers and middlemen in the colony. For example, imported bicycles and their parts, salt, and gunpowder were allocated to specific areas in the region as inducements to increase production of particular raw materials. For instance, the Tyre and Inner Tubes Order of 1942 placed the sale of tires and inner tubes under the control of transport officers. Only transporters involved in the export trade were allowed to purchase these scarce commodities, which they got at subsidized rates. In the Igbo region, bicycle parts were also

supplied at subsidized rates to induce farmers and middlemen to produce and bring palm produce to trading stations.[9] Salt, in acute scarcity
throughout the war, was stringently rationed to induce local producers,
traders, and middlemen to increase the production and supply of palm
produce and cassava starch.

During this period the colonial government introduced more oil
presses and nut-cracking machines to speed up processing of palm fruits
and kernels, to save labor, and to improve the quality of the oils. As a
result, the number of palm oil presses owned by indigenous producers in
Onitsha division increased from 32 in 1935 to 164 in 1941. In Orlu district
in 1941, local producers owned 130 palm oil presses. Only one belonged
to a woman, Mrs. Rose Uche, a trader and palm products producer from
Ndimoko village of Arondizuogu, who bought a large Duchscher that
cost about £18 at Aba.[10]

Southern Nigeria, the oil palm belt of the colony, was divided into
operational zones, each coordinated by a team. The Igbo area, where
most of the palm products were produced, was partitioned into five
zones, each headed by a palm produce officer, under the supervision of
J. W. Wallace, the senior agricultural officer at Umuahia.[11] In addition to
encouraging farmers to increase production, these teams also collected
information regarding production and marketing and examined proposals for improvement. They were empowered to investigate problems
and make recommendations regarding the distribution of imported and
locally produced goods and foodstuffs. Each zonal team had a transport
controller responsible for rational distribution of available transport and
spare parts.

### Igbo Women and the Wartime Export Production Drive

Igbo women's role in export production and the Win-the-War effort
must be considered in the context of their participation in the colonial
economy in southeastern Nigeria.[12] Like elsewhere in Nigeria, the colonial economic policy in the region favored export crop production at
the expense of food crops. Infrastructural development depended on
labor, which was forcibly obtained by enacting several ordinances that
empowered the local authorities (the warrant chiefs and native courts) to
carry out the exercise.[13] Many men (and at times women) were forcibly

recruited to engage in public works necessary to implement production and distribution policies, such as clearing waterways, constructing roads, bridges, and railway lines, and building houses for administrative officials. Others were employed on colonial farms and plantations, in mines, in native courts, and in trading firms as clerks, bookkeepers, security workers, and carriers. Some were employed as mission workers and teachers. With so many men engaged in waged and salaried employment, the burden of food production and processing in the Igbo area fell on women, resulting in a huge increase in their workload.

Expanded demands for primary agricultural crops as raw materials in metropolitan industries, coupled with the recruitment of able-bodied men for military activities, compounded the situation and further intensified women's economic activities. In the absence of their husbands, many women also assumed responsibility as heads of household. Women's new roles and increased workloads required them to devise new strategies in domestic and farm management. Some increased their working hours from 10–12 hours a day to 12–14, and some resorted to reciprocal rotational cooperative labor among themselves or to hired labor if they could afford it. Child labor was also important.

Traditionally Igbo women engaged in multiple economic activities, including agricultural cultivation, food processing, pottery, salt manufacturing, weaving, and trading. During the war they focused on palm oil and kernel production as well as on cassava starch manufacturing and marketing. Suffice it to say that the contributions of women in food production and processing (maize, taro, beans, cassava, yams, palm oil, and all kinds of vegetables) were enormously important and deserved commendation. Despite the government's neglect of local food production and the wartime measures devised to ensure increased export production, women persevered and intensified their agricultural activities to produce enough food, which not only sustained the dense Igbo population but also produced enough surplus for export to other parts of the colony.

### Production and Distribution of Palm Products

The oil palm was one of the indigenous economic trees exploited by the Igbo long before their contact with the Europeans. It has been a major factor in the economic development of southeastern Nigeria, generally referred to as the "oil palm belt of Nigeria." Palm oil and yams constituted major food items for the local population and for the slaves sold into the transatlantic trade. From the mid-nineteenth century, palm oil was a major staple of the "legitimate trade." Palm kernels, a byproduct of oil processing, also became an export of great commercial value after the 1870s. Both palm oil and palm kernels were traditionally regarded as women's products.

From the nineteenth century, when palm oil and kernels witnessed an unprecedented commercialization, major changes occurred in the ownership and control of the industry as well as in the introduction of new techniques to increase production. Every aspect of their processing was largely in the hands of the local people, especially women. As their commercial importance grew, changes occurred in the production and marketing system that affected women's role. Men assumed the ownership of oil palms and the control of palm produce, and they owned most of the new technology introduced in the production process. Nonetheless, women still constituted the largest labor force in the industry. They headloaded palm fruit from the farms to the processing centers, picked the palm seeds from the thorny fruits, fetched water and firewood, boiled and pounded the seeds, extracted oil from the fiber and nuts, separated the fiber from the nuts, and cracked the nuts to produce palm kernels. Each activity was very strenuous.

During the war, the acute shortage of vegetable oils and butter in Britain prompted the colonial government to intensify measures to expand palm production in the Igbo area. The focus on palm production and the introduction of oil presses to replace wooden mortars resulted in the overproduction of oil. Likewise, the increase in the number of kernel cracking machines yielded a kernel surplus. Unfortunately for the general population, the emphasis on the export production of palm produce caused a serious decline in food crops in the region, exacerbated by import control and shipping shortage.

Sometimes the colonial administration shifted its emphasis from the production of palm oil to cassava processing because starch was needed for the textile industry, especially for military uniforms, and as glue for the wood industry. In one of his national broadcasts in 1940, Governor Sir Bernard Bourdillon urged that all efforts should be diverted to the production of starch, noting, "One commodity which is not over pro-duced and which in fact is badly needed by the Imperial Government is cassava starch. Britain could take 10,000 tons of starch in a year and our duty is to make every effort to meet this demand."[14]

Colonial economic policy shifted according to war needs. In 1940 the focus was on starch production, but two years later it shifted back to kernel production. Administrators met with the producers and middle-men to explain the necessity for maximum production of kernel for export. In addition, the authorities introduced measures to control the gari trade. In 1942 the price of gari was reduced from 8s.9d to between 3s.6d and 4s. per ninety-pound bag at Aba, a major commercial center in the eastern provinces. Later the price was further reduced to 3s.7d for ninety-five pounds of gari or 1d for a salmon tin measure.[15]

Gari exportation to the northern provinces, where it had become very popular, was restricted. Southern immigrants (Igbo, Yoruba, Ibibio, Efik, Ijo, and others) serving in the military or employed in building army barracks, roads, and airfields created a large market for gari and palm oil. The presence of such a large local market made it more lucra-tive for women entrepreneurs to shift to gari production rather than oil or kernels. For example, while the average returns per man-and-woman-day in palm production was 4.4d, that of gari production was 6.6d.[16] The new government starch policy of the early 1940s, combined with the profitability of the gari industry, encouraged many local palm producers to turn to cassava production. In certain places in the oil palm belt—especially Ngwa, Asa, and Azumini—palm trees were left unharvested and palm nuts were scattered everywhere. Administrative officials, concerned about the decline in palm production and export, tried to find a way to reverse the situation.[17]

To revive palm produce production, the colonial government ad-opted a number of measures that seemed oppressive to local producers. Instead of offering attractive prices for palm produce, in 1943 the govern-ment promulgated the Food Controls Order, which restricted interre-gional and interdistrict trade in domestic produce. When this regulation proved ineffective, the MOF, which exercised the official monopoly of the purchase of major staples from British West African colonies, slightly increased the price of kernels, then the most needed product. It fixed the prices of export staples and ordered buying agents to adhere to them strictly. For instance, at Oguta in 1943 the price of kernels was increased from £5.8s.6d per ton to £7.8s.6d, from 8s.10d per bag to 12s.3d, and from 2s.5d per bushel to 3s.3d.[18]

This slight increase in prices, however, proved insufficient incentive because wartime prices were far lower than prewar prices. On the eve of the war, a four-gallon tin of palm kernel had sold for 3s and a puncheon of palm oil for £30, but after the war prices fell to 6d and £6.12s, respectively.[19] Moreover, government had no means of ensuring that the fixed prices were paid directly to the farmers. Middlemen manipulated the control price and further exploited the farmers. In 1941 the district officer in Aba complained to the senior resident in Owerri that the quota system had forced down prices paid to the women who sold the produce. Although the control price of kernels was 1s.10½d per measure, women traders and producers were paid less than 1s.2d by middlemen and government agents.[20] To improve the quality of produce, the WAPCB ordered that all palm oil and kernels offered for sale must be approved by the local inspectorate.

To enforce the measures that ensured quality control of palm produce and to promote greater production efforts, the government promulgated a series of regulations, including the Control of Export Produce (Palm Oil) (Prices) Order of 1944, which compelled local farmers to harvest and process palm fruits. If farmers failed to comply, the government authorized native authorities to grant local agents rights to harvest and process palm nuts and impose a £5 fine for noncompliance.[21] The 1944 order fixed prices of oil and kernel. In 1943, the government had set up a produce control board to regulate oil marketing in the colony.

Furthermore, women and children were made to crack more kernels. Schoolchildren were enlisted to crack kernels as a Win-the-War measure. J. A. C. McCall, the production officer of Owerri province, called on school proprietors and managers, teachers, and even clergymen to aid the administration in this effort, declaring that "this production business is our particular war effort, and surely that should come first, even if other duties of administration have to suffer."[22] The Niger Diocese board in the eastern provinces, all the mission schools, the district officers, the local councilors, and the warrant chiefs cooperated with McCall in the export production drive. Pupils spent many days at school engaged in palm kernel cracking competitions to support the Win-the-War effort.[23]

When the exercise did not yield the expected results, they were dismissed earlier than usual and urged to help their parents crack kernels at home during their holidays. In 1943, for instance, the school holiday started at the end of July instead of December. This measure was fairly successful, and the collected palm kernels were either presented to the military authority or sold. The proceeds were paid into the war fund.

A propaganda campaign was mounted to appeal to different classes of people, especially women. Posters with snappy sentences were posted everywhere, such as "CRACK KERNELS, CRACK HITLER" and "WOMEN, DOES CRACKING WORRY YOUR WAISTS?" "YES, BUT DON'T WORRY. YOUR CRACKING IS GIVING HITLER A SERIOUS HEADACHE."[24] These measures, plus the fact that kernel did not command as much value as oil in the domestic market, led to increased production of the commodity throughout the eastern provinces, especially Owerri province. For instance, exports of palm kernels from the eastern provinces increased from 157,715 tons in 1940 to 170,096 tons in 1941 and 170,451 tons in 1942.[25]

The task of cracking higher quantities of palm kernels entailed considerable sacrifice on the part of women and their children. It involved picking and crushing the hard nuts one after the other between stones. To produce two pounds of kernel required cracking more than 200 nuts. Women had to sit in one place, bending their backs for hours, to produce enough kernels to fetch enough money for a day's meal. It was strenuous, monotonous, and caused waist pain—hence the reference to women's waists in the propaganda advertisement. One can imagine the pain and other sacrifices these women went through to produce the tens and hundreds of thousands of tons of kernel that were exported from the region during the war.

As part of the palm kernel drive, three buying stations were opened at Owerri, Okigwe, and Okoko Item. Expanded production stimulated the growth of lorry transport from the collection points to Port Harcourt, Okigwe, and Uzuakoli, for bicycles had neither the capacity for large loads nor the speed to meet wartime demand. Furthermore, after 1942, lorry passenger traffic was diverted to produce export centers.[26]

The improved transportation system facilitated the export of food items to regions outside the Igbo area, particularly to Calabar and the northern provinces. A quota system was established to control palm oil export to other provinces. Under the Nigeria Defense Regulations, particularly the Food Controls (Removal of Palm Oil) Order of 1943, the shipment of palm oil to the north was restricted to a few licensed traders and agents who were issued specific quotas. The palm oil price was fixed at 3s.6d per four-gallon measure or 3d for a beer or soda bottle measure to discourage its export to the north. Buying agents were authorized to purchase oil in the eastern provinces as was the case with cocoa in the western provinces. These buying agents were required to purchase oil on the basis of naked ex-scale Bulk Oil Plant (BOP) prices prescribed by the order.[27] The less the impurity or fatty acid contents of the oil, the higher the price.

Oil bought by the government and trading firms was categorized into six grades according to the impurity and fatty acid contents:

Grade 1: 0–6%
Grade 2: 6–12%
Grade 3: 13–18%
Grade 4: 17–30%
Grade 5: 29–42%
Grade 6: above 43%

Grade 1 oil earned more money than grade 2 and others. In 1943, for example, special order oil was fixed at £53 per ton, grade 1 at £42.15s.0d, grade 2 at £37.2s.6d, and grade 3 at £33.[28] Approved buying agents were directed to sell oil after being passed by the local inspectorate on the basis of a fixed naked ex-scale price. This required the agents to be meticulous in inspecting and buying high-quality oil from the local producers if they wanted to make more money. Aware of the new regulations, local producers had to improve production methods to ensure high-quality oil with reduced fatty acid. Often they were cheated by the government agents, who subtracted four tins from every cask containing thirty-eight tins of oil, allegedly to cover leakages during transit.

Male producers and local traders manipulated some control measures by diverting oil from the export market to the domestic market because it was more profitable. Local demand for staple foods, including palm oil, was high. Men often did better than women in the distribution of food items because they had more access to the new British currency to invest in transport (bicycles, motor lorries, and train fare). Male traders also had more time than women, who were saddled with familial and other responsibilities, to engage in long-distance and regional trade. They were ready to pay a higher price for oil from the producers in local Igbo markets, which they then transported and sold to local middlemen either within or outside the Igbo area rather than buy it at the government's reduced rate and sell to the approved agents for export. At Agbani it was reported that army agents were unable to purchase palm oil even when they were prepared to pay 4s for a four-gallon measure, which held less oil than a gasoline can. Yet the control price was 3s.6d. Meanwhile, indigenous traders were ready to pay 5s to local producers and transport the oil to northern markets rather than sell to the army or government agents in Igbo markets because they knew the profit in the northern markets would be higher. When price control officers were present in the markets, local traders publicly paid the control price but made up the balance when the officers left.[29] Many decided not to sell in the markets at all, preferring instead to buy oil from the producers in their homes, thus evading the control officers.

As a result, the palm oil trade to northern towns boomed. The steady increase in the quantity of oil railed to northern markets confirms this. For example, oil railed to the north increased from 4,510 tons in 1941 to 6,504 tons in 1942, 8,297 tons in 1943, and 8,811 tons in 1944.[30] These figures do not include the quantity that went north from the Nsukka area by road and from Onitsha by canoe. On discovering the evasion, the colonial government decided to enforce the oil price control in the northern provinces. In addition, stationmasters were ordered not to rail any private oil north until all military quotas had been filled each month. Travelers going north were allowed to carry a specified small quantity for personal use.

The enforcement of restrictions in railing oil to northern markets resulted in making it scarce and expensive there. In response, more Hausa traders from the north traveled to the east to buy the produce directly from the source. A United Africa Company trading station that was opened at Ihiala during this time to evacuate palm oil had to be closed due to the influx of Hausa traders. Initially the station flourished and provided a nearby market for local women producers who had hitherto either sold to middlemen or traveled to Onitsha or Oguta to sell their produce. Because Hausa traders paid higher prices than the trading companies and their local middlemen, the Oguta market was adversely affected. Not only did it lose oil from Orlu district to the Hausa traders, but it also lost the oil it used to get from Onitsha to the same northern traders.

Hausa traders offered more attractive prices than did the agents at Oguta, Onitsha, and Ihiala. Moreover, Hausa traders paid cash and did not subject the producers to any inspection. For example, at Onitsha, Hausa traders paid 1s more for a four-gallon tin than the Oguta buying price.[31] In fact, while local traders in the northern markets were paying 7s.6d for a four-gallon tin of upgraded oil, the foreign trading companies at Onitsha were only paying 5s.3d.[32] The margin was so great that local producers and traders naturally preferred to sell to these northern traders. It reached the point where only those who faced geographical and transportation difficulties patronized the expatriate firms. Between January and December 1944, a total of 2,780 tons was shipped to the north, while in December of that year 156 tons of palm oil left Onitsha by canoe to the northern provinces.

To counter the Hausa traders and rechannel all oil into the Win-the-War effort for export and military use, the authorities recommended the complete prohibition of oil exports from Owerri and Onitsha provinces to the northern provinces. Local producers, who were mostly women, however, were determined to circumvent government measures and continue their trade with Hausa traders because of the higher prices they paid. Sometimes this was not possible because of the unavailability of transportation, which meant that they had to settle for the cheaper prices offered by agents of the trading firms and government.

### Cassava Production and Distribution

Portuguese traders had introduced cassava, which was indigenous to South America, in the Igbo area during the slave trade. At first, cassava did not receive an enthusiastic reception among the Igbo due to its high prussic acid content, the Igbo's lack of knowledge about processing, and other factors.[33] As a result, the crop's diffusion into the Igbo area was very slow; however, it gradually gained ascendancy over other crops in the region for two reasons. First, yam, the chief staple of the Igbo, sometimes has low yields. Second, cassava has important advantages over yam: it can adapt to a wider range of soil and climatic conditions and can be cultivated all year round. Yam cultivation, on the other hand, is seasonal. When matured, cassava can be left in the soil for up to three years. Other advantages of cassava are that it grows well on old farmland with diminished fertility, it is relatively productive even on poor soil, it is drought-resistant, and it is less vulnerable to insects and disease. Moreover, cassava cultivation requires less labor than yam, for it needs little weeding and no staking. Unlike yam, it can be planted and harvested anytime. L. C. Uzozie observes, "Cassava is not a true annual. At any time of the year, both new and old crops can be observed growing in the field."[34] According to A. G. Hopkins, the Igbo "fully" accepted cassava and took active part in its cultivation and processing only when they realized that the crop would yield higher return for the same input (or even less) than yam.[35] Cassava proved a welcome supplement in situations of acute food and labor shortages, and it has remained so ever since.

When cassava was first introduced, it was processed into *akpu* or *foufou* (mashed cassava). It could also be processed into tapioca and eaten with coconut or kernels. Later cassava was processed into gari (farina). Gari processing involved intensive labor using both manual and mechanical graters. Cassava tubers had to be peeled, washed, and grated. The mashed cassava was put into an *akpa aji* (a baft sack with tiny perforations made of cords) and tied on four wooden frames to drain the liquid. Two wooden frames were placed on the bag on top of another two frames, and it took a day or two to drain the liquid from the pulp. The hard dried pulp was sieved to remove impurities or fibers before frying. It took two hours or more to grate a fifty-pound bag of cassava and four hours or more to fry that quantity.

In Abakaliki, cassava was not introduced until the early 1940s, when the colonial government established cassava demonstration farms for the purposes of promoting the starch industry for wartime needs. Colonial agricultural officers taught men how to cultivate cassava and women how to extract the starch with simple grating machines that cost £2 each. At first Abakaliki villagers resented government pressure to cultivate cassava and produce starch. They complained that cassava ruined their soil for yam cultivation. Because they resented cassava, they were slow to learn how to process it into gari, but the educated stranger population in the area imported gari from Onitsha and Enugu. In a few places, mechanical graters were introduced to increase production, and the native administration provided gari pans and graters and employed demonstrators to teach new techniques in processing gari. But the installation of mechanized graters was expensive, and only a few people could afford one.[36] Eventually the local population developed a taste for gari, and now it is a dietary staple.

In such gari-producing centers as the Ngwa area and Umuahia, Ohaji, and Obiarukwu in Anioma, the producers more readily adopted the labor-saving technique of the mechanical grater. In these areas large-scale gari production already featured in the local export trade outside the Igbo area. Unfortunately, there is no record of women owning mechanized graters. This was partly because they could not afford one and partly because only men were trained to use them. Women had to take their cassava tubers to grating centers, where they paid men to grate their cassava. In many cases, the scarcity of graters meant that women had to trek long distances and then wait in long queues to have their cassava tubers grated.

The spread of cassava greatly increased the workload of women. Unlike the Yoruba area, where both men and women participated actively in the production of cassava, in the Igbo region, all aspects of cassava cultivation and processing had been done by women until it started to gain economic value. During the war women still did most of the work because of the government's Win-the-War measures discussed above. The continued effort to accelerate export production reduced the labor available for domestic food production, which caused a decline in food crop production. Consequently the demand for food and other farm produce outstripped the supply and resulted in high prices. During the war, gari production became very important and lucrative. Gari was a staple food of soldiers in the army. In addition, the huge growth of Igbo urban centers meant a concomitant growth in consumer demand for gari and other food supplies: Aba, Umuahia, Onitsha, Enugu, Owerri, Nsukka, and Abakaliki acted as the major stimuli for gari production and trade.

Government attempts to coerce farmers to concentrate on export production and its inability to offer attractive prices to the farmers drove many of them away from the export economy into the lucrative domestic market for local foodstuff. Many men moved into food production and distribution in gari, yam, fish, and palm oil. Since gari was the major staple of the region, it attracted the greatest number of local producers and distributors. In addition to local demand by Igbo consumers, a huge demand developed in the northern provinces and some non-Igbo districts in the southeast. According to a 1943 report by the department of agriculture at Umuahia, Aba was the chief center for gari export to the northern provinces. The quantity railed from Aba to the north stood as follows:

| | |
|---|---|
| 1938 | 4,011 tons (valued at £14,177.64) |
| 1939 | 5,428 tons (valued at £19,041.65) |
| 1940 | 4,000 tons (valued at £14,838.76) |
| 1941 | 6,000 tons (valued at £19,062.85) |
| 1942 | 21,000 tons (value not available)[37] |

Umuahia came next. In Awka, Onitsha, and Obiarukwu, gari production also increased in the 1940s. Even with increased production, gari was still scarce and expensive in the local markets due to its forced sale and exportation. In June 1943, for instance, two cups of gari sold for 1d against ten to fifteen cups for the same amount prior to the imposition of government regulations and the expansion of northern exports.

In 1944, 2.5 tons of gari were transported by lorry to Calabar township daily from Aba, and about 10 tons were sent weekly to the United African Company plantations in Calabar province. However, the quantity did not meet the needs of the Calabar population and neighboring cities. The control of the gari trade to the Calabar region became difficult because of the activities of black marketers, whose number increased due to price control and prosecution of price defaulters in the courts. As these measures drove foodstuffs, including gari, out of the open market, black marketers hiked their prices. In some places a near famine state developed. In November and December 1944, more than 5,000 hungry and angry men and women demonstrated against the gari shortage in the streets in Ikot Ekpene district.[38] Scarcity even raised gari prices in such major producing and distribution centers as Aba and Umuahia.

The high cost of gari continued for several years after the war had ended. In Aba, the gari price rose from 7s per cwt in 1948 to 20s.6d in 1949. Some of the factors contributing to high prices were poor cassava yields; increased inland trade between Aba, the Ibibio region, Calabar township, Cameroon, and Fernando Po; and population growth in Aba and other major urban centers.[39] The export of gari to Fernando Po and Cameroon was later banned, an indication of its growing popularity there. Many Igbo immigrants had been attracted to these places by job opportunities in the plantation economy and the civil service. Moreover, Igbo entrepreneurs dominated the trade in palm oil, local foodstuffs, and imported goods as well as the transport industry in these areas.[40] Although gari export to Calabar Province continued, the official quantity allowed was significantly reduced. The Food Controls Order of 1943 introduced quota restrictions on the export of gari and yam, the two major staples of the region. This regulation did not allow gari or yam exports over fifty pounds to leave Port Harcourt township "without the written permission of a competent authority."[41] This restriction was also extended to other cities. Individual travelers were only permitted a personal allowance of ten pounds per person.

The exportation of gari to the northern provinces, however, attracted the most concern from colonial officials during the war. A quota system was introduced to control the supply of gari to the north in the early 1940s. Gari permits were issued to only a few authorized agents by a quota issuing authority in alliance with a local authority. In 1942, about 800 gari traders at Aba complained that gari export to the north had dropped from 21,000 tons in 1942 to 1,640 tons in 1943, including the military quota.[42] Before this period, the Traders League at Aba and Umuahia had representatives in the northern cities. It took at most nine or ten days to deliver gari and receive payment from the northern agents. The quota system, however, encouraged monopoly. Under this arrangement, most of the traders and agents who had previously handled the gari trade were eliminated, and those who succeeded in getting government permits to engage in the gari trade could not handle the volume, leading to long delays and consequent spoilage of gari. Spoilt gari could not be sold and was returned to the producers or to traders in the Igbo area, thereby creating a huge loss.

Some gari dealers manipulated the quota system and still exported gari to the north. Others resorted to smuggling. Government officials at Aba met with local gari traders to discuss ways of alleviating this problem. At the meeting, traders were asked to act as middlemen between the producers and one Mr. Bresby, who was in charge of railing gari to the north. This decision meant the cancellation of the permit system, but it did not produce the result that the administration wanted. In August 1944, the resident accused the traders of cheating by smuggling in that month alone about 200 tons of gari to the north.[43] In their defense, the traders blamed the railway clerks in charge of railing gari to the north for the excess tonnage. The colonial government was not convinced and ordered the traders to recall their agents from the north. Thereafter, only Mr. Bresby had the authority to export gari to the north.

The same situation occurred in Onitsha province. At Agbani railway station market, the Gari Traders Union petitioned the chief secretary in Lagos against the ban on gari export to the north. They argued that since gari traders were mainly soldiers' wives and old men who had no other source of income, government price controls or a ban on gari export would seriously affect their livelihoods.[44] Wartime control measures fell hardest on women, for they were the main cultivators and processors of cassava. When these women were forced to sell gari below the market prices to appointed agents, their incomes suffered.

Thus government attempts to control gari prices and export failed woefully. Despite strict measures to restrict export, gari smuggling flourished. Local traders opposed colonial regulations, and the administration did not have the ability to enforce them effectively. Controls made the commodity scarce and very expensive, and this risked widespread discontent among the people. As a result, the residents of Bauchi, Kano, Katsina, Plateau, Sokoto, and Zaria provinces decided to lift the restrictions on gari railments to the north from the eastern provinces, effective 1 January 1945.

## Effects of the War on Igbo Women and Society

The Second World War had far-reaching consequences for the Igbo economy and gender relations. Although one could argue that the Igbo area was exploited during this period, a number of innovations to increase production facilitated economic diversification in the region. The increased number of palm oil presses and kernel crackers had important consequences for the area. They multiplied the quantity of produce exported from the region. The new techniques also economized on time and labor. Unfortunately, most women producers did not have the capital to acquire the new machinery or the skills to operate them.

While they continued to rely on the crude and more laborious means of production, the men benefited because they could afford the machinery and the training necessary to operate it.

The war brought about changes in gender roles. Igbo women had assumed greater responsibilities than before as heads of households when their husbands left for military duty and other war-related services. Many women became breadwinners for their families. They took on additional responsibilities and economic activities previously reserved for men. Their involvement in yam cultivation was a particularly important example, for before the war this was considered a male activity. Thus the war led to the diversification of women's economic activities. Women took part in the production of export crops as well as in the cultivation and processing of food crops.

Of all the food crops Igbo women produced, it was cassava that benefited them most. For women, cassava became a symbol of independence, wealth, and higher status. Their production of cassava products gave women economic independence and reduced their level of poverty. Not only did cassava cultivation alleviate the traditional *unwu* (hunger) and *ugani* (starvation) periods, especially during the period after yam planting, but it also profoundly altered the economic and social relations between husbands and wives. With little or no assistance from their husbands, women could bear the total financial responsibility of providing food and other domestic needs for the family. They could send their children to school, sponsor marriage ceremonies of their children, take high titles in their communities, and sponsor community ceremonies. Some began to challenge men in launching town development projects. Thus cassava has been important to Igbo women in terms of resource allocation, product utilization, and income generation.

Meanwhile, the war also resulted in the influx of men into economic activities hitherto regarded as female domains. From the time men gained control of the new technology introduced in the oil palm industry, women began to lose ground in the industry that had formerly been one of their main domains. The introduction of cassava graters broke women's monopoly of cassava production in the Igbo area. Worse still, men began to control the marketing of gari, especially outside the Igbo area. More men than women could afford the capital required for such trade. Unlike the women, men were not also constrained by child care and household chores. Thus, while men had the time required to organize long-distance and interregional trade, women were saddled with family and other responsibilities.

Apart from dominating long-distance trade, men also took over retail trade from women. When the war ended, many of the ex-servicemen, who returned with war bonuses and British money, went into trading because they were unable to secure employment in the formal sector. They rented or bought stalls in the city markets. Some went into the wholesale trade, but the majority of them took to selling imports and other merchandise. From the late 1940s until the present, Igbo women have not recovered their place in the city markets. Today, a visit to any city market reveals more men than women operating in the wholesale and retail trades. Women have been relegated to petty trade or pushed back to rural village markets.

In spite of these setbacks, some women traders, who had accumulated capital before the war, possessed the requisite business acumen and organizational skills to take advantage of the wartime economic stimulus to elevate their status from petty traders to prominent entrepreneurs. They competed favorably with Lebanese, Syrian, European, and African traders of Sierra Leonean and Brazilian descent in the major commercial centers in the region, especially Onitsha and Port Harcourt. Among these women merchants were Omu Okwei, Madam Iyaji Akaya, Iyom Victoria Amobi, Madam Izadi Ugboma, Mrs. Eleanor Brodie-Mends, Mrs. Eunice Nnoruka, Mrs. Janet Romaine, Mrs. Mary Nzimiro, and Lady Lydia Eze. Many of these women were successful agents of such major foreign trading companies as the United Africa Company (UAC), Societe Commerciale de l'Ouest Africain (SCOA), Compagnie Francaise (CFAO), G. B. Ollivant, Leventis, and John Holt. Some were real estate brokers and transporters.[45]

Igbo women merchants traveled widely and built powerful commercial networks inside and outside Nigeria. Their lifestyles blended multiple cultural values and practices derived from local, Euro-American, and African diasporic sources. Some entered marriages with Saro men and men from other ethnic groups; likewise, some Saro women married indigenous men. For instance, Janet Ifeyinwa, who was born in Eziowelle but grew up in Onitsha, married George Romaine, an Onitsha resident of Sierra Leonean descent. Amicitia Rosalind Babington Johnson, the daughter of I. B. Johnson, a prominent Saro in Port Harcourt, married the Igbo lawyer A. C. Nwapa when she returned from England, where she acquired her medical degree in 1948, thus becoming the third West African woman to qualify as a physician.

Many of these Igbo women appreciated the value of Western education and sent their children to study overseas in Britain and the United States. B. V. O. Amobi, the eldest son of Victoria Amobi, studied medicine in the United Kingdom in the 1940s; Priscilla Nzimiro, Mary Nzimiro's only daughter, trained as a physician in Glasgow in the 1940s. Priscilla's half-brothers—Richard, Nnamdi, and Ifediora—were also sent overseas by Mrs. Nzimiro for their university education. Zaccheus Eko, the only son of Mrs. Brodie-Mends, studied medicine in the United Kingdom in the early 1950s, and Lydia Eze's son Kingsley also studied in London. Their children were part of the earliest generation of Western-trained Igbo professionals and university graduates. Through this effort, these Igbo women contributed in no small way in building the Igbo and, by extension, African diasporic communities in Europe and the Americas.[46]

Igbo women also participated in the postwar nationalist movement that brought the British colonial rule in Nigeria to an end in 1960. Many became members of the National Council of Nigeria and the Cameroons (later renamed the National Council of Nigerian Citizens, or NCNC), and some led the local and regional branches of its women's wing.[47] There is no doubt that the interest in world gender reform that followed the establishment of the United Nations at the end of the war and the subsequent outreach by international women's organizations to expand African membership played a major role in the increased political and nationalist activities of Igbo and other Nigerian women. The women's wings of the political parties mobilized women in electoral campaigns, organized fund-raising activities, arranged entertainment for party events, developed communication networks to spread political information through the markets and local communities, hosted visiting party dignitaries, and contributed generously to party finances. For example, Mary Nzimiro's enthusiastic commitment to the NCNC earned her the title of "mother" of the party in Port Harcourt. She was instrumental in the election of her husband, Richard Nzimiro, as the first mayor of Port Harcourt municipality in 1956. Ironically, while the war ended Saro influence in the Port Harcourt politics, it marked a turning point in the rising importance of the indigenous elite in that city's political scene.[48]

## Conclusion

The increased economic activities of women in the war years proved to be a mixed blessing. On the one hand, women's labor was massively exploited due to the continuous decline in the prices of exports. Their workload also increased without much in the way of corresponding rewards. While women lost some of their economic power and independence to men, they also diversified their economic activities and increased their revenues. Some played an important role in sustaining their families as heads of household in the absence of their men. Some acquired wealth, economic independence, and empowerment, which enhanced their social status and political influence. Through their role in food production and processing, women sustained not only their respective families but also the Igbo domestic economy.

The multiethnic and multinational commercial networks built by some Igbo female entrepreneurs, their involvement in the decolonization politics, and the investment in the overseas education of their children fostered linkages and nationalist sentiments in Nigeria and in diasporic communities, especially after the late 1940s, when many Igbo deliberately chose to undertake higher education in the United States. Hopefully, this microstudy of how European colonialism and the Second World War affected Igbo women and their society will stimulate comparative studies of the impact of global events on gender relations in different parts of Africa and the African diaspora at home and abroad.

## Notes

1. Falola, "'Salt Is Gold': Management of Salt Scarcity in Nigeria during World War II"; Falola, "Cassava Starch for Export in Nigeria during the Second World War"; Njoku, "Contributions to War Efforts"; Njoku, "Export Production Drive in Nigeria during the Second World War"; Olusanya, *The Second World War and the Politics in Nigeria, 1939–1945;* and Olusanya, "The Role of Ex-Servicemen in Nigerian Politics."

2. See Falola, "The Lebanese in Colonial West Africa"; Winder, "The Lebanese in West Africa"; Dixon-Fyle, *A Saro Community in the Niger Delta, 1912–1984;* Dixon-Fyle, "The Saro in the Political Life of Early Port Harcourt, 1913–49."

3. Among the local newspapers were the *Daily Times of Nigeria,* the *Daily Service,* the *Nigerian Standard,* the *West African Pilot,* the *Comet,* the *Nigerian Observer,* and the *Eastern Nigerian Guardian.* See, for example, Idemili, "What the *West African Pilot* Did in the Movement for Nigerian Nationalism between 1937 and 1957."

4. See Chuku, "From Petty Traders to International Merchants"; Chuku, *Igbo Women and Economic Transformation in Southeastern Nigeria, 1900–1960;* Martin, *Palm Oil and Protest;* and Ekechi, "Aspects of Palm Oil Trade at Oguta (Eastern Nigeria), 1900–1950."

5. Dixon-Fyle, *A Saro Community,* 124.

6. Resident, Owerri province, to district officer [hereafter DO], Aba, 11 December 1944, ABADIST 1/26/707, National Archives of Nigeria, Enugu [hereafter NAE].

7. Memorandum, "The Nigerian War Relief Fund: Summary of Receipts and Payments, 1946," ABADIST1/26/707, NAE.

8. Njoku, "Contributions to War Efforts," 164.

9. "Control of Tyres and Inner Tubes Order, 1942"; CSE 1/85/8587; and DO, Orlu to the resident, Owerri province, 6 March 1946, file no. OR/C/181 B, vol. III, ORLDIST 3/1/255, NAE.

10. Onitsha Province Annual Report; 1935, file no. O. P. 1300, ONPROF 1/14/504; "Palm Oil Press Purchase," ORLDIST 3/1/200; and "Duchscher Palm Oil Press," AADIST 14/1/541, NAE.

11. Resident, Owerri Province, to DO, Aba, 29 May 1943, ABADIST 1/26/907, NAE.

12. The introduction of British colonial rule in the Igbo area was primarily by military conquest. The nature of the Igbo ministates and autonomous polities, combined with Igbo determination to protect their sovereignty, made the region one of the most difficult for the British to subdue and control. Igbo resistance, which started in the mid-nineteenth century, lasted through the second decade of the twentieth century. By 1900, however, most of the area had been conquered by the British.

13. In accordance with the Lugardian "indirect rule" system of colonial government, the British created and imposed on the Igbo certain local authorities that were not in existence before. For convenience and economic purposes, certain local individuals (some of whom were men of questionable character or from servile backgrounds) were given warrants of authority to assist the British in administering the region and running the native courts. These men were called warrant chiefs. Their appointment and their activities created many problems in Igbo society. See Afigbo, *The Warrant Chiefs.*

14. Governor's broadcast on food production, August 1940, AIDIST 2/1/306, NAE.

15. DO, Aba, 2 July 1943, file no. 1646, vol. II, ABADIST 14/1/1873, NAE; and memorandum, "Restriction on the Movement of Foodstuffs—Gari," 7 January 1943, file no. 4038/S.6, CCI 1/1, National Archives of Nigeria, Ibadan [hereafter NAI].

16. J. W. Wallace, senior agricultural officer, Umuahia to the resident, Owerri province, 14 May 1943, ABADIST 14/1/863, NAE.

17. John Holt agent, Aba, to DO, Aba, 5 August 1942, ABADIST 1/26/797, NAE.

18. Correspondence on palm produce, ABADIST 14/1/863, NAE.

19. Secretary, eastern provinces [hereafter SEP] Enugu, to resident, Owerri province, 26 July 1943, ABADIST 1/26/707, NAE.

20. DO, Aba, to senior resident, Owerri, 10 February 1941, ABADIST 1/26/797, NAE.

21. Memorandum, "Prosecution under the Oil Palm Production Regulations 89 of 1943," CSE 1/85/9915, NAE.

22. Memorandum, J. A. C. McCall, controller of oil palm production, Owerri province to DOs, Owerri province, 2 March 1944, ABADIST 1/26/907, NAE.

23. Correspondence and figures for palm oil railings north, CSE 1/85.9881, NAI; Olusanya, *Second World War*, 47. Two kernel cracking competitions held among Ishan schoolchildren in the western provinces yielded £39. Part of the money was paid to the Win-the-War Fund and another part to the Nigerian Troops Comfort Fund. In Ilesha district in the Western Provinces similar school competitions yielded £217.

24. Memorandum, DO, Aba, 2 July 1943, file no. 1646, vol. II, ABADIST 14/1/863, NAE.

25. Table for Palm Kernel Exports, Eastern Provinces (Excluding Cameroon), December 1940, p. 43, ABADIST 1/26/910, NAE. In 1940 the breakdown of kernel production by tons in each province was as follows: Onitsha—24,714, Oguta—15,272, Owerri—46,574, Calabar—42,956, Ogoja—3,855, Opobo—19,962, and Eastern Kabba—4,382.

26. See Chuku, *Igbo Women and Economic Transformation*; Njoku, "Development of Roads and Transport in Southeastern Nigeria, 1903–1939."

27. G. F. T. Colby, deputy director of supplies, Nigeria Secretariat, Lagos, 7 June 1943, ABADIST 14/1/863, NAE.

28. Ibid.

29. G. F. T. Colby, "Palm Oil Control Scheme"; interview with J. O. Okorocha, c. 81 years, trader and farmer, Umuomainta, Mbawsi, 26 May 1993; and interview with Pa Kanu Uga, c. 88 years, trader, Isimkpu, Arochukwu, 8 June 1993.

30. Memorandum on "Restriction on the Movement of Foodstuffs—Gari," 7 January 1943, file no. 4038/S.6, CCI 1/1, NAI.

31. DO, Orlu, to resident, Owerri province, 6 March 1946, OR/C/181 B, vol. III, ORLDIST 3/1/255, NAE.

32. DO, Aba, to resident, Owerri province, 24 May 1943, ABADIST 1/26/907, NAE.

33. Chuku, *Igbo Women and Economic Transformation*; and Ohadike, "The Influenza Pandemic of 1918–19 and the Spread of Cassava Cultivation on the Lower Niger."

34. Uzozie, "Patterns of Crop Combination in the Three Eastern States of Nigeria," 66.

35. Hopkins, *An Economic History of West Africa*, 31.

36. Memorandum, "Harvest Prospects, 1946–47," AIDIST 2/1/433, NAE.

37. Colby, "Palm Oil Control Scheme," and table, "Palm Oil Grading Figures, Eastern Provinces (Excluding Cameroons) in Tons, December 1944," ABADIST 1/26/910, NAE.

38. Chief Umana to senior resident, Calabar, 29 December 1943, CALPROF 7/1/95, NAE; Memorandum, SEP to residents, Eastern provinces, January/February, 1942; ABADIST 1/26/707, NAE; and memorandum, "Restriction on Movement of Foodstuffs—Gari, January 1943," file no. 4038/S.6, CCI 1/1, NAI.

39. Correspondence in file no. 1647: Rising Cost of Gari in Aba, April 1949, ABA-DIST 14/1/876, NAE.

40. See Kleis, "Confrontation and Incorporation: Igbo Ethnicity in Cameroon."

41. Njoku, "Export Production Drive," 23.

42. Memorandum, DO, Aba, 2 July 1943, file no. 1646, vol. II, ABADIST 14/1/873, NAE.

43. Memorandum, "Export of Gari to the North by Gari Traders Will Stop on 1st September 1944," file no. 1646, ABADIST 14/1/875, NAE.

44. Petition from the Traders' Union, Agbani, to the chief secretary, Lagos, 25 September 1944, file no. 185, vol. III, UDDIV 9/1/24, NAE.

45. Chuku, *Igbo Women and Economic Transformation*; Mbajekwe, "'Landlords of Onitsha': Urban Land, Accumulation, and Debates over Custom in Colonial Eastern Nigeria, ca. 1880–1945"; Ekejiuba, "Omu Okwei, the Merchant Queen of Ossomari: A Biographical Sketch"; Bauer, *West African Trade*.

46. The role of West African students overseas in building African diasporic communities and Pan-African networks and organizations with their Caribbean counterparts and in the leadership of nationalist movements in different parts of colonial Africa cannot be underestimated. See Adi, *West Africans in Britain*, and Denzer, "American Influences in Nigerian Culture." Through the American Council on African Education (ACAE) and the African Academy of Arts and Research (AAAR), two Pan-African cultural organizations founded between 1937 and 1943 by Nwafor Orizu, Mbonu Ojike, and Kingsley Mbadiwe in the United States, all Igbo graduates of American universities, scholarships were awarded to Nigerians to study in the United States. Out of the eight branches of the ACAE in Nigeria, four were located in the eastern towns of Port Harcourt, Aba, Enugu, and Onitsha. There is no doubt that the activities of these organizations helped to increase interest in American education, which ultimately led to the growth of an Igbo diasporic community in the United States.

47. See Chuku, "Igbo Women and Political Participation in Nigeria, 1800s–2005"; Mba, *Nigerian Women Mobilized*.

48. See Wolpe, "Port Harcourt," and Dixon-Fyle, "The Saro in the Political Life of Early Port Harcourt."

# References

Adi, Hakim. *West Africans in Britain, 1900–1960: Nationalism, Pan-Africanism, and Communism*. London: Lawrence and Wishart, 1998.

Afigbo, Adiele E. *The Warrant Chiefs: Indirect Rule in Southeastern Nigeria, 1891–1929*. London: Longman, 1972.

Bauer, Peter Thomas. *West African Trade: A Study of Competition, Oligopoly, and Monopoly in a Changing Economy*. Cambridge: Cambridge University Press, 1952.

Chuku, Gloria. "From Petty Traders to International Merchants: A Historical Account of Three Igbo Women of Nigeria in Trade and Commerce, 1886–1970." *African Economic History* 27 (1999): 1–22.

———. *Igbo Women and Economic Transformation of Southeastern Nigeria, 1900–1960*. London: Routledge, 2005.

———. "Igbo Women and Political Participation in Nigeria, 1800s–2005." *International Journal of African Historical Studies* 42 (2009).

Denzer, LaRay. "American Influences in Nigerian Culture: A Case Study of the American Council on African Education." *Journal of American Studies in Nigeria* 1 (1991).

Dixon-Fyle, Mac. "The Saro in the Political Life of Early Port Harcourt, 1913–49." *Journal of African History* 30 (1989): 125–38.

———. *A Saro Community in the Niger Delta, 1912–1984: The Potts-Johnsons of Port Harcourt and Their Heirs.* New York: University of Rochester Press, 1999.

Ekechi, Felix K. "Aspects of Palm Oil Trade at Oguta (Eastern Nigeria), 1900–1950." *African Economic History* 10 (1981): 35–65.

Ekejiuba, Felicia. "Omu Okwei, the Merchant Queen of Ossomari: A Biographical Sketch." *Journal of the Historical Society of Nigeria* 3 (1967): 633–46.

Falola, Toyin. "Cassava Starch for Export in Nigeria during the Second World War." *African Economic History* 18 (1989): 73–98.

———. "The Lebanese in Colonial West Africa." In *People and Empires in African History: Essays in Memory of Michael Crowder,* ed. J. F. Ade Ajayi and J. D. Y. Peel, 121–41. London: Longman, 1992.

———. "'Salt Is Gold': Management of Salt Scarcity in Nigeria during World War II." *Canadian Journal of African Studies* 26 (1992): 412–36.

Hopkins, A. G. *An Economic History of West Africa.* London: Longman, 1973.

Idemili, S. O. "What the West African Pilot Did in the Movement for Nigerian Nationalism between 1937 and 1957." *Black American Literature Forum* 12 (1978): 84–91.

Kleis, Gerald W. "Confrontation and Incorporation: Igbo Ethnicity in Cameroon." *African Studies Review* 23 (1980): 89–100.

Martin, Susan M. *Palm Oil and Protest: An Economic History of the Ngwa Region, South-Eastern Nigeria, 1800–1980.* Cambridge: Cambridge University Press, 1988.

Mba, N. *Nigerian Women Mobilized: Women's Political Activity in Southern Nigeria, 1900–1965.* Berkeley: University of California Press, 1982.

Mbajekwe, P. "'Landlords of Onitsha': Urban Land, Accumulation, and Debates over Custom in Colonial Eastern Nigeria, ca. 1880–1945." *International Journal of African Historical Studies* 39 (2006): 413–39.

Njoku, O. N. "Development of Roads and Transport in Southeastern Nigeria, 1903–1939." *Journal of African Studies* 5 (1978): 471–97.

———. "Export Production Drive in Nigeria during the Second World War." *Transafrican Journal of History* 10 (1981): 11–27.

———. "Contributions to War Efforts." In *Britain and Nigeria: Exploitation or Development?* ed. T. Falola, 164–85. London: Zed Books, 1987.

Ohadike, Don. "The Influenza Pandemic of 1918–19 and the Spread of Cassava Cultivation on the Lower Niger: A Study in Historical Linkages." *Journal of African History* 22 (1981): 379–91.

Olusanya, G. O. "The Role of Ex-Servicemen in Nigerian Politics." *Journal of Modern African Studies* 6 (1968): 221–32.

———. *The Second World War and the Politics in Nigeria, 1939–1945.* London: Garvase, 1973.

Sheldon, Sayre P., ed. *Her War Story: Twentieth-Century Women Write about War.* Carbondale: Southern Illinois University Press, 1999.

Turshen, Meredeth, and Clotilde Twagiramariya, eds. *What Women Do in Wartime: Gender and Conflict in Africa.* London: Zed Books, 1998.

Uzozie, L. C. "Patterns of Crop Combination in the Three Eastern States of Nigeria." *Journal of Tropical Geography* 33 (1971): 62–72.

Winder, R. Bayly. "The Lebanese in West Africa." *Comparative Studies in Society and History* 4 (1962): 296–333.

Wolpe, Howard. "Port Harcourt: Ibo Politics in Microcosm." *Journal of Modern African Studies* 7 (1969): 469–93.

# 11

# Intersections: Nigerian Episodes in the Careers of Three West Indian Women

### LARAY DENZER

Africa's debt to the West Indies can never be repaid. Not all the gold and diamonds dug from the bowels of this great continent are sufficient to give the West Indies the reward they deserve for the blood and toil and sweat which their sons and daughters had offered as an oblation to emancipate Africa from ignorance and superstition.

EDITORIAL, *WEST AFRICAN PILOT*, 26 MARCH 1943

We have looked upon ourselves as the heralds and beacons of a greater and glorious Africa.

H. M. DOUGLAS, *WEST AFRICAN PILOT*, 29 JUNE 1948

Significant linkages have existed between Nigeria and the West Indies since the nineteenth century. Although historically the size of the West Indian community in Lagos and other West African towns was small, West Indian men and women played distinguished roles as soldiers, railway workers, civil servants, teachers, missionaries, lawyers, judges, and entrepreneurs.[1] Some settled permanently in Nigeria while others returned to their original homes.[2] In the last quarter of the nineteenth century, the ideas of Edward Blyden, a Liberian of West Indian descent, interested the Lagosian intelligentsia, including his ideas about the re-patriation to Africa of peoples of African descent from the United States and the West Indies. His ideas were popularized by the *Lagos Weekly*

*Record*, which published articles about repatriation and African development.[3] Later in the 1920s the ideas of Marcus Garvey, the radical black populist who led the Universal Negro Improvement Association (UNIA) based in New York and who was influenced by Blyden, revived interest in repatriation as well as in black autonomy and self-help projects like Garvey's shipping venture, the Black Star Line. The Lagos branch of the UNIA was the strongest and most active of its several branches in West Africa.[4] Its leaders included two notable West Indian businessmen, John Ambleston of Antigua and Stanley Amos Wynter Shackleford of Jamaica, as well as local cultural nationalists, some with Sierra Leonean backgrounds.[5] In the 1940s, West Indians enjoyed particularly high regard among Nigerians because of the courage of Felix Éboué, the French Guyanese governor-general of French Equatorial Africa, who supported Free France and gave General Charles de Gaulle an important base for African operations during World War II.[6] The wartime Nigerian press, especially the *West African Pilot* and other newspapers in the Zik Group, highlighted transatlantic linkages among West African students overseas, international black news agencies, and Pan-African organizations. Editorials and other coverage heralded African American initiatives in Ethiopia and Liberia as hopeful signs of a new commitment of African Americans and West Indians to African postwar reconstruction and development. Occasionally, an article on black immigration and settlement echoed earlier interest in repatriation.[7] After the war a number of distinguished African American leaders visited Nigeria, partly inspired by the growing nationalist movement but also interested in exploring possible links between African Americans and Nigerians for education, development, and diasporic unity.

This chapter focuses on the Nigerian episodes in the lives of three women from the English-speaking West Indies who worked or stayed in Nigeria at different times from the late 1920s to the 1950s: Dahlia Whitbourne, a physician who practiced in Lagos from 1928 to 1930; Henrietta Millicent Douglas, a journalist who worked in Lagos from 1939 to 1955; and Amy Ashwood Garvey, a Pan-African organizer and businesswoman who made a lengthy visit to Nigeria in 1947–48. The common denominator linking their lives was the lure of Africa and the British colonial situation. They came from colonies undergoing the same sort of complex socioeconomic and political development that was taking place in Nigeria. All were single women, well-educated, with sufficient funds to travel and investigate opportunities beyond their homes. Family ties brought Whitbourne to Lagos, where she joined the small community of West Indian repatriates, a mobile and skilled group committed to economic advancement and African self-determination. Before coming to Nigeria, both Douglas and Garvey had already established connections with Pan-African organizations and diasporic networks at home, in the imperial metropole, in West Africa, and in the United States. Committed Pan-Africanists, they were interested in the pragmatic application of Pan-African ideas to the growth of Nigerian nationalism and gender equality. Their social backgrounds, financial situations, and networks facilitated the entry of these three women into Lagos society and permitted them to be independent and forthright in public life. While they did not necessarily share the same political philosophy, their lives demonstrated concern for Africa and its development.

The choice of life histories considered here rests on the accumulation of evidence collected from Nigerian newspapers and archives in the course of conducting other research projects on Nigerian women's history. The call for papers for the conference on which this volume is based presented an opportune time to explore the contribution of these three West Indian women to Nigerian social history. In 1998, Ula Taylor criticized Paul Gilroy for his "reluctance to offer any sustained discussion of the female intellectuals" whose travels "transformed them and their understanding of the Pan-African world."[8] Since then, the growing body of work on women in slavery, free women of color, colonial women's movements, and women's political participation has begun to illuminate the range of women's experience in diasporan movements. Scholars have unearthed new sources, asked new questions, developed new methodology, and noticed personalities who played important roles. Evidence of the importance of the three women considered in this chapter emerged from a close reading of the Nigerian press. It consists of many fragments that, when considered as a whole, illuminate the type of diasporan networks that women developed. Their careers traverse those of their Nigerian sisters who opened new frontiers in employment, leadership, and organization.

## Dahlia Whitbourne and Lagos Health Services

On 13 August 1926, the *Daily Times of Nigeria* reported that Dahlia Whitbourne had become the first girl from a Jamaican school to become a doctor. With a Wolmer's scholarship in 1920, she enrolled in the medical school of the Royal Free Hospital for Women in London. Six years later, she obtained her bachelor of medicine and bachelor of surgery degrees from the University of London, diplomas as a member of the Royal College of Surgeons, and a licentiate of the Royal College of Physicians of London. She took additional courses at the London School of Tropical Medicine and Hygiene and postgraduate study in midwifery, gynecology, and infant welfare at Rotunda Hospital, Dublin.[9] No doubt the reason why the newly qualified physician's success interested the Lagosian press was the fact that she was the eldest daughter of J. A. Whitbourne, a produce buyer and overseer employed by Lagos Stores. So far, the only other information we have about her father is that he lived with his wife and two sons in Ebute Metta, then a suburb of Lagos. She had other relatives in Lagos: the *African Messenger* mentions that she was the niece of Dr. J. A. Foster, a dental surgeon. It seems likely that this period of employment was her first, and perhaps only, time in Lagos, for the *Daily Times* described her father as "late of Kingston," suggesting fairly recent emigration.[10] Like their West African counterparts, elite West Indian daughters who were educated in Britain were usually sent when very young and remained there until completing their training.

On 8 March 1928, Whitbourne arrived in Lagos to assume a post as lady medical officer (LMO) in charge of maternal and infant welfare work for the Lagos Town Council (LTC). Her appointment made her one of the very few professional women, black or white, in the employ of any British West African colonial body at that time. The colonial service was largely a man's world, but beginning in the mid-1920s the Colonial Office, partly due to pressure from governors' wives and interested imperial women's groups, initiated a policy to promote maternity clinics and infant welfare services. Late in November 1924, the *Daily Telegraph* reported the first appointments of women medical officers, Mrs. G. Blacklook to Sierra Leone and Miss A. M. K. O'Halleren to the Gold Coast, and *West Africa* magazine added the name of Miss M. A. Robinson, who had gone to an unspecified West African colony in June.[11] According to the *Telegraph*, these appointments were significant for several reasons: there was no discrimination against married women; LMOs received the same pay and allowances as their male counterparts; and they were eligible for promotion on the same terms as men. The report suggested that this represented an "ever-widening field of women's activities" and anticipated more such appointments in the future; moreover, British West African governors noted the "special suitability of women doctors for welfare work in connection with women and children, particularly in regard to the schools and in maternity cases." Three years before Whitbourne's appointment, the Nigerian government had appointed four European LMOs, followed by a woman secretary to the Board of Education in 1926 and the appointment in 1927 of a European principal and two school mistresses to the newly established Queen's College, the first government girls' secondary school in Lagos.[12] Several West Indian women had applied for teaching posts in the new school. Although none gained appointment, one of them, Carmen Ferguson of Jamaica, wrote of her keen desire "to get a glimpse of the outside world—especially of Africa."[13] Unfortunately, these pioneer appointments of women officers to the senior colonial service failed to fulfill expectations of expanded opportunities for female civil servants—European or Africa—and their numbers remained low until the 1950s.[14] Nevertheless, these appointments signaled imperial recognition of the importance of improving female education and reproductive health, however slowly policy makers moved to expand education and health services.

Whitbourne's appointment coincided with an initiative by the colonial government to meet imperial directives to develop preventive infant and maternal health care services in the late 1920s. According to the LTC general purposes committee, infant mortality in Lagos was almost twice that of England and Wales, 127 in 1,000 compared with 69 in 1,000. The LTC appointed Whitbourne to develop antenatal, maternity, and child welfare programs. Lagosian elite women and the wives of European officials, led by the governor's wife, Lady Thomson, president of the Ladies League, a women's social welfare organization, promised assistance and support in developing a plan of action. Whitbourne was hired on similar terms as local African medical officers, whose salary and conditions of service was considerably less than European medical officers.

Her beginning salary was pegged at £400 plus a housing allowance of £60 and transport allowance of £94.[15] By contrast, the European LMO in charge of Massey Street Clinic in Lagos received a starting salary of £600, a furnished house with electricity, telephone service, and other allowances. This inequity was a source of contention among African medical officers until the 1950s.

By all accounts Whitbourne was well liked, efficient, and hardworking in setting up the LTC infant welfare clinic, but she soon resented the onerous conditions of service and resigned after her first tour of service. She had a heavy workload, which was probably not dissimilar from that of the European LMO at Massey Street Hospital, who attended to between 90 and 120 patients daily, supervised the women's wards at the African General Hospital, trained midwives, held infant welfare clinics several afternoons a week, and gave occasional lectures in mothercare and hygiene.[16] As Lagosians grew more accustomed to European maternal and infant health care, the numbers seeking treatment increased and the workloads of the attendant physicians became more arduous.

On 1 July 1930, Whitbourne went on leave to Jamaica with her mother and two brothers. Prior to her departure the local press carried reports concerning her resentment about the restrictive conditions of service. Some Lagos leaders pressed the LTC to reconsider her terms of appointment, but before such steps could be taken, the LTC announced her resignation at its meeting of 24 June 1930.[17] No reason for her decision was offered, so the councilors asked for further explanation. She replied that her salary was too low to buy a car or pay for return passage to Jamaica or England, and the work was too strenuous. Further, she complained that the stipulated period of leave did not provide enough time for a proper holiday in Jamaica: "You will recall that in the 27 months during which I worked in Lagos, I only once obtained a week's leave, and that had to be deducted from my general leave. . . . You will therefore agree that my health could not but suffer under such conditions, and that it was impossible for me, a stranger in Nigeria, to work under conditions which were laid down to natives of the country." Despite a LTC resolution to offer better terms of service, Whitbourne did not change her mind. Perhaps other factors were at work. Nigeria was then in the throes of economic depression, which may have affected her father's position in Lagos. There was no further news of her in the local press; however, it seems reasonable to expect that as a pioneer woman doctor, she pursued her profession in government service or private practice in the West Indies or elsewhere.[18]

### Henrietta Millicent Douglas, Journalist and Civil Servant

Henrietta Millicent Douglas arrived in Lagos on 1 August 1939, about seven weeks before Great Britain declared war on Germany. At the beginning of the year, a Jehovah's Witness friend had sent her some issues of the *West African Pilot,* which had articles on the youth movement and a report speculating about the rumors concerning the transfer of Nigeria to Germany. "The entire spirit of the paper fired my imagination," she wrote in her column in the *African Mirror* (2 June 1940, 5). So she wrote to Nnamdi Azikiwe about her interest in Nigeria and asked about employment possibilities. Perhaps she also mentioned to him that her interest in coming to Nigeria went back to 1918. In March she received a cable from Azikiwe offering her a three-year contract in his editorial office at £25 a month, but very little in the way of travel expenses (*African Mirror,* 21 June 1940, 3). Much to the surprise of her family and friends, she accepted the offer, settled her affairs in Grenada, and booked passage to England, where she would stay for a few months before her final departure to Nigeria. But she was not dissuaded.

Some months prior to her arrival, the *West African Pilot* had published a letter she had written to the editor, Azikiwe, on the front page of its 29 March 1939 issue. She referred to a packet of papers sent to her containing the *Pilot*'s run for the month of November 1938, enthusing that "This new paper, which has come across the ocean to me, seems to have a policy of driving force which, if handled in all essentials with soul satisfying sincerity, will go far to raise the hopes and aspirations of every true born African, in and out of Africa." She agreed with Azikiwe that youth and women must be reoriented to attain modern progress and development in Africa. Reciting James Aggrey's much-quoted axiom that "no race rose above its women," she urged Nigerian women to emulate their sisters in the colony of Grenada, where women sat on town boards, served as jurors, and could be nominated for seats in the legislature. She herself had served as a nominated member of St. George's (Grenada) Town Council since 1934.[19] In that letter, she did not mention the possibility of relocating to Lagos, but clearly it began an exchange of correspondence that resulted in her arrival in Nigeria and a position on the editorial staff of the *Pilot*. She resided there until she retired in 1955.

At the time of her arrival, Douglas was already an experienced public leader, businesswoman, and journalist with strong Pan-Africanist interests. She came from an elite political family in Grenada, a small West Indian colony in the Windward Islands. Two pen portraits published in 1953 in the *Nigerian Catholic Herald* and the *Daily Times of Nigeria* provide tantalizing biographical notes about a well-to-do, politically involved, and unmarried planter, and businesswoman temporarily down on her luck.[20] She was the eldest and only surviving child of Mr. and Mrs. Henry Mathew Douglas. Her father had been the last black politician elected to Grenada's Old House of Assembly before its replacement by a legislative council in the 1870s.[21] The accounts in the Nigerian press tell us very little about Douglas's mother, but she seems to have possessed the level of education and accomplishment typical of elite West Indian women of the time. Widowed in 1901, she taught Henrietta music and arranged for the best education available at private elementary schools in Grenada and Port of Spain, Trinidad. Sometime in 1917, mother and daughter went to England, where Henrietta attended St. Dominic's Convent School in Stone, Staffordshire. After obtaining the Oxford Senior Certificate Examination, she acquiesced to her mother's desire that she study medicine, which she did for only a few months before transferring to the Royal Academy of Music to study music and art, her real passions, and qualify for the intermediate licentiate in pianoforte.

Douglas lived in England with her mother, who died there in 1924. According to autobiographical comments in her 1939 columns for the *Pilot*, Douglas conducted research in the British Museum from 1917 to 1924, while she took musical training. At the same time she began her career in journalism as a columnist for the *Negro World*, the journal of Garvey's UNIA, writing under the pseudonym Nefetari, a choice that suggests interest in ancient Egyptian women's history. (Nefetari was the favorite wife of Ramses II, king of Egypt from 1304 to 1237 B.C.) Although her early writing career indicated an interest in Garveyism, she also gravitated to less radical forms of Pan-Africanism, such as Harold Moody's League of Coloured Peoples.

In London, Douglas was part of the small group of black colonial residents or visitors from the West Indies and West Africa. She participated in the formation and activities of the Society of Peoples of African Descent (SPAD), founded in 1917, which became the Union of Students of African Descent (USAD), and the African Progress Union (APU), which absorbed the SPAD in 1918 but not the USAD, which remained an independent student organization until the formation of the West African Students' Union (WASU) in 1925.[22] The broad objectives of these groups coincided. The APU had two main aims: to articulate African sentiments and to further African interests in colonial politics and business.[23] It took up issues connected with the spread of race riots of 1919, the contribution of black colonial troops to the Allied victory in World War I, the special interests of the growing black population in Great Britain, greater self-determination in the black colonies, and colonial commerce. Membership embraced Africans, West Indians, African Americans, and Latin Americans in Britain. Among the APU leaders who figured in Douglas's later life was the Guyanese activist E. F. Frederick of British Guiana, who later established the Negro Progress Convention in Georgetown.[24]

These organizations included young colonial women from the music conservatories or finishing schools or, in a few instances, commercial schools in Britain. H. Millicent Douglas's name appeared in a *West Africa* report of the first annual USAD dinner, along with those of Misses Royaards, M. Christian, G. Julien, M. Deerkin, E. M. Mocara, and Louie Douglas, who served as honorary assistant secretary.[25] Through their activities with these organizations, these young women met influential black leaders, colonial administrators, and a range of British liberals involved in commerce and philanthropy. Very likely, they would have been particularly excited about meeting Adelaide Casely Hayford, who addressed the West African students on education on 2 December 1922. Casely Hayford's ideas on girls' education in Sierra Leone had been widely publicized through a series of articles, coauthored with her niece Kathleen Easmon, published in *West Africa* in 1921 and 1922.[26] As the first West African women to publish at such length in the Anglo-African press as well as in the West African press, their careers served as an inspiration to these young women soon to return home.

In London, Douglas and her mother were very well known in black colonial circles, and they entertained many West African students and

Nigerians visiting London for business, politics, and social reasons. Among them were the barrister and politician Adeyemo Alakija and his wife, Ayo; physician and legislator Dr. Curtis Crispin Adeniyi-Jones; barrister and legislator Dr. Kofo Abayomi and his wife, Oyinkan, who later became influential in women's organizations and politics; businessman and newspaper proprietor T. A. Doherty; and barristers A. Soetan, Ayo Williams, and A. O. A. Abayomi.[27] Adeniyi-Jones attended Douglas's mother's funeral in 1924. Also resident in London was another Douglas family from Grenada who may have been connected to H. Millicent Douglas, for she was listed among the persons who attended the funeral of Mrs. Maria J. Douglas, who also died in 1924 and was the mother of Louie Douglas.[28]

After her mother's death, Douglas returned to Grenada, where she managed the family cocoa estate, established two thriving cinemas, and took part in organizing social services for youth. She organized a breakfast shelter for schoolchildren, for which she received the honor of the Member of Order of the British Empire (MBE) in 1933. In 1931 or 1934 (dates vary in existing accounts), she was appointed to the St. George's Town Council, on which she served until her departure for Nigeria. Because of her public role in Grenada as well as her earlier acquaintance with the leader of the Negro Progress Convention, she was invited in 1934 to chair the women's session of its annual convention in British Guiana. The governor's wife, Lady Douglas-Jones, attended this session, reported by the contemporary West Indian press as the first time that "the First Lady of the Land had attended such an assembly." She also held an "At Home" reception in honor of Douglas and her colleague from Boston, Dr. Theodore E. A. M. McCurdy, a British Guianan, who delivered the oration of the convention.[29]

In St. George's, Douglas continued her journalist career, writing a column and feature articles for the *West Indian,* a local newspaper that until 1934 was edited by the Honorable Theophilus Arthur Marryshow, an outspoken nationalist and federalist.[30] "Educate, Agitate, Federate" was his slogan in newspaper and political campaigns. Although Douglas's connection with the *West Indian* occurred for only a year or two of his editorship, she probably shared his convictions on the importance of West Indian self-government and perhaps the desirability of larger federation. In addition, she occasionally contributed articles to the

*Chronicle* of Georgetown, British Guiana. The content of her writing for these newspapers requires further research, but quite likely her columns covered the same issues as those she later wrote for the *Pilot* and other Lagos newspapers: cultural events, women's participation in public life, education, and current social issues.[31]

In the late 1930s, Douglas encountered financial difficulties and lost much of her wealth, which may have contributed to her decision to relocate in Lagos. Outward migration has been an important theme in Grenada's history.[32] It is the smallest of the Windward Islands and the most densely populated, and many islanders sought better opportunities elsewhere, principally to the United States, Trinidad, Cuba, Central America, and other parts of the Caribbean. So her decision to emigrate was not unusual, but her choice of West Africa as a destination was. Besides employment on the *Pilot* staff, we do not know what other motivations lay behind her decision to make this major move, but her funds covered travel and relocation expenses. The dynamic philosophy of her prospective employer, Nnamdi Azikiwe, may have persuaded her that Nigeria offered hope for Pan-African associations and political autonomy. Moreover, Nigeria was perhaps West Africa's most prosperous colony and offered prospects of an interesting career and comfortable lifestyle.

On 27 May 1929, Douglas left Grenada for Lagos via Britain. Breaking her journey in London, she stayed there for two months to renew old friendships and conduct a series of interviews for later use in her column for the *Pilot*. She stayed at Aggrey House, a hostel established for African students by the Colonial Office, which by 1939 had become a popular meeting place for Africans coming to Britain. During her stay, she met prominent black leaders and colonial administrators, including the Reverend Israel Oluwole Ransome-Kuti, then on an extensive educational tour of Britain.[33] She discussed contemporary West African issues with Sir Arnold Hodson, governor of the Gold Coast; G. C. Whiteley, who had just been appointed chief commissioner in Ibadan (Nigeria); Major Hanns Vischer of the Colonial Office; and Lady Thomson, the widow of Sir Graeme Thomson, governor of Nigeria from 1925 to 1931. Douglas took special note of Lady Thomson's views on Lady Violet Bourdillon, the popular wife of the incumbent Nigerian governor, and her work with the Ladies Progressive Club, an organization for the wives of European

officials and the wives and daughters of the Lagos professional and political elite.[34]

Douglas also met Lady Kathleen Simon (née Harvey), the American-
born wife of Sir John Simon, the chancellor of the exchequer, whom she
interviewed at her 11 Downing Street address.[35] An abolitionist, Lady
Simon had published in 1929 a comprehensive survey of contemporary
slavery and other forms of servitude in Africa and Asia based on League
of Nations and colonial government reports.[36] This work and her reputation for socializing with eminent black leaders had intrigued Douglas.
Their discussion ranged widely over topics like Africa House, the WASU
hostel, which Lady Simon had opened, and personalities with whom they
shared acquaintance (Paul Robeson, among others), and then turned to
the situation for women in Nigeria. When Douglas asked her to write
a personal message "for my paper" that would inspire young educated
women, Simon inquired if they were educated enough to take up nursing, a profession in which she had qualified.[37] Douglas replied that there
was considerable interest in nursing as a career and that two West African women—Elizabeth Akerele (later Awoliyi) in Nigeria and Agnes
Savage in the Gold Coast—had become physicians.[38]

Among other personalities interviewed by Douglas were two important Pan-Africanists: Harold Moody, the president of the League
of Colored Peoples (LCP), and Ohenenana Cobina Kessie, grandson of
Asantehene Prempeh II and a former editor of *WASU Magazine*. With
Moody she reminisced about the earlier Pan-African organizations with
which she had been connected. They also discussed the importance of an
all-black executive for effective Pan-African organization and his desire
to make the LCP into a more representative force.[39] She described Kessie as "a man of vision, whose enlightened views [bore] testimony to an
ancient heritage" and "cultured, in its true sense" at a WASU reunion.[40]
He had recently published a pamphlet entitled *Colonies: What Africa
Thinks,* a pamphlet that Douglas would find being vigorously advertised on the masthead of the *Pilot* when she arrived in Lagos. This small
pamphlet proclaimed the West African nationalist viewpoint that the
days of empire were soon to be over. "The fact is," declared Kessie, "the
average African is not interested in the bitter press war raging between
the European Powers for slices of 'places in the sun.' . . . The cherished
hopes of all Africans lie in the complete emancipation of their Moth-

erland, for, like all other human beings, the spirit of freedom is innate in them." Moreover, he warned, "There is at present among the youth of West Africa an ever-growing dissatisfaction, anger and resentment towards the British people. They no longer pay heed to the Colonial Official's grandmotherly wail of 'As-it-took-Great-Britain-centuries-to-get-her-freedom-so-it-will-take-you'; nor do they listen with respect to the parochial missionary's advice of God's time is the best."[41]

Douglas also attended cultural functions and ceremonies that featured black culture and performance. Some revived memories of her earlier associations in London. One of the most memorable events was the memorial service for Garland Anderson, the African American playwright, who had died in early May, at St. Peter's Church in Great Windmill Street.[42] Despite its overtly Christian message, his play, *Appearances,* a drama about the power of faith, had played to full houses in London in 1930. John Payne, an African American singer who had lived in Britain since 1919, sang several spirituals before the eulogy. Douglas recalled how thrilled she had been in 1919 when she had first heard his solos with the Four Harmony Kings in the Philharmonic Hall in Regent Street.

Finally, Douglas embarked for West Africa on the SS *Banfora,* arriving in Lagos on 1 August 1939. A photograph published with the *Pilot's* announcement of her arrival shows a dignified middle-aged woman of ample proportions with a forthright, somewhat stern expression, wearing a fashionable sleeveless dress with a large appliquéd bodice. She anticipated vibrant new experiences and the chance to participate in Nigeria's evolving modernity. She already knew many Nigerians. She had kept up with the Nigerian press, so she was well aware of the key issues of the day and the various viewpoints of the local intelligentsia. Her colonial background and network of Nigerian friends in London and Lagos oriented her to Nigerian life and society. No doubt she already knew some of the West Indian residents or had introductions to members of their community, led by Amos Stanley Wynter Shackleford, a businessman (popularly known as the bread king) and former leader of the Lagos UNIA, and his wife, Gwendolyn.[43] In the mid-1940s, Douglas joined forces with the Shacklefords in setting up the Lagos branch of the African Academy of Arts and Research (AAAR), led by Kingsley Ozuomba Mbadiwe.

While she looked for suitable living arrangements, Douglas stayed with Rita Akaje-Macaulay (née Dove), a mainstay of Lagos society, whom she may have known in London, for a Miss Dove had attended the same APU and USAD functions that she did.[44] As her guest, Douglas quickly met the leaders of Lagos society. Her hostess was the successful proprietor and principal of Ladi-Lak Institute, a center for training young women in domestic science and sewing before marriage. Akaje-Macaulay was the daughter of Frans W. Dove, a prominent Sierra Leonean barrister, formerly a leader in the National Congress of British West Africa, who eschewed conventional Christian monogamy and had children by various "outside" wives, resulting in a complex family network with branches in major West African coastal cities. Born in Freetown, she was connected to the Blaize family of Lagos, one of the richest merchant families in the nineteenth and early twentieth centuries.[45] In 1931 she became the first female librarian in Nigeria. She also cofounded an elite literary club with a membership drawn from political and professional circles. At the time of Douglas's arrival, however, she was best known for her play *Frei-ghine* (*The Horned Woman*), which had been performed in 1932 as part of a program at Glover Memorial Hall featuring the music of Samuel Coleridge-Taylor, the celebrated Sierra Leonean composer.[46] Like Douglas, she was interested in journalism and contributed articles to the local newspapers, though which ones remains unclear, for she wrote under a pseudonym.[47]

How did Douglas regard her new home? Her eight-part series, "My Impressions of Lagos Colony," published in the *Pilot* from 12 to 30 December 1939, provide a vivid view of rapidly changing Lagos life in wartime. She had looked forward, she wrote, to coming to Lagos, and as a journalist, she no doubt kept careful notes. The greetings, the "splendid" bus service, the noise, the colors, the migration from the countryside, the prevalence of food traders, the open drains in need of reconstruction, and the large number of beggars in the street—all permeated her senses, even if she did not necessarily like every aspect of the urban scene. She loved the sociability of the people, especially during the holidays. She appreciated the etiquette of Yoruba greetings, but she hated the "drab, inartistic, and crude patterns of imported cloths."[48] Caustically, she observed that foreign firms were "Not content to kill the local and extensive industry which [had] existed for thousands of years" and that they were "gradually instilling a liking for the crudest colours which are also liable to degrade the people's sense of beauty." She urged the Lagos elite to follow the example of the Akan elites in the Gold Coast who had protected their textile tradition and "their ancient sense of beauty" from European competition.

By the time she arrived, Azikiwe was completing plans to expand his newspaper operations. Within a month, he moved his staff and printing operations into a new building in Commercial Avenue in Yaba, Lagos. On 25 September, he announced that the *Pilot* was increasing its editorial staff and its print run, returning to its former eight-page size, and launching an evening edition.[49] Douglas was named as the society editor and seems to have been in charge of page 2, on which her personal column, "My Daily Diary," began publication on 25 September. Other popular columns were "Milady's Bower," society news reported by "Miss Silva." With this appointment, Douglas enlarged the field for women journalists in Lagos, building on the work of the first Nigerian female editor, E. Ronke Ajayi, who had published the *Nigerian Daily Herald* in 1931–32. Throughout the 1930s most Lagos newspapers published a women's column, which may or may not have actually been written by a woman. Mabel Dove (Mrs. J. B. Danquah), a cousin of Rita Akaje-Macaulay, had briefly contributed a column under the pen name Ebun Alakija as a freelance journalist shortly after the *Pilot* began publication in November 1937, but she decided that the payment for her work was too small.[50]

Douglas began "My Daily Diary" with a three-part account of her interview with Lady Simon (discussed above). The third part published Simon's message to Lagosian women in full, prefaced by the comment that this message was "particularly opportune at this time."[51] Simon dwelt on the dignity of nursing as an employment choice for modern women, observing that "such work teaches that the ideal of life is Service," now "accepted as one of the highest careers for women in every social grade." Even though nursing may seem a rather narrow focus for addressing modern women in Nigeria, this message can be read more broadly as support for widening employment opportunities for women beyond nursing and greater equality in public life. Such a message found a ready audience among the girls then entering the secondary schools of Lagos. From 1938 through the war years, these students included Folayegbe Akintunde (later Akintunde-Ighodalo), Felicia Adetoun Banjo (later Ogunsheye), and Deborah Fasan (later Jibowu), who eventually rose to the top of their chosen professions and widened the scope for women's leadership.[52]

During her tenure with the *Pilot*, Douglas's columns covered many topics, including her London experience, values, local transportation, churches, local industries, music, and education. They reflected the everyday interests of her readers caught up in the social change brought about by mass transportation, the growth of literacy, new forms of popular culture, and development. Her interest in business produced articles on the prerequisites and perils of self-employment. She urged her readers to investigate thoroughly the requirements of industries like sugar manufacturing before investing their hard-earned capital in such enterprises.[53] In another column, she urged women to develop a commercial canning industry based on local produce.[54] Concerning the local cinema, her suggestions for improvements derived from her personal experience as a cinema proprietor in St. George's. In her view, "Cinema going is a boon to any community, it advances education, especially what films of an ennobling type are screened, and now that there is a 'cleaner picture' campaign, there has been a marked improvement in the plots and in the general make-up of the pictures."[55] Very deliberately, she avoided the topics featured in "Milady's Bower" and similar columns in competitors' newspapers: marriage, love, problems in modern relationships, childcare, and etiquette.

Like Azikiwe and other popular journalists, Douglas also published serialized articles. One series was devoted to women, and a second concerned education. At this time, intense debate on both subjects engaged the Lagos press and continued to do so until the coming of independence in 1960. From its foundation, the *Pilot* featured more news about women leaders, women's organizations, women's achievements, and girls' education than other newspapers. At the same time, it urged the expansion of education at all levels and regularly publicized the departure of students for overseas education in the United States and Great Britain. Thus Douglas's contribution to the ongoing discussion reflects the concerns of the Lagosian elite, particularly elite women. In the six-part series entitled "On Women," she decried gender discrimination and the limited opportunities open to women. Paying obligatory lip-service to the notion that women must develop their domestic skills as part of their training for national leadership, she pointed out that British women had not only demonstrated their domestic accomplishments but had also taken risks and endured numerous indignities in their struggle for equality. Urging women to make their own opportunities, she observed: "They must forge ahead, or remain stagnant." African women worked hard, but they had to enter modern life, which emphasized equal opportunities. They had to organize to improve opportunities no matter what their situation was. Even in India and Turkey, where women often led cloistered lives, there were nevertheless hundreds of women doctors and other professionals. African women did not suffer the same restraints, yet to her mind they seemed slow in uniting for a common cause. They must formulate definite programs and hone their occupational skills. In the last installment of this series, she declared, "Women should be on the City Councils, in the Legislature, and other political bodies where they would help to frame economical programmers to further the prosperity of the community."[56]

In a five-part series on education, she observed that in "progressive" countries, education was free, resulting in the inculcation of "the methods of correct living, and thinking" among the masses. In Nigeria, however, education was largely in the hands of missions or private proprietors who now needed greater financial assistance from the state. She stressed the importance of schools in shaping morality and inculcating the notion of service to the family and community among students. "Education," she wrote, "which helps the pupil to steer clear of the many pitfalls which lie in wait for the careless, is the best way of leading the one taught through the narrow by-way of true Culture."[57] Her views stressed personal development and happiness—the creation of well-rounded individuals—as the cornerstone of society. Such beliefs were echoed throughout the educational establishment; however, the *Pilot* pushed discussion on education further. Education was also the source of the skills and technological know-how needed for a modern self-governing nation. The sooner Nigerians obtained higher qualifications in every discipline, the sooner they could take over policy making and their own affairs.

Douglas did not remain on the *Pilot*'s staff very long. "My Daily Diary" stopped at the end of 1939, and she resigned after what she regarded as humiliating circumstances in April 1940. Almost immediately she joined the editorial staff of a new paper, the *African Mirror,* launched on 20 June 1940. There she gave a detailed account of "astonishing avalanches of abuse and insults" from the *Pilot's* business and works managers, concluding with the statement: "I am a fighter, not a whiner, but I am not ashamed to say that I cried."[58] Soon after joining the new paper, she was elected treasurer of the reconstituted Press Association.[59] In October, she took over as editor-in-chief of the *Mirror,* becoming the second female editor of a Nigerian newspaper.[60] Its maiden editorial clearly indicated its moderate tone: "to pull our own weight in the great task of building up in Nigeria, a social order in which the ideals of freedom, justice, moral and material progress shall thrive—a social order which would make Nigeria fit not only for heroes to live in but also for lesser people to have the opportunity of self-realisation."[61] Unfortunately, its content proved far less exciting than the *Pilot,* and the newspaper failed after a short time.[62]

The content of the *Mirror,* however, showed that Douglas was moving away from adult readership toward a more educational format for schoolchildren. In her column "From My Diary," she began to publish simply written articles about places, behavior, and historical figures. Examples from the period of July to September include articles on selfishness, honesty, rowdiness, Lady Astor, James Buchanan, the empress Josephine, and places like Gibraltar, Paris, and Rumania. This type of writing may have caught the eye of the colonial officials who wanted to experiment with new types of publications for the schools, for on 11 February 1944, she was appointed to a senior civil service post in the newly created Public Relations Office.[63] In this capacity, she founded and edited the *Children's Own Newspaper,* part of the administration's effort to respond to public pressure for more innovative programs in education and to stimulate interest in recreational reading. It began as a supplement to the *Nigeria Review,* first published on 12 February 1944. Seven months later, the *Pilot* reported that it had gained so much popularity that the government had decided to turn it into a separate newspaper aiming for an initial circulation of 100,000.[64] It was intended to be used in schools and to promote extracurricular activities. It organized a Pen Club and the Sunray Club, and encouraged children to participate in a variety of competitions in painting, drawing, and essay writing. This newspaper was Douglas's most successful effort: tens of thousands of children read it, and her connection with it is one that many people still remember.[65]

From her arrival, Douglas impressed Lagosians by her enthusiastic embrace of the city's social life. She joined several organizations involved in social welfare work, serving as a member in the general council of the Young Women's Christian Association (YWCA) and as president of the Ladies Progressive Club. She supported the work of Olufunmilayo Ransome-Kuti and the growth of women's participation in public life. At the First Nigerian Women's Congress held in Abeokuta on 31 July 1953, she observed, "A meeting of this kind has been taking place all over the world, but in Nigeria this is the first meeting for all Nigerian women to sit together. The first thing to [be] tackled is the unity for all Nigerian women. As you know without unity there is nothing we can do."[66] She also joined the Reformed Ogboni Fraternity, founded in 1914 as a modernized form of a traditional Yoruba secret society that sought to incorporate Christian and Muslim leaders.[67] Her experience in the cinema business led to her appointment to the board of censors. Although accounts of her activities between 1944 and 1954 are sporadic, they reveal a busy professional journalist who, besides working as a public relations officer, also contributed articles on a freelance basis to various newspapers, including the *Daily Service* and the *Pilot*, on much the same themes as those in her earlier *Pilot* column.[68] Being a government servant, however, meant that she had to avoid politics in her writing.

Douglas had an abiding interest in Pan-Africanism and so was a constant figure in activities related to furthering Pan-African interests of all kinds in Lagos. World War II had intensified interest in African affairs among African Americans and other peoples of African descent. Two main reasons account for this. Azikiwe's career after his return to West Africa in 1936 interested his former African American colleagues, who now read the *Pilot* on a regular basis and found him a reliable source on West African events. He maintained connections with Lincoln University and the African American press. Further, in the United States, the work of a talented Nigerian trio, Kingsley Ozuomba Mbadiwe, Mbonu Ojike, and Nwafor Orizu, sometimes collectively, sometimes individually, promoted greater awareness of Nigerian and African culture and aspirations. During and after their university careers, they campaigned intensely for greater cross-cultural understanding and the expansion of

American scholarships through speaking tours, publications, and the establishment of two interconnected organizations, the African Academy for Arts and Research (AAAR), founded in 1943, and the American Council on African Education (ACAE), founded in 1944.[69] Mbadiwe's *British and Axis Aims in Africa* (1942), Orizu's *Without Bitterness: Western Nations in Post-war Africa* (1944), and Ojike's two autobiographies, *My Africa* (1946) and *I Have Two Countries* (1947) circulated widely and received good reviews in both the black and white presses. Moreover, Eleanor Roosevelt's public reception of these authors at the White House enhanced their prestige at home, underscored by her serving as a patron of the AAAR and even appearing onstage at various performances.[70] At the close of the war, these three Nigerians returned to their country, where they were to lead distinguished political careers.

Already engaged in educational journalism, Douglas recognized the importance of expanding educational and political opportunities at home and abroad. She became the vice president of the Lagos branch of the AAAR, which Mbadiwe established after his return to Nigeria in June 1948. Fellow West Indian Amos Shackleford was the president.[71] The main goal of the AAAR in Nigeria was to organize scholarships for Nigerian students to study in the United States. It was patterned on an earlier scholarship program organized in 1945–47 by the Nigerian branch of the ACAE established by Orizu. Although the ACAE program had run afoul of the authorities, it had revealed considerable public enthusiasm for any scheme that facilitated overseas education.[72] Knowing the problems experienced by the ACAE, Mbadiwe took a more cautious approach in promoting his scheme. Like the previous plan, however, it gained active support of many prominent leaders in Lagos and other urban centers.

Douglas met Horace Mann Bond, the president of Lincoln University, when he visited Nigeria in 1949 as a guest of Mbadiwe.[73] It appears that they discussed nationalist politics and the local press. In February 1950, she wrote him a letter, thanking him for a "Xmas token," and mentioning the recent Enugu colliery strike during which some unarmed miners had been shot.[74] She concluded, "That's the outcome of 'mad politics.' The mob got mad, too!" Furthermore, she believed that "They [the Nigerians] should push ahead with education *cum* . . . culture." Bond had also introduced her to various popular African American periodicals and suggests that she read *Color* and *Our World,* both magazines covering black issues and culture, following up by sending her a copy of *Color.* Meanwhile, the editor of *Color,* I. J. K. Wells, had contacted her to market the magazine in Nigeria, which she promised to do, starting with twelve issues each moth. She confided that she found the magazine so interesting that she wanted to explore possibilities of a similar magazine in Nigeria, but first wanted to see how *Color* sold.[75] We do not know the extent to which she pursued this idea, but it was not until 1958 that this type of magazine appeared in Nigeria, with the start of the Lagos edition of *Drum* magazine, an offshoot of the popular South African journal.

In 1953 the publication of the two profiles in the *Daily Times of Nigeria* and the *Nigerian Catholic Herald* testified to Douglas's position in Lagos society. The *Daily Times* article appeared in a series entitled Women Who Matter, edited by the rising star in women's journalism, Theresa Ogunbiyi (later Bowyer), who changed the focus of the women's page in the *Daily Times* in the early 1950s and influenced the direction of the women's press in other periodicals.[76] Ogunbiyi benefited immensely from the model of woman journalist established by Douglas. The next we hear of Douglas, she was in Monrovia, where she landed on 27 September 1955 after her retirement from Nigerian government service. Writing on the eve of Ghana's independence to Horace Mann Bond, whom she had met on his triumphal tour of Nigeria for the AAAR in 1949, she reported that she was now attaché to Liberia's Bureau of Information. She wrote that she had heard his "fervent message" to people of Ghana on this evening broadcast: "It was grand. I could not attend but I listened with great pride and joy on the 5th, 6th, and up to now. All I can say is 'Thank God.' We have begun to move and move we shall with great alacrity." She thanked him for his gift of a subscription to *Color,* an African American periodical published from 1944 to 1957, and remarked on how her new position gave her further opportunities to maintain her acquaintance with African American leaders, including entrepreneur Claude Barnett and his wife, musical star Etta Moten, who had accompanied Vice President Richard Nixon on his 1957 West African tour, as well as I. J. K. Wells, the editor of *Color,* who had visited Liberia in 1955.[77] Further research on Douglas's career needs to be done, but it is clear that she was a passionate Pan-Africanist and African nationalist whose life contributed to African, and especially Nigerian, politics and educational development.

## Amy Ashwood Garvey, Pan-African
## Traveler and Businesswoman

Of the three women under consideration in this chapter, Amy Ashwood Garvey was the best known to the Nigerian elite before her arrival in Lagos in May 1947.[78] The Garvey name had great resonance in Lagos, where Marcus Garvey's ideas influenced nationalist thinking and where a branch of UNIA was established in the 1920s. Shackleford, former president of the UNIA branch, remained an important leader in the city in the 1940s. Azikiwe, one of the main nationalist leaders in the campaign for self-government, acknowledged Garvey's influence on his political ideas.[79] Amy Ashwood Garvey's status as Marcus Garvey's first wife was well known, but even more important was the personal network she formed among Nigerian students and the elite as a result of her role in founding the Nigerian Progress Union (NPU) and her support of the Lagos Women's League petition to the Lagos government pressing for more facilities for girls' education, modern employment for young women, and other social welfare programs in 1924.[80] This network further expanded during the interwar period because of her association with the London-based Pan-African movements as well as West African patronage of her popular restaurant in London's West End in the late 1930s.

Although Africa was a central element in Ashwood Garvey's ideology for most of her career, it was not until 1946 that she traveled to West Africa, beginning a journey that lasted two years and took her to Liberia, Senegal, Sierra Leone, the Gold Coast (Ghana), Nigeria, the Cameroons, and Spanish Guinea. In this chapter the focus is on her visit to Nigeria. Evidence about this episode in her life is limited to reports in the Nigerian newspapers and the brief accounts in biographies by Lionel Yard and Tony Martin.[81] More questions than answers arise from these sources. While the press reports provide information about some of her public meetings in Lagos and other towns, they reveal little about the nature of her trip, her overall activities, and only a rough idea of her itinerary. Yard provides a brief description of her notebooks on the Birom of

Jos Plateau and the Efik of Calabar, but so far access to these documents has been limited.[82] Martin's account of her activities in Nigeria augments and clarifies Yard's account, but it is not extensive. Nigerian press accounts extend our knowledge further, but we still do not get a complete idea of her activities. According to George Padmore, she "intend[ed] to go into business with a firm of native merchants, but this objective was not articulated until her later visits to West Africa."[83] Martin refers to an agreement she signed in 1947 to serve in London as an agent for the Mein Trading Company of Owo, a commercial center in Yorubaland, but there is no further information about this connection.[84]

Some of the Lagos elite were also acquainted with the work and ideas of Ashwood Garvey's lifelong rival, Amy Jacques Garvey, the second wife and widow of Marcus Garvey as well as the bitter public feud between the two women. Some regarded their legal struggle over the disinterment and custody of Marcus Garvey's remains as unseemly, and the *West African Pilot* urged them to settle their differences in a way that did not distract from Garvey's legacy.[85] The contribution of both women to Pan-Africanism and their rivalry has been well documented elsewhere and need not be dealt with extensively here.[86] For the purposes of this chapter, however, it is relevant that Azikiwe maintained a friendship and correspondence with Jacques Garvey and published extracts from her letters and some of her articles in his newspapers.[87] He was well aware of her anger over what she believed was Ashwood Garvey's usurpation of her place at the Manchester Pan-African Congress.[88] In 1960 it was Jacques Garvey, not Ashwood Garvey, whom he honored with an invitation to attend Nigeria's independence celebrations and his inauguration as the country's first African governor-general.[89]

The *Pilot's* initial account of Ashwood Garvey's arrival briefly recounted how, during her stay in the Gold Coast before coming to Nigeria, she had discovered her Asante ancestry, had been accepted as a member of a Juaben family, and had acquired her new Akan name, Yaa Buahimaa. This story of the discovery of her African roots, the personal intervention of the Asantehene, Osei Tutu Agyeman Prempheh II, in the investigation, and the public ceremony of the Damanhene family was reported at the time in the *Ashanti Pioneer* and has been detailed by Tony Martin.[90] According to Garvey, her great-grandmother had been captured from the village of Daman (Darmang) during a war between Juaben and Kumasi in 1824 and then shipped to Jamaica.[91] This date, seventeen years after the abolition of the British slave trade, means that her grandmother was sold illegally. In the Gold Coast, Garvey was treated as a celebrity, where the people of Juaben organized a durbar in her honor, and she was invited to address the joint provincial council of the colony. But Nigerians appeared relatively unimpressed by the affirmation of her Akan identity, perhaps because in Nigeria transnational family links were not so unusual.[92]

When Ashwood Garvey arrived in Lagos, the press briefly referred to her role in founding the Nigeria Progress Union in London and the Universal Negro Improvement Association in the West Indies and the United States.[93] The *Pilot* observed that her concern about "the backwardness of the African woman" had persuaded her to investigate girls' education and ways to improve the status of Nigerian women, both subjects she had been interested in since her association with the NPU. From the beginning, her plans appeared fluid. She told the *Pilot* she meant to stay for "several weeks" during which she would visit the provinces to gain direct information about the problems of African women. But, in fact, her stay in Nigeria was to last for two years.

Initially, Ashwood Garvey resided with Mrs. Jessica A. Otunba-Payne, an important Lagos socialite and the widow of John Payne Jackson, who had been a strong supporter of the UNIA.[94] Garvey was accompanied by three young Liberian women, Mrs. Carolina Lewis, who is later identified as the founder and president of the Liberia Charity Society, and Misses Moore and Morris.[95] Miss Morris may have been Garvey's adopted Liberian daughter, Eva, who was one of her business partners in the 1950s.[96] Her visit was initially facilitated by T. Morocco-Clarke, a West Indian baker, whom she had met twenty years before when he was in the United States.[97] At a meeting he organized, she wore Ghanaian attire, described as a "rich Accra style." Her choice of dress was symbolic and asserted her new Ghanaian identity, and she remarked that "it was something of her own and represented something spiritual to her." No doubt the audience appreciated this gesture, for Nigerian civil servants had just begun to wear African attire to their offices.[98] After describing her joy in at last realizing her lifelong dream of traveling in Africa and describing the epiphany of discovering her ancestral roots, she focused on her interest in African women's education and her intention to visit schools in the provinces. She met with Oyinkan

Abayomi, a founder of the Women's Party and a city councilor, to discuss the problem.[99] Abayomi was then perhaps the most influential woman in Lagos politics and educational circles, but no great rapport seems to have developed between the two women. Although the Women's Party sponsored a concert featuring Garvey and her three Liberian associates, it is not known whether there were other connections with the organization or its leaders.[100]

In Lagos Garvey visited the offices of the *Daily Times of Nigeria, the West African Pilot,* and the African Book Company.[101] One of the highlights of her visit was a visit to Abeokuta on 22 May, a town well known to Pan-Africanists because of Martin R. Delaney's visit there in 1858, where she had an audience with the Oba Oladapo Ademola, the Alake, traditional ruler of the town. They discussed African women's education and other women's issues. In her association with the NPU in 1924, the executive had given her the title of "Iyalode" of the organization, so she was well aware of the importance of Yoruba women's traditional titles, which after her visits to Sierra Leone and the Gold Coast was further underscored by her knowledge of titled women in Mende and Akan society.[102] She expressed surprise that the town had allowed the Iyalode title to lay dormant since the death of Madam Jojolola in 1932, and she urged the Alake to resuscitate the title.[103] According to the *Pilot*'s account, the Alake promised her that he would consider this, but Ademola, who did not like to be told by foreigners what to do, did nothing, and the title remained unfilled until 1982.[104] She also asked to see a girls' school, so she was taken to the Baptist Girls' High School at Idi Aba, considered to be the best girls' school in the town.[105] Interestingly, she was not taken to Abeokuta Girls' School run by Olufunmilayo Ransome-Kuti, an influential women's leader and educator, just then beginning her powerful opposition to the traditional ruler. In fact, Garvey's visit to Abeokuta coincided with the beginning of the women's tax protest in the town, one of the most important occurrences in Nigerian gender history, but there is no hint of a meeting between the two women either at this time or later when Garvey would not have been bound by diplomatic constraints.[106]

Initially, Ashwood Garvey was well received in official circles in Lagos and the provinces. On 13 June, Ashwood Garvey and her Liberian entourage gave a charity concert under the patronage of Governor Sir Arthur and Lady Richards, one of the social events of the year. She delighted the audience by singing a Yoruba song and expressing her great pleasure in being in Nigeria. She declared, "We have come to learn. We have learned. We have looked and found the scene." At the close of the concert, she urged the audience to ensure the preservation of their songs, for they represented the origins of the African American spirituals that she had just performed for them. Ten days later, Garvey and her three Liberian companions staged another concert at Glover Memorial Hall in Lagos under the patronage of the Alake of Abeokuta, Lady Alakija, and Oyinkan Abayomi of the Women's Party, but this event received little attention in the press. Unfortunately for Ashwood Garvey's group, their concerts were eclipsed by a rival musical event starring Broadway celebrity Etta Moten, who accompanied her husband, the prominent journalist and head of the Associated Negro Press. Their visit occurred during the same month as Garvey's.[107]

Press reports give little evidence of the range of Ashwood Garvey's various meetings, but a memorandum on her interview with the deputy director of education of the southern provinces, J. B. Gott, on 27 December 1947, provides a glimpse of her concerns and the respect for her among colonial administrators. Their discussion focused on girls' education. The deputy director explained that the early marriage age and seclusion had accounted for the late start in setting up girls' schools, but that the enrollment of girls in elementary school had steadily increased. He also discussed the history of the northern provinces, the views of the northern educated elite, the difficulties of building a teaching staff, and the obstacles of importing trained women teachers from the southern provinces. She suggested that more domestic science centers should be established, but basically she limited herself to gathering information. Gott observed, "The Northern Provinces in general was evidently something quite new to Mrs. Garvey, and she did little but enquire, she did not offer suggestions." He noted on his memorandum that she was to meet the secretary of the northern provinces after she left his office, but if notes were made of that meeting, they have not yet surfaced.[108] Martin refers to a letter she wrote to the resident of Onitsha province in which she stated that she was conducting a survey of girls' education in Nigeria and had "received kind courtesies from the Education Department and from Officials everywhere I have gone."[109]

Not much more is heard about Garvey's activities in Nigeria until July and August 1948, when she gave two talks in Onitsha, both entitled "The Survival of the Negro," one of which was sponsored by the radical Zikist Movement. These talks repeated basically the same message: she had come to Nigeria on a fact-finding mission to investigate the conditions of women. She wanted to raise their awareness about new ideas, the struggle for emancipation, and the expansion of women's education.[110] She also harked back to Garvey's plan for repatriation to Africa, calling for African unity and renewal of the repatriation project. Moreover, she averred that Africans had the duty to bring African Americans back.[111] Earlier in 1943 and 1944, the *Pilot* had expressed some interest in resuscitating the idea of repatriation of North Americans, now for the purposes of hastening modern development and industrialization, an idea that had some currency in the African American postwar press, but these sentiments were not mentioned in conjunction with Ashwood Garvey's visit.[112]

In October, the *Pilot* published a report about Garvey's "anthropological mission" in Cameroon during the period 13–27 September. According to this account, in an unnamed town, she had lectured to an audience of 1,000. Describing her as "a compact revolutionary intelligence," it noted her concern for the plight of Cameroonian women, their dignity crushed by "unilateral social conventions, and centuries of traditional usage."[113] On her return from Cameroon, she again spent time in Nigeria. At the close of her Nigerian tour, she visited Aba, one of the sites associated with the women's war of 1929, although she did not refer to this famous event in her speech. She ended her lecture on much the same note that had permeated her other lectures:

> I am happy to say that I had opportunity of studying the conditions of women in all stages of our African civilization.... I found her fettered and kept back by social traditions stretching back to countless ages.... I have now found within Africa itself a ray of hope in the growing understanding of the people and in the ever widening scope of liberal education.[114]

The date of Garvey's departure from Nigeria is unclear, but this seems to be her last reported public meeting in Nigeria. According to Martin, she returned to England on 12 July 1949.[115]

This account has considered only material in existing biographies and accounts of Garvey's visit in Nigerian newspapers. More research is needed to establish the network that she established and her actual itinerary. It is clear that her visit centered on towns that were strongholds of the National Council of Nigeria and the Cameroons (NCNC), but we only have a few accounts of her public talks. When they are reported, it is clear that she could draw a crowd and that her audience was as interested in the Garvey movement as they were in her.

Clearly, Garvey did not receive the enthusiastic welcome she had experienced in the earlier part of her journey in Liberia, where she may have received a proposal of marriage from President Tubman, and the Gold Coast, where she was formally adopted by her Juaben family. Part of the reason for this might be that news of her rivalry with Amy Jacques Garvey had preceded her. Amy Jacques had written a letter to Azikiwe complaining in detail about Amy Ashwood's effort to usurp her identity and rights as Garvey's widow.[116] At the time of her arrival in Nigeria, Azikiwe was in the United States receiving an honorary doctorate at Lincoln University, where he received a hero's welcome. As a friend and correspondent of Amy Jacques, Azikiwe may not have been particularly welcoming to Amy Ashwood.

Perhaps the most important thing about the accounts of Garvey's visits and speeches are in what they do not contain. There is little mention of the resident West Indian community celebrating her arrival, apart from her association with Morocco-Clark. Neither the Shacklefords nor Douglas appear to have hosted public receptions for her, nor are they mentioned in the various accounts of her activities. There are few mentions of Garvey holding extensive meetings with the many women's groups existing in Lagos and other urban centers, except for her early meeting with Abayomi and the Women's Party. There is no mention of meetings with organizations like the ACAE and the AAAR, both of which by the time of her trip had mounted dynamic scholarship schemes for sending Nigerians and other West Africans to U.S. colleges and universities.[117] There is no mention of meetings with Orizu of the ACAE or Mbadiwe of the AAAR, although both of them had established links with the Garvey movement in the United States during their student days in the early 1940s. Although she interviewed colonial educational administrators and visited some girls' schools, there does not seem to be any extensive development networking with independent schools' proprietors or the leadership of the Nigerian Union of

Teachers (NUT). While meetings with mission educators or colonial officials were important, the independent proprietors who worked outside the system and the NUT led the push for reform and expansion of the education system.

Nor did the press take up Garvey's views on women's education, which were very vague and did not connect all that much with contemporary developments in Nigerian educational policy. In fact, education was one of the burning issues of the day and formed an essential part of the public discourse on development. The contemporary press often took up issues related to girls' education and had forced the government to expand provision for girls' schools after World War II, with a corresponding increase in new opportunities in employment. Nigerian women leaders like Abayomi and Ransome-Kuti were in the frontline shaping these trends. Not only were many of them educationists, including some who were independent school proprietors, but they were also in the forefront of mobilizing women in strikes, tax resistance, political campaigns, and numerous women's organizations.[118] Thus Nigerian women may have found Ashwood Garvey's views patronizing, inadequate, and irrelevant to the Nigerian situation.

Nevertheless, the Nigerian press continued to take note of Ashwood Garvey's activities after she left Nigeria. Three years later, the *Pilot* published Ashwood Garvey's statement on the 1951 elections, which included an extensive roll call of African heroes, ranging from Osei Tutu and Jaja to J. B. Danquah, W. E. B. Du Bois, and George Padmore. She closed her manifesto with an appeal to African women, "Go out and take your place in the line of struggle for Africa's freedom and sustain your men in the battles ahead."[119] She was also interested in the World Federal Government (WFG) group, formed in 1945 with Boyd Orr (London) as chair and Fenner Brockway as deputy chairman. She emphasized that, although she supported the general objectives of the WFG, she was particularly interested in the woman's angle.[120] For the rest of her career, Ashwood Garvey maintained her interest in Pan-Africanism and organizing black women wherever she happened to be. She also tried her hand at a number of enterprises in Liberia and the Gold Coast/Ghana, including diamond mining, a duracrete factory, collecting African art, and setting up a girls' school.[121] Her talent lay in initiating organizational work, but not in the arduous day-to-day work that sustained programs.

## Conclusion

This study has examined the experience of three modern West Indian women in colonial Nigeria. They offer three models of interaction. Of the three, Henrietta Millicent Douglas was more fully accepted by local Nigerian elite society, including the West Indian expatriates, and her ideas seem to have been more in keeping with what Nigerians themselves were exploring. As a person who became deeply integrated into Nigerian society and culture during a long stay, she had both specific and more general interests that accorded with major questions being confronted by Nigerians in general, especially with regard to the expansion of education and women's issues. Whitbourne was a professional who brought specialized skills and apparently used them effectively but stayed for only two years and as far as we know did not get heavily involved in wider issues. Nevertheless, her medical career began at a moment when colonial women gained entry to a profession formerly dominated by men, a moment in which male policy makers realized that women professionals were better equipped to expand infant and maternal health services. Her success promoted acceptance for Nigerian women physicians in government service. As a traveler, Ashwood Garvey represented the growing interest among African Americans and West Indians in the postwar world in gaining firsthand knowledge of African conditions aroused by the growth of the nationalist movement there and publicized by the black press. She wanted to observe the specific aspects of Nigerian life and culture that she had been interested in throughout her career in Pan-African organizing and perhaps investigate future business possibilities, but she did not find Nigeria as welcoming or agreeable as other parts of West Africa that she had visited. Moreover, the degree of Nigeria women's participation in political life and expansion of girls' education had overtaken her ideas.

The common denominators linking their lives were the pull of Africa, the colonial situation, and travel. The idea of Africa, differently imagined and realized by each woman, formed the ideological backdrop to their experience. The colonial situation offered opportunities for professional careers, entrepreneurship, and organizational work beyond the colony of origin in somewhat familiar sociocultural and

political contexts. Travel broadened their horizons, providing comparative perspectives and firsthand knowledge of other colonial peoples, and
specifically the wide variety of women's status and conditions. All three
women expressed an interest in improving colonial women's and girls'
education. Their life histories reflected new interests in improving colonial women's status and social welfare through new forms of health
care and education. Pan-African ideas informed each woman's efforts to
gain firsthand experience of different sections of the black world. They
also played an important role in shaping the approach of Douglas and
Ashwood Garvey in establishing organizations to promote black unity
and to shape black identity on the basis of shared cultural and historical
heritage. Nigeria featured as an episode in each of their lives. Whether
of short or long duration, these episodes formed part of their search for
employment or entrepreneurial opportunities or a desire to contribute
to women's social welfare and education in an African country in the
diaspora.

## Notes

I would like to thank Judith Byfield, Karen Tranberg Hansen, Elisha Renne, Chris
Bankole, Tunji Ojo, and Marjorie McIntosh for their comments on this chapter.

   The first epigraph is from an editorial in *West African Pilot,* 26 March 1943. The
editorial was written in honor of Canon L. A. Lennon, a West Indian clergyman-
politician who had made a strong speech in the Nigerian Legislative Council in support of greater autonomy for the unofficial Nigerian members.

   1. For an analysis of the West Indian contribution to West Africa, see Blyden,
*West Indians in West Africa, 1808–1880,* and Nicol, "West Indians in West Africa."

   2. Talbot, *Peoples of Southern Nigeria,* 4:152. This work includes the 1921 census,
which enumerates 194 West Indian residents in Lagos. Some Nigerian families with
West Indian roots include the Clintons, the McCormacks, the Harts, the Morocco-
Clarkes, the Renwicks, the Wells-Palmers, the Ricketts, the Jones, the Thompsons,
and the McEwens.

   3. Omu, *Press and Politics in Nigeria, 1880–1937,* 33–36. The editor of the *Lagos
Weekly Record* was John Payne Jackson, who was born in the small African Ameri-
can colony of Maryland, which became part of Liberia in the late 1850s. His African
American emigrant father was a local politician and Methodist missionary.

   4. For accounts of the UNIA in West Africa, see Okonkwo, "The Garvey Movement in British West Africa" and "The Garvey Movement in Nigeria."

   5. For a brief biographical note on Ambleston, see Macmillan, *The Red Book of
West Africa,* 114. Born in Antigua in 1856, he came to West Africa in 1895, settling
first in Sierra Leone, then in the Gold Coast, and finally in 1916 to Lagos, where he
set up a sawmill. For a short biography, see Okonkwo, "Amos Stanley Wynter Shack-

leford: Bread King and Nationalist." Shackleford, a Jamaican, first came to Lagos in 1913 to work on the railroad. After a brief return to Jamaica, he returned to Nigeria and worked for several Nigerian-owned businesses before establishing a successful bakery, which earned him the sobriquet "the bread king." He was active in various Pan-African and nationalist endeavors throughout his lifetime.

6. Weinstein, *Éboué*.

7. The *West African Pilot*'s editorial of 18 April 1944 proclaimed, "Let the doors of West Africa be thrown open to any American Negro who is prepared to come out to assist us in materializing our social and economic programmes of reconstruction. There are thousands of qualified American Negro medical practitioners, dentists, social workers, economists, agriculturalists, veterinary surgeons, engineers, technicians, etc., who could immigrate to West Africa and be of invaluable service, officially and privately, to us." See also "American Universities and Colonies," editorial, *West African Pilot* [hereafter *WAP*], 30 January 1945, 2; and "America Can Help Nigeria," editorial, *WAP*, 30 January 1945, 2.

8. Taylor, "Intellectual Pan-African Feminists," 10.

9. "Jamaica Lady Doctor," *Daily Times of Nigeria* [hereafter *DTN*], 13 August 1926, 1.

10. "Dr. Dahlia Whitbourne," *Nigerian Spectator*, 10 March 1928, 5; "Infant Welfare Work in Lagos: Appointment of Lady Medical Officer," *DTN*, 23 March 1928, 4; "Personal and Social," *African Messenger*, 11 March 1928, 7.

11. "Women Doctors for West Africa," *West Africa*, 27 December 1924, 1300, reprinting a report in the *Daily Telegraph*, 29 November 1924.

12. Denzer, *Women in Government Service in Colonial Nigeria, 1862–1945*; Callaway, *Gender, Culture, and Empire*, 95, 112.

13. Carmen Ferguson to Director of Education, 15 July 1936, MED(FED)½, DE240, National Archives of Nigeria, Ibadan.

14. The LMOs were Honoria Somerville Kerr, Greta Lowe (later Lowe-Jellicoe), Mary Joseph Farrell, and Beatrice Emily Ebden. Sylvia Leith-Ross was the secretary to the Board of Education, and Faith Wordsworth was appointed foundation principal of Queen's College with two supporting women teachers.

15. G. J. Pirie for director of medical and sanitary service to chief secretary to the government, 15 February 1928, p. 2, ComCol 1/397, NAI.

16. Callaway, *Gender, Culture, and Empire*, 95–98. Callaway's description of the work of a LMO is based on the letters of Dr. Greta Lowe-Jellicoe, one of the first four European LMOs appointed to Nigeria in 1925.

17. "Personal and Social," *DTN*, 5 July 1930, 4.

18. "Resignation of Dr. Dahlia Whitbourne," *Lagos Daily News*, 29 July and 1 November 1930.

19. "West Indian Lady Writes in Praise of Policy of 'Pilot,'" *WAP*, 29 March 1939, 1, 8.

20. "A Great Woman: Miss Millicent Douglas," *Nigerian Catholic Herald*, 10 April 1953, 7; "Henrietta Millicent Douglas," Women Who Matter, *DTN*, 18 April 1953. Unless otherwise indicated, information about Douglas's early life derives from these two accounts.

21. Steele, "Grenada, an Island State, Its History, and Its People," 14.

22. "Ramble in London (3)," *WAP*, 11 October 1939, 2.

23. Adi, "West African Students in Britain, 1900–60," 112.

24. Langley, *Pan-Africanism and Nationalism in West Africa, 1900–1945*, 245–46; H. M. D., "Dr. Moody," *WAP*, 12 October 1939, 2. Other founders included the organizing secretary and militant Nigerian journalist Thomas Horatio Jackson; the Pan-African journalist Duse Mohammed Ali, who settled in Lagos in the early 1930s; the Sierra Leonean entrepreneur John Eldred Taylor, who published the *African Telegraph* in London from 1917 to 1919; onetime mayor of Battersea John Archer; the Trinidadian physician Dr. John Alcindor, who served as senior district medical officer in Paddington from 1921 until his death in 1924; and Robert Broadhurst, an Afro-British commercial agent who was involved in the establishment of many Pan-African organizations in Britain from 1911 to the 1950s.

25. "Union of Students of African Descent," *West Africa*, 10 June 1922, 585.

26. Adelaide Casely Hayford and Kathleen Easmon, "Technical School for Girls Tour," *West Africa*, 26 February 1921, 128; "A Visit to Tuskegee," *West Africa*, 4 June 1921, 444; and "Sierra Leone Delegates at Boston," *West Africa*, 15 August 1921, 878; and Casely Hayford, "Afro-American Clubland," *West Africa*, 19 November 1921, 1469; "West Africa in America," *West Africa*, 7 January 1922, 1656; "Sierra Leone Girls' School," *West Africa*, 1 April 1922, 277; "Interesting Ceremony at Tuskegee," *West Africa*, 5 August 1922, 870. See also the report of Casely Hayford's speech to the Scottish Mission conference at Glasgow, "Women's Education in West Africa," *West Africa*, 18 November 1922, 1386 and 1389. For a biography of Casely Hayford, see Cromwell, *An African Victorian Feminist*.

27. "Miss H. Millicent Douglas Is a Prominent Social Worker," *WAP*, 5 August 1939, 1, 7; *WAP*, 17 October 1939; H. M. Douglas, "My Impressions of Lagos Colony (1)," *WAP*, 12 December 1939, 5; and photo caption, *African Mirror*, 27 June 1940, 2. Adeniyi-Jones (1876–1957) was a Sierra Leonean who in 1904 took up medical practice in Lagos, where he remained. A prominent member of the Saro community there, he became a major factor in early electoral and later nationalist politics.

28. "Mrs. Maria J. Douglas," obituary, *West Africa*, 30 August 1924, 899.

29. "Miss H. Millicent Douglas Is a Prominent Social Worker," *WAP*, 5 August 1939, 1, 7; photo caption, *African Mirror*, 27 June 1940, 2.

30. For a brief biography, see "T. A. Marryshow," at http://uwichill.edu.bb/bnccde/grenada/centre/tam.htm.

31. "Miss H. Millicent Douglas Is a Prominent Social Worker."

32. Steele, "Grenada," 16, 30–31.

33. "Executives of Nigeria Teachers Union Give Send-off to Their President," *WAP*, 30 May 1939, 3; and H. M. D., "Prince Kessie," *WAP*, 16 October 1939, 2.

34. In its issue of 5 June 1936, the *Lagos Daily News* published the names of the African members as follows: Mrs. E. J. Alex Taylor (vice president), Mrs. B. Ajose, Mrs. O. Alakija, Mrs. Oyejoki, Mrs. K. A. Abayomi (secretary), Mrs. H. Balogun, and Misses Adeniyi Jones, A. Adebayo, L. Sasegbon, Shola Vaughan, F. Dawodu, Ebun Moore, and Titi Pearse. Among the West Indian and European members were Mesdames Melville Jones, Graham Paul, Wilcock, Thompson, Dixon, Hollist, Young, and Wynter-Shackleford. Concerning Douglas's meeting with Lady Thomson, see *WAP*, 17 October 1939, 1. Lady Bourdillon enjoyed enormous popularity among the Lagosian elite and the market women. See Pearce, "Violet Bourdillon, Colonial Governor's Wife."

35. H. M. D., "I Meet Lady Simon," parts 1–3, *WAP*, 26–28 September 1939.

36. Simon, *Slavery*.

37. H. M. D., "I Meet Lady Simon (2)," *WAP*, 27 September 1939, 2.

38. Agnes Yewande Savage received her medical degrees from the University of Edinburgh in 1929, after which she practiced in Accra. "Miss Agnes Yewande Savage," *Lagos Daily News*, 13 July 1929, 1; "Nigerian Girl Medical Student," *DTN*, 28 December 1935, 7. Elizabeth Akerele qualified as a surgeon of the Royal College of Surgeons in Dublin in 1935 and returned in 1938 to Lagos, where she took up a post in the government medical service. "Dr. Elizabeth Akerele Returns from Medical Study in UK," *WAP*, 25 February 1938, 1, 5.

39. H. M. D., "Ramble in London (3)," *WAP*, 11 October 1939, 2; and "Dr. Moody," *WAP*, 12 October 1939, 2.

40. Sankoh, introduction to *Colonies: What Africa Thinks*, by Ohenenana Kessie of Ashanti; and H. M. D., "Prince Kessie," *WAP*, 16 October 1939, 2. Ohenenana Cobina Kessie completed a three-year course in economics and political science at the University of London, after which he studied anthropology with Malinowski at the School of Economics and then read law at the Middle Temple. After he returned to the Gold Coast, he practiced law and became deeply involved in politics. He was a member of J. B. Danquah's United Gold Coast Convention and later a founding member of the National Liberation Movement, which opposed Kwame Nkrumah.

41. Kessie, *Colonies: What Africa Thinks*, 7, 24.

42. H. M. D., "A Memorial Service," *WAP*, 4 October 1939, 2; "Memorial Services," *WAP*, 5 October 1939, 2.

43. For more on the West Indian community of the interwar period, see "West Indian Community Fetes Canon Lennon with Dinner," *WAP*, 27 March 1943, 1.

44. Jimmie, "Another Lady in Nigeria," *Nigerian Daily Herald*, 2 June 1931, 1; "'Frei-ghine' by Rita Macaulay," *Lagos Daily News*, 22 November 1932, 1; Ted Mackie, "Me and My Diary," *Nigerian Daily Telegraph*, 8 December 1932, 4; "Rita Akaje-Macaulay," Women Who Matter, *DTN*, 11 April 1953.

45. For more on the Blaize family, see Hopkins, "Richard Beale Blaize, 1845–1904: Merchant Prince of West Africa."

46. *Lagos Daily News*, 8 December 1932.

47. Eugene Shawnd, "Journalism and Our Young Ones," *Nigerian Daily Telegraph*, 4 September 1933, 5.

48. *WAP*, 23 December 1939, 5.

49. "An Evening Newspaper," *WAP*, 25 September 1939, 1–2.

50. *WAP*, 23 November 1937.

51. "Lady Simon's Message," *WAP*, 28 September 1939, 2.

52. Denzer, *Folayegbe M. Akintunde-Ighodalo*, 25–39.

53. H. M. D., "Local Enterprises," *WAP*, 2 November 1939, 5.

54. H. M. D., "Local Enterprises (2)," *WAP*, 6 November 1939, 5.

55. H. M. D., "Local Amusements," *WAP*, 1 November 1939, 2; and "Voice Recording," *WAP*, 3 November 1939, 5.

56. "Our Women," 5 parts, *WAP*, 24–28 October 1939.

57. H. M. D., "Education (4)," *WAP*, 10 November 1939.

58. H. M. D., "My Story," *African Mirror*, 22 and 26 June 1940.

59. "Rebirth of Press Association," *African Mirror*, 29 August 1940, 1. The president was Duse Muhammed Ali, then the oldest journalist in Nigeria.

60. Photo caption, *African Mirror,* 10 October 1940.

61. "Our Policy," *African Mirror,* 20 June 1940, 3.

62. There is only a small bound volume of this newspaper in the NAI.

63. CSO 26/03571/s.2, vol. 1, p. 20, National Archives of Nigeria, Ibadan.

64. Zik, "Bright Prospects for Children's Newspaper," Inside Stuff, *WAP,* 28 November 1944, 2.

65. Information from Lady Kofoworola Ademola.

66. Minutes of the meeting of the First Nigerian Women's Congress, Centenary Hall, Abeokuta, 31 July 1953, FNWO-Box 2, Ransome-Kuti Papers, Manuscript Collection, Kenneth Dike Memorial Library, University of Ibadan.

67. Alao, "Yoruba: An Enduring Legacy."

68. See, for example, "The Nigerian Police: A Tribute," *Daily Service,* 17 January 1946; "The Afro-American's Case for Yesterday and Today," *WAP,* 29 June 1948, 2; "'While Sun Shines'—A Review," *WAP,* 7 November 1948, 3; "Choice of Career for Nigerian Girls," *Daily Service,* 13 and 15 August 1949; and *WAP,* 27 October 1949; "Nigerian Girl Wins Scholarship" [a profile of Minjiba Felicia Karibo], *Daily Service,* 20 December 1954, 3.

69. For detailed studies of these two organizations, see Denzer, "Black Cultural Nationalist Networking in the United States and Nigeria after World War II," and "American Education and Nigerian Nationalism."

70. "Mbadiwe Is Received by Mrs. F. D. Roosevelt," *WAP,* 13 May 1943, 1.

71. Okonkwo, "Amos Stanley Wynter Shackleford."

72. Denzer, "The Popularization of American Education in Nigeria."

73. For an account of this visit, see Bond, "Howe and Isaacs in the Bush."

74. See Akpala, "The Background of the Colliery Shooting Incident in 1949.".

75. Douglas to H. M. Bond, 7 February 1950, Horace Mann Bond Papers, reel 1, part 2, Library of Congress.

76. This series presented brief accounts of the lives of about fifty prominent women leaders in Nigerian politics, business, and society; as an aggregate, they provide invaluable information about women's leadership in the 1950s. For an account of Ogunbiyi's career, see David Bowyer, "Theresa: A Husband's Frank Appraisal of His Own Wife," *DTN,* 31 August and 1–2 September 1964.

77. H. M. Douglas, Bureau of Information, State Department, Monrovia, Liberia, to H. M. Bond, 13 March 1957, reel 1, part 2, Horace Mann Bond Papers, Library of Congress. Wells, the editor of *Color,* published many articles in his magazine about his tricontinental trip to Europe, Palestine, and Africa. He was particularly enthusiastic about political and economic developments in Nigeria and Liberia. See "Strange Safari across Africa," October 1955: 51–53; "Miracle in Monrovia," November 1955: 44; "Liberia: Land of Marvels," December 1955: 9–10; "Azikiwe—Wonder Man of Africa," December 1955: 32–33; and "The Smartest Statesman in the World," May 1956: 9.

78. "Mrs. Amy Ashwood Garvey Arrives in Lagos Colony," *WAP,* 2 May 1947, 1.

79. For example, see Azikiwe, *My Odyssey,* 34–35, 162.

80. "News and Notes," *Eleti Ofe* (Lagos), 26 March 1924, 10. This brief report refers to the "encomiastic letter written by Mrs. Amy Ashwood Garvey from America to Mrs. C. O. Obasa and her associates with regard to their recent petition to the Government," published in the *Lagos Weekly Record,* 1–8 March 1924. For more information

on the Lagos Women's League and Charlotte Olajumoke Obasa, see Johnson, "Grass-roots Organizing Women in Anti-Colonial Activity in South-western Nigeria," and Olusanya, "Charlotte Olajumoke Obasa."

81. Martin, *Amy Ashwood Garvey.*

82. Yard, *Amy Ashwood Garvey, 1897–1969,* 188–90.

83. George Padmore, "Garvey Widows Fight over Body of Leader," *Chicago Defender,* 16 February 1946, 1.

84. Martin, *Amy Ashwood Garvey,* 224.

85. George Padmore, "West African Press Hits Garvey Widows' Battle," *Chicago Defender,* 27 April 1946, 4.

86. For biographies of Amy Ashwood Garvey, see Yard, *Amy Ashwood Garvey, 1897–1969;* Martin, "Discovering African Roots"; and Martin, "Amy Ashwood Garvey: Wife No. 1." For the life of Amy Jacques Garvey, see Taylor, *The Veiled Garvey.* Also see Taylor's useful comparison of the two leaders in "Intellectual Pan-African Feminists."

87. For example, see "Mrs. Garvey Seeks Formation of African Council as Part of the United Nations," *WAP,* 29 May 1944, 1, 4; Zik, "The Spirit of Marcus Garvey Lives," Inside Stuff, *WAP,* 1 June 1944, 2; "Mrs. Marcus Garvey Writes from Jamaica," *WAP,* 14 September 1944, 2; and A. J. Garvey, "The Battle of Bread Plus Butter Goes On after All the Jeopardies of an All Out Scientific War," *WAP,* 16 August 1946, 2. In these letters, she urged support for the creation of an African Council as part of the proposed United Nations structure, which would include African leaders from the continent and the diaspora. She also praised his long-running series Ambassadors of Goodwill, which described in great detail the accomplishments of the West African Press Delegation in England in August 1944, a major milestone in West Africa's march toward self-government and independence.

88. Taylor, *The Veiled Garvey,* 172–73. Taylor cites a letter from Jacques Garvey to Azikiwe, 28 November 1944, in which she warns him that Ashwood Garvey "is slippery and most immoral."

89. Ibid., 24.

90. Martin, "Discovering African Roots"; Martin, *Amy Ashwood Garvey,* 212–22.

91. "Mrs. Garvey—The Story of an Ashanti Woman," *Ashanti Pioneer,* 15 February 1947; Yard, *Amy Ashwood Garvey,* 165–75; and Martin, "Discovering African Roots," 123–25.

92. For accounts of Garvey's activities in the Gold Coast, see "Meet Amy Ashwood Garvey," *Ashanti Pioneer,* 7 December 1946, 2; "Joint Provincial Council Meeting Open at Guggisberg Memorial Hall, Dodowa," *Ashanti Pioneer,* 28 December 1946; 1; "Juaben-man Welcome Mrs. Garvey," *Ashanti Pioneer,* 19 February 1947, 1; and "Grand Durbar in Honour of Mrs. Amy Ashwood Garvey," *Ashanti Pioneer,* 20 February 1947, 1. Examples of Nigerian families having links with the overseas branches are the Vaughan, Alakija, and Asumpcão families.

93. "Mrs. Amy Ashwood Garvey Arrives in Lagos Colony," *WAP,* 2 May 1947, 1.

94. For a profile of Jessica Otunba-Payne (née Bruce), see "Victorian Lagos Lady," *West Africa,* 14 January 1956, 29–30. She had been a schoolmate of Victoria Forbes-Davies, Queen Victoria's goddaughter.

95. "Three Liberian Visitors Will Stage Concert," *WAP,* 23 June 1947, 1; "Liberian Stands in 'Lone Star' Defence," *WAP,* 29 May 1947, 1 and 3.

96. See Yard, *Amy Ashwood Garvey*, 151 and 151n16.

97. "Revolution Is Divorced for Slow Coast in Evolution; Wife of Late Garvey Speaks," *WAP*, 19 May 1947, 1 & 3; and "Mrs. Marcus Garvey on Women's Education," *DTN*, 15 May 1947, 1.

98. "Civil Servants Report for Work in Their African Attires: Ladies Take Accra Way," *WAP*, 2 May 1947, 1.

99. For more on Oyinkan Abayomi, see Coker, *A Lady*, and Cheryl Johnson-Odim, "Lady Oyinkan Abayomi."

100. *WAP*, 23 June 1947, 1.

101. "Mrs. Marcus Garvey on Women's Education," *Daily Times*, 15 May 1947; *WAP*, 15 May 1947.

102. Titled women positions in West Africa greatly interested Ashwood Garvey. On hearing about a woman paramount chief during her visit to Sierra Leone, she traveled 150 miles to visit Madam Woki Massaquoi of Gallians Perri, Pujehun district, who ruled from 1925 to 1971. Ashwood Garvey did not seem to realize that about 10 percent of Mende and Sherbro paramount chiefs were women. In the Gold Coast, she also saw how important queen mothers were in Akan society. Martin, "Discovering African Roots," 122; Worldwide Guide to Women in Leadership: Sierra Leone Heads, www.guide2womenleaders.com/Sierra_Leone_Heads.htm.

103. For information on Jojolola, see Byfield, *The Bluest Hands*, 46–47, 97–100.

104. For women's chieftaincy organization in Abeokuta, see Karunwi, *A Woman Industrialist*, 55–66.

105. *WAP*, 30 May 1947.

106. For contemporary accounts of Ransome-Kuti's tax protest, see "8,000 People Attend Ake Grade 'A' Court to Hear Result of Income Tax Charge against Mrs. Kuti," *Daily Service*, 29 April 1947; "Judgment in Sensational Abeokuta Tax Case Reserved for Monday," *Daily Service*, 8 May 1947; and "Mrs. Ransome-Kuti, President, Abeokuta Women's Union, Fined £3 in Tax Case," *Daily Service*, 13 May 1947.

107. Caption of photograph of Amy Ashwood Garvey, *WAP*, 23 June 1947, 1, and "3 Liberian Visitors Will Stage Concert," in the same issue; "Famed Musical Prodigy to Stage Play on June 13 Has a Distinguished Career," *WAP*, 16 June 1947, 1 and 3; and "Distinguished Broadway Star Thrills Lagos with Odes and Lyrics," *WAP*, 16 June 1947, 1 and 4.

108. J. B. Gott, deputy director of education, Northern provinces, to secretary of the Northern Provinces, Kaduna, interview with Mrs. Garvey, 29 December 1947, CSO 26 file 11133, vol. 3, National Archives of Nigeria, Ibadan.

109. Quoted in Martin, *Amy Ashwood Garvey*, 234n89; this letter is dated 16 July 1948.

110. "Mrs. A. Garvey Urges Africans to Hope: Says They Cannot Achieve Their Objective without Their Women," *Nigerian Spokesman*, 21 July 1948, 1, 3.

111. "Mrs. Ashwood Garvey Speaks on the Survival of the Negro," *WAP*, 27 August 1948, 1.

112. For example, see "Interpreting Africa to Aframerica," *WAP*, 18 April 1944, 2. This editorial declares: "After the war, West Africans look forward to a change of policy. Let the doors of West Africa be thrown open to any American Negro who is prepared to come out to assist us in materializing our social and economic programmes of reconstruction. There are thousands of qualified American Negro

medical practitioners, dentists, social workers, economists, agriculturists, veterinary surgeons, engineers, technicians, etc. who could immigrate to West Africa and be of invaluable service, officially and privately, to us."

113. L. N. Namme, "Mrs. Amy Garvey Lectures on Position of Women in World," *WAP*, 16 October 1948, 3.

114. "Mrs. Amy Garvey Sends Message of Hope to Nigerians," *Nigerian Spokesman*, 20 October 1948, 1, 4.

115. Martin, *Amy Ashwood Garvey*, 225.

116. Taylor, *The Veiled Garvey*, 171–75, 268n20.

117. For the ACAE, see LaRay Denzer, "The Popularization of American Education in Nigeria."

118. For a discussion of this trend, see Denzer, *Folayegbe M. Akintunde-Ighodalo*, 171–95.

119. George Padmore, "Marcus Garvey's Wife Sends Greetings to Gold Coasters on Occasion of New Elections—Coloured World Watching Outcome of Big Day," *WAP*, 7 February 1951.

120. *WAP*, 3 April 1951.

121. Martin, "Amy Ashwood Garvey: Wife No. 1," 35.

# References

Adi, Hakim. "West African Students in Britain, 1900–60: The Politics of Exile." In *Africans in Britain*, ed. David Killingray. London: Frank Cass, 1994.

Akpala, Agwu. "The Background of the Colliery Shooting Incident in 1949." *Journal of the Historical Society of Nigeria* 3 (1965): 335–64.

Alao, Akin. "Yoruba: An Enduring Legacy." Paper presented at the Center for African and African-American Studies, University of Texas at Austin, 24 January 2003.

Associated Press. "Pioneering Black Actress, Singer, Dies at 102. Etta Moten Barnett Played Dignified Role in Pictures." Associated Press, 5 January 2004, http://msnbc.msn.com/id/3880383.

Azikiwe, Nnamdi. *My Odyssey: An Autobiography*. New York and Washington: Praeger, 1970.

Blyden, Nemata Amelia. *West Indians in West Africa, 1808–1880: The African Diaspora in Reverse*. Rochester, N.Y.: University of Rochester Press, 2000.

Bond, Horace Mann. "Howe and Isaacs in the Bush: The Ram in the Thicket." In *Apropos of Africa: Sentiments of Negro American Leaders on Africa from the 1800s to the 1950s*, ed. Adelaide Cromwell Hill and Martin Kilson, 278–88. London: Frank Cass, 1969.

Byfield, Judith A. *The Bluest Hands: A Social and Economic History of Women Dyers in Abeokuta (Nigeria), 1890–1940*. Portsmouth, N.H.: Heinemann, 2002.

Callaway, Helen. *Gender, Culture, and Empire: European Women in Colonial Nigeria*. London: Macmillan in association with St. Antony's College, Oxford, 1987.

Coker, Folarin. *A Lady: A Biography of Lady Oyinkan Abayomi*. Ibadan: Evans Brothers, 1987.

Cromwell, Adelaide M. *An African Victorian Feminist: The Life and Times of Adelaide Smith Casely Hayford*. Totowa, N.J.: Frank Cass, 1986.

Denzer, LaRay. *Women in Government Service in Colonial Nigeria, 1862–1945.* Boston: African Studies Center, Boston University, 1989.

———. "The Popularization of American Education in Nigeria: A Case Study of the American Council on African Education." Paper presented to the American Studies Association in Nigeria, University of Jos, 23–24 May 1990.

———. "Black Cultural Nationalist Networking in the United States and Nigeria after World War II: The Example of the African Academy of Arts and Research." *Nigerian Journal of American Studies* 3 (1993): 180–96.

———. "American Education and Nigerian Nationalism: Nwafor Orizu and the American Council on African Education, 1944–1955." Paper presented to the Black Atlantic Seminar, Rutgers University, 23 January 2003.

———. *Folayegbe M. Akintunde-Ighodalo: A Public Life.* Ibadan: Sam Bookman, 2003.

Hopkins, A. G. "Richard Beale Blaize, 1845–1904: Merchant Prince of West Africa." *Tarikh* 1 (1966): 70–79.

Johnson, Cheryl P. "Grassroots Organizing Women in Anti-Colonial Activity in South-western Nigeria." *African Studies Review* 14 (1982): 137–58.

Johnson-Odim, Cheryl. "Lady Oyinkan Abayomi." In *Nigerian Women in Historical Perspective,* ed. Bolanle Awe, 149–62. Lagos and Ibadan: Sankore Publishers Ltd. and Bookcraft Ltd., 1992.

Karunwi, Omodele. *A Woman Industrialist: A Biography of Chief (Mrs.) Bisoye Tejuoso, Yeye-Oba Oke-Ona Egba, 3rd Iyalode of Egbaland.* Lagos Cow-Lad Ent. Nig. Ltd., 1991.

Kessie, Ohenenana Cobina. *Colonies: What Africa Thinks.* 2nd ed. London: African Economic Union, 1939.

Langley, J. Ayodele. *Pan-Africanism and Nationalism in West Africa, 1900–1945: A Study in Ideology and Social Classes.* Oxford: Clarendon Press, 1973.

Macmillan, Allister, ed. *The Red Book of West Africa: Historical and Descriptive, Commercial and Industrial Facts, Figures, and Resources.* London: W. H. and L. Collingridge, 1920.

Martin, Tony. "Amy Ashwood Garvey: Wife No. 1." *Jamaican Journal* 20 (1987): 32–36.

———. "Discovering African Roots: Amy Ashwood Garvey's Pan-Africanist Journey." *Comparative Studies of South Asia, Africa, and the Middle East* 17 (1997): 118–26.

———. *Amy Ashwood Garvey: Pan-Africanist, Feminist, and Mrs. Marcus Garvey No. 1; or, A Tale of Two Amies.* Dover, Mass.: Majority Press, 2007.

Nicol, Abioseh. "West Indians in West Africa." *Sierra Leone Studies* n.s. 13 (June 1960): 14–23.

Olusanya, G. O. "Charlotte Olajumoke Obasa." In *Nigerian Women in Historical Perspective,* ed. Bolanle Awe, 105–20. Lagos: Sankore; Ibadan: Bookcraft, 1992.

Okonkwo, Rina L. "The Garvey Movement in Nigeria." *Calabar Historical Journal* 2, no. 1 (June 1978): 98–113.

———. "The Garvey Movement in British West Africa." *Journal of African History* 21 (1980): 105–17.

———. "Amos Stanley Wynter Shackleford: Bread King and Nationalist." In her *Heroes of West African Nationalism,* 45–58. Enugu, Anambra State: Delta, 1985.

Omu, Fred I. A. *Press and Politics in Nigeria, 1880–1937.* London: Longman, 1978.
Pearce, R. D. "Violet Bourdillon, Colonial Governor's Wife." *African Affairs* 82 (1983): 267–77.
Sankoh, Laminoh. Introduction to *Colonies: What Africa Thinks,* by Ohenenana Kessie. London: African Economic Union, 1939.
Simon, Kathleen. *Slavery.* London: Hodder and Stoughton, 1929.
Steele, Beverly. "Grenada, an Island State, Its History, and Its People." *Caribbean Quarterly* 20 (1974): 5–43.
Talbot, P. A. *Peoples of Southern Nigeria.* 4 vols. London: Oxford University Press, 1926.
Taylor, Ula Yvette. "Intellectual Pan-African Feminists: Amy Ashwood-Garvey and Amy Jacques-Garvey." *Abafazi* 9 (1998): 10–18.
———. *The Veiled Garvey: The Life and Times of Amy Jacques Garvey.* Chapel Hill: University of North Carolina Press, 2002.
Weinstein, Brian. *Éboué.* New York: Oxford University Press, 1972.
Yard, Lionel M. *Amy Ashwood Garvey, 1897–1969: Co-founder of the United Negro Improvement Association.* Silver Springs, Md.: Associated Publishers for the Association for the Study of Afro-American Life and History, n.d.

## 12

# Immigrant Voices in Cyberspace: Spinning Continental and Diasporan Africans into the World Wide Web

### MOJÚBÀOLÚ OLÚFÚNKÉ OKOME

One of the significant and enduring effects of contemporary globalization is that it generates population movements from African countries in the throes of deep economic crisis to countries with buoyant economies. Globalization also facilitates "real-time" virtual connections between immigrants and those in the African continent, with African immigrants in the various contemporary diasporas and with Africans from older diasporas. Consequently, new transnational communities, some of them epistemic, are being created. Thus the changes wrought by globalization impinge on the lives of ordinary people in new and remarkable ways. Among these changes, the communications that bind Africa and its diasporas together are manifested and deployed in discussions in on-line social networks, chat rooms, instant messaging systems, electronic mail, web pages, electronic journals, and various other ways. They provide a wealth of information for scholarly research on globalization and contribute to our understanding of the antinomies of globalization from the perspective of ordinary people. We can also focus on how people articulate their experiences and give meaning to their lives. Immigrants and populations in their home countries are being woven into connective webs of political, economic, and social life. Thus communities are being developed in the absence of propinquity, challenging the assumptions that for a group of people to form a community, they must live in close proximity to one another.[1]

Much analysis remains to be done on these communities. For example, who has power within them, and to what effect? Power here is defined as the ability to command obedience; to determine the agenda; to fully participate in a community, with the capacity to voice opinions and engage in a variety of other activities that generate social capital; and ultimately, to participate in developing shared norms, values, principles, and institutions that shape the nature and processes of everyday life. The primary focus here is on gender relations within the burgeoning African immigrant virtual communities of the information age. Gender is an important consideration due to the pervasiveness of the assumption that there is a technological divide that privileges those with better access to technology in capturing the power to shape the nature, form, and type of relations within the virtual communities spawned by new technologies.

Howard, Rainie, and Jones contend that more men than women use the World Wide Web.[2] They also show that more young than old and more affluent educated people than poor uneducated ones use the medium. If the assumption is that more privilege means better access to the World Wide Web and that more African immigrant men than women access it, then it stands to reason that there will be a domination of male over female voices in the communications and relationships that develop, and men will have more power than women in these virtual communities.

This study considers the extent to which communities without propinquity are being established. It also examines how Africans on the continent and African immigrants themselves in the old and new diasporas understand these processes. This study is based on information gathered from primary research focused upon online groups engaged in discussions on political, economic, and social issues on the World Wide Web. It explores how a regionally and linguistically diverse African community that is also diverse in socioeconomic class origins perceives its role in shaping the political economy of an increasingly globalized world. Finally, it considers the extent to which male voices may dominate women's voices in cyberspace and offers some explanations. A complex and rich story emerges about the use of technological tools (some of the positive effects of globalization) to communicate and, ultimately, to build communities by ordinary people, most of them pushed to emigrate from their home countries by economic and political crisis (some of the negative effects of globalization).

## A New African Diaspora

To address the concerns of this chapter, certain analytical concepts must be defined and/or refined. What is a community? There are numerous definitions, and in general terms, a community is often applied to people who share some characteristics, although scholars disagree on what those characteristics might be. According to Kazmer and Haythornwaite, who studied an online community developed from an internet-based library science course, the markers of an online community are much the same as those for real-life communities. They include the provision of social support, companionship, emotional support, sociability, and a place where there is shared activity, shared space, and technology. Activities, people, tasks involved in the online community become the foci of participants' thoughts in descriptions or explanations of their activities in the community to others.[3] Anderson and Tracey contend that the internet plays a rich and varied role in people's lives, making it difficult to pinpoint its diverse effects on socioeconomic and political interactions.[4] Rheingold categorically claims that communities can be developed virtually that could be as vibrant, complex, and multidimensional as real-life ones.[5] Yet there are elements of community that propinquity (close proximity) enriches. Rich virtual communication may be possible, but it is also possible to pretend to be something that one is not and get away with it, as many find out when they are duped in financial or emotional transactions. With more recent development of social networks and the increased power of search engines, some have argued that the capacity to pretend to be something that one is not on the internet has been lost forever.[6] There is also much comfort derived from face-to-face interaction, and numerous people still prefer this mode of relating to the virtual, particularly when serious negotiations are at issue and the ability to read and interpret nonverbal cues is desired.

Is "diaspora" an appropriate concept for an analysis on the emergence of virtual communities that include contemporary African immigrants and the old diaspora? Clearly, there are many definitions of diaspora. Campt reminds us that diaspora has been used coterminously with the ideas of dispersal, migration, displacement, and "complex relationships between real and imagined communities in the homeland

and places of settlement." However, unlike most other black diasporas, black Germans do not share a common narrative of origination, for they include people of African, Asian, and Arab heritage. Thus shared ethnicity and cultural pluralism fail to capture the nature of this community, which challenges orthodox understandings of diversity, pluralism, and cultural difference.[7]

Defining diaspora is no less complex even when there is a common narrative of origin. Drawing on the insights of Sundiata as well as those of Patterson and Kelly, Alpers gives an extensive review of the concept of diaspora and identifies several critical points. First, many African diasporas exist; furthermore, they may overlap and intersect to forge new African identities that may not remain constant over time. Second, there are internal African diasporas that result as much from forced migration as diasporas created outside Africa. Third, diasporas are essentially constructed and reproduced in the scholarly and intellectual imagination as well as in popular life. Finally, the idea of diaspora obscures differences and emphasizes sameness, producing different and shifting understandings among Africans about Africa, Africans, and the diaspora itself.[8]

Temporality must also be considered in discussions of diaspora, for much of the scholarship on African diaspora has focused on communities created outside of Africa during the era of the slave trades across the Atlantic and the Indian oceans. Although recent African immigrants were not subjected to the harsh inhumanity of being ripped away from Africa by those Everett calls "European body snatchers," nor have they endured the ordeal of the middle passage, Ifekwunigwe contends that recent African immigrants may be considered diasporan. Many who leave Africa "by any means necessary," as Ifekwunigwe puts it, are compelled by circumstances created by being on the losing side of the calculus as globalization progresses.[9] Being so compelled, many who flock out of the continent lack volition, forming a constant outflow into more affluent parts of the world as recruits into the underground economy to serve as menial labor or as bodies in the sex industry.

According to the 2000 census, the total number of black and African Americans in the United States is 34,658,190, of which 16,465,185 are male and 18,193,005 are female. Of these, African immigrants in the United States number 1,781,877 (which excludes Africans of Arab descent) and West Indians number 1,869,504.[10] As labor, contemporary African immigrants may either be skilled, and therefore desired and courted by capital and by their host country for skilled technical and professional employment, or they may be unskilled, and hence repulsed and reviled by the host country's unfriendly policies, transforming them into undocumented immigrants, pushing them into the informal or underground economy, subject to gross exploitation by capital. If lucky, they might work their way up the socioeconomic ladder. For this second category of African immigrants/migrants, the likelihood of being stuck in vicious cycles of perpetual informalization and underremuneration for their labor is very high. Paradoxically, skilled and technical workers may also enter the global North as undocumented workers, beginning their labor force participation in the informal economy as underpaid, underemployed, and overexploited workers.

Although diasporan African women and men experience many of the same challenges, some challenges are peculiar to women. First, it is well documented that the gender wage gap negatively impacts all women.[11] According to the U.S. Census Bureau, women's earnings average seventy-four cents of every dollar men earn. The difference is attributable to socioeconomic factors, since labor markets are highly segregated by gender, and jobs dominated by men attract higher salaries than where women dominate. This differential is also documented in Europe and elsewhere.[12] The glass ceiling is another well-documented barrier to male-female parity in the labor market.[13] Both the wage gap and the glass ceiling affect diasporan African women who face additional challenges that other women may not necessarily face as a consequence of racial discrimination, bias, and, for the new immigrants among them, xenophobia. It is well-nigh impossible for most new immigrant women to compete on an even footing or even participate equally with female citizens or legal residents of their host country until they secure a firm toehold in the economy, which may take years of sweat, blood, tears, and possible exploitation.

Unlike most other migrations, African out-migrations have both women and men initiating migration, although women may also follow spouses who departed earlier to secure a toehold in the buoyant labor markets of the West.[14] When this happens, the women sometimes face subtle and not-so-subtle pressures to be subservient to their husbands

290 · MOJÚBÀOLÚ OLÚFÚNKÉ OKOME

or the threat of losing immigration status and facing deportation. Even without this kind of duress, women must also combine whatever job they find with household and family responsibilities. This may create time pressures that curtail or prevent meaningful participation in either virtual or real life communities, except when their services are required for food preparation or cleaning connected with social events involving their families.

On balance, globalization fosters the growth of African out-migration as a survival strategy.[15] Some scholars point out the possibility of transforming this disability into an asset through remittances that immigrants send to their families back home, and through using innovations in communications technology made available through contemporary globalization, to create connections that were formerly impossible.[16] Converting out-migration into an asset, however, requires much more than remittances. To begin the process of understanding what it means, we need better data on African migrants in the West, why they do what they do, and the consequences.

## Transnationalization of African Immigrant Communities: Old and New Diasporas

In both past and present eras of globalization, African labor has been extracted from the continent into the "new world" and into today's global north, as a result of what Okpewho, Boyce Davies, and Mazrui describe as the "labor imperative" and the "territorial imperative."[17] I argue that while both imperatives drove the creation of the old diaspora, the creation of the contemporary African diaspora is driven by the "labor imperative." Of course, imperialism is taking new forms. Today's imperialism does not entail the physical presence of the imperialists on the soil of the empire; instead, neocolonial relations of power maintain imperialistic domination through the extraction of economic and financial resources, the extraction of labor, and its uses in new ways in the peripheries of the empire. Today's imperialism, unlike the old, is not necessarily driven by the direct action of states, but predominantly by transnational capital, principally by the multinational corporations located in the global north, and supported by state policies in both the North and the newly liberalized global South that is compelled to integrate more rapidly into the global economy. This indicates a significant and fundamental change in the nature of globalization.

Both old and new imperialisms developed global political economies, which created distinct African diasporas. Both imperialisms caused the emergence of transnational populations, with the old African diaspora maintaining its connectedness with Africa through social practices, aesthetics, religious ritual, and the literary and scholarly imagination. The process of maintaining connectedness with Africa was, and remains, as much social as ideological as Patterson and Kelly contend.[18] Further, the new diaspora, being in formation, is dynamic. I date its emergence from the period after the Second World War, but its most rapid growth was experienced very recently, coinciding with the growth of economic crises, unsustainable debt, and the use of the International Monetary Fund's policies of structural adjustment programs as corrective mechanisms in Africa.

The new transnationalization of the African diaspora creates novel linkages between the old and new African diasporas and also strengthens existing linkages. The most vibrant of these linkages depend on ideologically driven constructions of African identity. Simultaneously, this process creates tensions, characterized by Watkins-Owens as intraracial ethnicity, that is, where groups that may be seen by those outside their group as belonging to the same race, but within the group, fine distinctions are made based on differences in ethnicity and national origin, which prevent unity, collaboration, and coalition building to solve common problems.[19] To a significant extent, nationality rather than racial identity still drives, and substantively divides, the various African diasporas, creating tensions, and subverting the promise of Pan-Africanism. The Pan-Africanists had contended that the continent is an integral whole and can only achieve progress by building a united front to ensure that governance and wealth creation on the continent are taken over by Africans for Africans. This has yet to happen, and although the African Union has embraced the diaspora as its sixth region, the new structure is not operationalized.

The intellectual work of diaspora must take new forms as well, and it requires a new subjectively of its architects. Mazrui suggests that diasporan Africans use the transatlantic traffic in education as their primary mechanism for cultural penetration of the West. Migrant African intellectuals would then represent Africa in the West as spokespersons and emissaries who build linkages with African Americans to strike back at the imperial centers of power that formerly exploited and dominated them. They would also revive the moribund and tenuous connections between mother Africa and her widely dispersed children who were scattered by the transatlantic slave trade. It is easy to extend this vision into a scenario where Pan-African proactive and conscious effort generates the development of Africa into a world power.[20]

For Edward Said, exiled intellectuals from the Third World are the elite vanguard of forces that can engage the West intellectually to liberate the world from the forces of oppression. These elite soldier-intellectuals experience existential flux, being located between cultures, homes, and nations.[21] Thus Third World intellectuals are in a voyage into the heart of the old metropoles:

> The voyage in, then, constitutes an especially interesting variety of hybrid cultural work. And that it exists at all is a sign of adversarial internationalization in an age of continued imperial structures. No longer does the logos dwell exclusively, as it were, in London and Paris. No longer does history run unilaterally, as Hegel believed, from east to west, or from south to north, becoming more sophisticated and developed, less primitive and backward as it goes. Instead, the weapons of criticism have become part of the historical legacy of empire, in which the separations and exclusions of "divide and rule" are erased and surprising new configurations spring up.[22]

Third World migrant intellectuals are then particularly well situated to challenge the empire from within by striking at its heart, thereby transforming history and the nature of the world.

The new intellectual constructions of diaspora consider space and place differently. Appadurai maintains that in this contemporary global era characterized by mass migration, electronic communication, and a new global cultural economy, the fixed temporal world has become irrelevant. It is replaced by dynamic and mobile landscapes that contain ideas, technology, finance, images, and people who do not necessarily identify with one and/or any nation-states. The existence of these communities and landscape does not depend on the pleasure or desire of states but indicates the development of new kinds of nations; their actions respect no territorial boundaries and cannot be subjected to them. Among the variety of postnational communities that can be formed are diasporas that transnationalize religion, ethnicity, race, and identity. Appadurai's transnational communities are not immutably positive and progressive. More than the imagined communities of the preindustrial and industrial ages, these imagined communities are moved by ideas, images, and financial resources that are transmitted instantaneously to millions of people in the world in a manner never before experienced.[23]

One of the critical concerns of this chapter is where and how we can locate women in the transnationalization of the African diaspora and its intellectual construction. Transnationalism is considered in immigration literature as the process through which geographical, political, and cultural boundaries are breached by new immigrant-created social relations. These networks challenge existing conceptions of migration, citizenship, ethnicity, and culture. They are bound together by the volitional or coerced action of immigrants who move from one locale to another.[24] Host and source countries of immigrants respond to changes in transnational social relations among migrant communities by devising new policy responses and strategies that seek to domesticate and discipline transnational communities as well as access and control the resources they generate, whether these are financial, informational, social, or political. Sending countries may, as Nigeria and South Africa have done, extend dual citizenship to their immigrant indigenes. Or they may, like Ghana (similar to Liberia in the nineteenth century), extend the right to claim dual citizenship to Africans from the old diasporas and the franchise to contemporary migrants from their shores.[25] Immigrants may campaign for an extension of these and other rights, as the members of the Uganda–North American Convention did in 2000 with respect to the demand for dual citizenship and as the Ghanaians did in 2006.[26] These kinds of policies are sought by transnational immigrants, who seek to extend their power vis-à-vis the state. Much of the discussion tends to be presented in gender-neutral terms. It is critical that we delineate women's voices in this virtual political arena, for it has implications for political praxis both in Africa and immigrant host countries.

Communications in African transnational networks have not reached their full potential, but they occur and are significant. They can be seen in news groups, discussion groups, signature drives, websites, e-journals, e-newsletters, and commercial advertisements that are created and maintained by both the new and the old African diasporas. The business-owned websites are incredibly diverse and extensive. A cursory overview of these websites illuminates numerous spaces where women are located—food, books, clothing, and home decorations. Matchmaking services in cyberspace are bountiful and are an especially rich place to observe changes in gender discourse and expectations. These sites together compose popular sources of a diasporic consciousness that also links old and new diasporas.

The World Wide Web has become an essential space for the intellectual construction of the diaspora. It is one of the most important tools for African intellectuals in the continent's universities, research centers, and the contemporary migrant diaspora. It facilitates the ongoing collaboration, contact, and conversations that must be undertaken by all these communities in order for the migrant intellectual to achieve the promise of being "productive and progressive for Africa."[27] It is a site where scholarly research and publications, novels, and other forms of artistic expression demonstrate the connection between Africa and its diasporas as well as their tensions and contradictions. Finally, it is a space where women intellectuals of the old and new diasporas debate the politics of gender, nation, and empire.

### Technology and the Lack Thereof: Effects on Transnational Networks

In negotiating the socioeconomic and political relations of their relocated and dislocated lives, African diasporan communities today engage in networks of communication that use old and new technologies to communicate. Old technologies include communications tools like letters ("snail mail"), telephone, telegrams, radio, and television. Communication and exchange of information before the information age also utilized paper books, journals, newsletters, and magazines. In the information age, electronic "real-time" virtual connections are used for communications between immigrants and those left behind in the African continent, with African immigrants who are scattered in the various contemporary diasporas, as well as with Africans from older diasporas. Such communication utilizes electronic mail, chat rooms, instant messaging, and web pages as well as open discussion fora that operate as news lists. Cable and satellite communication have also revolutionized media like television, radio, and even electronic mail and web communication because of the effect of broadband communication systems on making electronic communication faster, cheaper, and more reliable.

For some, information technology provides the exciting opportunity of building communities that contribute to creating social capital.[28] However, the effect of inexpensive, faster, and more reliable technology should not be overstated, for the existence of a technology divide is widely acknowledged.[29] As with many effects of globalization, access to information technology is determined by the antinomies of globalization. There are clearly fundamental contradictions integral to the process of globalization. While many scholars assume that the process has positive consequences, it is obvious that it also has negative consequences on the lives of many people in Africa, Asia, Latin America, the Middle East, the Caribbean, and even parts of Western Europe and North America. Moreover, the negative and positive consequences of globalization often relate to each other in a dialectical manner. In consequence, affluence is created in the global north, poverty in the global South. Regional differentiation in poverty and affluence exist within the same country's borders.[30]

In terms of the technological divide, one sees the operation of antinomies in graphic relief. There is widespread availability of information technology and all the exciting possibilities that it presents to those who can afford it and who have reliable electricity, telecommunications, or broadband technology.[31] At the same time, the majority of the world's population, particularly in the South, can neither afford nor use this technology. Even within the United States, a country on the cutting edge of the new information age, which in many ways leads the trends, it is widely believed that there is a technological divide determined by race, class, and gender. As such, nonwhites, those low on the socioeconomic scale, and women are assumed to be underrepresented in using and accessing information technology.[32]

No doubt, unequal access to information technology is a typical example of the antinomies of globalization. To focus specifically on gender, the operation of antinomies implies that women have less presence, voice, and power in this medium; however, it is also possible to use the new medium in a counterhegemonic manner that challenges entrenched power interests and structures of inequality, because it offers anonymity, and transgression is easier, and also because the cost of access is relatively inexpensive, making it possible for even people without private access to use internet cafés in Africa, Asia, the Caribbean, and Europe (to a greater extent than in North America) or to use public libraries in North America. With such access, asynchronous and intermittent use is possible, but those who have full-time broadband access may dominate discussions, negotiations, and agenda-setting.

Antinomies are integral to the process of globalization. This same phenomenon causes diametrically opposite effects, and paradoxically, each effect occurs as a logical consequence of the operation of antinomies. As argued above, globalization routinely produces wealth in some parts of the world or in regions within countries. It is also normal for it to produce poverty in some countries and within given regions. Ability to afford, access, and use technological innovation is as much a consequence of globalization as is the lack of access to technology or the inability to utilize or to afford to purchase technology. As a consequence of globalization, many developing countries have become no more than labor reserves for the more affluent, postindustrial countries of the global North, which have become magnets that draw migrants and immigrants to seek an end to the problems of unmitigated poverty, social and political conflict, unemployment, and underemployment.[33]

In spite of a digital divide, the transnationalization of African diasporan communities has produced complex webs of relationships, including social, political, economic, and intellectual linkages that take the nature of epistemic communities. An epistemic community is one with a network of colleagues who maintain close ties, share beliefs that influence their positions on social problems and issues, share ideas on what is valid, use similar approaches and methods in their work, desire common policy outcomes, and exchange information. These communities, if composed of people with a significant amount of name recognition and stature, will impact the theory and practice in areas of their expertise.[34]

The amount of time that a scholar can devote to nonessential or non-work-related communication and collaboration may determine how much and how well she or he can participate in the formation or strengthening of an epistemic community. Those with more seniority, more job security, and more time will dominate. Because the top echelons of higher education are dominated by men, more men than women will probably have hegemonic power within the community. More research should be undertaken to evaluate the extent to which this is categorically true or otherwise. However, initial research on internet usage suggests that more men than women regularly use the medium.[35] Everett provides some intriguing arguments that challenge this assumption because there is indeed some level of automaticity to assuming women and black people's technophobia. Instead, she contends that there is significant, and not yet generally acknowledged, black technophilia.[36] Her analysis suggests that information technology and the communications it fosters offer significant liberatory prognosis. Not only do African online communities exist, but they also proliferate constantly and demonstrate technophilia. They challenge temporally bound notions of the nation, community, and relationships and demonstrate how formerly marginalized individuals and groups can use technology to subvert and resist oppression and domination.

As a case in point, Naijanet, a Nigerian virtual community, was fashioned to transcend Nigeria's plethora of ethnic divisions, but it maintained the tendency to marginalize women, which of course was resisted by the women, who decamped to form an independent virtual community. To find more examples of Nigerian World Wide Web communities, I asked the moderator of Naija-women, Omolola Ijeoma Ogunyemi: How many members does the Naija-women group have? How many are women? How many are men? Is it really possible to tell if a member is male or female? Who communicates more, men or women? Would you characterize the Naija-women group as a community? If so, why? Ogunyemi responded:

> Naija-women has 254 members. It's impossible for me to tell how many are women or men or who on the list is a woman or man aside from those I know personally. Naija-women was set up as a list primarily for discussing issues of importance to Nigerian women, and membership was made open to women and men interested in this. Naija-women started out as a small mailing list based out of UPenn at inception; there were mostly women on the list (at least, people who had identified themselves

as women on the naijanet list and were fed up with sexist attitudes on
that list), and it was a community in the sense that many members actually got to know each other outside of cyberspace; I got advice for my
thesis defense from other netters who had already been through the process, naija-women netters contributed funds to various Nigerian causes
through the list, etc. Once the list grew to more than 100 people, it became
a lot more impersonal; most of the pioneering members from 1994 are no
longer on the list.[37]

The same inquiry went out to Martin Akindana, the moderator of
the general group Chat Afrik, who responded that the groups were a
community because there were both virtual and real-life interactions
between members, and while it is impossible to categorically determine
whether participants are male or female, there are more male than female contributors to the discussions in the general groups. Efforts were
being made to encourage women's participation, including establishing
women-only groups.

What does it mean if indeed more men than women participate? Are
women less interested in virtual communities? Do they have less time
on their hands than men? Are the issues being discussed uninteresting
and/or irrelevant to them? Are these communities being patterned on
real-life communities where some issues are believed to be the special
preserve of men? Are the communities perceived as hostile to women?
Without broader, in-depth research, no conclusive answer can be offered; however, women Naijanet members' refusal to be intimidated by
the male members and their formation of an autonomous virtual community suggests that the answers to all the questions, except those that
focus on women's lack of time, is a resounding "Yes."

There is evidence that epistemic communities are being created to
link old and new African diasporas. For example, I began research on
African immigration to the United States in 1995. At that time, an internet search in electronic and physical databases revealed that very little
was being published on contemporary African migration outside the
continent. Today, such a search produces massive lists of bibliographic
sources. This shows evidence of a concerted desire to study, research,
and write about the contemporary immigrant experience by people who
are recent immigrants and by people who are members of Africa's old
diasporas. One also sees research projects on the subject of contempo-

rary African immigration and conferences that seek to study both old and new diasporas. New virtual databases are being created that document the work of these research projects.

### E-journals, E-newsletters, and Virtual Cybercommunities

The creation and maintenance of e-journals, e-newsletters, and virtual cyber communities is ongoing among African intellectual and wider immigrant communities. These efforts are relatively new but very significant. There are many examples. *Safundi: The Journal of South African and American Comparative Studies* was founded by Andrew Offenburger, who is also the editor.[38] Africa Resource Center was founded by Nkiru Nzegwu, a scholar who is also general editor of four of the five journals published by the center: *JENDA: A Journal of Culture & African Women Studies; African Philosophy: Journal on African Philosophy; ProudFlesh: New Afrikan Journal of Culture, Politics and Consciousness; W.A.R: West Africa Review;* and *IJELE: Art eJournal of the African World.*[39] Bertrade Ngo-Ngijol Banoum and I are coeditors of *Ìrìnkèrindò: A Journal of African Migration.*[40] *GWS Africa: Gender and Women's Studies for African Transformation* is a Ford Foundation project based at the University of Cape Town, South Africa, headed by Amina Mama, a Nigerian immigrant to South Africa.[41] The program has an e-journal titled *Feminist Africa.*[42] Seven of these eight journals have women as founders and coeditors. This challenges, but does not entirely eliminate, the assumption that cyberspace is dominated by male intellectuals. As we move further into the information age, more women will participate in such ventures, even though they will still have to juggle multiple familial and professional responsibilities. These journals are a useful addition to the process of the production of knowledge on Africa. For them to succeed and thrive, they need the dedicated sacrifice of committed scholars who contribute as editors, submit papers, and collaborate in acquiring funding. Given the constant breadth and depth of the adoption of information technology, these e-journals and e-newsletters may be more important than their paper counterparts in the future, although it seems unlikely that the world will become entirely paperless anytime soon.

The claim that new epistemic communities are developing should not be taken as an indication of the adequacy of these communities in numbers or in the range of subjects and issues that they engage. Indeed, the promise of intense, consistent, and fruitful transnational collaboration has yet to be fully realized.[43] It is worthwhile to consider why African diasporan scholars have not intensively utilized information and communications technology to foster enduring linkages with their peers in the continent. Such linkages, if properly deployed, would yield the development of collaborative research that adds significantly to the production of knowledge on the continent, its people, and its diasporas. Zeleza presents this as a problem involving the lack of vision, absence of will, and lack of resources both in the continent and the diaspora. Tettey contends that this problem arises from capricious and punitive decisions by African governments that favor foreign expertise and repulse indigenous expertise in the African diasporan scholarly community.

This refusal to consult with and draw upon the knowledge base of African experts in the diaspora is also imposed by conditionalities that are attached to foreign "aid." Further, there is the passivity of African-based professionals who often wait to be "discovered," and there are government policies that create barriers to the acquisition of computers and information technology through the imposition of high tariffs on the importation of these goods. Finally, there is gross inadequacy in the exercise of what Tettey describes as the "diaspora option" through the use of new information and technological innovation to build communities of knowledge. The yet-unexplored possibilities that Tettey identifies include the establishment of joint economic initiatives by cybergroups that connect "credible individuals who use the internet to establish networks of mutual trust on the basis of which to launch economic ventures and undertakings whose ultimate mission is tailored toward the development of their countries." These networks can connect African intellectuals in the continent with those in its diasporas to produce knowledge, wealth, and power.[44]

Zeleza rightly contends that unsustainable debt, consequent economic crises, political conflict—including war and the dislocations that attend these phenomena, particularly from the 1970s—led to the decimation of research and development capacity in the universities. He argues that African intellectuals in the continent have become integrated into the global political economy as captured peons of Northern philanthropic and NGO sectors, whose agenda, whims, and fads drive research projects; however, he underestimates the power of the antinomies of globalization in forcing both diasporan and continentally located African intellectuals into either migrant or home-based labor that is drawn from increasingly segregated and impoverished labor reserves and made into wage slaves in or for the North.

African diasporan intellectuals in the North remain low in the pecking order of Northern hegemonic intellectual structures and networks. Many work in institutions where teaching rather than research is the focus, or in historically black colleges and universities that, like the teaching universities, are underfunded. As a group these scholars have not accumulated sufficient social capital to access the biggest and most prestigious grants that enable predominantly white Northern intellectuals to dominate the enterprise of producing and reproducing knowledge on Africa and Africans. Lacking access to significant research funds and to the pipelines and gatekeepers that manage the enterprise of scholarly publications, diasporan African scholars are also, in the main, unable to engage in the poaching-type, patron-client relations that often exist between African and Northern scholars on the one hand, and between African intellectuals and Northern grantmakers on the other, to produce studies that unreflectingly homogenize the products of research projects on Africa and Africans.

Zeleza suggests that African intellectuals in the diaspora and those in the continent must build transnational bridges that assault and destroy old orthodoxies that stymie the production of socially and politically conscious, relevant, and timely knowledge on Africa. He contends that such a radical break from the past is only possible with institutional, financial, ideational, and scholarly commitment to building epistemic communities. In the effort to accomplish these goals, scholarly networks that collaborate in teaching, research, publication, and the dissemination of ideas through the use of old and new technologies are crucial. While some such networks exist, the majority remain dependent on patronage from the Northern intellectual market. Such research centers are underfunded. They are also undersupported by intellectual exchange from colleagues in Northern "Babylons," and as such, they can only do so much. Being strapped for cash, lacking access to innovations in technology and telecommunications, such research centers are ripe and ready for colonization by those with purchasing power denominated in "hard currency."

Tools exist to bridge the divide between the few better endowed African intellectuals in the continent and its diasporas and the majority of impoverished, marginalized wage slaves that other African intellectuals have become in the era of structural adjustment. Many African intellectuals in the diaspora have access through their universities to new instructional technology. They can, at the very least, establish or join discussion groups, mailing lists, and online communities that help the operations of transnational epistemic communities. All that is needed in this regard is the will to act through the development and cultivation of face-to-face linkages that are nurtured by streams of online communication. Many African intellectuals in the North can also apply for institution-to-institution collaborative funding for exchange programs between universities in the North and their African counterparts to be not only possible but affordable. Unfortunately, most of the funding for collaborative research across continental boundaries goes to Northern scholars. Despite the significant difficulties involved, efforts must be made to bring diasporan immigrant and African continentally based scholars into close intellectual contact with one another, with students, and with African societies. Collaborative relationships can be strengthened and enriched through the use of instructional and telecommunications technologies. Tragically, many African countries are still on the negative side of the information divide. There are not enough computers or telecommunications links and definitely not enough money to purchase new, and sometimes even old, technologies.

There is increasing evidence that vigorous efforts are underway to create virtual communities with the express intention of reversing the brain drain. Some of these include the digital diaspora. One example is Network Africa, an organization established by a group of technology firms, nonprofit organizations, and United Nations agencies to undo the negative effects of Africa's brain drain by harnessing skills that have been lost to the continent.[45] Scholars are also able to use virtual technology to conduct discussions. H-Net, the humanities and social sciences online community (www2.h-net.msu.edu), includes scholars of Africa who may be Africans in the continent, Africans of the old diaspora, Africans of the new diaspora, and Africanists who may be

North American, South American, European, and Asian. H–Net describes itself as

> an international interdisciplinary organization of scholars and teachers dedicated to developing the enormous educational potential of the internet and the World Wide Web. Our edited lists and web sites publish peer-reviewed essays, multimedia materials, and discussion for colleagues and the interested public. The computing heart of H-Net resides at MATRIX: The Center for Humane Arts, Letters, and Social Sciences Online, Michigan State University, but H-Net officers, editors, and subscribers come from all over the globe.

The following Africa-specific groups belong to the H-Net community: H-Africa, H-Hausa, H-Luso-Africa, H-West Africa, H-SAfrica, H-Afrlitcine, and H-Afrarts.

There are numerous African and African diaspora discussion groups on the World Wide Web. Ackee.com is an example of a Jamaican online community. A Google search for the words "African discussion groups" returned 5,960,000 listings on 26 October 2008. Not all of them are active, and there is bound to be some duplication. A sampling of the first page of the Google listing shows a diversity of groups, engaged in a disparate number of issues, including scholarly research, education, HIV-AIDS, economics, literature, music, and so on. Some are academic databases, some commercial, and some social. A researcher has an infinite set of possibilities to explore in accessing materials for research on Africa.

In chat rooms, discussion groups among people who meet in cyberspace fora have anonymity and enjoy a presumption of the equality of all participants. Here the most engaging conversations and communications occur. Chat-Afrik provides a good example of one of these. It advertises itself as a group that is open to all Africans, but the majority of its members tend to be Nigerian immigrants living in North America, Europe, and home-based communities. Topics taken up in its discussion groups include information on lectures by scholars and public intellectuals on Afrocentric issues, values, and politics (African, African American, and to a lesser extent, Caribbean politics). Comparison is often made between African and African American sociopolitical values, tending to lead to valorization of what is presented as authentic African values. Because Nigerians form the core of the group, Nigerian issues dominate in the forum. For example, topics covered on 17 November 2002 included the Nigerian in Diaspora Organization in the United States, a conference on "Reform and Privatization of the Nigerian Electricity Sector," the extension of the ANA scholarship deadline, job openings on Capitol Hill, the first inaugural meeting of the Nigerians in Diaspora Organization Europe, and the Yoruba Oscar Night.

Increasingly, there are new services that closely resemble or replace real-life interactions. Many news groups and cybercommunities provide dating services and various opportunities for social interactions not just online but face-to-face. These are rapidly becoming alternatives or supplements to traditional modes of socializing. Parties, conferences, reunions, town hall meetings, political rallies, and other get-togethers are advertised, promoted, and broadcast on the World Wide Web in the various groups and communities that proliferate daily. Rich, thick communications linkages are being formed by these and other groups.

## Conclusion

Community interactions among old and new African diasporas occur through telephone conversations, faxes, chat rooms, and instant messaging systems. These communications are massive and largely undocumented. Potentially they provide a vibrant database for research. A quick survey of a few internet news groups reveals a concern for a contemporary political economy and social relations. There is also the development of relationships of friendship and mutual respect, as well as those of dislike and mutual derision. In essence, these groups create virtual communities where people are able to have intense or superficial discussions about matters of mutual concern. Information is exchanged, celebrations and social events are advertised, and signature drives for global justice are initiated. One prominent example was the campaign on behalf of Amina Lawal, the Nigerian woman who was sentenced to death by stoning by a Shari'a Court. Many of the groups that undertook the signature drives were women's groups. Significantly, the Nigerian women's group, Baobab for Human Rights, which spearheaded Amina's defense, was largely ignored in the signature drive, thus foreclosing an opportunity for cross-fertilization and accurate information on the situation on the ground in Nigeria by those who had firsthand information and knowledge of the case. To underline the need for access to technology, Ayesha Imam, one of the members of the group in North America, eventually provided accurate information and protested the tactics of the signature drive, which had propagated a certain amount of misinformation in the West about the case.

Due to the innovations in technology, it is possible for advertisements and calls for action to reach people all over the world. Becoming a member of a discussion group is as easy as subscribing for most, although for some groups a recommendation is required. It is true that revolutions in information technology create transnational communities that are not restricted by geographical boundaries and cannot be subjected to state control. The existence of these communities is creating revolutionary changes in the concepts that we use to make meaning. When communities are formed of people who may never have met one another and may never meet, who is a stranger? Who is a citizen? What constitutes community? What are the rules of the game? Clearly, the world as we know it is changing before our very eyes. These changes occur in a manner that impinges on the lives of ordinary people in very new and remarkable ways.

In physical and temporal terms, new ethnic minorities are being created and increased, new ethnicities are being formed, and new identities are being asserted, both in the immigrants'/migrants' country of origin and the host country.[46] There are increases in transnational transfers of financial, intellectual, and material resources, new trade and business relations, and new cultural interactions between sending and receiving countries. Inevitably, new tensions are also developing between ethnic minorities that are indigenous or "native born" (in the parlance of migration studies) and those that are relative newcomers. There are even tensions among old-timers and newcomers within immigrant populations that originate from the same country. Among African migrants and immigrants, subtle and not-so-subtle tensions may arise from differences in class, gender, language, culture, religion, and national origin.

In virtual terms, old social constructions and the effects of socialization may well inform the ideas and sensibilities of members of communities, but the lack of face-to-face contact removes or restricts the ability to identify and or classify people as belonging to a particular race, class, or gender. Virtual relationships also develop into physical ones. Particularly among the younger generation, dating and social friendships develop from virtual relationships. For the older generation, these interactions are also possible, given the proliferation of internet dating services, the ubiquity of chat rooms, and the growing use of the World Wide Web as a global mart, although professional relations may well dominate.

Misinformation and disinformation are possible with sole reliance on information from the World Wide Web. At the moment, it is better to depend on the websites of research institutions and bodies, peer-reviewed e-journals, scholarly groups, libraries, established NGOs, and universities. Government sites can misinform as much as they inform. Researchers must also follow established rules of verification. Through library database-driven research, scholars and researchers can also access information on African communities, particularly in the form of papers that result in the findings of scholars on a given subject. These sources can be used to verify information that is available on the web.

The traditional means of production and dissemination of knowledge about Africa is increasingly recognized as just one mechanism. The increasing number of web-based journals augments in a significant way and may even replace paper journals if the paper-free world of the new information age is ever actualized. A growing number of journals solely dedicated to African studies has appeared on the Web. They provide opportunities for the exchange of scholarly ideas and debates. These exchanges still privilege populations in the global North to the disadvantage of groups in the global South. It is unbelievably difficult to engage in instant communication when dealing with power failures and unreliable internet service providers.

Cybercommunications and cybercommunities are arenas where one can hear the cybervoices of African diasporan communities. In considering these communications and communities, it would be remiss if we do not consider questions of power. Who has voice and presence in these arenas? Who sets the agenda? Who establishes the rules? Who shapes the consciousness of the members of the community? Who forces and/or imposes the silences? Transnational networks may give voice to all comers in a democratic manner, but the reality is that access to technology, to wealth, to ideas, and to political power would naturally privilege some and disadvantage others. As things stand, populations in most of Africa are grossly disadvantaged in these networks. Overcoming such a disadvantageous situation can be accomplished by conscious, consistent, and proactive action of Africans in the continent and its diaspora, but requires conscious volitional action by people who enthusiastically embrace the use of constantly changing technology.

## Notes

1. Pfeiffer, "'Community,' Adaptation, and the Vietnamese in Toronto."
2. Howard, Rainie, and Jones, "Days and Nights on the Internet," 387.
3. Kazmer and Haythornwaite, "Juggling Multiple Social Worlds," 511, 514, and 526.
4. Anderson and Tracey, "Digital Living."
5. Rheingold, *The Virtual Community*.
6. Thompson, "Brave New World of Digital Intimacy"; Kinsley "Like I Care."
7. Campt, "Reading the Black German Experience," 289–91, and "Converging Spectres of an Other Within."
8. Alpers, "Defining the African Diaspora," 19–26. For more discussion on the definition of diaspora, see Chivallon, "Beyond Gilroy's Black Atlantic: The Experience of the African Diaspora," 359–61; and DeCosmo, "Pariah Status, Identity, and Creativity in Babylon."
9. Everett, "The Revolution Will Be Digitized," 126–27; Ifekwunigwe, "An Inhospitable Port in the Storm."
10. U.S. Census Bureau, American FactFinder, QT-P13: Ancestry 2000, http://factfinder.census.gov/servlet/QTTable?_bm=yand -geo_id=Dand -qr_name=DEC_2000 _SF3_U_QTP13and -ds_name=Dand -_lang=en. Unfortunately, the figures for African and West Indian immigrants do not provide information on gender. In addition, this data does not tell us whether or not undocumented immigrants are included.
11. "The Gender Wage Gap: Progress of the 1980s Fails to Carry Through"; and Lips, "The Gender Wage Gap: Debunking the Rationalizations."
12. "Towards Closing the Gender Wage Gap in Europe?"
13. Wirth, *Breaking through the Glass Ceiling*; Loutfi, *Women, Gender, and Work*. Both publications are available online at www.ilo.org/public/english/support/publ/online.htm.
14. See Hughes, "Gender, Remittances, and Development," 9.
15. See Di Marie and Stryzowski, "Brain Drain and Distance to Frontier," for an argument that the effect of the brain drain is positive for developed receiving countries while the phenomenon has ambiguous consequences for developing sending countries.
16. Stark and Wang, *Inducing Human Capital Formation*; Cho, "A Foot in Each Country."
17. Okpewho, Davies, and Mazrui, *The African Diaspora*.
18. Patterson and Kelly, "Reflections on the African Diaspora and the Making of the Modern World."
19. Watkins-Owens, *Blood Relations*.
20. Mazrui, *Political Values and the Educated Class in Africa*.

21. Said, *Culture and Imperialism,* 332–33.

22. Ibid., 295.

23. Appadurai, *Modernity at Large.* For more on the multiple uses of internet-driven communication to build religious and other communities by Trinidadian Muslims, Catholics, and Hindus, see Miller and Slater, *The Internet: An Ethnographic Approach,* 178–79.

24. Zeleza, "African Labor and International Migrations to the North."

25. "President Praised in Harlem."

26. "Dual Citizenship Beneficial"; "Ghanaians Meet in Montreal to Discuss Diaspora Vote Implementation."

27. Zeleza, "African Labor and International Migrations to the North."

28. Cavanaugh and Patterson, "The Impact of Community Computer Networks on Social Capital and Community Involvement."

29. U.S. Government, Office of Educational Technology, "Digital Divide."

30. Mojúbàolú Olúfúnké Okome, "The Antinomies of Globalization: Some Consequences of Contemporary African Immigration to the United States of America."

31. Hampton and Wellman, "Long-Distance Community in the Network Society."

32. U.S. House of Representatives, *Bridging the Information Technology Divide in Africa;* United States Office of Educational Technology, "Digital Divide"

33. Okome, "The Antinomies of Globalization."

34. Haas, "Introduction: Epistemic Communities and the International Policy Coordination."

35. Howard, Rainie, and Jones, "Days and Nights on the Internet," 387.

36. Everett, "The Revolution Will Be Digitized," 132–40.

37. Personal communication from Omolola Ijeoma Ogunyemi, 17 February 2004.

38. *Safundi* can be accessed at www.safundi.com/.

39. The journals of the Africa Resource Center can be accessed at www.africa resource.com/index.htm.

40. *Ìrìnkèrindò* is available at www.africamigration.com.

41. *Gender and Women's Studies for African Transformation* is available at www .gwsafrica.org/.

42. *Feminist Africa* can be found at www.gwsafrica.org/e-journal/index.html.

43. Zeleza, "African Labor and Intellectual Migrations;" Tettey, "Africa's Brain Drain."

44. Tettey, "Africa's Brain Drain," 12–13.

45. Mutume, "Reversing Africa's 'Brain Drain.'"

46. Zeleza, "African Labor and Intellectual Migrations," 7.

# References

Alpers, Edward A. "Defining the African Diaspora." Paper presented to the Center for Comparative Analysis Workshop, 25 October 2001.

Anderson, Ben, and Karina Tracey. "Digital Living: The Impact (or Otherwise) of the Internet on Everyday Life." *American Behavioral Scientist* 45 (2001): 450–75.

Appadurai, Arjun. *Modernity at Large: Cultural Dimensions of Globalization.* Minneapolis: University of Minnesota Press, 1996.

Campt, Tina M. "Converging Spectres of an Other Within: Race and Gender in Prewar Afro-German History." *Callaloo* 26 (2003): 322–41.

———. "Reading the Black German Experience: An Introduction." *Callaloo* 26 (2003): 288–94.

Cavanaugh, Andrea L., and Scott J. Patterson. "The Impact of Community Computer Networks on Social Capital and Community Involvement." *American Behavioral Scientist* 45 (2001): 496–509.

Chivallon, Christine. "Beyond Gilroy's Black Atlantic: The Experience of the African Diaspora." Trans. Karen E. Fields. *Diaspora: A Journal of Transnational Studies* 11 (2002): 359–82.

Cho, Adrian. "A Foot in Each Country." *Science* 304 (28 May 2004): 1286–88. Accessed at www.sciencemag.org/cgi/reprint/304/5675/1286.pdf?ijkey=nHqSBu3w.TU3I& keytype=ref&siteid=sci.

DeCosmo, Janet L. "Pariah Status, Identity, and Creativity in Babylon: Utopian Visions of 'Home' in the African Diaspora." *Identity: An International Journal of Theory and Research* 2 (2002): 147–56.

Di Marie, Corrado, and Piotr Stryzowski. "Brain Drain and Distance to Frontier." Center and Department of Economics, Tilburg University, draft dated 2 June 2006. Accessed at http://papers.ssrn.com/so13/papers.cfm?abstract_id=930347 #PaperDownload.

"Dual Citizenship Beneficial." *New Vision* (Kampala), 30 December 2000. Accessed at http://fr.allafrica.com/stories/200101020422.html.

Everett, Anna. "The Revolution Will Be Digitized: Afrocentricity and the Digital Public Sphere." *Social Text* 20 (2002): 125–46.

"The Gender Wage Gap: Progress of the 1980s Fails to Carry Through." *Institute for Women's Policy Research Fact Sheet.* IWPR Publication #353, November 2003. Accessed at www.iwpr.org/pdf/C353.pdf.

"Ghanaians meet in Montreal to Discuss Diaspora Vote Implementation" *Diasporian News,* 8 June 2006, at www.ghanaweb.com/GhanaHomePage/NewsArchive/artikel .php?ID=105544.

Haas, Peter M. "Introduction: Epistemic Communities and the International Policy Coordination." *International Organization* 46 (1992): 1–36.

Hampton, Keith, and Barry Wellman. "Long-Distance Community in the Network Society." *American Behavioral Scientist* 45 (2001): 476–95.

Howard, Philip E. N., Lee Rainie, and Steve Jones. "Days and Nights on the Internet: The Impact of a Diffusing Technology." *American Behavioral Scientist* 45 (November 2001): 382–404.

Hughes, Tim. "Gender, Remittances, and Development: Preliminary Findings from Selected SADC Countries." Santo Domingo: UN-INSTRAW, 3 April 2008.

Ifekwunigwe, Jayne. "An Inhospitable Port in the Storm: Recent Clandestine African Migrants and the Quest for Diasporic Recognition." Paper presented at the conference on "Imagining Diasporas: Space, Identity, and Social Change," University of Windsor, Ontario, 14–16 May 2004.

Kazmer, Michelle M., and Caroline Haythornthwaite. "Juggling Multiple Social Worlds: Distance Students Online and Offline." *American Behavioral Scientist* 45 (2001): 510–29.

Kinsley, Michael. "Like I Care: On the Internet, Everybody Knows You're a Dog." *Slate* *.com*, 27 November 2006. Available at www.slate.com/id/2154507.

Light, Ivan, Parminder Bhachu, and Stavros Karageorgis. "Migration Networks and Immigrant Entrepreneurship." Institute for Social Science Research Papers, vol. 5: paper 1. Los Angeles: University of California at Los Angeles, 1989. Accessed at http://repositories.cdlib.org/issr/volume5/1/.

Lips, Hilary M. "The Gender Wage Gap: Debunking the Rationalizations." Accessed at www.womensmedia.com/new/Lips-Hilary-gender-wage-gap.shtml.

Loutfi, Martha Fetherolf. *Women, Gender, and Work: What Is Equality, and How Do We Get There?* Geneva: International Labor Organization, 2001.

Mazrui, Ali. *Political Values and the Educated Class in Africa*. London: Heinemann, 1978.

Miller, Daniel, and Don Slater. *The Internet: An Ethnographic Approach*. Oxford: Berg, 2000.

Mutume, Gumisai. "Reversing Africa's 'Brain Drain': New Initiatives Tap Skills of African Expatriates." *Africa Recovery* 17 (2003): 1.

Njubi, Francis N. "African Intellectuals in the Belly of the Beast: Migration, Identity, and the Politics of Exile." *Mots Pluriels* 20 (February 2002). Accessed at http://motspluriels.arts.uwa.edu.au/MP2002fnn.html.

Okome, Mojúbàolú Olúfúnké. "The Antinomies of Globalization: Some Consequences of Contemporary African Immigration to the United States of America." Accessed at www.africamigration.com/archive_01/m_okome_globalization_02.pdf.

Okpewho, Isidore, Carole Boyce Davies, and Ali A. Mazrui. *The African Diaspora: African Origins and New World Identities*. Bloomington: Indiana University Press, 1999.

Patterson, Tiffany, and Robin D. G. Kelly. "Reflections on the African Diaspora and the Making of the Modern World." *African Studies Review* 43 (2000): 11–45.

Pfeiffer, Mark Edward. "Community, Adaptation, and the Vietnamese in Toronto." 1999. Accessed at http://ceris.metropolis.net/Virtual%20Library/community/pfeifer2/pfeifer2chapt7a.html.

"President Praised in Harlem. Hints on Dual Citizenship for Americans of African Decent [sic]." *Ghanaian Newsrunner*, 21–23 October 1995. Accessed at www.newsrunner.com/archive/NW241095.HTM.

Rheingold, Howard. *The Virtual Community*. Accessed at www.well.com/user/hlr/vcbook.

Rimer, Sara, and Karen W. Arenson. "Top Colleges Take More Blacks, But Which Ones?" *New York Times*, 24 June 2004, A1. Accessed at www.nuatc.org/articles/pdf/CollegesTakeMoreTopBlacks.pdf.

Said, Edward. *Culture and Imperialism*. New York: Vintage Books, 1994.

Stark, Oded, and Yong Wang. *Inducing Human Capital Formation: Migration as a Substitute for Subsidies*. Vienna: Institute for Advanced Studies, 2001. Accessed at www.ihs.ac.at/publications/eco/es-100.pdf.

Tettey, Wisdom J. "Africa's Brain Drain: Exploring Possibilities for Its Positive Utilization through Networked Communities." *Mots Pluriels* 20 (February 2002). Accessed at http://motspluriels.arts.uwa.edu.au/MP2002wjt.html.

Thompson, Clive. "Brave New World of Digital Intimacy." *New York Times Magazine*, 5 September 2008. Accessed at www.nytimes.com/2008/09/07/magazine/07awareness-t.html/.

"Towards Closing the Gender Wage Gap in Europe?" *European Industrial Relations Observatory Online* 12 (2002). Accessed at www.eiro.eurofound.ie/2002/12/Feature/NO0212103F.html.

U.S. Census Bureau. American FactFinder QT-P13: Ancestry 2000. Accessed at http://factfinder.census.gov/servlet/QTTable?_bm=y&-geo_id=D&-qr_name=DEC_2000_SF3_U_QTP13&-ds_name=D&-_lang=en.

U.S. Census 2000. Table 3: Black or African American Population, by Age and Sex for the United States, 2000. Accessed at www.census.gov/population/cen2000/phc-t08/tab03.pdf.

U.S. Government. Office of Educational Technology. "Digital Divide." Accessed at www.ed.gov/Technology/digdiv.html.

U.S. House of Representatives. *Bridging the Information Technology Divide in Africa.* Hearing before the Subcommittee on Africa of the Committee on International Relations, 107th Cong., 1st sess., 2001. Accessed at http://commdocs.house.gov/committees/intlrel/hfa72637.000/hfa72637_0f.htm.

Watkins-Owens, Irma. *Blood Relations: Caribbean Immigrants and the Harlem Community, 1900–1930.* Bloomington: Indiana University Press, 1996.

Wirth, Linda. *Breaking through the Glass Ceiling: Women in Management.* Geneva: International Labor Organization, 2001.

Zeleza, Paul Tiyambe. "African Labor and International Migrations to the North: Building New Transatlantic Bridges." Paper presented to the African Studies Interdisciplinary Seminar, Center for African Studies, University of Illinois at Urbana-Champaign, 4 February 2000.

**Hakim Adi** is a British Academy/Leverhulme Trust senior research fellow. His major publications include *West Africans in Britain, 1900–1960: Nationalism, Pan-Africanism, and Communism* and (with Marika Sherwood) *Pan-African History: Political Figures from Africa and the Diaspora since 1787.*

**Judith A. Byfield** is Associate Professor in the Africana Studies and Research Center at Cornell University. She is author of *The Bluest Hands: A Social and Economic History of Women Dyers in Abeokuta (Nigeria), 1890–1940.* She is working on a manuscript tentatively titled "The Egba Women's Tax Revolt: Gender and Nationalist Politics in Nigeria."

**Gloria Chuku** is Associate Professor of Africana Studies with a specialty in African history at the University of Maryland, Baltimore County. Her research has focused primarily on Igbo history and culture, gender relations, women, and economic and political development in Nigeria and Africa. She is author of *Igbo Women and Economic Transformation in Southeastern Nigeria, 1900–1960.*

**LaRay Denzer** is a historian specializing in the social history of Sierra Leone and Nigeria. She has authored many articles and a major biography of Folayegbe M. Akintunde-Igodalo, the first female permanent secretary in Nigeria's civil service, edited a mediated autobiography of Constance A. Cummings-Johns, and co-edited several volumes. Currently, she is a visiting scholar in the Department of History, Santa Clara University.

**Janice Mayers** is national coordinator of the UNESCO Transatlantic Slave Trade Education Project. She has served as head of the history department at the Combermere School in Barbados, and she has published articles on child welfare, education, and health.

**Olatunji Ojo** is Assistant Professor of History at Brock University, St. Catharines, Ontario. His research focuses on West African history (social and economic), African diaspora, and gender. He is co-editor (with Paul E. Lovejoy) of *Documents in Yoruba History* (forthcoming), and author of several articles, including "Slavery and Human Sacrifice in Yorubaland: Ondo c. 1870–1894," published in the *Journal of African History*.

**Antonia MacDonald-Smythe** is Professor and Senior Associate Dean in the School of Arts and Sciences, and Assistant Dean in the Graduate Studies Program at St. George's University, Grenada. She has published articles in journals such as *Callaloo* and is author of *Making Homes in the West/Indies: Constructions of Subjectivity in the Writings of Michelle Cliff and Jamaica Kincaid.*

**Anthea Morrison** is Senior Lecturer and head of the Department of Literatures in English at the Mona campus of the University of the West Indies. She has published articles on Caribbean women writers and French West Indian poetry, and she is working on a study of Maryse Condé.

**Mojúbàolú Olúfúnké Okome** is Associate Professor of Political Science at Brooklyn College, CUNY. She is author of *A Sapped Democracy: The Political Economy of the Structural Adjustment Program and the Political Transition in Nigeria, 1983–1993* and co-editor of the online journals *Jenda: Journal of African Culture and Women Studies* and *Ìrìnkèrindò: A Journal of African Migration.*

**Judith Salmon**, a native of Jamaica, studied at the Chicago Academy of Fine Art and received her BA degree in liberal arts from Norwich University in Vermont. She has exhibited internationally, and her work is held in numerous public and private collections, including the National Museum for Women in the Arts, Washington, D.C.

**Brinsley Samaroo** is Senior Research Fellow at the University of Trinidad and Tobago. For some three decades, up until 2005, he taught New

World and Indian history at the St. Augustine campus of the University of the West Indies. His main research areas have been Caribbean labor history and the Indian diaspora in the Caribbean.

**Verene A. Shepherd** is Professor of Social History at the Mona campus of the University of the West Indies and current president of the Association of Caribbean Historians. She is the author, co-author, editor, or co-editor of several publications, including *I Want to Disturb My Neighbour: Lectures on Slavery, Emancipation, and Postcolonial Jamaica, Maharani's Misery: Narratives of a Passage from India to the Caribbean,* and *Slavery without Sugar: Diversity in Caribbean Economy and Society since the Seventeenth Century.*

**Faith Lois Smith** is Associate Professor in the African and Afro-American Studies and English and American Literature Departments at Brandeis University. Her chapter in this volume is part of a book project on Caribbean people's ideas about modernity and the future in the late nineteenth and early twentieth centuries, entitled "Whose Modern?"

**Linda L. Sturtz** is George Russell Corlis Professor of History and chair of the History Department at Beloit College. She wrote *Within Her Power: Propertied Women in Colonial Virginia.* She is working on gender and racial construction in eighteenth-century Jamaica and a project on music as history.

# INDEX

Aba (Nigeria), 210, 220, 222, 225, 226, 232, 233, 234, 242n46, 271
Aba division (Nigeria), 221
Abadu-Bentsi, D. K.: correspondence with Harry Williamson, 4–5
Abakaliki (Nigeria), 231, 232
Abayomi, Dr. Kofo, 254
Abayomi, Oyinkan, 254, 269, 270, 272, 273, 277n34
Abeokuta (Nigeria), 210, 213, 214n3, 263, 269, 270
Abeokuta Girls' School, 269
abolition, 6, 8, 9, 158, 163; antislavery laws in Nigeria, 157, 163, 164; British antislavery squadron, 145; in Britain, 268; in Nigeria, 145, 155, 154–159, 164, 165, 167; in the West Indies, 26, 89, 115, 116, 117; in the United States, 117
Abrego, Luisa de, 85n65
Ademola, Oba Oladapo (Alake of Abeokuta), 269, 270
Adeniyi-Jones, Dr. Curtis Crispin, 205, 207, 254, 277n27
Adisatu, 163, 172n77
adultery in eastern Yorubaland, 151, 152–154, 157, 159, 160, 161
African Association, 200
African Academy of Arts and Research (AAAR), Lagos branch, 242n46, 257, 264, 265, 272

African General Hospital, Lagos, 250
*African Mirror* (Lagos), 262
African Progress Union (APU), 209, 211, 253, 258
African Students' Union, 201
Afro-Women's Center, 213
Ajayi, E. Ronke, 259
Akaje-Macaulay (née Dove), Rita, 258, 259
Akerele (later Awoliyi), Elizabeth, 256, 278n38
Akindana, Martin, 298
Akintunde-Ighodalo, Chief Folayegbe M., 150–151, 259
Aladin, 119–120
Alakija, Adeyemo, 254
Alakija, Ebun. *See* Mabel Dove
Alakija, Lady, 270
Alcindor, John, 277n24
Aldred, George, 67, 69, 84n56
Alexander, A. H., 114, 125
Ali, Duse Mohammed, 277n24
*Allanshaw,* 115, 116, 117, 121, 122, 123, 124, 125
Ambleston, John, 246, 275n5
Ambrose, Captain W. Gerald, 164
American Council on African Education (ACAE), 242n46, 264, 272
Amobi, B. V. O., 238
Amobi, Victoria, 237, 238

World War I, 2–3, 185, 201, 253; participation of colonial black soldiers, 3; racial discrimination, 3, interethnic tension among soldiers, 3.

World War II (WWII), 10; Africa as base for Free France, 246; African experience, 212; defense regulations in Nigeria, 221–222; demand for reforms, 180, 273, 291; Igbo experience, 219, 220–221, 227, 235, 239

World Wide Web, 286, 294, 297, 303, 304; drawbacks, 306

Wynter, Thomas, 63, 65, 81n18, 82n27, 85n67

Wynter, William Rose, 63, 81n18

Yam cultivation, 230–231, 234, 236

Yard, Lionel, 267–268

Yoni Temne (Sierra Leone), 33

Yoruba Christians, 160, 161, 162

Yoruba culture in diaspora: impact in the Caribbean, 6, 8; networks, 8; religion, 35n16, 140; repatriates in West Africa, 7

Yoruba Oscar Night, 304

Yorubaland (Nigeria): *See* adultery; Christian missions; concubinage; divorce; slave wives; slavery

Yaa Buahimaa, 267

Young, Charles, 151–152, 156, 161

Young Women's Christian Association (YWCA), 263

Zik Group, 246